Schwenckfeld and Early Schwenkfeldianism:
Papers Presented at the Colloquium
on Schwenckfeld and the Schwenkfelders

Schwenckfeld
and Early Schwenkfeldianism:
Papers Presented
at the Colloquium
on Schwenckfeld
and the Schwenkfelders

Pennsburg, Pa.
September 17-22, 1984

edited by

Peter C. Erb

Pennsburg, Pa.
Schwenkfelder Library
1986

ISBN 0-935980-05-9

Table of Contents

Abbreviations

CR   *Corpus Reformatorum* (Zurich und Berlin, 1834-1982)

CS   *Corpus Schwenckfeldianorum* edited by Chester D. Hartranft, Elmer E. S. Johnson, and Selina Gerhard Schultz (19 vols.; Leipzig and Pennsburg, 1907-1961)

GCS   *Die Griechischen Christlichen Schriftsteller der Ersten Jahrhunderte*, (Berlin, 1897-)

LW   *Luther's Works* edited by Jaroslav Pelikan (55 vols.; St. Louis, Mo., 1958-1967)

PL   *Patrologiae cursus completus, series latina* edited by J. P. Migne (Paris, 1878-1890)

Schiess   Traugott Schiess (hrsg.), *Briefwechsel der Brüder Thomas und Ambrosius Blaurer* (3 Bde; Freiburg, 1908)

Schultz   Selina Gerhard Schultz, *Caspar Schwenckfeld von Ossig (1489-1561)* with an Introduction by Peter C. Erb (4th ed.; Pennsburg, 1977)

QGT, 1   *Quellen zur Geschichte der Täufer, 1: Württemberg*, hrsg. von Gustav Bossert (Leipzig, 1930)

QGT, 4   *Quellen zur Geschichte der Täufer, 4: Baden und Pfalz*, hrsg. von Manfred Krebs (Güterloh, 1951)

QGT, 7   *Quellen zur Geschichte der Täufer, 7: Elsass, 1. Teil. Stadt Strassburg, 1522-1532*, hrsg. von Manfred Krebs und Hans Georg Rott (Güterloh, 1959)

QGT, 8   *Quellen zur Geschichte der Täufer, 8: Elsass, 2. Teil. Stadt Strassburg, 1522-1532*, hrsg. von Manfred Krebs und Hans Georg Rott (Güterloh, 1960)

WA   *Luthers Werke. Kritische Gesamtausgabe* (Weimar, 1883-)

WA Br   *Luthers Werke. Kritische Gesamtausgabe. Briefwechsel* (Weimar, 1883-)

WA Tr   *Luthers Werke. Kritische Gesamtausgabe. Tischreden* (Weimar, 1883-)

Preface

The year 1984 marked the 250th anniversary of the arrival in America on September 22, 1734 of the principal band of Schwenkfelder emigrants from Silesia. It also marked the 100th anniversary of the year 1884 when the Schwenkfelder Conference initiated the *Corpus Schwenckfeldianorum* project and formalized the collection of Schwenkfelder historical materials, later Schwenkfelder Library. To honor the anniversary year appropriately Schwenkfelder Library sponsored a week-long colloquium, attracting to Pennsburg an international group of scholars, currently active in Reformation, historical, and theological study. Papers delivered or prepared for this occasion on Schwenckfeld and early Schwenkfeldianism are printed in this volume. A second series of papers concerned with aspects of Schwenkfelder life in America will be presented in a companion volume *Schwenkfelders in America*.

Throughout their history the Schwenkfelders have attended closely to the maintenance, perpetuation, and study of the written sources of their tradition. A full review of that concern in the past century is well presented in W. Kyrel Meschter's *Twentieth Century Schwenkfelders: A Narrative History* (Pennsburg, 1984). Professor Horst Weigelt's *The Schwenkfelders in Silesia* (Pennsburg, 1985) provides ready information on the European period. Schwenkfelder scholarly interest is first seen in the detailed biblical and patristic studies and in the careful theological work of the founders of the movement, Valentine Crautwald and Caspar Schwenckfeld among others. It was continued in the extensive collecting and publishing enterprises of men like Daniel Sudermann in the early seventeenth century, and in the work of numerous lay scholars, collectors, and scribes who struggled tirelessly throughout the next two centuries to preserve the records of their intellectual and religious heritage in spite of the great turmoil caused by their persecution in Silesia following the initiation of a Jesuit mission against them in 1719 and their eventual emigration to south eastern Pennsylvania in the 1730s.

The projects which the Schwenkfelders undertook in 1884 at their 150th anniversary celebrations are not surprising as a result. Their critical edition of the works of Caspar Schwenckfeld, the *Corpus Schwenckfeldianorum*, was eventually completed in nineteen volumes in 1961, and Schwenkfelder Library which served so significant a role in supporting research for the *Corpus* was eventually incorporated in 1946 and housed in its present building in 1951.

In consideration of such a history of intellectual endeavors, the organization of a colloquium was planned as the most suitable event to celebrate the initiation of both the *Corpus* project and Schwenkfelder Library. It was the hope of the Library Board that such a colloquium would serve two purposes. In the first place, it was to bring together major scholars working on Schwenkfelder related topics to provide opportunity for their interaction, to support scholarship presently underway, and to encourage further research in the area: in the second, it was to provide an opportunity for persons of Schwenkfelder descent or those who had chosen to join the tradition to become more fully acquainted with the broad sources of their background, the various ways in which it was being approached in the scholarly community, and the significance of earlier Schwenkfelders' attention to scholarly concerns.

In one sense the endeavor to hold a colloquium and to publish papers for both a professional academic and a lay 'confessional' audience may appear contradictory. There is a strong anti-intellectual strain in the North-American lay public, especially relating to religious topics. Scholars at the same time tend to retreat to book-lined towers, insisting that academic freedom means the bracketing of all confessional interests, that their studies are 'value-free,' and that any attempt to 'apply' the results of scholarship is the responsibility of the cleric or other persons with immediate religious concerns. From the beginning Schwenkfelders have opposed such a dichotomy. Schwenckfeld and his colleagues attended closely to current developments in biblical, historical, and systematic theology, always for the fuller edification of the lay public which did not have the opportunity to gain the philological and philosophical expertise necessary for academic work. The generation immediately following Schwenckfeld's death carried out a massive editorial and publishing program to make certain that the truth

as they saw it would not be lost. Among the Silesian Schwenkfelder exiles who fled to Pennsylvania in the eighteenth century.
a significant number of men and women copied manuscripts so
as to preserve their tradition. Pastoral leaders like Balthasar
Hoffman and Christopher Schultz continued careful linguistic
and theological study, while maintaining normal 'lay' responsibilities. The publication of the massive *Corpus Schwenckfeldianorum* and the establishment of Schwenkfelder Library
would have been impossible without a broad scholarly interest
on the part of the lay supporters of the projects and a direct
'confessional' concern on the part of the scholars who led in the
direction of the two projects. The majority of Schwenkfelder
lay persons at the end of the nineteenth century knew that the
results of Hartranft's seemingly arcane studies had an immediate value for them. and even non-Schwenkfelder scholars like
Professor Ernesti seldom interpreted their academic work aside
from its 'use' in the Schwenkfelder community.

The papers which follow are published within this framework. They are gathered into major sections: the first section
treats some major themes of Schwenckfeld's thought, the second outlines historically significant events in Schwenckfeld's
career. the third discusses important figures in early Schwenkfeldianism and Schwenckfeld's influence, and the fourth treats
aspects of Schwenckfeld's thought in a more contemporary setting.

Plans for the Colloquium were initiated some five years
prior to 1984 and were successfully completed only because of
the generous financial and personal assistance of a great number of interested people. Dr. Claude A. Schultz. Jr.. President
of the Library Board. never ceased to encourage and offer suggestions. W. Kyrel Meschter. Vice-President and Treasurer of
Schwenkfelder Library. worked tirelessly. making certain that
all energies were continuously directed to their proper end.
Local arrangements were the responsibility of Dr. Ruth Har-
ris who graciously volunteered her time for a full year before
the opening of the Colloquium and for many months after its
conclusion. overseeing all logistical matters. The Library staff.
Dennis Moyer. Director. and Claire Conway. gave regular attention to all aspects of the celebration in addition to their
many regular duties and in this they were helped enormously
by the inspiring energy and optimism of Mrs. Lib Dewey who

volunteered generous service to the Library for four years prior to the 1984 celebration and has continued to do the same since that time. The Colloquium program was my responsibility. but in this I was helped by my colleagues at the Library, Dennis Moyer and Claire Conway. The editing of the papers was greatly aided by the consistent and careful work of Alice Croft. The Computing Centre at Wilfrid Laurier University is especially to be thanked for time and advice in preparing the final typeset pages.

Peter C. Erb.
Associate Director.
Schwenkfelder Library

I

Caspar Schwenckfeld
and the Royal Way

George H. Williams

In August 1884, less than a month before the celebration of
the 150th anniversary of the coming of the Schwenkfelders
to America. Dr. Chester D. Hartranft of Hartford Theological Seminary circulated an open letter to the Schwenkfelder
community. suggesting that a critical edition of the works of
Caspar Schwenckfeld be undertaken. For him the project was
to be a 'suitable memorial of the greatness of our fathers. and of
our gratitude to God.' He felt Schwenkfelders could not 'make
a nobler contribution to theological science and righteous living' than such an edition. On *Gedächtnisstag* (the memorial of
the arrival of the largest group of Schwenkfelders in America
in 1734) September 24. 1884. Hartranft pressed his point once
more. and the project was taken up by the community with
enthusiasm. The scope. toil. scholarly and religious treasure to
be embodied in that project by 1961, few Schwenkfelders who
were present on that day in 1884 could have comprehended.

The seventy-six years of scholarship that brought the *Corpus Schwenckfeldianorum* to completion. and with it the
Schwenkfelder Library, a collection initially begun to support
the *Corpus* publication, are fully recounted in the second and
third chapters of Mr. Kyrel Meschter's *Twentieth Century
Schwenkfelders.* Many persons dedicated their lives and resources to the *Corpus*. It is difficult to imagine the inception
of such a program of publication without the dream of Chester
David Hartranft. His original plan to include a complete bibliographical. philological. historical. and theological treatment
of every treatise by every sixteenth-century Schwenkfelder. as
well as a complete critical edition and translation of each document. was curtailed by the commonsense considerations of
the many Schwenkfelders who were supporting the enterprise.
We look with near incredulity at Hartranft's ambitious and allegedly 'foolhardy' suggestion exemplified in Volume 1 of the

Corpus. We now realize that had he had his way, the complete project would have included about 400 volumes for what we presently have in nineteen. This estimate does not take into account the works of several early Schwenkfelders not in the end included in the *Corpus.* Nevertheless, we are all thankful that Hartranft had the vision of such a project and the energy of enterprise to inspire the community with a sense of responsibility for collecting these documents, many of which by now might well have perished forever.

Of course, even the simplest account of the *Corpus* is incomplete without reference to Selina Gerhard Schultz. Born in 1880, she graduated from Perkiomen Seminary in 1898, and after some years teaching in the Montgomery County School system she took up the momentous role of associate editor and then editor of the *Corpus.* In 1919 she married Eugene S. Schultz, following a number of years spent in Germany working on the *Corpus* with her brother-in-law, Elmer E. S. Johnson, the other major figure in the *Corpus* and above all in the collection of books for the Schwenkfelder Library. In 1961, more than half a century after she began her work, she saw the project to its end, and was rewarded an honorary doctorate by Tübingen University.

I had read her life of Schwenckfeld (Norristown, 1946) and in connection with my research for *The Radical Reformation* (Philadelphia, 1962) I visited the Library and called on Mrs. Schultz. In her gracious welcome and in her hands of scholarly toil I sensed at once the enormous responsibility she had borne so long for amassing in stately tomes the documentary witness to her faith. Her face registered some traces of inexplicable anxiety and sadness, largely effaced, however, by serene joy on her welcoming countenance. She was reflecting perhaps the sense that something great, deep, and enduring had been substantially brought, through scholarly publication, to the consciousness of all those of us who enter into the joy and the anguish of sixteenth-century Christendom in the throes of reformation, revolt, counter-reform, confessional strife and religious war. Her's was, in any event, an older scholar's benediction on a younger one. She was aware of the taxing burden as well as the great privilege of being called uniquely to become the custodian of a heritage, to keep track of the heirlooms of faith still redolent and throbbing with life that is past and yet

continuous with us and future generations. She was the weaver
of the web of historical recollection. I came to the celebrative 1984 colloquium in part to pay tribute to Selina Gerhardt
Schultz. whose countenance before and since her death in 1969.
has strangely come before me often. even when not thinking of
Caspar Schwenckfeld. as if she might be beckoning me to that
better way.

Selina Schultz subtitled her major biography of the Silesian
nobleman 'Spiritual Interpreter of Christianity' and 'Apostle
of the Middle Way.' In this biography and with this theme
she was carrying out one of the implications of the conceivers
of the *Corpus*. In their first volume the editors had said in
anticipation: 'It is our purpose to write a full history of the
Middle Way. That will involve not only the biography and
writings of its exponents but its adjustments to other currents
which were in unchecked flow and the multitudinous springs
that broke forth from every quarter in Europe.' It is true that
Selina Schultz had carried into her work certain modernizing
trends taken over from Hartranft: she stressed Schwenckfeld's
early years and in general dealt with him as though he had
been of essentially the same outlook from the inception to the
close of his career as reformer.[1] And it is probably fair to say
that she may not have fully grasped the degree to which the
devout and disciplined. astute. and learned lay Reformer was
for a season held to be on a par with the major figures of his
age. She had esteemed her hero as a gallant loner and ret-
rospectively conceived of his loyal following as even from the
beginning a conventicle apart. I was considerably influenced
by her perspective. and in trying to locate Schwenckfeld as a
spiritualizer among the eminences and the minor figures of his
age in my *Radical Reformation* I made of him more of a loner
among the sectarians than he was. and I did not sufficiently sit-
uate him in. and then disengage him from. his Silesian setting:[2]
nor did I attend adequately to his christological development.
My doctoral student. Ernest Lashlee. however. in his unpublished Harvard thesis of 1969. drew attention to the dynamic
of Schwenckfeld's thought. centering on the conception of human being created and then recreated to the image of God.
that is. to the person of Christ's two natures. particularly his
human nature of celestial origin. Lashlee. like Schultz. inciden-
tally gave prominence in the title of his work to a key term of

Schwenckfeld, the *Via Regia,* without having directly taken up
the origin and meaning of the phrase.[3] It is to this concept of
the Middle or Royal Way that I wish now to turn, although I
do not presume to do in these few pages what the editors of
the *Corpus* did not quite manage in their nineteen volumes.

The Middle Way is in one enduring sense the way of mag-
nanimous toleration that can be taken by believers between
clusterings of conviction. when on either side the intensity
is such that dialogue has become impossible and is even replaced by strife. So often in religious, social, and political, the
most conspicuous counselors of dialogue and mutual toleration are often themselves somewhat drained of that conviction
that once motivated their forebearers or that impels still the
more intense of antagonists. Caspar Schwenckfeld. in contrast,
towers physically. spiritually. and morally from the sixteenth-
century religious plain as a wayfarer of the Middle Way whose
experiential and scholarly conviction was at once intense and
yet benignant. It is in the context of mutual toleration. a topic
treated in the papers below by Professor Franklin Littell. that
I place my celebrative reflections. remarking in passing that it
was Littell's set of the *Corpus* that I borrowed for my *Radical
Reformation* and I thank him publicly for this and his many
other generous, thoughtful, and enabling acts of kindness towards me and others.

In nineteenth-century England the term Via Media was
prominently used by John Henry Newman and the other
Tractarians. in reference to properly re-catholicized or high
Church Anglicanism as the middle way between Popery, as
they then called it. and Dissenter nonconformity to the established Church of England. The Tractarians were repristi-
nating a term already in use in the same sense in the seventeenth century. by George Herbert. the poet and divine. and
brother of Edward. Lord Herbert of Cherbury. the 'father of
Deism.' I have not ascertained whether these seventeenth- and
nineteenth-century Anglicans were acquainted with Schwenckfeld's use of the term. but such a connection is improbable.
Martin Bucer. exponent of a middle way in eucharistic theology between Luther and Zwingli. did visit England and would
have been a more likely source. But the Latin term used by
the Tractarians and by Schwenckfeld for a middle way. was a
generic metaphor of no obvious single classical or scriptural
source.

Schwenckfeld, calling the *via media* the Royal Way (*via regia*), evidently intended by the term something both Christian and classical and wished to apply it to more than the eucharistic controversy.[4] He was in his usage classical and specifically Aristotelian in the counsel and practice of being temperate, moderate, and proportionate—of doing nothing to excess. But for him the term was also informed by deep experiential conviction and was grounded in Scripture. The confessional and civil toleration fostered by Schwenckfeld was based on deep commitment, although he was himself always open to dialogue along the way.

The route of the Middle Way, so to speak, and the eminences on either side changed in the course of Schwenckfeld's life much more than the editors of the *Corpus* indicated. It was always a way between the old order and the brusk and all too heartily 'libertine' reformation espoused by Luther. But early in Schwenckfeld's career the term came to designate for him the Middle Way in his Evangelized part of Silesia (as well as in southwest Germany and in some of the Swiss cantons) between the Lutheran and Zwinglian extremes regarding eucharistic theology and practice. Eventually, as Schwenckfeld became a more marginal figure in the Reformation, the Middle Way was his attempted mediation among the Anabaptists who were, from his point of view, wilfully sectarian and separatist. For him this was true even of the more conciliatory among them like Pilgram Marpeck and various spiritualists, some of whom seemed to him to have settled for a religious life apart from religious fellowship. As well, almost to the end of his life, he retained the term to designate the proper way between Catholic and Protestant sacramentality and spirituality.

Schwenckfeld is too often looked upon as a loner, but his concern with a middle way marks him as almost unique in his troubled and anguished but courteously articulated concern for the whole fabric of Christian society, ripped and lacerated as it was by what he experienced as heartless contention either to the right (*ad dexteram*) or to the left (*ad sinistram*) of what was for him the correct way, the *recta via*.

Although the referents of 'right' and 'left' along the Way were not always sufficiently brought out in the *Corpus* annotations and in the standard life issuing therefrom, Schwenckfeld's early editors and biographers were right in sensing a sustained continuity in his thought and particularly in his concept of royal mediation as at all times a strategy for committed persons to deal with others equally committed to opposing positions. It was a strategy which proposed mutual toleration and common aspiration on both sides in a dialogue undertaken to gain fuller clarification on various theological points. Seen in this light, the changes in Schwenckfeld's theological terrain testify to the authenticity of his principle of dialogue. And it is possible that his principal message to us in pluralistic America, where church and state are constitutionally separated, is that there is a way yet to be found between individualistic religious indifference to the common political good in self-absorbed piety on the one side and, on the other, corporate religious intrusion into public affairs. Perhaps even more important, his ecumenical message is that one can be deeply convinced, engaged in candid theological exchange and possible change, and at the same time be charitable.

Initially, Schwenckfeld's concern was with a general reform of abuses within the Church. At this point his Middle Way was the formation of an Evangelical Catholicism midway between conventional beliefs and practices and the new reform movement from Wittenberg. When addressing the sisters of a convent at Naumberg in 1523, Schwenckfeld opposed the abuses of the monastic system, but in his critique he still insisted that sisters who wished to serve their Lord within the context of their monastic covenantal vows should be left free to do so, providing they truly did reform the abuses. When he wrote to his bishop in Breslau in 1524, he worked through a long list of abuses troubling the Church of his day. Yet there is little in that letter that would separate him from other humanists in the diocese of Breslau, loyally critical, inspired by Luther, but scarcely aware of the impending rupture of Christendom. In a treatise written with Hans Magus von Langenwaldau, Schwenckfeld drew up a list of reforms for the duke of Liegnitz which he believed should be carried out in his domains with speed. Much of what he treated was, to be sure, in keeping with the Wittenberg reform as he understood it. When he discussed the sacrament of the altar and called for communion in both kinds, he added: 'Let the priests be no longer permitted to read masses for money.' His criticism was primarily directed against the priestly traffic in chantry masses for souls of the departed. Schwenckfeld was nevertheless still open to the view 'that this service should be observed when there existed an actual hungering and desire for the most venerable sacrament of Christ.' And clearly aware of the implication of his words, he went on immediately to add: 'Another and weighty subject of reform do we now propose: Let no one in matters of conscience be compelled to render obedience to merely human precepts. On the contrary, since we are called into Christian liberty, we are therefore urged to stand fast therein; nevertheless, we have no right to pervert this into a liberty of the flesh.'[5]

The first instance of Schwenckfeld's use of the term Middle Way for his approach occurs in his *Admonition to All the Brethren in Silesia* written in 1524. The passage in which he uses it sums up his purpose for the whole work: 'We are prone, dear brothers, to swerve from the left hand to the right, contrary to the Lord's command [cf. Matt. 7:13 f., but especially Isaiah 30:21]: Turn not to the right hand nor to the left. We must walk on the royal road and seek to find the Middle Way between the former hypocritical life and the present carnal liberty. Otherwise all will be futile.'[6]

Several aspects of this passage invite attention. First, Schwenckfeld was identifying the royal road with the Middle Way. The 'right' (*recta*) direction for the reformation in Silesia was the middle road between what he deemed the too 'wide and easy' way of Lutheranism and the muddy road of unreformed Christendom; he followed the Lord's injunction to keep to the 'hard' and 'narrow way' of personal self-discipline and interiorized piety. Secondly, the Middle Way, in this early formulation, was that between what he felt to be two extremes: lethargy and recklessness. As of 1524 Schwenckfeld welcomed the reform movement from Wittenberg but feared any extreme that might tear the fabric of Christendom. His extremes were that of hypocritical conformity to the old order with all its built-in privileges and excessive reformation under what he considered the too permissive slogan of faith alone (*sola fide*). His major concern was for the sanctification of life and that is how he had originally understood Luther's reform. The right (correct) way for Schwenckfeld as of 1524 was the Middle Way of evangelical Catholic reform over against the oppressive old order and what he considered the Lutheran rupture. Thirdly, Schwenckfeld's persistent references to straight, correct (*recta*) and right

(*ad dexteram*) throughout the *Corpus* evidently go back to Isaiah 30:20 with what was for him an allusion to baptism, the
eucharist. and the eternal Christ. The whole scriptural passage Schwenckfeld had in mind is: 'And though the Lord give
you the bread of adversity and the water of affliction, yet your
teacher will not hide himself any more, but your eyes shall see
your teacher. And your ears shall hear a word behind you,
saying, "This is the way; Walk in it" when you turn to the
right or when you turn to the *left*.' The prophet's counsel
was striking when Schwenckfeld considered the images or possible types of the context of the correct. the Middle Way, in
relation to Luther's great reformatory emphasis on faith by
the hearing of the word (Rom. 10:17). With this text of Isaiah Schwenckfeld held that it was Christ himself by his inner
word who directs the faithful onto the Middle Way. Here, indeed. is a paradigm of the whole of Schwenckfeld's spiritual
theology with its emphasis on the inner Word and the inner
teacher leading the believer through baptism (preferably postponed into childhood) into the school of Christ and then to the
eventually inward eucharistic communion.

As is well known, in an encyclical letter of April. 1526.
Schwenckfeld and Valentine Crautwald called for the suspension of the Lord's Supper until the ferocity of the eucharistic
controversy calmed down between Catholics and Lutherans.
Lutherans and Zwinglians. and even among various groups of
Anabaptists. Only Schwenckfeld's followers in Silesia heeded
this irenic but reductionist proposal. a confessional armistic,
as it were, a spiritually disciplined and watchful *Stillstand* between the warring militias of Christ who could not even hear
the call above the din. By this action Schwenckfeld found
himself increasingly isolated from the main body of reformers. Henceforth his dialogue would be increasingly much more
with sectarians and evangelical and conventual Catholics than
with the magisterial Reformers. He would become a 'Reluctant
Radical.'[7]

Since the eucharistic *Stillstand* became a central and then
permanent aspect of Schwenckfeld's eucharistic theology and
piety (hence also of his Christology and doctrine of sanctification). we momentarily leave the main road of our reflection to
recall what this was. It was initially a provisional strategy for
spiritual communion, pending the resumption of sacramental

intercommunion. Schwenckfeld had corresponded with several of the leading theologians as far west as Basel and Strassburg on the relationship of the Last Supper. the sacrifice on Calvary. the real presence at liturgical communion. the worthiness of the participants, and inner eating. The idea of an inward feeding on the celestial flesh of Christ Schwenckfeld had received in its first formulation from his learned colleague Valentine Craut-wald who had long been perplexed by the eucharistic issue raised by Luther's persistence in holding that all who partook of the sacramental bread participated in the communion with Christ. Crautwald had a protracted experience of illumina-tion and joy in Christ's very presence. and following further study. meditation, and prayer, he was convinced by the expe-rience of the eternal nowness of Christ's 'sacramental.' 'myste-rious' presence beyond the elements themselves and within the transformed heart of the believer. Instructed by Crautwald. Schwenckfeld was in his turn vouchsafed a 'tremendous' expe-rience, 'a gracious visitation.'which was decisive in his career.

In his eucharist teaching Schwenckfeld and Crautwald to-gether were appropriating a high medieval tradition of great awe in the presence of the high altar or the consecrated ex-posed Host. Schwenckfeld was not at all a sacramentarian in the sense that Luther derisively gave that term. that is. he was not one who (from the Lutheran or Catholic point of view) hollowed out the meaning of the sacrament of the altar into a simple commemoration as with Zwingli.

All this is quite familiar but it remains to be observed that Schwenckfeld seems to have come to feel that the eucharist was both experientially once for all and yet also continuous, as Luther said of baptism. once for all, yet life-long. In the eu-charistic theology and experience of Schwenckfeld it was not of the last Holy Communion in which he had participated that he thought but of some experiential eating of the heavenly manna. Yet in the resonance of memory he seems to have heard. amid progressive deafness. the recurrent ring of the Sanctus bell of the Mass in his native Silesia.

When Schwenckfeld read Deuteronomy 8 about the God of the Commandments and of the Exodus 'who fed you in the wilderness with manna' (vs. 16). he thought of the heavenly nourishment of Christ as available to all peoples in their pil-grimage through all the deserts of life. When he wrote of the

Royal Way in reference to the inner eucharist. he had also in mind making 'straight in the wilderness the highway of our God' (Is. 40:3) and perhaps the injunction of Jeremiah (6:16): 'Stand by the roads.... ask where the good way is, and walk in it.'

With this high but spiritualized experience of the inward eucharist, Schwenckfeld created new problems with his Duke in Silesia and with the Anabaptist refugees there who for their part celebrated the Lord's Supper. simply. in imitation of the original scene as described in the Gospels. Schwenckfeld had welcomed these Anabaptists, many of them Sabbatarians. and sought to protect them in their Silesian asylum. He invited them into discussions that turned acrimonious and he would carry memories of these misunderstandings into his later encounters with Pilgram Marpeck and other Anabaptists.

Early in 1527 Schwenckfeld prepared an *apologia* for the faith of the Silesians to be set forth in the name of Duke Friedrich II of Liegnitz. It contains a great many distinctively Schwenkfeldian stylistic and conceptual patterns. Among these stands another formulation of the Middle Way.[8] Later in the same year Schwenckfeld dealt again in his *De cursu verbi Dei* (printed by Oecolampadius in Basel in 1528) with the Middle Way between the the transubstantiationist and the consubstantiationist positions. the Catholic/Lutheran sacramental accessibility to every mouth. on the one side, and. on the other, the extreme represented by Zwingli. Like so many of the South German Protestants Schwenckfeld was seeking a theological basis for the exclusion of the unworthy. Judas included, from any true participation in Christ through the elements— hence his new stress on the eternal Word accessible only to the righteous. Again he argued that the interior Word as Teacher directed the believer to the Middle Way in allusion to Isaiah 30:20.

Without his knowledge or approval two of his eucharistic tracts. the foregoing and another. were printed in Zurich and Basel. alarming King Ferdinand of Bohemia under whom the Duke of Liegnitz stood vassal. While things grew difficult under the Catholic overlord. Schwenckfeld wrote defenses of religious toleration under the Duke's name. promoting the Middle Way.

Schwenckfeld discretely withdrew to Strassburg in 1529 and found himself among congenial mediating theologians, like Bucer and Wolfgang Capito. Increasingly he became involved with the various separatist groups in the city, trying to resolve the differences between the various Anabaptists and spiritualists, who like himself stressed the fruits of justification in sanctification. Thereby he increasingly alienated himself from the city's principal reformers. Having been excluded from the Marburg Colloquy of 1529 on the central issue of concern to him, he found himself eventually ridiculed for withholding from communion and for his eucharistic theology, until at length he was ostracized for having based it all on a day-dream, on an exalted moment of allegedly divine revelation, even though Zwingli, with his merely commemorative view of the Supper, had also appealed for sanction to a dream of the night.[9]

By 1534 it had become clear that his concern with concord was not compatible with the policy of Bucer,[10] and he was forced to leave Strassburg. From then on his life was one of continual movement, but he never ceased to work for a concord among rival religious groups. For a time he lived at the Franciscan convent at Esslingen and then in the Benedictine monastery at Kempten, and his correspondence indicates an ongoing interest in all confessional groups.

That Schwenckfeld continued to think of all of Christendom together in the flux of reformation is evident by his letter of September 12, 1539. Writing to Hans Conrad Thumb von Neuburg, Schwenckfeld made it clear that his distinctive teaching on the sacrament as mediated to him and the visionary revelation granted to Crautwald lay at the basis of his principle of the Middle Way: 'The time came when merciful God revealed to certain simple people that some parties moved too much to the left and others too much to the right in their understanding of the body and blood of Christ and that a 'right' (correct) Middle Way of the true knowledge of Christ as well as a proper understanding of his Supper must be found and held to. One of these simple people admonished and warned both parties faithfully.' Schwenckfeld then goes on to point out what he had said to each of the groups, Catholic and Protestant.[11]

In 1546, deeply disturbed about the religious intolerance raging and soon to result in religious war, Schwenckfeld made another attempt to identify once again the mediating position

in writing his book *On the Three-Fold Life of Man*. In a letter
to Sybilla Eisler, Schwenckfeld, referring to his intentions in
the book, wrote: 'In this book on works and what they merit,
I hope to teach the right Middle Way between the Papists and
the Lutherans: the one party has left the royal road which
is Christ by going too far to the right, the other too far to
the left.'[12] An initial reading of this statement would seem to
suggest that Schwenckfeld no longer considered his doctrine of
the spiritual eating of the body of Christ as the only issue in
persevering in the Middle Way, but his further comment on
the royal road 'which is Christ' indicates that this is not the
case. The Middle Way was the way which is committed to
the person and work of Christ, to his redeeming activity ever
present among men spiritually in his body and blood which can
be eaten by faith at all times and places without the need for
any institutional mediation, directly accessible to the worthy
in the realm of the Spirit or the uncreated Light.

Early in 1552 Schwenckfeld wrote a lengthy treatise *On the
Gospel of Christ and its Misuses* in which he developed a section outlining the alleged misappropriations of the Gospel by
both Protestants and Catholics, the one sinning by turning
too far to the left, the other too far to the right, making it impossible for him to ascribe to either with certainty the greater
guilt for the schism. One was not to flee one church nor the
other, he averred, but rather to refrain from so insisting on
one's own position as though no further truth from historic
revelation or from above could break through to illuminate all,
as though each had the exclusively correct way.[13] This counsel
represented a kind of German 'Nicodemizing' strategy (cf. John
3:1 f.), except that such conduct was not primarily determined
by fear of the coercion from the dominant territorial church
and the consequences of nonconformity, as it was, for example,
in Italy. This German 'Nicodemism' was, in effect, prudential conformity but without sacramental communion in the inward affirmation of the universal accessibility of Christ and the
catholicity of his Church of the redeemed. Yet in point of fact
by this time Schwenckfeld was in effect stubbornly making his
own way the only correct way and came close to compromising
an earlier insight as to the royalty of the high, straight, and
narrow way. Indeed, in his letter to Blasius Seyfried on 1555,
the year of the Religious Peace of Augsburg, Schwenckfeld suggested that all who were able were to flee from 'Babylon' and

its confusion of tongues. He was deeply disappointed in the Council of Trent which condemned the Lutheran and Calvinist formulations of eucharistic theology and practice. The flight of the inwardly faithful was to be taken along the Middle Way, as he wrote: 'There is a sure, right Middle Way between the Papists and the Protestants, namely, the true and saving knowledge of Christ. He who has that knowledge has Christ, and he who has Christ has God and all righteousness.'[14]

The Middle Way had by now become the route of spiritual refugees. Schwenckfeld may have lost in this formulation his original Silesian vision of the way on which the knights and the nobles, the artisans and the peasants, the clerics of all kinds could find a thoroughfare to spiritual freedom under ascetic discipline of the kind he imposed on himself to his death in Ulm in 1561.

In a closing salute to Caspar Schwenckfeld himself particularly in the presence of the assembled community of memory and hope that here bears his name in the New World, let me say that it is our primary purpose as scholars in the papers which follow to refocus on the past, to get a clearer view of Schwenckfeld among his contemporaries than we had before, to strip off some of the patina of piety in order to reglimpse the original self-portrait as it were. Nevertheless, in my own more generalist opening message, I wish to say a further ecumenical word about the vision of Schwenckfeld on the contemporary scene, to share a possible message from the unwitting founder of the Schwenkfelders to the vaster global Church, now fissured by the uncertainities of life and nearing the close of two millennia of Christian history.

In a very comprehensive perspective Caspar Schwenckfeld embodied almost uniquely the transformation in the Era of the Reformation of two medieval Catholic ideals in Protestantized guise. He was the Grand Master of a wholly spiritual military order of Christ under gentle but consistent discipline, subduing spiritual terrain. He was also the Pilgrim, the Wayfarer, the Viator, on his way to the heavenly city.

In today's ecumenically aware context Schwenckfeld's Middle Way also reaches from the divisions of the sixteenth century into our general yearnings for greater Christian unity around the globe.

Whether we are Protestant. Catholic. Orthodox. of some other line of development from antiquity. or of more recent origin, many of us know the difficulty of intra-Christian communication and the absence of sacramental communion. And this is experienced as theologically scandalous even if historically, socio-psychologically. and canonically explicable. Moreover, we are confronted with this problem religiously perhaps more often in the last quarter of the twentieth century than our ancestors were in the first quarter of the sixteenth century, since we participate vicariously at nuptial and funeral masses and in rites and religious confessions other than our own. whether through television or at quasi-liturgical public events. On some of these occasions we find ourselves in the presence of a eucharistic celebration, not of our tradition. Are we indifferent observers? Or is such a eucharistic event something in which we. too, participate at a canonical distance. albeit spiritually? Schwenckfeld had a eucharistic theology that might fit in here perhaps better than we could have imagined. Suspension was for Schwenckfeld. we remember. a tactical or provisional Middle Way toward the eventual resolution of eucharistic theology and praxis and then renewed intercommunion. On the sacramental level his strategy did not effect a change of disposition. The divisions hardened. And Schwenckfeld's suspension became itself fixated at a place and a moment in the history of Christendom to become for generations a mark of the Schwenkfeldian community. as if Schwenckfeld's tactical counsel had become a new canon and as if the non-observance of sacramental communion had the same anti-sacramental basis as the asacramental spirituality of groups such as the Quakers. for example. The belated resumption of the observance of the Lord's Supper among American Schwenkfelders could have obscured the deep and truly ecumenical character of Schwenckfeld's original vision of the spiritually omnipresent Christ.

To be sure, Schwenckfeld's eucharistic piety presupposed a late medieval thought-world that is no longer ours. Moreover, for him the spiritualization of the sense of taste represented the most personal way of avoiding the contamination of the divine Body by the unworthy. We of today are all sufficiently participant in the heritage of Luther to acknowledge that we recognise ourselves at once saints and sinners. and we have been too profoundly sensitized by Darwin. Marx. and Freud ever to be serene about our sanctifications. But *mutatis mutandis* we can still appropriate much from the intense and extensive writings of Schwenckfeld on the inner nourishment from the bread of heaven.

Schwenckfeld's Middle Way can still be an approximation of communion within a theology of appropriation and participation above canon and custom. His eucharistic theology and intention might be worked through with this intent in our new ecumenical climate among the Friends of God, would-be confessors of the glory of Christ.

The Middle Way, the Royal Way of Schwenckfeld, then, belongs to all the descendants of the time of the Reformation, Catholics included, for his devotion was an updating of medieval asceticism for the common life. He was, indeed, a kind of tertiary of the Protestant Reformation. And as belonging in a sense to all of us, as I have postulated more than proved, his Royal or Middle Way, once set forth in the name of the Duke in the interest of the reform in Silesia, can become accessible again in at least the specialized ecumenical context of spiritual Communion.

In his earlier usage of the terms *via media* and *via regia*, Schwenckfeld seems to have been especially aware of the ambiguities of the Way. He and his contemporaries would have known, at least in general, about the royal road of the Persian kings that ran from Susa to Sardis and was described by Herodotus.[15] And the later prophets, if not Second Isaiah himself, knew of such a royal highway in the Persian Empire. The great roads of the Roman Empire were given not this name but rather were called consular roads. It is clear that Schwenckfeld's frequent employment of the term *via regia/via media* and of *recta via, neque ad dexteram, neque ad sinistram*, owes more to Scripture than to classical tradition, to his intuition that Christ as King of Kings had built, as it were, the highway in the desert, made straight in the wilderness for the experiential coming of the Lord.

Caspar Schwenckfeld was a pilgrim or wayfarer on the royal road, the King's Highway, the route of pilgrimage to the earthly and especially to the heavenly Jerusalem. He walked the Middle Way, a man of conviction and benignity, somewhat alone, eager to share words of Christian greeting and consolation, to exchange the intelligence of the inbreaking Reformation with fellow wayfarers, and to proffer light and consolation when it became dark. His Middle Way was not some piece of the road but the inner means of travelling that road. It was a way pointed out by the Grand Master of his life, by Christ the Teacher, his Lord and King.

Notes

1 Peter C. Erb, in his admirably lucid Introduction to the fourth edition of the the Schultz biography, places Schwenckfeld in the midst of the scholarly literature on him since Mrs. Schultz laid down her pen in 1961.

2 Subsequently Horst Weigelt has admirably placed Schwenckfeld within the Reformation of Silesia and also in controversy with the Sabbatarian Anabaptists and others. See his *The Schwenkfelders in Silesia*, translated by Peter C. Erb (Pennsburg, 1984). Schwenckfeld's Latin writings evidently influenced some Polish-speaking noblemen: from Vilna, Rakow, and elsewhere we have references to the adhesion of some of the *szlachta* to Schwenckfeld's principles, as well as the Ducal Prussian Germans, including Albert of Hohenzollern, whom he directly addressed in Königsberg. I have noted these instances in my annotation of Stanislas Lubieniecki's *History of the Polish Reformation* (Amsterdam, 1685). *Harvard Theological Studies*, 34 (1986).

3 'The Via Regia: A Study of Caspar Schwenckfeld's Ideas of Personal Renewal and Church Reform,' (Harvard Ph.D., 1969). In my enlarged and updated Spanish edition, *La Reforma Radical* (Mexico City and Madrid: Fondo de Cultura Economica, 1983) I was able to nuance and deepen my treatment of Schwenckfeld in light of the intervening research.

4 Walther Kohler dealt with the *via media* in the eucharistic context in *Zwingli und Luther, ihr Streit über das Abendmahl* (Leipzig, 1924).

5 Schultz quotes both these passages, 49.

6 CS 2:62.

7 See R. Emmet McLaughlin, *Caspar Schwenckfeld, Reluctant Radical* (New Haven, 1986).

8 CS 17:150.

9 CS 2:681.

10 Cf. Gottfried Hammann, *Entre la secte et la cité: le project d'église du reformateur* (Geneva, 1984).

11 CS 6:573-757.

12 CS 9:823.

13 CS 12:855 ff.

14 CS 14:258.

15 Herodotus, *Histories* 52, 53. Lorenzo Valla translated the Greek *it reguim*; this suggests that *via regia* was not a common term at the time and reinforces the impression that for Schwenckfeld it was as much scriptural and christological as it was classical.

The Abomination of Desolation: Schwenckfeld's Christological Apocalyptic

Walter Klaassen

Very little attention has been given so far to Schwenckfeld's views on the endtimes and to his interpretation of history. That is perhaps because Schwenckfeld is viewed as a spiritualist and mystic, and therefore concerned primarily with the inner world of faith and the comprehension of God. But even though it was not an independent feature of his thought, he did have an interpretation of history, and he was interested in the future, for he, like his contemporaries, believed he was living in the Last Days.

His writings contain many references to the manifestation of the Antichrist as a sign of the nearness of the End. Like Luther he identified the Antichrist with the Papacy. Like the Anabaptists he located the depredations of the Antichrist especially in the Catholic and Lutheran practices of the sacraments. Like most contemporary church leaders, he wrote expositions on most of the standard apocalyptic passages in both Old and New Testatments, and a full-length, if uneven, commentary on the Apocalypse.

Still, Schwenckfeld's interest was not primarily historical but rather theological. Even Martin Luther was more concerned than he about the apocalyptic timetable. Schwenckfeld made absolutely no attempt to identify the persons, nations, places, and times of the apocalyptic landscape as was done by Justus Jonas, Martin Bucer, Andreas Osiander, Hans Hut, and Melchior Hoffman. There is no identification of the church as the apocalyptic kingdom as in Bernhard Rothmann and Menno Simons. Although he did not identify a role for himself in the events of the endtime like Thomas Müntzer or Jan van Leiden, others did it for him, identifying him as Elijah, one of the two witnesses of Revelation 11.[1]

However, although Schwenckfeld used all the standard words of apocalyptic employed also by his contemporaries, one cannot speak of his apocalyptic if we define the word in the sense of a cataclysmic clashing of kingdoms and rival authorities ending with the inbreaking of the power of God to annihilate his enemies. We can, however, speak of Schwenckfeld's apocalyptic if it is defined as the uncovering of mysteries which had hitherto remained hidden. With that clarification of the term I proceed.

For a man who, as he said about himself, was more concerned for the manageable things of the present, and who in any case did not have the gift of prophecy,[2] he expressed himself relatively often on the subject of apocalyptic. Approximately 200 pages of the *Corpus Schwenckfeldianorum* are devoted to the subject. Usually he wrote in response to the inquiries of friends or in refutation of attacks on him by his many opponents. The original stimulus to study the Apocalypse came from a friend. He writes that once he began reading it he was not sorry he had begun because he had found in the book many splendid testimonies to the glory of Christ.[3] I would rather, he writes in another instance, discuss passages from the Gospels, Paul, and the prophets, than the book of mysteries, many of which I do not understand myself.[4]

The main reason for his use of apocalyptic language and imagery was that it was biblical, and the Bible was always the main source of his thought and language. He also found this language in the church Fathers, especially Jerome, even though he infrequently cites them on this subject.[5] Finally, it was evidently language that was sufficiently expressive and descriptive to suit his purposes. He did what everyone else in the sixteenth century did, namely mine the Scriptures for those images and metaphors that best expressed the views he developed.

Since the beginning Christians had been 'bewitched, bothered, and bewildered' by the figure of the Antichrist, who, as incarnate evil, was to appear at the end of time as Satan's agent in a doomed attempt to wrest cosmic sovereignty from the hand of Christ. Schwenckfeld, too, gave considerable attention to this figure, but in doing so clearly revealed himself to stand in the tradition of apocalyptic symbolism which had been developed by Tyconius, the Donatist theologian who died about the year A.D. 400, and which was transmitted to Latin theology by Augustine. The symbolic interpretation was then

carried forward by writers like Gerhoh von Reichersberg and
Otto von Freising in the twelfth century. Schwenckfeld never
refers to these people and likely never read their work, but he
belonged to their company nevertheless. He had, of course,
read Augustine.

Schwenckfeld's views on the Antichrist and related issues
remained virtually constant throughout his life which makes
it relatively easy to sketch out his views. The reason why
there was no development nor any changes of substance is that
Schwenckfeld did not pursue apocalyptic for its own sake but
only to explain the present deplorable state of the church and in
particular to show how the Lord's Supper had been destroyed.

In his letter to Johann Hess in 1522, Schwenckfeld stated
his conviction that the kingdom of the Antichrist was present
in the church,[6] a theme that was repeated the next year in
a letter to the nuns at Naumburg. There he cites the two
passages of Scripture which were to be the core of his apocalyptic thought throughout his life, 2 Thessalonians 2:3-10, and
Matthew 24:23-26. But at this stage his arguments reveal the
general early Reformation view that the papal church was the
Antichrist. Since at this time Schwenckfeld was an avid partisan of Luther, he was probably simply following his mentor. In
his 1520 work *The Babylonian Captivity of the Church*, Luther
had written that the 'abomination of desolation' described the
Papacy. Its main guilt, according to Luther, was to claim divine sanction for human traditions and to smother the true
Word of God.

In 1525 Schwenckfeld began to be especially exercised by the
increasing intra-evangelical controversy concerning the Lord's
Supper. He became convinced that all transubstantiationist and impanationist theories were in error.[7] He studied the
Fathers, and the writings of Carlstadt, Oecolampadius, and
Zwingli and began to develop his own views, especially influenced by the Church Fathers. He submitted his written views
to his friend Valentine Crautwald, who, after some study of
his own, confirmed Schwenckfeld's view that both Luther and
Zwingli were mistaken and that a spiritual interpretation in
which the spiritual person actually feeds spiritually upon the
spiritual glorified body of Christ was the true one. The actual
bread of the eucharist was the material parallel to the spiritual bread. Its function is purely to stimulate remembrance of

Christ. The body of Christ is the bread: hence he concluded
that the *est* remained intact and that Zwingli was wrong when
he said that the bread *signifies* the body.[8] Schwenckfeld, then,
had come to his own unique view of the Lord's Supper which
he was to explicate and defend until the end of his life.

His thoroughgoing matter-spirit dualism determined his
apocalyptic views. It was in *A General Epistle... Concerning the Lord's Supper*, written in February, 1527, in response
to Luther's *Von dem Sacrament des Leibs und Blutes Christi
wider die Schwarmgeister* that Schwenckfeld first located the
heart of the destruction of the Antichrist in the perversion of
the understanding of the sacrament of the bread and wine.
Where, he asks, did the error come from 'to regard the bread
as the body of Christ and the creature as God?' And why is it,
he asks further, that it is impossible today to agree that this is
the error? Is is easy to see, he answers, that we have here the
fulfillment of the prophecy of 2 Thessalonians 2 and Matthew
24.[9] In those passages we read that before the Last Day comes
the man of lawlessness will be revealed who opposes God, takes
his seat in God's temple, and claims to be God. This process,
writes Schwenckfeld, is already at work. The abomination is
that a creature, the bread, is taken to be the very body of
Christ, the second person of the Trinity.

The Antichrist in the History of the Church

It is because of the connexion between the Antichrist and the
Eucharist that Schwenckfeld gives more attention to the Antichrist than to any other aspect of apocalyptic. Following the
tradition of the symbolists he warned against identifying the
Antichrist as a specific person. Hence also Schwenckfeld did
not share the widespread preoccupation in the popular apocalyptic tracts of the sixteenth century with the biography of the
Antichrist.

The Antichrist, he wrote, had been active in the world from
shortly after the time of Christ. At the beginning Christ ruled
visibly in the church, and in the work of the Apostles and
his appointed servants prevented the breaking out of the mystery of iniquity. But once the Apostles had gone, this mystery, which is the Antichrist and the adversary of the glory of
Christ, broke forth and even now holds power.[10] The mark of

the change was that the true knowledge of Christ was darkened and human wisdom became paramount in the church.[11] Thus, as in the time of the Apostles Christ ruled openly and the Antichrist was hidden. So after their time Christ was hidden and the Antichrist ruled openly; and this condition has not yet changed.[12]

A major sign that the church had fallen from the truth, wrote Schwenckfeld, was its adoption of coercion and tyranny. This happened already during the second century as reported by Eusebius in his *Ecclesiastical History* and was a clear indication that the church had abandoned the gentle, patient spirit of Christ. Now the church protected its teaching by means of worldly power rather than by the sword of the spirit.[13] And this has been the practice of the church since then.

The Character and Activity of the Antichrist

But Schwenckfeld does not long dwell on past history. He was far more interested in describing the Antichrist and his work in the present as he observed it. He returned to this theme again and again.[14]

The Antichrist, according to Schwenckfeld, is in the first place the one who establishes himself in God's temple, the church, in his own power and with the worldly sword. There he will assume sovereignty and the right to teach and will exalt himself against God and his Word, Jesus Christ. What makes the Antichrist so difficult to detect is that he masquerades as Christ and an angel of light.[15] This is achieved by making Christian clergy and teachers his followers. He leads them to apostasy by offering them earthly wealth, position, and reputation. They live and work by the power of the Antichrist by virtue of their office and the protection of the secular rulers.[16] The deception is so convincing because the Antichrist appears to be building the temple of God, the church, and to be concerned for its security. He has endowed the church with esteem, with pomp and glory and success and promotes its worship and the sacraments. In fact, however, he was always determined to destroy the church and the gospel by concentrating on the letter rather than the Spirit, and by corrupting the clergy with the promise of worldly enjoyments and success.

This church of the Antichrist was identified by Schwenckfeld primarily as the papal church. In his commentary on the

Apocalypse Schwenckfeld identifies the beast of 13:1 as the pope and those who are with him. He appears to accept the older interpretation of the words 'the dragon gave [the beast] his power' (v. 2) as a reference to the Roman Empire which became subject to the papacy when the emperors gave Rome to the popes, became their vassals, and had to be confirmed in their office by the popes. And everyone, Schwenckfeld writes, marvelled at 'the beast' (v. 3) and ran to Rome to receive its grace and indulgences.[17]

Schwenckfeld did not regard the Antichrist to be a particular person. He had been present in the church since the days following the apostles, and was now identified by Schwenckfeld with Catholics, Lutherans, and Anabaptists. Indeed, he repeatedly said that the Antichrist is not a person but a 'corpus,' the body of all those who, under the name of Christ, oppose the living Word of God and the saving teaching and life of Christ. He has been in the world since the time of Paul and can therefore not be a person. If he were, he, like Christ, would before now have died. But then, even as people can't discern the body of Christ, so they can't discern the body of Antichrist either.

Schwenckfeld's description of the Antichrist was a description of the papal church as he saw it. The Antichrist attempts to administrate divine mysteries and direct Christ's church without a mandate and authorization from Christ whose it is. He calls himself the vicar of Christ and insists that his law is divine law. He wants to feed the flock of Christ but without love for Christ. Indeed, all he does opposes Christ. The Antichrist is the evil shepherd who climbs into the sheepfold because he does not desire to enter by the door which is Christ.

When he identifies the Antichrist as the one who sells the Christian birthright of the Spirit for the dead letter and God's Word for man's word, we get very close to the heart of Schwenckfeld's concerns. The outward appearance of the Antichrist and his work is that of the holy church but appearance is all there is; there is no substance, no Spirit. He makes a worldly estate out of the spiritual so that all that remains is the spiritual name, title, and comportment. Otherwise all is worldly and carnal. The Antichrist interposes all these externals between men and God and will not allow people to come to Christ directly without the mediation of creaturely things.

He is characterized specifically by false teaching, an evil life, and especially by perverted worship. Finally, the Antichrist is everyone who denies that Jesus is the Christ and that Jesus is God's son. All the creaturists make this denial. The creaturists are the Catholics but also the Lutherans who regard Christ as a creature because, according to them, he is one with the creaturely bread of the eucharist.[18] By all this in particular we can know, says Schwenckfeld, that the Antichrist is present now.

A further sign which confirms the presence of the Antichrist is his persecution of the true followers of Christ. Anyone who persecutes the godly cannot be Christ's and must belong to the Antichrist since there are only these two. The Antichrist, since he is the opposite of Christ, coerces and forces people to do his will by means of the sword of the secular rulers.[19] This is especially typified by the killing of the two witnesses of Revelation 11. The purpose of the persecution is to stifle and suppress the truth. Schwenckfeld adds that all this is happening today.[20]

Although Schwenckfeld rarely attempted to fit historical particulars into his scheme of the endtime, he did say that the prophets had set forth and typified the kingdom of Christ by means of worldly kingdoms. Thus, he was always glad to find something in their writings that witnessed to Christ and his glory.[21] Thus, Antiochus Epiphanes, while he was a historical king who set up the abomination of desolation in Jerusalem, is also a type of the Antichrist who has similarly desecrated the Christian church. As he suspended the daily sacrifice in Jerusalem so he has suspended true worship in Christendom by the introduction of the Mass.[22] Nebuchadnezzar, too, is a type of the Antichrist because Isaiah referred to him as the foolish, useless shepherd who has no concern for the health and safety of the flock. In another place Schwenckfeld identifies the Smalcald War as a sign of the nearness of the end. There is a sense of excitement in the letter in which this appears because, according to Jerome, the Roman Empire would fall just before the end would come. Schwenckfeld notes that the Protestants are in good spirits expecting to win. The defeat of Rome could be the beginning of the end. In any case, both of these kingdoms, the papal and the Lutheran, are very close to the final kingdom of the Antichrist. Perhaps it matters little which one wins.[23]

Finally, in his description of the character and work of the Antichrist, Schwenckfeld follows earlier exegetes in describing the Antichrist in terms precisely opposite those of Christ. He bases himself on 2 Thessalonians 2:3-14. The Antichrist is a man of sin; Christ a man of grace. Antichrist is a son of perdition and destroyer of the temple of God; Christ is the son of love and the builder of the house of god. Antichrist is an adversary of God, a teacher of error and unrighteousness, the bearer of the mystery of wickedness; Christ is the friend and counselor of the Most High, a teacher of the word of justice, and a distributor of sacred, heavenly treasures. There is no middle ground between these two; one must choose one or the other.

Several times Schwenckfeld draws attention to the mark of the beast of Revelation 13:16-17 and indulges in a little word-play. The Greek word for mark is *charagma*, which he interprets as a mark of identity like a family's coat of arms. By the livery one knows to whom a servant belongs. All who belong to the Antichrist have this *charagma*. But those who belong to Christ have the mark of Christ which is *charisma*, namely the Holy Spirit. *Charagma* or the mark of the Antichrist is therefore a sign of the absence of the Spirit.[24]

The Second Party of the Antichrist

It is clear that Schwenckfeld was enormously disappointed by his failure to convince Luther that his own view of the eucharist represented a middle way on which all Christians would walk together. He was grieved by the malediction Luther hurled against him in December of 1543 as a response to Schwenckfeld's last attempt to win Luther over to his interpretation. Luther, he wrote in reply, curses those who bless him, and persecutes those who pray for him. Words like those from such a man are hard to bear.[25] Schwenckfeld and his associates were always respectful towards Luther and tried hard to avoid offending him. But that did not deter them from articulating the truth as they had perceived it. Their view of the Supper was especially critical of the Lutheran practice which they perceived as a reversion to the papal externalization of Christian faith.

Schwenckfeld was forced by Luther's own statements to ask whether Lutheranism was not also part of the church of the

Antichrist. Already in 1530[26] in a tract on the church, the keys, and the sacraments, he put the matter as follows: How can the Lutherans who call the papal church the assembly of Satan and the pope the Antichrist, at the same time accept the sacraments of that church as true and legitimate? Can the Antichrist be part of God's service?[27] This cannot be since Christ and Antichrist are mutually exclusive, and therefore the Lutherans are wrong when they say that the church of the Antichrist can have the true mysteries and sacraments of Christ. In the church of the Antichrist there is neither divine grace nor Holy Spirit; no body and blood of Christ nor forgiveness of sins are available there. The prophets, and especially the Apocalypse, say much about this church which is drunk with the blood of the saints and witnesses of Christ. She is the receptacle of all unclean spirits and haunt of every foul and hateful bird (Rev. 18:2) Therefore, the prophet admonishes all to come out of her so that one does not become a participant in her sin. How, asks Schwenckfeld, after having known the truth, could one boast about the sacraments of the papal church and regularly participate in them? He is reluctant to come right out and say at this time that the Lutheran church is part of the church of the Antichrist, but he asks the reader to consider what Christ meant when he said, 'He that is not with me is against me.'[28]

Despite all this, he writes, Lutheranism presents itself as having the true gospel, the Word of God and the sacraments, but it is all bound to the letter. This church ridicules and persecutes as *Schwärmer* those who teach about the Holy Spirit.

When in 1544 Schwenckfeld commented on Osiander's work on the Apocalypse, he wrote that the details of historical prediction in which Osiander was so interested, were not important at all. What was omitted by him, however, and deemed unimportant, was the apostasy from the living Word to the letter, from the living regnant Christ to the Antichrist, and from the work of the Holy Spirit in the heart to the external ritual.

The beast of Daniel 7:20, wrote Schwenckfeld, is a clear reference to Lutheranism which has spoken 'great things,' all of which have been blasphemy.[29] This interpretation then appears again in his commentary on the Apocalypse 13:11. This other

beast, some say, means Lutheranism. Schwenckfeld evidently
accepted this interpretation because he also explains that the
deadly wound suffered by the first beast (13:3) was inflicted
by Luther on the papal teaching on the Mass. However, now
that Luther had made common cause with the papacy on the
interpretation of the eucharist, the deadly wound had been
healed. This happened after the Peasant War.[30] Lutheranism,
too, claims that its teaching is the gospel and God's Word,
that its sacraments are the true ones, but it is as bound to the
letter as the papacy. It decries the teaching of the Holy Spirit
as *Schwärmerei*.[31]

When Schwenckfeld prepared his commentary on Revelation he no longer hesitated to put the Lutherans in the Antichrist's camp. Commenting on 13:15, he identifies the image of the beast with the servants, preachers, teachers, and
priests of the Antichrist who promote his abominations, in
all things acting against the reigning king Jesus Christ, his
glory and kingdom. He identifies the speech of the image with
Luther's attempt to force the Holy Spirit into the external
rites by means of the dead letter. Not only has he erected the
papacy again and confirmed its false understanding and idolatry, but he actually increased the coercion and the hypocrisy of
the sacraments more that ever before.[32] Here there is no doubt
that Schwenckfeld regarded Lutheranism as part of the church
of the Antichrist. What was it that drove Schwenckfeld to this
desperate identification?

The Eucharist and the Abomination of Desolation

It was in the eucharistic doctrine and practice of the Catholics
and Lutherans that Schwenckfeld saw the burning focus of
the destruction of the Antichrist. As already mentioned,
Schwenckfeld took the reference from Daniel 8:11 to be a
prophecy of the end of true worship in the Christian church.
In its place would come the complete devastation of all true
teaching and worship, and the corruption of God's people. He
described this in some detail in his work *Von dreierley leben
der Menschen* in 1546, complete with numerous references to
the Psalms, Prophets, Gospels, and works of Paul.[33]

The abomination of desolation is identified by Schwenckfeld
in particular with the eucharist and its perversion in thought

and practice. As early as 1527 in his long explication of the sacrament of the Lord's Supper, Schwenckfeld thus identified the Catholic view of the Supper. He reminded his readers of Jesus' words that the time would come when it would be said: 'He is here' or 'He is there.' That is precisely what has happened now, he says, when we are told he is in the bread, he is in the cup, and that means that the end is near.[34]

What else could the Mass be but the 'abomination of desolation,' implies Schwenckfeld, when by action of the priest, as they claim, the bread and wine are changed into the very body and blood of Jesus? For that means that the priest, a sinful man, has control of the Holy Trinity and heaven too. This is patently false, since Christ never instituted the Mass. Indeed, the whole idea is preposterous. But Christ did say that the kingdom does not come with signs to be observed but is within us. Now, if the kingdom does not come with external signs, neither will the King himself come through the external motions, words or consecration in the Mass. But Christ, the heavenly king, is not on earth hidden under the form of the bread but is exalted in heaven and present to all believers through faith.[35]

Schwenckfeld's position on the Supper was unique in that he began with John 6:55 rather that with the words of institution. The John text says: 'My flesh is bread indeed and my blood is drink indeed.' These words, so Schwenckfeld believed, are the interpretation of the words of institution at the Last Supper where Jesus said: 'This is my body and blood.' Thus, instead of saying 'The bread is my body' and going no further so that a completely erroneous understanding emerges, we should accept Jesus' words in the Gospel of John which say 'My body is the bread,' and come to the right understanding. The word 'indeed' or *wahrhaftig*, says Schwenckfeld, is meant in particular to exclude everything material.[36] To secure the point he adds the words *exclusiva particula*. That means that the body of Jesus, glorified already during his life-time,[37] and by the resurrection,[38] had been taken up into God where the glorification of his flesh was now complete.[39] This heavenly flesh is the bread upon which the believer feeds in faith.

The materialization which Schwenckfeld saw in the Mass and also in the Lutheran Supper was therefore for him a terrible perversion of the truth. It was an upending of the order

of God. It was a spiritless ceremony based on the dead letter
which darkened and obscured the saving knowledge of Christ.[40]
It was substituting a creature for God, and the external sign
for the internal saving reality.[41] In fact the mass was simply another crucifixion of Christ every time it was done.[42] The whole
perversion was a product of the sophists and philosophers but
not of true believers.[43]

Schwenckfeld felt if anything even more strongly about the
fact that Luther had followed the papal church into the same
externalization than he did about the original apostasy.[44] The
Lutherans claimed to have the restored sacrament, but alas,
it too was tied to the dead letter.[45] The glory of Christ is
regarded by them as an unnecessary fantasm. But the whole
thing with them is so carnal as to horrify an honest, godfearing
person.[46] This insistence on the materiality of Christ and his
ministry, charges Schwenckfeld, is done for the sake of carnal
security.[47]

It was therefore in the destroyed eucharist that the Antichrist had been victorious in his campaign of desolation. He
had succeeded in diverting attention from the spiritual glorified Christ by locating a creaturely Christ in the sacrament of
bread and wine, thereby making it into a material ceremony
whose external glory blinded everyone. And now even Luther,
the great champion of the renewed gospel, had fallen prey to
the Antichrist. But Schwenckfeld was not discouraged. He
knew that the Antichrist would be defeated and that it would
not be long.

The End of all Things

Although Schwenckfeld was reluctant to assign specific contemporary times, places, and persons to the details of prophetic
oracles, he, like virtually all his contemporaries,[48] did look to
apocalyptic literature for light on the future. In 1558 he wrote
that Christians should carefully consider especially Daniel and
the apocalypse since they provide an irrefutable portrayal of
the present state of the church and Christendom. To be sure,
the godless will pay no attention, as Daniel says, but those who
understand will comprehend.[49]

Even the relentless critics of Luther, the Anabaptists, and
Schwenckfeld, always acknowledged that Luther had been the

first to restore the gospel. 'A great light has arisen in our time' writes Schwenckfeld, 'by which God has revealed to us the spurious worship, human ignorance, idolatry, sin, and blindness.'[50] But the appearance of the light also brought out the powers of darkness. Satan has been loosed and has come out to do battle against the truth.[51] And he has been successful for he subverted the Lutherans to abandon the Word of God and instead to depend on the secular rulers. This began after the Peasant War when Luther abandoned his earlier dependence on God's Word. The result is that the true church has again gone into hiding as it had done before. That is the meaning of the words 'the heavens vanished' (Rev. 6:14). Heaven was frequently a symbol for the church.[52] Schwenckfeld was, of course, thinking of the little conventicles of his followers who had to lead a clandestine existence and who had, at his direction, suspended the celebration of the Lord's Supper, a mark of visibility, for the time being.

In his commentary on the Apocalypse Schwenckfeld can be seen to be using traditional interpretations of Christian history as well as his own. He does this with respect to the vision of the Four Horsemen in 6:1-8. The four horsemen represent four ages of the church. The white horse is the first age, the age of purity, of clarity, and of joy. The red represents blood, the period of the martyrs of the Roman imperial persecutions. The black horse stands for the age of the heretics and the philosophers who distorted and falsified the true teaching. The fourth and pale horse represents the age of the papacy and Luther. Especially with respect to Luther, Schwenckfeld comments that the horse is pale, that is, half-white, because externally everything appears to be genuine, but in fact people are given soft cushions to make them comfortable and lull them to sleep. It is the time of the *falsi fratres*, a feature already identified with the time of the Antichrist by Tyconius and Augustine.[53]

A variant of this interpretation is found in Schwenckfeld's exposition of Zechariah I in 1541. The three horses which appear there, red, brown, and white represent in turn the suffering and humiliation of Christ and his followers, the moderation of the suffering as the final liberation approaches, and finally, Jesus in glory on a white horse, leading the army of the redeemed.[54] This image of the horsemen was much more congenial to Schwenckfeld that the one from the Apocalypse because it included the image of Christ in his heavenly glory.

Another image that encompassed the whole sweep of the story of redemption from incarnation to consummation was that of the stone which destroyed the great image seen by Nebuchadnezzar (Dan. 2:34-5, 45). It spoke to him of the incarnation of Christ which took place 'without hands.'[55] It assured him of his interpretation of the glory of Christ. 'It must be understood to be speaking,' he wrote, 'of the glory and adoration of the flesh of Christ, a mystery set forth by the stone. It was torn from the mountain without hands, struck the great image, shattered it, and became a great mountain that filled the whole world. It signifies not only the *mysterium incarnationis Christi* but also the *mysterium apotheoseos*, the divinising (*Gottwerdung*) of Christ.'[56] Beyond that it spoke to Schwenckfeld of the eternal kingdom and perpetual glory of Christ at the consummation of all things.[57]

But Schwenckfeld did not only look to written prophecy. Like his contemporaries he also looked out over Europe and saw signs there of the nearness of the end. In 1545, after having just heard of the death of Valentine Crautwald, he wrote to his friend Hans Wilhelm von Laubenberg about these signs.[58] He lists six of them. The first is the Smalcald War, which might, if Jerome is correct, mean the end of the Roman Empire, and therewith a clear sign of the approaching end. The second sign is the revelation of the Antichrist with his spurious worship, unjust coercion and false teaching. Thirdly, there is the appearance of false prophets and apostles. When have there been more preachers who run without ever having been called, and who promise the kingdom of heaven for a piece of bread without repentance? The ceremonial sacrament is their cure for everything. But they will have nothing to do with repentance and the gracious work of the Holy Spirit. A particularly clear sign is that people are more inclined to believe lies than truth. Truth has no home today and is driven out and scattered. But every error has its crowds. The fifth sign is the persecution of the true church which is the most severe that has ever been. In one of his letters Schwenckfeld mentions the execution of a number of English churchmen because they confessed that Christ was not in the bread but in heaven at the right hand of God.[59] He also mentions the death of five martyrs in Paris. At this very time Anabaptists everywhere found themselves persecuted, especially in the Netherlands. The present persecution, he wrote, is the fiercest of all the ten persecutions and worse than those by the pagans because it is Christians persecuting each other.[60] And finally, there are signs in sun and moon. In his commentary on Revelation 6:12 Schwenckfeld explains this to mean the blotting out of the knowledge of Christ in the Spirit, and that under the Antichrist the church will be blood and flesh, that is, it will be carnally minded.[61] That is all taking place now in Catholicism and Lutheranism. God be praised, he writes, that these two are not far from the consummated kingdom of the Antichrist.[62] The end is near, and that calls for all true Christians to be vigilant.

For all that Schwenckfeld was by no means discouraged since he regarded the final appearance and defeat of the Antichrist, and all his minions as the prelude to a reformation of the church. He discussed this at length in his 1546 work *Von dreyerley leben der Menschen*,[63] basing himself primarily on the Apocalypse with some references to Romans at the end. The Apocalypse proves, he writes, that this reformation will come since it is a book that tells the story of the church from the beginning to the end of the world. This reformation and reconstruction of the church will take place before the Last Day, and therefore within human history. The conversion of Israel will be part of this reformation. That it will not take place with the church in its present divided and corrupt state is clear enough. But since Israel's conversion is to be within history according to Paul in Romans, Schwenckfeld can hope for a reformation within history.

But he wants to be certain that he is not misunderstood. The reformation will not be the millennium. The number 1000 is to be interpreted spiritually in any case; it is a number which denotes perfection, and means the whole period of the kingdom of Christ.[64]

The new reformation is also not the erection of a pure sinless church, whose members no longer need to be forgiven. That is not possible within history. And finally, it is also not the extermination of evil as though it were possible to have perfect justice in a mutable world. These are all clearly the rejection of manifestations of perfectionism within Anabaptism.

For the positive statement of what this reformation will be it is best to listen to Schwenckfeld's own words:

In a word our consolation, hope, and prayer to God is,
that our Lord Jesus Christ might, in the present lan-
guishing state of the church, use the only proper means,
that is, establish a bond of unity between his people, to
send forth many pious, faithful teachers into his vine-
yard, who will not mix or adulterate the word with the
doctrines of men, but holy men, who will only seek the
honor of God and the salvation of men. Teachers who
will preach the gospel not only in the outward form or
letter, but with the spirit and power, in the demonstra-
tion of the Spirit, that the blessing of God may richly
descend upon his heritage and give a gracious increase.
In this way will the Lord purify and renew the hearts of
his people.... In like manner will he re-establish the lan-
guishing worship of god, in spirit and in truth, and build
up the waste places, and greatly multiply the number of
true Christians, that the earth, according to the predictions of the prophets, may be covered with the glory of
Christ and the knowledge of the Lord as the waters cover
the sea.[65]

That is, all in all, a very modest expectation, calling for no
spectacular incursions of divine wisdom and power such as we
find, for instance, in the expectations of Melchior Hoffman.[66]

But he also has some things to say about the faithful teachers and holy men who will be instrumental in this future reformation. The seven angels with seven trumpets and seven
plagues of Revelation 11 are the messengers and teachers sent
by God to bring about the reformation. When their work is
finished 'the temple of God in heaven will be a reality.' He
also identifies the two witnesses of chapter 9 as those who
will restore the church. Finally, he refers to 'another angel'
(Rev. 14:6), the one proclaiming the everlasting gospel, and
appends a reflection about Elijah. There have been two so
far, Elijah the Tishbite and John the Baptist. 'Even so the
Holy Spirit will have his special Elijah who will serve him by
restoring and setting right everything in the church that has
been scattered and devastated by the Antichrist.'[67] Do we detect here an unspoken, wistful hope that it might be he, even
though when others suggested it, he modestly put it aside?[68]

The New Jerusalem that comes down from God out of
heaven (Rev. 21:10) is very simply identified with the newly

built reformed church in her divine ornaments, adorned with the glory of God.

But it is still all part of human history. In the meantime the souls of those who had been killed for the witness of Jesus were under the altar (Rev. 6:9-11). That means, writes Schwenckfeld, that they have not yet been united with their bodies which are still on earth. They are not yet completely glorified as Christ their head is who lives now in heaven in his flesh. They will be reunited with their bodies when those who are on earth are transformed into the glorious spiritual body with Christ at the Second Coming, for, writes Schwenckfeld quoting Hebrews 11:40, 'apart from us they should not be made perfect.' This is not the doctrine of soul-sleep which was not uncommon in the sixteenth century. Rather, the souls under the altar are fully conscious, contemplating in awe and wonderment the perfection of the glory of Christ. They are to wait there until the number of martyrs is complete, and this completion, writes Schwenckfeld, is taking place now since this is the worst of all the persecutions.[69]

Once we are beyond this point in Schwenckfeld's chronology of the end we are beyond history. He has virtually no interest in the Second Coming and Judgment, otherwise standard features in sixteenth century apocalyptic. He refers to these 'events' in various passages but gives no further attention to them, not even in his commentary on Revelation.[70]

But he gives a lot of attention to the final 'event,' that of Christ's surrender of the kingdom to God according to I Corinthians 15:24. This is an important passage for Schwenckfeld because the 'creaturists' use it to dispute his view of the heavenly glory of Christ. To their criticisms he replies that it is here by no means a question of Christ doing homage to God as though he were the Father's feudal vassal. The surrender of the kingdom is not surrender of his equality but rather of the kingship which Christ has exercised in history. In this time Christ rules over his own both physically and spiritually. The kingdom is composed of those who believe in him and, as used here, is not a general designation of Christ's eternal sovereignty as the Second Person of the Trinity. All whom Christ in his flesh conquered from Satan and his horde are his kingdom, '*Land und Leute*, and the souls and consciences' which are subject to Christ the king. When all his own are gathered into his kingdom and all his enemies have been defeated, then he will surrender this temporal kingdom. and present all those who comprise it to God. It is the final uniting of all things, Christ with his own, his own with Christ, and all with God.[71] Now it is no longer a secret kingdom of faith and hope, but the all-encompassing kingdom of eternal seeing (*Schauen*) in the clarity of God, in the perfection of Christ.[72]

Conclusion

From the foregoing it appears fair to conclude that Schwenckfeld was interested only in those aspects of apocalyptic which in his view related directly to his view of Christ, exalted in heaven in his glorified flesh, and his interpretation of the eucharist which was determined by his christology. The Antichrist was the evil corporate power, extended through history, that sought specially to deny the heavenly glory of Christ as Schwenckfeld understood it and to reduce him to a creature. The future reformation of the church within history just before the end meant primarily the departure from the literal-creaturely understanding of Christ and of the eucharist to his spiritual understanding. The final consummation and surrender of the kingdom by Christ to the Father was the eternal vindication of Schwenckfeld's view of Jesus as the man of flesh even in his heavenly glory as the eternally supreme sovereign and Second Person of the Trinity. His apocalyptic has, as it were, no ontology of its own. It lived and thrived on the body of his doctrine of the heavenly flesh. In this he appears to have been unique in his time.

Notes

[1] CS 11:919.
[2] CS 9:706.
[3] Ibid.
[4] CS 9:364.
[5] CS 9:923.
[6] CS 1:41.
[7] CS 1:129-40.
[8] CS 1:310-33.
[9] CS 2:453-54.
[10] CS 19:205, 920-22; CS 10:113; CS 11:365.
[11] CS 19:332.

12 CS 9:205.

13 CS 4:190.

14 The main summaries are in CS 3:845; 4:189-92; 9:920-21; 10:113-14; 11:365-66. The passages form the basis of the following summary without detailed documentation. Any references that do not follow are taken from elsewhere in Schwenckfeld's works.

15 CS 9:901; 19:338.

16 CS 19:310.

17 CS 19:339. I identify the commentary included in the *Corpus* as Schwenckfeld's with the awareness of the multiple authorship. But Professor Packull (see his article in this volume) identifies the Corpus version as closest to Schwenckfeld's own views.

18 CS 9:205.

19 CS 19:289, 310

20 CS 9:321.

21 CS 9:204.

22 CS 9:899-900.

23 CS 9:497-99.

24 CS 19:345. Cf. CS 11:366-67.

25 CS 9:33-34.

26 CS 3:824 indicates that this date is somewhat conjectural.

27 CS 3:827.

28 CS 4:189-92.

29 CS 9:208.

30 CS 19:339, 341.

31 CS 19:342; CS 9:499.

32 CS 19:343-44.

33 CS 9:900-04.

34 CS 3:527-28.

35 CS 11:985-87.

36 CS 2:575.

37 CS 8:365.

38 CS 7:773.

39 CS 9:911-15.

40 CS 11:365.

41 CS 9:900; CS 16:287; CS 19:322.

42 CS 19:323.

43 CS 11:365.

44 CS 19:356.

45 CS 19:342.

46 CS 9:208.

47 CS 16:287.

48 The only notable exception was Zwingli.

49 CS 16:289.

50 Ibid.

51 CS 19:365.

[52] CS 19:299.

[53] CS 19:294-96. Similar schemes are found in Anselm of Havelberg (1100-1158) and Otto von Freising (1114-1158), although there is no evidence that Schwenckfeld knew the writings of these men. See Horst D. Rauh, *Das Bild des Antichrist im Mittelalter: Von Tyconius zum deutschen Symbolismus*. (Münster, 1973), 276-77 and 349.

[54] CS 7:403-05.

[55] CS 12:611.

[56] CS 17:157.

[57] CS 7:847.

[58] CS 9:497-99.

[59] This letter is dated 1557. We have here therefore a reference to the deaths of Cranmer, Ridley, Latimer (1556) and Hooper (1555) and others in the Marian persecution.

[60] CS 15:194. It was a feature of some medieval interpretations of history that there had been ten persecutions. One such was Bonaventure (1217-1274). See B. McGinn, *Visions of the End*, (New York, 1979), 199.

[61] CS 19:298-99.

[62] CS 9:499.

[63] CS 9:904-20.

[64] CS 9:242-43; CS 19:366; Cf. CS 17:827.

[65] CS 9:906-07. Translation in *The Three-Fold Life of Man*, trans. by F. R. Anspach (Baltimore, 1858), 170-71.

[66] CS 17:827.

[67] CS 19:349-50.

[68] CS 11:919.

[69] CS 19:297-98.

[70] Some references are CS 18:256; 19:267.

[71] CS 6:246-49; CS 3:330.

[72] CS 10:704.

The Schwenkfeldian Commentary on the Apocalypse

Werner O. Packull

The *Corpus Schwenckfeldianorum* contains a Commentary on the Apocalypse attributed to Caspar Schwenckfeld. This 'semi-critical edition' was based on a manuscript copied by Daniel Sudermann in 1610. It varies in content and in terms of Bibles used from two other manuscripts of the same Commentary, copies of which have survived in German archives. The oldest of these, in the script of Adam Reisner and dating from May 6, 1556, lacks positive identification of author, raising the question of whether the original Commentary should be attributed to Schwenckfeld. Although this was duly noted by the editors of the *Corpus*, they were unable to clarify the problem of authorship or the relationship of the manuscripts to each other. Consequently this study had to begin with an attempt to clear the interrelationship of the surviving manuscripts, to date the approximate time of origin of the *Urtext*, and to clarify its authorship. Only after these problems had been adequately addressed was it deemed fruitful to probe the oldest surviving manuscript for its hermeneutic and content.

Historical Background

(1) The Manuscripts

The editors of the *Corpus* designated the three known manuscripts found in libraries and archives of Berlin, Munich, and Nürnberg as A, B, and C respectively. For the sake of convenience these designations have been retained. By way of background, the known facts about the three manuscripts are here briefly rehearsed.

Of the three, A and C were at one time in the possession of Daniel Sudermann. A was given to Sudermann around 1595. An entry at the beginning indicates that Burckhardt Schilling, son of a Schwenkfeldian preacher by the same name, was the donor. The manuscript itself originated around 1571 and was a copy made by Hans Georg Schid, preacher in Lampertheim. It carries the title 'Ein Kurtze Auslegung Der Offenbarunge Johannis' with the initials CS.[1]

C, in Sudermann's own hand, carried his initials on the inside of the back cover with the information that he had 'collected' the materials and brought them into a 'proper order.' His declared intentions were to edify the 'lovers and confessors of the glory of Christ.' Dating from 1610, C carries exactly the same title as A, and claims Schwenckfeld under the pseudonym, D. Eliander,[2] as its author.[3]

The editors noted the disparity in size between A and C, and were able to provide helpful cross-references to various sources from which Sudermann 'collected' some of the additional materials. Although they did not critically evaluate the relationship of C to A they did render valuable service by providing extensive footnotes comparing variations in the texts of the manuscripts. For purposes of this study, it was most helpful to compare the edition in the *Corpus* and its cross references to A with the third manuscript, B.[4]

In the script of Adam Reisner,[5] B was completed on May 6, 1556. It carries the simple designation 'Apocalypsis,' with the subtitle 'Auslegung der Offenbarung Johannis.' Hence the title varies slightly from that found in A and C. More significantly, the manuscript provides no identification of its author. Since B is the oldest of the three extant versions, the lack of positive identification of author is significant. Interestingly, B was initially bound into one codex with Valentine Crautwald's 'Hoffhaltung des Herren Christi, contra impugnatores Graciae,'[6] also in Reisner's hand. Less than two years earlier (Oct. 1554), Reisner completed the transcription of Crautwald's 'Collectanea.'[7] B was therefore copied during a time period when Reisner was otherwise preoccupied with Crautwald's works. As is also well known, Reisner translated several of Crautwald's Latin works. Schwenckfeld in turn edited and published several of Crautwald's treatises without clear identification of the author or under the initials V.C.S. (Valentine Crautwald of Silesia).[8] The initials confused contemporaries, who, at times, credited the better-known Schwenckfeld with authorship. Schwenckfeld, interested in protecting his friend, seems not to have been adverse to such confusion. Moreover, at times he took editorial liberties which suggest that he treated Crautwald's statements as the collective wisdom of the 'lovers and confessors of the glory of Christ.' None of this proves helpful when investigating questions of authenticity. As will be seen, it is open to debate whether the original version of the Commentary on the Apocalypse can be attributed to Schwenckfeld.

(2) A Comparison of the Manuscripts

A comparison of B with the edition in the *Corpus* and its variations from A, as indicated by the editorial apparatus, suggests that B or its prototype served as the basis for A and C. According to the principle of modern critical method, when seeking to establish the *Urtext*, it is a fair assumption that in the process of transmission additions are more likely than omissions.[9] The manuscripts in question provide a perfect illustration of this maxim. As noted above. C contains considerable additional information beyond A. Or to put it differently, with few exceptions, everything contained in A is repeated and elaborated in C. It may be inferred therefore that C constitutes an expanded version of A, a conclusion supported by the fact that A had come into Sudermann's possession fifteen years before he completed C. The dependence of C on A is further demonstrated by the fact that in cases where A varies from B, C follows A (Appendix 1). Meanwhile a comparison of B with A indicates a close generic relationship between these two. Indeed. the conclusion is inescapable that A was a copy either of B or of its prototype. Both A and B were certainly closer to the initial version of the Commentary than the manuscript included in the *Corpus*.

Both A and B differ from C in chapter divisions and in citations of biblical texts. As the editors of the *Corpus* correctly surmised, different Bibles were used in preparation of the manuscripts. The Bible used for B and A can now be identified as Luther's Bible of 1536. Perhaps the most convincing evidence for this contention is found in the divisions of chapters 10 and 11. Both A and B begin chapter 11 with what is the third verse of chapter 11 in the King James version. Both open chapter 12 with what is verse 15 of chapter 11 in the King James version. Thus, these sources provide a shortened

chapter 11, the content of which is limited to the ministry of
the two prophets. These divisions correspond to the divisions
found in Luther's Bible of 1536. C, however, shows divisions
parallel to those found in the Vulgate and the King James version. Frequent references to original Greek texts suggest that
Sudermann may have consulted a Greek New Testament.[10]

Other evidence for the use of Luther's Bible in A and B
may be gleaned from the exegesis of the four beasts around the
throne (Rev. 4:6). The 'four times six' wings of the beasts are
said to represent the twenty-four books of the Old Testament.[11]
A glance at the table of contents of Luther's Bible of 1536 indicates that Luther had arranged the Old Testament into twenty-
four sections. The twelve 'Minor prophets' were combined in
the twenty-fourth section. Whether by mistake or deliberately
C as given in the *Corpus* speaks of twenty-five books of the Old
Testament. Thus, the analogy between the twenty-four wings
of the Beasts and the twenty-four books of the Old Testament
loses its meaning. The agreement between the commentary
and the Bible originally used is broken.[12]

A few expressions citing Luther's translation in A and B but
changed in C may further illustrate the above point. Thus,
where A and B have *werck*, C speaks of *Arbeit*.[13] Similarly,
where A and B bring Luther's expression *scharfe Hippe*, C
has *Sichel*.[14] Where Luther translated *arge drus*, Sudermann
used *arge geschwer*.[15] Interestingly, on at least one occasion,
A and B provide a rider to Luther's translation, indicating
that the *Urtext* used a different biblical version, perhaps the
Vulgate. The case in point concerned Luther's translation of
Revelation 11:2 as a reference to the inner *Chor* of the Temple.
Here the commentator or the copyist noted, 'the old Bible has
outer court of the temple.'[16] The observation was repeated in
C where Sudermann added that 'some Greek texts' and the
'Old Translation' have 'outer court.'[17]

The point to be made here is that both A and B used
Luther's Bible as a basis for their Commentary while the same
case cannot be made for C. We can summarize our findings so
far by means of a list as follows:

Urtext, author and date of origin unknown. Bible used
described as 'old Bible,' possibly Vulgate.

Manuscript A, 1571 by Schilling. Luther's Bible of
1536 used.

Manuscript B, 1556 by Reisner. Luther's Bible of 1536 used.

Manuscript C, 1610 by Sudermann. Greek New Testament used. Additional information gleaned from Schwenckfeld's writings.

Corpus edition. Compared to A in notes.

We can now resume our examination of the question of authorship, and attempt a dating of the original Commentary.

(3) Authorship and Time of Origin

As noted above, B makes no mention of the author. A case will be made here for Crautwald as the originator of the initial Commentary. Indirect evidence comes from a letter, dated April 18, 1546, by Schwenckfeld to Gregor Tag [Emaranus], preacher at Wohlau, Silesia.[18] Schwenckfeld responded to a previous letter by Tag in which Tag implied that it was providential that certain writings by Crautwald had not become public knowledge. Otherwise Crautwald rather than God would have received credit for key ideas cherished in Schwenckfeld's circle. Schwenckfeld did not entirely agree with this appraisal. He lamented the fact that Crautwald's writings had been confiscated and their anxiously awaited arrival delayed. The writings in question included, among others, Crautwald's *Collectanea*.[19] Of special interest for our study is the indirect evidence that Tag had come into possession of a Commentary on the Apocalypse by Crautwald. He sent it on to Schwenckfeld with apologies for the delay caused by his keeping it awhile for his own perusal. Schwenckfeld wrote:

> I have nothing against the fact that you have kept the Apocalypse of the blessed father for a while and perused it. Although I too, just as you, consoled myself to find more therein. I hope the other *Collectanea* will bring something greater of Christ... than is spoken of in this book.[20]

Thus, according to the statement made by Schwenckfeld in April 1546, Crautwald had written a Commentary on the Apocalypse which proved somewhat of a disappointment. Nevertheless, Schwenckfeld then went on to praise Crautwald for having aroused his own interest in the Apocalypse. As a result he had studied it with greater benefit than in previous times,

finding much 'glorious witness' of the *Gloria Christi* there. Tag
had apparently expressed disappointment with Crautwald's exegesis of particular passages, or lack thereof. Schwenckfeld
found it necessary to apologize for his late friend, described
as a 'weak, sick man,' who may have had good reasons to
hold back.[21] From this exchange, we can infer therefore that
Schwenckfeld had received Crautwald's Commentary on the
Apocalypse sometime prior to April 1546. The Commentary
had first gone through the hands of Gregor Tag who presumably received it sometime after Crautwald's death, September
5, 1545. Perhaps Crautwald's former *famulus*, Sebastian Eisenmann, who joined other Schwenkfelders in Glatz after the death
of Crautwald, had brought it to the apocalyptically-minded
Tag.[22]

At any rate, both Tag and Schwenckfeld seemed disappointed with Crautwald's initial effort—the former because of
its brevity and because it failed to answer some of his questions relating to the end time, the latter because he hoped to
find a greater witness to his peculiar christology. As a result
Schwenckfeld undertook his own reexamination of the Book
of Revelation. Eventually he appears to have rewritten and
fleshed out Crautwald's original Commentary.

This sequence of events is borne out by a careful analysis of
one of Schwenckfeld's treatises written at this time. The document in question is the *Three Kinds of Human Life*, completed
prior to June 1546.[23] Although intended as a little book on
'good works and their reward,' the lengthy treatise, not published until 1547, contains a six-chapter exegetical digression
into the Apocalypse.[24] What Schwenckfeld found of special interest in the Apocalypse is indicated by the relevant chapter
headings: chapter 40: 'Of the dissolution of the daily sacrifice and ruin of the true worship by Antichrist'; chapter 41:
'Wherein may be recognized the anti-Christian kingdom in its
members, false teachers, and servants'; chapter 42: 'About the
last dangerous times of the church and the common (general)
decline of the Christian life'; chapter 43: 'About reforming of
the church and the restoration of true worship through the
Spirit of the Lord'; chapter 44: 'Testimony of the glory of
Christ and the future reforming of the church through Christ,
from the Book of Revelation by John'; chapter 45' 'What from
the Holy Scriptures should be understood by the name Antichrist.'

A survey of the content of these chapters indicates that Schwenckfeld searched the Apocalypse primarily for statements supportive of his christology, prophetic statements concerning deviations from true worship, and promises of a spiritual Reformation. Christology took obvious priority among these topics. Schwenckfeld listed ten major passages illustrative of the notion that the ascended Christ is 'one in power, being, and glory with the Father in eternity.'[25] A similar tour de force provided evidence for the 'falling away, dissension, and destruction of the church in the last days' under Antichrist.[26] Set over against it were visions that promised a 'Reformation or rebuilding of the church.' Passages about the New Jerusalem and its temple were therefore of special interest to Schwenckfeld. The promised restoration of the church implied above all a renewed recognition of the glorified Christ as 'ruling king' in his church.

Thus, the evidence indicates that Schwenckfeld searched the Apocalypse carefully for the topics of interest to him. No attempt was made to seek a comprehensive meaning of its visions. The exegesis itself moved along the lines of the devotional and meditative tradition. In the process of exegesis, any 'chiliastic' interpretation was explicitly rejected.[27]

For the purposes of this paper, the significance of Schwenckfeld's discussion of the Apocalypse in his *Three Kinds of Human Life* is as follows: (1) It confirms that Schwenckfeld studied John's Revelation very carefully early in 1546. (2) It can be assumed that the inspiration for this enterprise came from Crautwald's initial exegesis. (3) Perhaps most importantly, a comparison of Schwenckfeld's interpretation of specific texts of the Apocalypse given in 1546 with the exegesis of the same texts given in Reisner's manuscript of 1556 (B) indicates a very close relationship between the two. It is possible to infer that Schwenckfeld's statements made in *Three Kinds of Human Life* of 1546 represent polished paraphrases of pertinent passages in the Commentary as given in B. On occasion the 1546 statements seem to be verbatim citations of B.[28] All this suggests, as best as can be reconstructed, that while studying the Apocalypse in 1546 Schwenckfeld rewrote and expanded the cursory Commentary by Crautwald. This expanded version must have served as the original text for Reisner's copy of B ten years later.

The above description of the origin of the Commentary finds support in the disparate composition of B. At least two layers of commentary may by discerned. The first and presumably older statements take the form of key-word captions. It seems that these were originally in the shape of marginal glosses on the biblical text.[29] A second layer of comment reads like an amplification of the key-word captions. In other words, the second layer constitutes an elaboration on the original comments. This gives the entire composition the appearance of repetitiveness and redundancy (Appendix 2). Given the information above, it is conceivable that the cursory key-word captions originated with Crautwald while the second layer was the work of Schwenckfeld originating in 1546. Curiously, in the *Three Kinds of Human Life* Schwenckfeld cited Crautwald in Latin as his source for the interpretation of at least one of the texts. The editors of the *Corpus* were unable to identify the Crautwald source cited. Presumably it was Crautwald's Commentary on the Apocalypse. At least this could help to explain why B provided the same interpretation in German translation without reference to Crautwald;[30] for if our reasoning is correct, Crautwald's initial annotations were in Latin. They were either translated and elaborated by Schwenckfeld himself in 1546 or by Reisner ten years later. At any rate, the oldest version of the Commentary is credited to the co-authorship of Crautwald and Schwenckfeld.

One further aspect relating to Schwenckfeld's study of the Apocalypse in 1546 is of significance in this context. A careful comparison of Schwenckfeld's statements in the *Three Kinds of Human Life* with C reveals that Sudermann utilized practically all of them to expand his copy of the Commentary (Appendix 3). Indeed, he placed Schwenckfeld's concluding statement at the end of C.[31] Thus, we have found the single most important source for the additional material with which Sudermann embellished C. Paradoxically then, C, although furthest removed in time and composition from the *Urtext*, is more Schwenkfeldian than the earlier manuscripts.

We may now turn to an examination of B with the specific intention of searching for statements revealing non-Schwenkfeldian origins. A case in point is the comment on the church of Laodicea (Rev. 3:14ff.). B identifies the lukewarm church, without qualification, with the Lutherans.[32] However, in his treatise of 1546, Schwenckfeld specifically attributed this identification to others, designating them simply as 'some.'[33] This point takes on greater significance in that the entire Commentary as preserved in B is polemically directed above all against Lutherans. However, Schwenckfeld's express purpose in his treatise of 1546 was to find a 'proper medium,' a Christian Concordia, between the Lutheran and Papal parties.[34] The strong anti-Lutheran undercurrent of the Commentary therefore appears to be at odds with Schwenckfeld's declared intentions in 1546. Indeed, the anti-Lutheran polemics suggest a Silesian context. If they did not originate with Crautwald himself, then they must have reflected the feelings of other Schwenkfeldians in Silesia.

Evidence that others added to the original manuscript could be contained in a letter by Schwenckfeld in August 1549. While paying respects to Gregor Tag, who had passed away several weeks earlier. Schwenckfeld recalled: 'Our prophet Tag sent us concerning the Apocalypse. His interpretation of the two witnesses, Rev. 11, is done only too well. I cannot permit it to be read. I must erase the names....'[35] The reference was to the identification of Crautwald and Schwenckfeld as the apocalyptic Enoch and Elijah. By inference, Tag had added the identification on a manuscript circulating among the brothers. Whether the manuscript in question was Crautwald's original Commentary can not be ascertained. It will be recalled that Tag had studied the latter before sending it on to Schwenckfeld.

Curiously, B, produced by Reisner, makes no explicit reference to the identification of the two witnesses as Crautwald and Schwenckfeld. Sudermann, however, must have seen the comments and Schwenckfeld's instructions. In the margin to the exegesis of the two witnesses, he wrote: 'It stated thus: *V.C. and C.S.. as has been revealed to some.* This can be left out.'[36] Sudermann's marginalia therefore included both Tag's identification and Schwenckfeld's instruction to delete the same. Since he added the information in the margin, Sudermann did not conceive of it as an integral part of the Commentary. But this did not prevent him from elaborating on the role of Crautwald and Schwenckfeld as the two witnesses.

The point to be made here is that although the Commentary, especially in the form incorporated in the *Corpus,* bore Schwenckfeld's stamp, it was not the product of a single mind. Evidence indicates that Crautwald was its original inspiration and author. Early in 1546 Schwenckfeld apologetically reworked the annotations of his esteemed colleague. He thus gave the Commentary its peculiar christological thrust. B must have been copied from this revised commentary. It was no longer purely Crautwaldian, but not solely Schwenkfeldian either. Perhaps this explains why B failed to name the author. Sudermann later felt that the Commentary needed further Schwenkfeldianization. He supplemented it with information gleaned from other writings by Schwenckfeld, above all, Schwenckfeld's more polished and systematic statements in *Three Kinds of Human Life*. Sudermann's final product was therefore closer in interpretation to Schwenckfeld's intentions than the earlier manuscripts. The editors of the *Corpus* are therefore at least partially vindicated for choosing C for inclusion in the collected works of Schwenckfeld. However, B remains without question closer to the original composition. It must be the starting point for any attempted examination of Crautwald's initial contribution and the approximate dates of origin.

The Internal Evidence for Crautwald's Authorship

To unscramble the Commentary with the intention of identifying what was Crautwald's initial contribution and what genuine Schwenckfeld would prove well nigh impossible. The aim here is more modest—to highlight some of the statements that appear to predate Schwenckfeld's preoccupation with the Apocalypse in 1546, and hence provide a possible case for Crautwald's authorship.

A careful reading of B suggests that at least some of the concerns expressed there date from around 1536, that is, ten years before Schwenckfeld devoted himself to the subject. One clue comes in the context of an exegesis of the third trumpet (Rev. 8:10) and the falling star named Wormwood. According to the initial commentary, Wormwood represented 'a great Pharisee, a learned cleric, Martin Bucer or an Anabaptist.' Bucer is singled out as fallen from grace because he has joined with Luther in a *Concordia*. Presumably, this was a reference to the *Wittenberg Concord* of 1536 and not as Sudermann in

C believed, a reference to the method of biblical annotation used by Luther and Bucer![37] Horst Weigelt has recently drawn attention to the fact that Crautwald was particularly sensitive to any rapprochement between Strassburg and Wittenberg. Crautwald felt not only further isolated by the *Concord*, but viewed it as a betrayal by Bucer of the cherished position of God's unmediated grace, *Heilsgewirklichkeit*.[38]

The reference to an Anabaptist leader could also reflect concerns of the mid-thirties. The designation, 'great Pharisee and learned cleric,' could be an allusion to Bernd Rothmann. 'Some' of the interpreters, the more elaborate statement explains, believe that the fallen star Wormwood refers to the Anabaptists, 'who have embittered everything... and have made the authorities suspicious of everything, including the rising pure divine truth.'[39] This could describe the impact of Münster, if read in the same time context as the reference to the *Concordat* of 1536.[40] If this statement can be traced to Crautwald, then it is plausible to argue that the Commentary had its genesis some time after 1536 and before his death on September 5, 1545.

At any rate, the attitude toward the Anabaptists throughout the Commentary is highly suggestive of authorship by Crautwald. It seems at odds with the more amiable attitude encountered in Schwenckfeld's earlier writings. Although he clashed with Melchior Hoffman at the Strassburg Synod of 1533 and later fought a war of words with Pilgrim Marpeck, Schwenckfeld's attitude remained genteel. True, he criticized Anabaptists for their self-righteous attitude toward outsiders, but to persecute them was to touch 'the apple of God's eye.'[41] Crautwald, on the other hand encountered a different branch of Anabaptism in the late 1520s and early 30s which, led by Oswald Glaidt and Andreas Fischer, developed highly legalistic and Sabbatarian attitudes. Later some went so far as to make circumcision a sign of the true faith. They were decried by Crautwald as above all Old Testament legalists and literalists.[42]

This was precisely the description of Anabaptists offered in B. They were identified with the church of Sardis, who had 'a name that thou livest, and art dead' (Rev. 3:1). According to the commentator, it was the 'hypocritical church of literalists, who dealt with the Scriptures according to flesh and

blood.'[43] Suprisingly, the Commentary makes no mention of
Carlstadt or Zwingli. This again suggests the environment of
Crautwald's Liegnitz. Crautwald's own understanding of the
contemporary religious scene has been fittingly described as
that of a *Stubengelehrter*.[44]

Other clues could similarly point to the aging Crautwald.
Certain passages suggest a preoccupation with the frailties of
old age. Thus, the promise that 'God shall wipe away all tears'
(Rev. 21:4) provokes the comment that this will not only bring
an end to persecution but also an end to old age![45] 'No ill or
feeble person will be found in the New Jerusalem.'[46] At the
same time, the author laments that the young are being attracted to the 'false teachers' [Lutherans].[47] surely these statements reveal something about the fear of aging. As is well
known Crautwald repeatedly cited old age and failing health
as the reason why he no longer travelled. Commenting on the
dismissal of his colleague Johann Werner in 1539, he wrote
gratefully that God has spared him in his 'old age. He had not
been forced into the street, but had been permitted to remain
in his corner.'[48]

Other circumstantial evidence could also point to Crautwald. Emmet McLaughlin has drawn attention to the fact that
the early Schwenckfeld thought of society in the rural or feudal
terms of priests, nobles, and princes. The citizen [Bürger] appeared to have no function in his religious imagery.[49] Yet, the
Commentary contains several such references. Not all spring
from the text dealing with the heavenly Jerusalem.[50] Thus,
the comment on Revelation 1:6 suggests that in the kingdom
of Christ all citizens will be 'raised to the status of priests and
kings.'[51]

To be sure, none of this is compelling proof for Crautwald's
original authorship, but the cumulative weight of the evidence
is in Crautwald's favour. We can therefore summarize our
findings as follows: The initial Commentary in all probability
originated with Crautwald. After Crautwald's work reached
Schwenckfeld, the latter undertook his own reexamination of
the Book of Revelation. At the same time he rewrote or expanded Crautwald's Exposition. The oft repeated phrase 'some
say' suggests that Schwenckfeld treated the Commentary as a
collective depository of the insights of the 'lovers and confessors
of the glory of Christ.'

Hermeneutic Principles of the Commentary

The principles of interpretation were clearly spelled out by the author(s) at the beginning of the Commentary. A threefold mode of revelation was possible. First, God could convey his message through physical means or through the senses, 'as when Balthasar saw a hand visibly writing on the wall.' Secondly, God could reveal himself through figurative means such as occurred 'in dreams or ecstasy.' Thirdly, God revealed himself by spiritual means (*intellectualis*), when through the Holy Spirit he granted clear understanding to the 'believing heart.'[52] This highest degree of revelation had imparted to the apostle John an understanding of the 'infinite glory of the body, flesh, and blood of Christ.'[53] At the very heart of Schwenckfeld's Exposition was therefore a heightened eucharistic concern, an almost sacramental reading of scripture in search of the revelation of Christ's heavenly body.[54] By means of inner contemplation the believer could spiritually taste and enjoy this body in the present, while longing for its eschatological fulfillment in the Last Supper and Marriage Feast. Schwenckfeld and Crautwald, it seems, turned to the Apocalypse above all for comfort, for devotional reading for food to the inner man. Exegesis itself was the product of meditation and contemplation. Its aim was to instruct the pious heart.[55] Indeed, in several passages the author(s) burst into personal prayer and praise.[56] Understandably, such an approach did not lend itself to treating the Apocalypse as a structural whole. Nor did it deal with John's Revelation as a plan of church history or a chiliastic manifesto.

If the three modes of revelation indicated in the introduction implied a three-layer interpretive key to the Apocalypse, then it is possible that the author(s) originally intended a threefold interpretation of key texts. However, this assignment was never carried out. It is therefore more likely that the three fold distinction was intended to underline the authority of Scriptural revelation and the importance of spiritual allegorical exegesis. At any rate, the attitude informing the exegesis of the Commentary indicates striking parallels to Origen's view of Scripture. About the latter, Beryl Smalley writes:

> Scripture for him was a mirror, which reflected the divinity now darkly, now brightly; it had body, soul, and spirit, a literal, moral and allegorical sense, the first two

for simple believers, who were unable to understand pro-
founder meanings, the third for the initiates, the Christian gnostics, who were able to investigate the wisdom
in a mystery, the hidden wisdom of God.[57]

Schwenckfeld's and Crautwald's study of Scripture concerned itself with the wisdom of God in Christ. In a circle
of friends that included some given to direct revelation, an
emphasis on allegorical spiritual exegesis enhanced the importance of the gifted exegete. Perhaps this helps to explain the
esteem enjoyed by Crautwald.

That Crautwald and Schwenckfeld were indebted to both
late medieval and patristic traditions of exegesis becomes clear
at a variety of points. According to the author(s)' axiom of
interpretation, 'The Apocalypse contained as many secrets as
words.'[58] St. Jerome was cited in support of this view, and
rightly so. According to St. Jerome, who here simply echoed
the Alexandrians,[59] the Apocalypse contained as many *sacra-
menta* as words.[60]

About Jerome's exegetical legacy on the Western church in
general, it has been alleged that he 'left... on one hand a fanciful
spiritual, on the other hand a scholarly literal interpretation.
Medieval students could take their choice.'[61] The esteem held
for St. Jerome in late fifteenth and early sixteenth century
humanist circles needs no elaboration here. His writings were
known to both Crautwald and Schwenckfeld.

That Crautwald consulted patristic and perhaps medieval
commentaries in their study of John's Revelation seems confirmed by their reference to Primasius, a sixth-century North
African bishop.[62] The reference concerns the second beast and
its miraculous power (Rev. 13:11-13). Primasius is cited as
stating that 'The servants of the beast will distribute and praise
many languages as gifts of the Holy Spirit.'[63] Unfortunately it
could not be determined whether the citation was authentic;
nor is it clear whether the author(s) had direct knowledge of
Primasius' influential Commentary. In all probability, they
knew of him only from secondary sources. Nevertheless Primasius' significance for the Western exegetical tradition of the
Apocalypse is worth noting. It was Primasius who domesti-
cated an earlier work by the Donatist, Ticonius.[64] As a result,
key features of Ticonius' interpretation of the Apocalypse were

mediated to the medieval period.[65] As a moderate Donatist, Ticonius read the Apocalypse as an indictment of the world-liness of the 'universal church' and of its 'false bishops and priests.' As a moderate, he nevertheless conceded to the universal church proper efficacy in administering the sacraments, and rejected rebaptism as demanded by radical Donatists. He therefore rejected outright the chiliastic reading of St. John's Revelation by the radical Donatists, thus muting vestiges of the 'historical realistic interpretation.'[66]

Primasius, who literally rewrote Ticonius' Commentary, moderated the Donatist elements even further, but also re-instated some elements of historical interpretation; as, for instance, in his identification of the witnesses with historical persons, a second Enoch and a second Elijah. The second Elijah was expected to play an apocalyptic role as preacher of repentance to the Jews. Antichrist, according to Primasius, would come from the tribe of Dan.[67] But Primasius was not the only mediator of Ticonius to subsequent students. St. Augustine had also found Ticonius' interpretation of the Apocalypse to his liking. Lines became further blurred because Primasius was widely cited in psuedo-Augustinian homilies. It is therefore no longer possible to determine from what source the allusion to Primasius by Schwenckfeld and Crautwald was taken. Possibly they knew of him[68] through one of the 'old teachers' referred to repeatedly. Primasius' Commentary on the Apocalypse, as that of Ticonius, was cited extensively by the venerable Bede (d. 735). The latter was read by Schwenckfeld.[69] This is not the place to trace the actual transmission of the tradition utilized by the author(s). Suffice it to state that such an investigation could throw new light on the hermeneutical presuppositions that informed their understanding of Scripture in general and their reading of the Apocalypse in particular. At least this writer has the impression that both Crautwald and Schwenck-feld were more traditional than previously suggested.

At any rate, the imagery of the Commentary remains strikingly traditional. Thus, angels are throughout interpreted to mean preachers in the church.[70] Stars symbolize teachers.[71] Fallen stars are obviously false teachers. Earthquakes spell insurrection.[72] The seven trumpets are preachers of judgment.[73] Thunder and lightning refer to the preaching

of the Word in judgment. The seven thunders of Rev. 10:4
signify seven false preachers.[74] Smoke is symbolic of the spirit
of prayer.[75] The sea indicates the world or people in general.
White dress means clarification in the spirit, but is also symbolic of regenerational washing in baptism. Thus, the Apocalypse represents a quarry of traditional allegorical types. The
major visions of the Apocalypse can be applied to both the
spiritual odyssey of the single soul and to the church. Certain peculiarities of interpretation such as the Schwenkfeldian
christology do not unduly disturb the traditional patterns.

The above point is best illustrated with reference to the
statements concerning the papal church. Some of these seem
contradictory and provide further circumstantial evidence that
more than one commentator contributed to this interpretation
of John's Revelation. Of special interest in this context are the
key statements regarding the nature of the fallen church and
Antichrist. The passages concerned deal with the 'great red
dragon' (Rev. 12:3), the 'beast from the sea' (Rev. 13:1) and
the 'beast from the earth' (Rev. 13:11).

In traditional exegesis the great red dragon had long been
identified with the beast in Daniel 8. Crautwald and Schwenckfeld took a concordance between the texts in Daniel and Revelation for granted. For them the little horn of the beast in
Daniel 8:9-10 corresponded with the notorious horn of the
dragon. The object of the references in Daniel was historically identified as Antiochus Epiphanes. By means of allegorical interpretation, Antiochus becomes a type of a 'spiritual'
tyrant, that is, of Antichrist, who persecutes the true church
spiritually.[76] The seven heads of the great red dragon of Revelation are described as protectors of the Babylonian whore.
The ten horns are seen as ten persecutors in the tradition of
Antiochus.[77] Obviously Crautwald and Schwenckfeld here drew
on a typology long established in patristic and medieval exegetical traditions.[78]

However, the commentary also reflects the general Reformation climate. As early as 1522, Schwenckfeld identified the
papal church as an instrument of Antichrist.[79] The Commentary generally concurs with this assessment.[80] The church of
Rome is the beast that arose from the sea (Rev. 13:1). The
Lutherans, included in the kingdom of Antichrist, are identified
as the beast that rose out of the earth (Rev. 13:11).[81] Luther

was credited with at first wounding the great beast. But since the great Peasant War. its wound had healed[82] because Luther returned to a creaturely understanding of the presence in the sacrament. Herein then lay what Schwenckfeld considered the essence of anti-Christian practice. Thus, Luther could also be identified with the fallen star or false teacher of the third and fifth trumpets (Rev. 8:10; 9:1). Having thrown away the key to heaven in his rejection of the spiritual understanding of the sacrament, he now held the key to the pit of hell.[83] Apart from suggesting a preoccupation with Luther's view of the creaturely presence, these statements reveal a partial attempt at giving the visions historical and polemical significance; but the attempt seems secondary to Schwenckfeld's preferred allegorical method. Indeed. the injection of the historical interpretation gives the Commentary a *dilettantisch* flavour.

A certain eclecticism and ambivalence remains also in regard to statements about the true church. Key passages of the Apocalypse are given a traditional meaning. Thus, the angel ascending from the East (Rev. 7:2) is interpreted to be the Emperor Constantine, who gave peace to the persecuted church of Christ. Eusebius and the 'papists' are cited without attempt at refutation of this view.[84] Similarly the angel with 'the key to the bottomless pit' (Rev. 20:1 ff.) is identified as Constantine who, according to 'old teachers,' gave the church peace. After Constantine's reign Satan's role as persecutor had been for a thousand years 'limited to the thoughts of the godless.'[85] Consistent with this view. the author speaks of a thousand years 'when pious persons were held in honour.' This time contrasts with the contemporary situation when pious persons are once again persecuted.[86] All this suggests that the traditional interpretation was never radically rethought, or that Schwenckfeld and Crautwald postulated a rather late fall of the church.[87] Aspects of a medieval understanding of the Apocalypse and of church history were retained. Unlike other Reformation interpreters, the author(s) of these comments did not totally reject the papal church. Their concern was primarily with the nature of Christ's presence in the eucharist. A certain ambivalence therefore remains in spite of the identification of the papal church as anti-Christian. Thus, the author can ask the rhetorical question: That St. Peter's little ship shall not perish is well put. But who were they that navigated in it? They were poor fishermen. It is questionable, however, whether the pope's prelates and the learned new and old doctors can be considered St. Peter's little ship.[88]

Obviously the rhetorical question had been answered. Schwenckfeld expected Antichrist and the Babylonian whore, meaning the papal as well as Lutheran churches, to be punished, precisely because they had adopted the anti-Christian view that removed the glorified Christ from his position of honour and placed him in creaturely elements. He therefore expected that a spiritual reformation would supersede the literalist one begun by Luther. The purified spiritual church, consisting of those participating in the first resurrection, that is, the spiritual rebirth from sin, death, and error,[89] constituted the new Jerusalem. Within its gates, the blessed would reach the status of 'joyful beholding and enjoyment of God.' Christ himself was to be the street and light of this city (Rev. 21:23), for he had promised to be present in his church and in his faithful 'without any medium.' The Apocalypse, including the passages concerning the millennium, was therefore ultimately given an other-worldly and spiritual interpretation.[90]

We can therefore summarize our findings as follows: The author(s) of the Commentary were indebted to exegetical traditions that reached back to the patristics. The author(s) searched the Apocalypse primarily for statements supportive of their christology. Of equal importance were prophetic statements that warned of deviations from true worship, as well as passages that could be applied to a coming spiritual reformation. Among these topics christology took obvious precedent. The allegorical method was found particularly suitable for the Christocentric interpretation. When the historical interpretation intruded, particularly in relation to identifying the fallen and the true church, the results were not always consistent. Nevertheless, for purposes of this essay, the ambivalent statements concerning the church are of special interest, precisely because in them a skeletal outline of the author(s)' view of church history become visible.

The Contents

As noted above, the author(s) of the commentary did not attempt a systematic exposition of the major visions of the Apocalypse. Indeed they treated the text as if each word contained a revelation of divine mystery. And yet a careful survey of the interpretation of the key visions suggests that consciously or unconsciously the author(s) accepted an implied larger pattern of revelation relating to church history and contemporary events. It is to these statements, rather that the devotional and meditative aspects of the exegesis that we here draw attention.

Thus, a glance at the exegesis relating to the letters of the seven churches indicates that the author(s) were familiar with a historical application of the texts. The church of Ephesus (Rev. 2:1) is described as the 'first church.' Its falling away indicates a turning to the 'flesh.' Smyrna is designated as the church of martyrs. The tribulation of Revelation 2:10, we are told, refers to ten historical persecutions, [91] but these can also be applied to 'all the times of this miserable life.' Pergamon, the third church, is historically identified as a time of conflict with heresy. Up to this point the implied chronological stages of church history have been traditional. Pergamon is also interpreted to be the papal church.[92] 'Balaam's error' found in this church is identified with the intrigue of spiritual leaders and secular authorities against God's people. The church of Thyatirra is designated as the church of the 'rising gospel' of Wycliffe, Hus, and the Waldensians (Picarts). Their followers are criticized as still too close to the papal church in belief and practice. Adultery with Jezebel, the mother of all false prophets, practised in Thyatirra, allegedly referred to all those 'wives of preachers, who mislead their husbands to avarice, unchastity, and idolatry.'[93] Not clear is whether this statement was directed against the practice of pre-Reformation concubinage or to Reformation marriages. Whatever the case, the statement seems to indicate continued attachment to the traditional ideal of celibacy.

The fifth and sixth churches were given contemporary significance. The church of Sardis symbolized the Anabaptists who were faulted for their literalism.[94] Statements about the church of Philadelphia, or of true brotherly love in possession of the key of David, applied to Schwenckfeld's circle of friends. It was the church with the true spiritual understanding of the Scriptures. Neither the pope, Luther, nor any heretic could claim control over the keys of David. Only Christ himself opened the secrets to the humble and closed them to the proud. The power of the keys was therefore interpreted spiritually, meaning an opening or revealing of the true nature of Christ as found in Scripture.

The church of Laodicea, on the other hand, described as neither cold nor warm, symbolized the 'Lutherans in their pride.' Like the Anabaptists they were faulted for being 'literalists' (*Buchstäbler*). Given the Schwenkfeldian perspective, it was also possible to identify Laodicea as the church of 'works righteousness, collecting works without faith, heart or spirit and putting its trust therein.'[95] Obviously in the mind of the author(s), Luther and Catholics belonged to the same camp because of their insistence on the objective presence in the creaturely elements.

While the interpretation of the letters to the seven churches thus combined a mixture of pedantic traditionalism with gropings for an identification of contemporary movements, the interpretation of the vision of the four beasts and twenty-four elders (Rev. 4:4ff)] followed almost entirely traditional lines. The beasts were understood as the four evangelists, witnessing to four stages of Christ's life. The human face demonstrated the incarnation, the calf suffering, the lion resurrection and the eagle Christ's ascension and glory.[96]

Traditional is also the interpretation of the book with the seven seals (Rev. 5:11) Its opening brings true understanding of the Scriptures, that is, of the mystery and glory of Christ like 'Moses, Isaiah, and the Prophets who foretold of Christ.' The time of opening coincides with the beginning of 'the dispensation of Christ' or the beginning of the true *Ecclesia*. The latter is spoken of in traditional terms,[97] but she is not so much the depository of God's grace as the guardian of his wisdom. She 'invites to the true knowledge of God.' True knowledge means a proper understanding of the stages of Christ's career, of his incarnation, suffering, resurrection, and exaltation. Only by understanding his final glorification is it possible to understand that in subsequent chapters, the Son receives equal honour and worship with the Father and that the Father and Son are now one. Without doubt, we encounter here Schwenckfeld's central concern with christology which had matured by 1530.[98] Coupled to it, was the theme of rebirth and of the new man, a subject already of special interest to Crautwald.

Turning to the seven seals and the opening scene of the white horse (Rev. 6) a skeletal outline of church history becomes visible once more. The white horse indicates the good

times for the church which began after Christ's ascension and
the sending of the Spirit. The opening of the seal itself reveals the secret that the rider is none other than the 'glorified
reigning Christ.' However, his reign is internalized in spiritualist fashion as a ruling of hearts. The opening of the next two
seals, featuring the red and black horse respectively, indicates
persecution and perversion, thus corresponding to the second
and third stage of the church as the church of martyrs and the
church struggling with heresy. The rider of the red horse is
identified as Nero, a type of Antichrist. By means of this same
horse, that is, by means of persecution, all saints must ride to
glory. The black horse indicated a time of doctrinal perversion by heretics. It meant the introduction into the church of
human wisdom by false teachers.[99] No specific chronological
details were given. Only the elect remained immune to these
errors. In them, the true church continues on to the end. A
comparison of the meaning of the first three seals with what
was said about the first three churches therefore indicates that
the author(s) of the Commentary read the Apocalypse in the
light of an assumed course of church history. In this, they
followed a well established exegetical pattern that sought to
coordinate the information about the seven churches with information about the opening of the seven seals, recapitulating
the seven stages of church development.

A break with the traditional pattern is noticeable with the
opening of the fourth seal and the pale horse. It signifies the
'reign of hypocrites.' These are identified as the papacy and
Lutheranism. Both ride without the 'reigning Christ,' that
is lack of proper christology. The hypocrites allegedly fail to
confront the sinners with the 'reigning king, Christ,' lest the
sinners become 'melancholy and weep about their sins.' Thus,
their ministry is faulted because it lacks a serious penitential
element.[100]

The fifth seal (Rev. 6:9) signified further persecution of the
true church, similar in kind to the one experienced by the
church of martyrs. The opening of the sixth seal (Rev. 6:12)
initiated great changes in the status of the *Ecclesia* and of the
'teachers of this generation,' that is to say, it had special application to the contemporary scene. Although it marked the
renewal of the church it was also to be a time when many fell
away from Christ to the letter and creatures. Surveying the

progress of the Reformation. the author(s) criticized the fact
that the preachers looked to the authorities for safety and support. The magistrates. in turn. manipulated the preachers who
now concerned themselves more with the wishes of the secular
lords than with Christ, the head of the church. As a result, the
'heavens departed as a scroll,' meaning that the 'secrets of the
kingdom' where hid once more. The author(s) repeated the assertion made elsewhere that a turning point was reached with
the peasant insurrection. Luther and his followers were deemed
especially blame-worthy because they returned to a creaturely
conception of the presence of Christ in the sacraments.[101]

A peculiar blending of Schwenkfeldian concerns and traditional exegesis becomes evident in the interpretation of the
'four angels' to whom was given to hurt the earth' (Rev. 7:11).
They represent tyrants, opposed to the 'living word.' Unfortunately the author(s) did not identify these any further. The
'other angel ascending from the east, having the seal of the
living God, (Rev. 7:22) is identified in accordance with 'papist' exegesis as emperor Constantine who brought peace to
the persecuted church.[102] However, on another level of exegesis, he becomes Christ who seals the 144,000, an innumerable
(*unentlich*) multitude with the seal of peace and joy in the
Holy Spirit.

The author(s) draw special attention to those passages in
which the multitude worships both God and the Lamb. These
'witness to the glorified Christ,' that is, to his divine nature.
'God and man, father and son' are seen to be 'one in divine status and being.' That the Lamb in the midst of the throne will
'feed' the chosen is interpreted in the context of the Schwenkfeldian understanding of the eucharist. Not surprisingly, John
6 is brought in as a supporting text. Christ, the lamb, feeds his
own with 'the bread of life,' that is, himself.[103] Only an inner
spiritual feasting nourishes the new man and provides comfort for the distressed conscience. These comments highlight
the internalizing thrust of much of the *Exposition*. Both the
salvation of the individual and the collective salvation of the
church depend on a proper understanding of the nature of the
post-ascendant Christ. To understand the glorified nature of
Christ is a prerequisite to understanding the nature of the eucharist. A heightened desire for true communion with Christ,
a 'soul-nourishing consumption of the very Word of God,'[104] is

at the very heart of the author's reading of Scripture. Without question this is genuine Schwenckfeld.

With the opening of the seventh seal, the restoration (*Widerbringung*) of the church resumes. What is meant is, above all, a restoration of proper spirituality. Significantly, it begins with a new outpouring of the Spirit, manifest in a restoration of the spirit of prayer.[105]

The seven trumpets are interpreted in the context of the restoration of the church. They indicate seven preachers of judgment or of repentance and reform. No specific identifications are made. The commotion triggered by the sound of the first trumpet (Rev. 8:7) suggests renewed tribulation. A third of those 'green and unfruitful in the faith' are said to perish. That a third part of the 'sea' turned to blood during the sound of the second trumpet (Rev. 8:8) meant that Scripture would be wrongly interpreted according to human understanding, leading thus to the damnation of many souls. The 'great star' named 'Wormwood,' who during the sound of the third trumpet (Rev. 8:10ff) made the waters bitter, is described as a 'mighty pharisee' or 'learned man' according to human standards. Both Martin Bucer and an unnamed Anabaptist leader are suggested as fitting this description.[106] But in more elaborate comments that follow Bucer and Luther seem to be the real villains. Held against them is the rejection of the 'reigning, glorified king of grace' and their claim to a monopoly on the 'office of justification.' There follows a somewhat surprising attack on the humanist emphasis on linguistic and rhetorical skills (*Die Kunst, die Zungen, die Ingenien, der gelernten Vernunft und wolredenheit*) as barring the way to a true understanding of the Scriptures. By these means, the author(s) complain, the Scriptures are treated no differently from other books.[107]

These accusations return in the commentary on the fifth trumpet (Rev. 9:11).[108] The fallen star with the key to the bottomless pit is identified as Luther and Bucer. Theirs was the error of having left a spiritual understanding of the sacraments for a creaturely one; Luther in regard to the Supper, Bucer in regard to baptism. Having thus thrown away the keys to heaven, Luther now held the keys to the pit into which he leads his unsuspecting followers.[109] The locusts, released from the pit were interpreted by 'some' to mean Turks. Our

author(s) preferred to think of them as proud false preachers
in the church. Thus, the author(s) restricted the meaning of
the visions consistently to ecclesiastical matters. A larger application to world events was foreign to them.[110]

The sounding of the sixth trumpet saw the loosing of the
four evil angels (Rev. 9:14). These personified four qualities
of Satan and stood in contrast to the four beasts and evangelists who witnessed to the four stages or qualities of Christ.
The influence of the four evil angels manifested itself by 'false
religion, a false being (*wesen*) and evil practices.' Their host
on horses with lions's heads represented secular 'authorities,
against Christ and his truth.'[111] In this case the author(s) were
satisfied with an identification of the principal powers of evil
without particular identification.

Opposed to the Satanic forces was the 'other mighty angel
with the face like the sun' (Rev. 10:1). In keeping with traditional exegesis, he was identified as Christ 'in his apostles.'[112]
The 'face like the sun' constituted a 'revelation of the glory of
Christ' perceivable only through the Spirit. The little book in
the hand of the angel represented the New Testament with its
secret message of the glorified Christ. The mystery of the glorified Christ had been concealed for a long time in the sacraments
of baptism and the eucharist but their true understanding was
now preached far and wide. The seven thunders during the seventh trumpet were seven false preachers (Rev. 10:4) attempting
but unable to hold back the message of the 'glorified, reigning
king, Christ.'[113] Obviously here again we meet Schwenckfeld's
central christological concerns. The whole progress of the Reformation was judged from this vantage point.

The discussion of the witnesses (Rev. 11:3ff.) falls into this
context. Identified by 'old teachers' as Enoch and Elijah,[114]
their role is to unmask the false teachings, misuses, and abuses
in the church. Elsewhere these had been identified as idolatry,
immorality, and avarice.[115] The two witnesses are described as
unassuming preachers of repentance (*Busse*). Their service is
to be one of tender-heartedness and of healing. They witness
courageously against Antichrist and restore the true witness
of the little book. To them are given the powers of the keys
thrown away by Luther. That means, above all, that they
will expose the false literal understanding of Scripture and the

sacraments by revealing their spiritual essence, that is, the glorified nature of Christ.

Although an explicit identification of the witnesses is avoided, the description of these *Gottsgelerten* struggling with the *Schriftgelerten* fits perfectly Crautwald's and Schwenckfeld's own self-understanding. That the two witnesses are overcome by the beast means that they are 'driven into exile and want' and that their writings are suppressed. Their death and miraculous resurrection indicate that the 'Pharisees and Scribes' will rule in the 'false church,' but that a true spiritual resurrection will bring a true reformation in the Spirit.[116]

The seventh and final trumpet (Rev. 10:7) brings an end to persecution and ushers in Christ's return.[117] The author(s) share the common expectation of an end-time conversion of many Jews.[118] These will become participants in the 'blessed life' offered by Christ.[119] However, the return of Christ does not usher in a visible millennium. Indeed, it is not entirely clear whether the 'blessed life' refers to life hereafter or to a spiritual Sabbath of the church. At times, the two possible interpretations melt into one.

At any rate, with the seventh trumpet the 'mystery of the kingdom' was to be fully revealed. This was indicated by the measuring of the temple (Rev. 11:14ff). The measuring rod for this purpose was the *Verbum incarnatum*. The action of measuring designated a sifting, weighing and reforming of the church and its teachings especially in respect to a proper understanding of the sacraments.[120] It concerned the spiritual reformation of the church the beginnings of which Schwenckfeld dated and identified with his own movement. Thus, the Reformation was viewed through the Apocalypse and the Apocalypse through Schwenckfeld's peculiar 'sacramentist' concerns and christology. Interestingly, this kind of reading of the text seems more prominent in the later chapters.

Half way through the Commentary, the author(s) inform the reader that the visions still to come are 'clearer than the previous ones, and may be considered interpretations of the former.'[121] A quick review of the remaining commentary confirms that the rest merely recapitulates and develops themes already discussed earlier.

As noted above, the 'great red dragon' (Rev. 12:3) signified Lucifer and his followers.[122] His expulsion from heaven by the archangel Michael meant an expulsion 'from the hearts' of believers. A similar internalized spiritual interpretation is given of the 'woman clothed with the sun' (Rev. 12:1). She represents the church, but the male child born by her symbolized the 'daily rebirth' of Christ in his own. The caption-like comments on the woman's flight into the desert (Rev. 12:6) read: 'exile, safe place, contempt by the world, lonely penitent conscience, cross of Christ, comfort in the world.' Thus, once again, an internal and external meaning of the text seems implied. In the desert the church is nourished in communion with the glorified Christ. The two wings given for her protection are interpreted to mean 'the two stati' (natures?) of Christ.[123]

The 'beast from the sea' (Rev. 13:1) is interpreted 'by some' to mean 'the papacy and Antichrist.'[124] Its blasphemy is that it attributes to the external elements what belongs solely to the glorified Christ. This is the ultimate in blasphemy, the 'desolation of abomination.' Luther is credited with initially wounding the beast, but since the Peasant Uprising the wound is said to have healed.[125] The meaning of the forty-two months of power given to the beast, the readers are told, is deliberately obscured 'in this and other books.'[126]

What is said about Luther in this context repeats the assessment given under the fifth seal and the fifth trumpet. His falling away is elaborated by his identification with the 'beast from the land' (Rev. 13:11). Its two horns symbolize Luther's 'literalist' approach to the testaments and his insistence on the creaturely presence of Christ in the sacrament of baptism and eucharist. Although he had originally wounded the 'beast from the sea,' he had also helped to heal its wounds with his German mass[127] by reintroducing coercion in the matter of the sacraments. The accusation is repeated that the importance of linguistic skills has been substituted for the Spirit in seeking a true understanding of Scripture.[128] Saxony is cited as the place where the beast from the land reigns. Without its 'sign' and approval no one is permitted to buy or sell.[129] Thus, as in the literature of the radicals in general, Luther was stamped as the new pope of Wittenberg. He was subsumed under the kingdom of Antichrist.

The next chapters bring little else that is new. The seven vials, like the trumpets, represent preachers of divine wrath. The first and second produce 'blindness, ignorance, quarrels, pride. and jealousy among the learned.' who 'worship the image of the beast,' identified as outer ceremonies. The third vial which saw water turn into blood applied specifically to the Lutherans. It signified their literalism and reliance on human wisdom. The fifth vail poured on the 'seat of the beast' (Rev. 16:10) applied to the seat of the 'scribes.' The sixth saw judgment on Rome as the new Babylon. The drying-up of the Euphrates indicated the fate of the 'spiritual estate.'[130] The seventh vial with its thunder and lightning brought 'division and dissension among the clergy in regard to religious matters.'[131] The church of Antichrist now separated into three parts. It was assumed that the three parties were known to the reader.[132] By inference they were Catholics, Lutherans, and Anabaptists.[133] Since all three were part of the church of Antichrist it was possible to dismiss them summarily. Thus, the vials like the trumpets were given contemporary significance.

After the seven punishments indicated by the vials, which presumably recapitulated the message of the seven trumpets, Christ, the 'king of the orient,' would repossess the governance of his church.[134]

Conclusion

By way of conclusion we may summarize the findings of our study as follows:

(1) Careful scrutiny of all evidence suggests that the Commentary evolved over an extended period of time, perhaps from 1536 to 1546. The initial Commentary in all probability originated with Crautwald. In 1546 Schwenckfeld appears to have rewritten Crautwald's work to which others may have contributed. The Commentary may therefore be viewed as a collective effort. This may help to explain some of its inconsistencies.

(2) Of the three manuscripts that have survived, the script in Reisner's hand (B), dating from 1556, must be considered closest in time and content to the original text. The Sudermann manuscript of 1610, published in the *Corpus*, contains considerable additional material gleaned from other Schwenkfeldian sources. Key among these was Schwenckfeld's *Three Kinds of Human Life* published in 1547. Thus, although the *Corpus* edition is furthest removed in content and time from

the original composition, it seems more representative of the Schwenkfeldian tendency toward spiritual exposition than the older manuscripts. The question arises to what extent the history of transmission of this Commentary must be considered typical. To what extent does the Commentary hold a special place in Schwenkfeldian documents?

(3) Luther's Bible of 1536 provided the biblical text as well as the chapter outline for Reisner's manuscript. References to the 'old Bible' seem to suggest that the Vulgate or some other pre-Reformation translations were consulted.

(4) The Commentary was not conceived as a systematic exposition of the Apocalypse. The Book of Revelation was approached like the rest of Scripture, as spiritually edifying literature. The allegorical method was considered especially suitable for the enterprise of discovering the hidden spiritual meaning. The author(s) showed special interest in the passages that witnessed to Christ, to the corruption in the church or to its spiritual restitution. In regard to the latter two points the historical interpretation asserted itself.

(5) In the exegesis, Crautwald and Schwenckfeld were indebted to traditions of hermeneutics that reached back through the medieval period to patristic sources. Among other things, they rejected the critical linguistic method that tended to approach Scripture no differently than other literature. In this the author(s) proved themselves conservative. Because Scripture was considered paramount by the author(s), their reading and understanding of Scripture must be considered a starting point for any study of their ideas. Hopefully future research on the exegetical traditions that influenced them will provide further insights into the unique reformation advocated by them.

(6) Analysis of the contents reveals that specific Schwenkfeldian concerns with christology and the eucharist mingled with attempts to interpret the past and contemporary religious scene through the Apocalypse. In this context, a skeletal outline of church history becomes visible which in many respects remains indebted to pre-Reformation traditions which in all probability contained a similar mingling of allegorical types and historical attempts at identification.

(7) Given the apocalyptic climate of the Reformation period, the Schwenkfeldian commentary on the Apocalypse must be considered an exegetical exercise in sobriety. Although it

contains polemical tendencies, it fares well when compared to similar enterprises of the magisterial reformers[135] or the more militant chiliasm of other members of the left wing of the Reformation.

Notes

1 Attempts to obtain a photo or microfilm copy from Berlin in time for publication met with no success. It is possible that the manuscript is now in Wolfenbüttel under the signature Cod. Aug. 45.9. Unfortunately I was unable to verify the Woifenbüttel location.

2 CS 11:210.

3 An entry under the date 1680 indicated at that time the treatise was in the possession of an unknown A. Pfaff.

4 A photocopy of B now at the Bavarian Staats-Archiv at Munich under the signature CGM 4102 a. qu. was made available to me through the Schwenkfelder Library. The Commentary takes up pages 182-288 in the Codex.

5 About his relationship to Schwenckfeld see Peter Erb, 'Adam Reisner, His Learning and Influence on Schwenckfeld,' *Mennonite Quarterly Review*, 54 (1980), 32-41.

6 This constitutes 1-180 of the Codex.

7 CLM 718, Munich.

8 I would here like to acknowledge my indebtedness to graduate student Douglas Shantz who, in one of his dissertation chapters, has examined the distribution of Crautwald's works in Schwenckfeld's circle.

9 Bruce M. Metzger, *The Text of the New Testament. Its Transmission, Corruption and Restoration* (2nd ed.; New York, 1968), 120.

10 CS 19:288, 301, 312, 317, 328, 336, 352. Sudermann's chapter divisions do not agree with the Froschauer Bible either.

11 B 206a and b.

12 I cannot be sure that this was not an editorial or printing error that found its way into the *Corpus*.

13 B 189b; CS 19: C 272.

14 B 258a; CS 19: 354.

15 B 160a; CS, 19:356.

16 B 237a.

17 CS, 19:317.

18 CS 9:701-12.

19 CS 9: Doc. 526, 705: 'Da ir schreibt es sey recht, dz uns seine bucher nicht worden, Damit Gott sein Ehr rein behalte, sonst möchte man sagen, Dz ist Crautwaldts, kan ich nicht mit euch stimmen... und gar nicht recht, noch gut were, dz dieselbigen anfencklich uns entwandt oder entnommen weren.... Er (God) wölle auch Crautw: Collectanea gnediglich fürkommen lassen....

20 CS 9: Doc. 526, 706.

21 Tag's complaint about the brevity of Crautwald's statements supports
    what we know of Crautwald's deliberate and cautious work habits (QGT
    7:123 n. 1: CLM, 718, fol. 407 Munich; CS 3:583).

22 Horst Weigelt, *Spiritualistische Tradition im Protestantismus* (Berlin
    and New York, 1973), 183.

23 *Von Dreyerley Leben der Menschen* (CS 9:826 ff).

24 After the digression, Schwenckfeld wrote: 'Nu kommen wir widerumb
    zu unserem anfencklichen fürnemen, vom Gots dinst, und den guten
    wercken, damit wir dann wollen beschliessen.' *Von Dreyerley Leben der
    Menschen* (CS 9:924).

25 CS 9:915. Among the passages listed and expounded were (1) the Son of
    Man (Rev. 1:13), (2) the Lion of Judah (Rev. 5:5-6), (3) the Lamb with
    seven horns (Rev. 2:17, 18), (4) the worship of the Lamb by the four
    beasts and twenty-four elders (Rev. 5:14; 7:9, 10), (5) those who had
    'washed their robes and made them white in the blood of the Lamb'
    (Rev. 7:14), (6) the loud voice saying, 'Now is come salvation,....and
    the kingdom of our God, and the power of his Christ' (Rev. 12:10;
    17:14; 19:6), (7) the marriage feast of the Lamb (Rev. 19:7,9; 2:7; 3:19-
    20), (8) the opening of heaven (Rev. 19:11-15), (9) the new Jerusalem
    (Rev. 21,22, 24) and (10) the clear, pure stream of water (Rev. 22:1-2)
    and the throne (Rev. 22:3-5).

26 CS 9:916.

27 He ruled out the idea that the millennium referred to a 'physical king-
    dom,' rejecting a visible gathered church, as well as the idea of cleansing
    the world of the godless (CS 9:906).

28 Cf. statements by Schwenckfeld, 914 l.29, 915 l.29-31; 916 l.10-15; 918
    l.12-14; with B 370b, 201a, 245a, 265b respectively.

29 They were not in Schwenckfeld's personal Bible which has survived. See
    CS 18:600ff.

30 *Von Dreyerley Leben* (CS 9:914 n. 1). The Latin comment on Rev.
    21:32 reads: 'Agnus, Lucerna continens in se lumen diu nitatis.' B gives
    'Das Lamb, ist die leucht, in der Kirche, auch im Himel ewiglich.' B
    284a. In *Three Kinds of Human Life* Schwenckfeld had elaborated: 'das
    Lamb die leuchte der statt Gottes,... der Christlichen Kirchen, und aller
    derselben glider ist' (913).

31 Cf. C 373-74 with CS 9:918.

32 B 201a: 'Du sprichst ich bin reich; Lutherische hoffart, und das
    Lutherthumb, heut kennet sich selbs nicht.'

33 CS 9:915.

34 CS 9:906, 929.

35 CS 11:919.

36 CS 19:318 n.

37 This is a case where the original meaning was lost to the copiest. C
    reads, with their 'concordieren verbittert' (308).

38 Weigelt, 157.

39 B 226b-27a.

40 A reference to events of the same year may be contained in the inter-
    pretation of the gathering of the 'beast and the kings of the earth...
    to make war' (Rev. 19:19). Allegedly, this signified 'a *Concilia* against
    Christ and his church. In 1537 Paul III convened a council to meet in
    Mantua, and Charles V entered war against France. B 273b-27a.

41 CS 4:818, 882; CS 5:522-33; CS 8: 281-85.

42 Daniel Lichty, 'Andreas Fischer: A Brief Biographical Sketch,' *Men-
    nonite Quarterly Review* 58 (1984), 125-32. Horst Weigelt , 'Die Au-
    seinandersetzung der Anhänger Schwenckfelds insbesondere Valentin
    Krautwald, mit dem Täufertum in Schlesien' (paper read at the Inter-
    national Colloquium of Sixteenth-Century Anabaptism, July 20, 1984
    at Strassburg, France.)

43 It is revealing and further evidence that Sudermann lacked a proper
    understanding of the original intention of the author, that C also applies
    elements of the description of the church of Sardis to Lutherans. C 278.

44 Weigelt, 158.

45 B 279b.

46 B 281b.

47 B 233. C again blurs the meaning; instead of 'die Jungen nach sich
    ziehen,' it speaks of disciples, 'Jünger nach ihnen ziehen' C 314.

48 Letter to Katherine Streicher, September 29, 1539 cited in Weigelt,
    1807. In connection with the two witnesses (Rev. 11], the author laments
    that the 'Gotsgelerten' are not 'permitted to print or market their writ-
    ings and are driven into want.' B 240b. It is not clear whether this too
    reflects Crautwald's situation or is an additional comment made by
    Schwenckfeld in 1546.

49 Robert E. McLaughlin, *Caspar Schwenckfeld von Ossig 1489-1561). No-
    bility and Religious commitment—Crisis and Decision in the Early Ref-
    ormation* (Ph.D., Yale University, 1980), 112-13.

50 The concept is used in relation to the heavenly Jerusalem on 281a, 283a.

51 B 185a-b. Interestingly, C carries the additional comment that they
    will reign over sin in Christian *Ritterschaft*. C 267. This imagery of the
    Christian knight is also found in B 190b.

52 B 182b.

53 B 281a: 'In freudenreichen anschauen und niessung gottes durch Chris-
    tum dess man alhie, einen vorschmack impfindet, durch den glauben.'

54 Schwenckfeld's thrust is reminiscent of Hugh St. Victor's sacramental
    reading of Scripture, in which Scripture contained the bread or body of
    Christ in analogy to the sacrament. Cf. Beryl Smalley, *The Study of
    the Bible in the Middle Ages* (2nd ed.; Oxford, 1983), 91.

55 What Beryl Smalley writes about—the 'spiritual exposition' —seems to
    describe the attitude manifest in the Commentary: It 'generally consists
    of pious meditations or religious teaching for which the text is used
    merely as a convenient starting point' (2).

[56] B, e.g., 202b: 'O Jesus, give us ears to hear your voice ....'; 257a: 'O Jesus, I give you thanks that you make those blessed in heaven who die in you on earth....'; 270b: 'O God, help us through your son Jesus Christ our Lord, that we may become rich in heavenly property....' 284a: 'If only we were there, hallelujah'; 286b: The Lord give it soon. Amen.'

[57] Smalley, 9.

[58] B 182a.

[59] Smalley noted that for the Alexandrians 'each word concealed a mystery' (22).

[60] Wilhelm Bousset, *Die Offenbarung Johannis* (Göttingen, 1906), 62-63.

[61] Smalley, 22. Bousset summarized Jerome's impact on the exegesis of the Apocalypse as follows: 'Heironymus steht deutlich in der Uebergangsperiode von einer in der Lateinischen Kirche allegemein herrschenden realistischen Auslegungsmethode zu einer spiritualistischen' (62-63).

[62] About him, see *Die Religion in Geschichte und Gegenwart* (3 Aufl.) Vol. 5:583.

[63] B 253: 'Die diener der Bestien, werden, ir viel sprachen, fur gaben des heiligen geists asstheillen, und rümen schreibt, Primasius.' Given the humanist training of Crautwald, the intention of this attack on languages is not clear. Earlier the author(s) attacked Luther's German mass. See also 34, n. 107 and 38, 128.

[64] About Ticonius, see the *Catholic Encyclopedia* (1912 ed.), Vol. 1:721. His Commentary on the Apocalypse was at St. Gall in the ninth century but has since been lost.

[65] Bousset, 65.

[66] Bousset, 59: 'Mit dem letzten Rest historisch-realistischer Deutung ist hier aufgeräumt.'

[67] Bousset, 66-67. Schwenckfeld never speculated about Antichrist as a particular historical personage.

[68] Peter Erb who has listed the number of Patristic citations in Schwenckfeld's *Corpus* does not cite Primasius. 'Schwenckfeld and Augustine' (Paper delivered at Anabaptist Colloquium, Eastern Mennonite College, Harrisonburg, Virginia, November, 1983); see Appendix.

[69] Although Bede is not mentioned by name in B he is frequently cited in C. Others mentioned there are Ignatius, Eusebius, Augustine and Tertullian: 273, 304, 317.

[70] This interpretation can be traced back via the Glossa Ordinaria of Walafried Strabo who influenced Richard of St. Victor, to Primasius and Ticonius (Bossuet, 70).

[71] B 278.

[72] B 277b.

[73] B 223b.

[74] B 235a.

[75] B 224a, b.

76 In *Of Three Kinds of Human Life* Schwenckfeld cited Jerome for his source (CS 9:899). Here he gave a more thorough interpretation of Daniel 8.

77 On another level, the tyrants were described as 'Jews, false apostles, Roman emperors, heretics, unbelievers, bishops, prelates, monks, lovers of this world, and the same' (B 245b).

78 Smalley writes: 'The types are so real and so familiar that they may be used as arguments from authority, as well as for illustration' (25-26).

79 CS 1:37, 118-23.

80 The cursory comment reads 'Bestia Bapstum.' Then follows the explanation 'Etlich legens aus, Es sei vom Bapstumb. Es ist der antichrist' (B 249b). Other examples could be given. Thus, the fifth vial indicates judgment on the new Babylon and the entire spiritual estate (B 261b).

81 B 251b. The comment reads 'Bestia, Luther.'

82 B 250b.

83 B 227a-29b.

84 B 221a.

85 He was now lose again, but not for long (B 275-76).

86 B 273b-74a.

87 Crautwald saw the fall occurring with the acceptance of transubstantiation under Gregory VII around 1085 (McLaughlin, 270). Schwenckfeld dated it also in the eleventh century. At other times he dated it earlier. (CS 2:247-48; 446 ff.). In contrast, many of the Reformation radicals dated the fall right after the apostles or with Constantine.

88 Comment on Rev. 18:7, B 268a.

89 B 274b.

90 B 276a; also 280b, 281a, 285a. See especially the discussion of the thousand years. Those who place their faith in outward sacraments are seen as 'sacramentierer' and as dogs (Ibid., 288a).

91 B 192a. C provides the names of three tyrants in this context: Domitianus, Traisnus, and Maximinus. In reference to those who have come out of great tribulation (Rev. 7:14), C adds: 'some interpret this to mean the time of Diocletian, Maximian, Maxentian and Nero.' B had been satisfied with the comment that these martyrs had been 'pressed and thrashed out' (B 222 b). However, A had already mentioned 'the time of Diocletian and Nero, etc.' This is an example of the dependence of C on A (C 274, 304).

92 This. if held to consistently. would imply a fall of the church in its third stage, a position espoused by other Reformation radicals. See my 'A Reinterpretation of Spiritualist Franciscan Eschatology with Special Reference to Peter John Olivi,' in *The Dutch Dissenters* ed. by Irwin Horst (Leiden, 1981), 32-61.

93 B 194a-b.

94 See above. In 1546/47 Schwenckfeld criticized the Münster Anabaptists because they attempted to have 'only righteousness in this passing world' (CS 9:906).

95 B 201a. Perhaps this is one more piece of evidence that several persons contributed to the Commentary at various times. Presumably this would have been generally more descriptive of Catholic practice.

96 B 206a and b. The identification of the beasts with the evangelists can be traced to Irenaeus of Lyons (140-202). See Calvin Pater, *Karlstadt as the Father of the Baptist Movements: The Emergence of Lay Protestantism* (Toronto, 1984), 204, n. 50.

97 B 208b-209: 'Kirche, volck der Kirchen.'

98 Erb, 'Schwenckfeld and Augustine,' 5.

99 This interpretation comes close to that given by Melchior Hoffman. Here, too, common traditional sources rather than dependence provides the most likely explanation. See my 'A Reinterpretation' (see note 92).

100 For the medieval teachings on contrition, see Thomas N. Tentler, *Sin and Confession on the Eve of the Reformation* (Princeton, 1977), esp. the chapter 'Sorrow and the Keys,' 233ff.

101 B 219b. The suggestion that the Peasant Uprising constituted a turning point is repeated in conjunction with the wounding of the beast.

102 The author cites Eusebius, *Ecclesiastical History*, lib:9.

103 B 221a-23a.

104 A phrase borrowed from Maier.

105 B 224a, b.

106 B 226-27. See discussion above 24. It is not clear who was meant by the Anabaptist. One thinks here of Marpeck, Hoffman or of Rothmann.

107 The anti-humanist thrust was noted above. See n. 63. It will be remembered that at one point in his life Crautwald destroyed his earlier writings.

108 The fourth produced only sparce comments.

109 B 228a-29b. Curiously C does not mention Luther in this context.

110 B 230a. The false preachers were identified by Paul in II Timothy 3.

111 B 231b.

112 A similar identification was given by Melchior Hoffman.

113 B 234a.

114 B 238a-b.

115 B 267a-b. The original comment spoke of the simony of the 'false doctors.'

116 See above n. 36 and 105.

117 B 234b.

118 B 242b.

119 Heiko Oberman has shown how wide-spread was the expectation of an 'extensive conversion of the Jews.' See his *The Roots of Anti Semitism in the Age of Renaissance and Reformation*, trans. by James J. Porter (Philadelphia, 1984).

120 B 236b-37a.

121 B 243b.

122 See above.

123 Presumably the author means the two natures of Christ, son of man and son of God. He comments that this is 'fulfilled today' (B 249a).

124 B 250a.

125 B 250b. *Cf.* 53, n. 1 above.

126 B 251a: '... nicht ohne ursach, in diesen und anderen Büchern verdunkelt.'

127 See above 53, 56-67. The anti-Lutheran thrust may have been provoked by Luther's publication against Schwenckfeld on the Lord's Supper in 1544.

128 Cf. 21, n. 663 and 34, n. 107.

129 B 253b. Interestingly, this comment is left out of both A and C.

130 B 261b.

131 B 262b.

132 The Commentary simply states: 'Merck... wer sie sein' (B 263a). Presumably they were the Catholics, Lutherans, and Anabaptists. Zwingli is not mentioned at all, perhaps because he was long dead. Bucer, as noted, did not come in for criticism.

133 The author writes that not 'everyone recognizes the Antichrist in his members (B 265b).

134 See above n. 89-90.

135 Cf. for example Luther's views as noted in Hans-Ulrich Hofmann, 'Luther und die Johannes-Apokalypse' (Th.D. diss., Erlangen, Germany, 1977), 180.

Appendix 1

Examples of agreement between A and B where C in CS differs:

B 184a

Christus hat auch gezeuget, vom Ewigen Leben, durch sein auff erstehung, und hats ahn Im *Erstlich* beweiset, nach dem er ist der Erst geboren aus den todten ist worden.

CS, 266

und hats an Ihme *eusserlich* beweiset. A like B gives *erstlich*.

B 189b

Dein gedult In der *Widerwertigkeit*.

CS, 272

Gedult die du hast in *gegenwertigkeit*. A here has *Widerwertigkeit* as in B.

B 193b

will ich zu essen geben, Des Herren Nachtmal, das ist die ewige gloria, die *unsichtbare* Speise.

CS, 275

zu essen geben das wahre himmelbrott des worts Gottes, ist *verborgen* in die *hülse* seines angenommen fleischs. Joh. 6 (48-51). Es wirt auch verborgen genant,.... A has the same as B.

B 237a

Die Alte Bibel, hat aber den vorhoff dess Tempels das ist die Ketzer und falschen Christen.

CS, 317

Etliche Griechischen Text lesen also: Den Vorhoff, der ausserhalb des Tempels ist. Also liset auch die Alte Translatz: Hieron:ad Paulum, August: und Beda. A reads: Die Alte Bibel hat aber den vorhoff des Tempels, Das ist, ein ausmusterung der Ketzer, und falschen Christen von dem volck gottes.

B 239b

Ezech: 3 Wollt Gott den Propheten nicht reden lassen, macht Ihm zu einen Stummen, von des ungehorsamen Volcks wegen.

CS, 320

CS leaves this phrase out altogether, but A has it verbatim.

B 287b

Das holtz des lebens ist Christus, welchen wir wie die Reben dem Weinstock eingepflantz, und eingeleibt sein sollen, Joha: 17.

Both CS and A give the same reading, but correct the reference to John 15.

Other evidence that A or a similar copy served as the original for Sudermann's manuscript (C) comes from additional information found in both A and C but not found in B Thus, for example, A and C tell us that St John had sent his disciple Polycarp to the church of Smyrna, that this was duly recorded by Eusebius, and that Ignatius had written on the nature of Christ to the church of Smyrna (CS 19:273).

Appendix 2

Examples of the caption-like Commentary and its elaboration, here translated into English:

(Rev. 6:22)

and behold a white horse, the white horse is the good time of the church, Acts 9.

and he that sat on him had a bow, the missiles of God, Psalm 45.

The bow on the white horse means the power of the Word of Christ, through which the hearts are wounded to conversion, and are shot through, hereof Psalm 45. Sharp are your arrows so that the nations fall down before you, and Hebrews 4: the Word of God is living and powerful and sharper than a two-edged sword.

The bow with its missiles means also the court endictment, judgment and punishment with which Christ judges his enemies, and also resists their power, as previous with the seven horns.

(Rev. 6:4)
And there went out another horse that was red, the spilling of blood of saints; the red horse means the time of persecution and of torture.

We have to ride to heaven on the red horse, which means a life of blood and cross, and follow the one on the white horse, that is, the glorified, ruling Christ.

All saints of God must ride to heaven on the red horse; in addition to heathens, Antichrist and the unbelieving servants. *was given to take peace*, Nero, Antichrist, I am not come to send peace, Matth. 10.

Because in this struggle the danger is greater than that pertaining to blood and flesh, help has been promised to the Christian knights.

(Rev. 6:5)
and lo, a black horse, a hoard of darkness, Christ's judgment on the false teachers, who through their fleshly wisdom, darkened the secrets of God, and introduced the *philosophia* into Christendom, by means of which they lead the hearts away from the simplicity which is in Christ.

The black horse, the time of error and deception of the church, and of the heretics and of philosophy.

(Rev. 11:4)
(and the two candlesticks) standing before the God of the earth.
Some read, placed before the God of the world, Zach. 4, that is, against Antichrist.
Enoch and Elijah shall, in the midst of all error, bring the little book again to the fore, and vigorously act against Antichrist, but they have no other help or assistance than Christ.

The old teachers interpret these two witnesses to be Enoch and Elijah who, in the midst of the deception and all kinds of error, shall bring the little book with its content again to the fore, to uncover the errors, act vigorously against Antichrist, and serve to the end that Christ bring all things back into order. But first [they must be] killed; their doctrine shall be driven into the [secret] corner, condemned, and persecuted. Thereafter they shall rise and come to the fore.

(Rev. 13:1)
and saw a beast, Bestia Papism,

The beast is greatly honoured by its own; beast or animal, a derogatory name, is set over against the lamb.

Appendix 3

We give here for comparison one example of the text of *Three Kinds of Human Life* and following it the texts inserted by Sudermann in the 'Commentary of the Apocalypse.'

Von Dreyerley Leben der Menschen in CS 9:917
Damit dann klarlich die offenbarung des Antichrists/ und seiner Synagoga/ Reichs/ und verfurung/ Dessgleichen auch die wider erbawung der kirchen/ unnd die erlössung der (vii) glaubigen durch die zukunfft oder erscheinung des gaistes Gottes wirt bedeutet.

So wil das gesicht von den zweien zeugen/ die Gott in den letsten tagen seiner Kirchen verhaisst zesenden/ nichts anders dann die reformirung und wider erbawung der verwüsten/ armen/ betrubten Kirchen Christi anzaigen/ wie dann auch die Vater/ Tertullianus/ Ambrosius/ Augustinus/ und andere mehr solichs auff die zukunft Enoch und Helie gedeutt haben/ die in mitten alles irrtumbs/ zerstrewung und verfurung/ wider das Antichristische Reich sich mit der krafft Gottes werden legen/ dawider schreiben/ predigen/ und leren/ ja die raine gotliche warhait widerumb herfur bringen/ Whelch auch den Herrn Christo darzu dienen sollen/ das er seine zurstrewte ellende/ vom Antichrist verwuste Kirche/ durch den H. gaist wirt reformiren/ den waren gottsdinst/ und ain rechtschaffen Christlich leben wider anrichten/ und alles so unterm Reiche der menschlichen Tradition/ auch des buchstabens/ mit Philosophischer Sophistischer unrechten leer inn Kirchen vermenget/ vertunckelt/ und mit mancherlai falschem Gottsdinst/ Abgötterey/ und gleissnerey/ unterm Antichrist verwustet/ widerumb wirt zu recht bringen/ bessern/ den Tempel Gottes massen und seine gmaind imm h. gaist erbawen/ mehren/ und versamlen/ Das die Kirch widerumb alssdenn durch den gnaden Konig Jesum Christum/ zum hailigen tempel Gottes wachse/ und Christus in den hertzen der glaubigen standhafftig wone/ das er auch durch sie inn der Liebe leuchte/ und mit seiner herlichait und glorien recht erkandt/ unnd seine macht und reich/ aller welt bekandt werden.

(The following passage was left out by Sudermann.)
Christus wirt den Alltar/ und die darinnen anbeten/ messen/ Aber den Fürhof der imm Tempel ist/ wirt ir hinauss werffen/ und nicht messen.

Zu solchem ambte/ sprich ich/ so der Herr Christus imm H. gaiste alssdenn mit mehr krafft wirt furen/ sollen ihm die zwene propheten/ Enoch und Helias/ ja vil andere mehr/ noch für der wellt ende dienen. Damit dann auch der menschen gewissen nicht mehr auf den sandt/ sonder auff den grund/ velss und Eckstain Jesum Christum/ seliglich sollen gegründet und erbawet werden.

Compare the above to the following found in: 'Ein kürtz Ausslegung Der Offenbarunge Johannis,' CS 19:351

Alhie wirt die offenbarung des Antichrists, und seine Synagoga, Reichs und verfürung, dessgleichen auch die widerbawung der kirchen, und die erlösung, der gläubigen, durch die zukunfft, oder erscheinung des geists bedeütet.

Dan dise zwen propheten. das gesicht von den zweyen zeügen, die Gott in den letsten tagen, seiner kirchen, verheist zusenden, wil nicht anders, dan die Reformierung, und wider erbawung der verwüsten, armen, betrübten kirchen Christi anzeigen, wie dan auch die Vetter Tertullianus, Ambrosius, Augustinus. und andere mehr, sölchs auff die zukunfft henoch und helias gedeut haben (wie droben gemeldet) Die in mitten aller Irrthumb, zerstrewung und verfurung, wider das Antichristische Reich, sich mit der krafft Gottes, werden legen, dawider schreiben, predigen und lehren, Ja die reine Göttliche warheit widerümb herfur bringen. Welche auch dem herren Christo darzu dienen sollen, das Er seine zerstrewte, ellende, vom Antichrist verwüste kirche, durch den h: Geiste wirt

Reformieren, Den wahren Gottesdienst und ein rechtschaffen Chrislich leben wider anrichten, und alles so underm Reich der Menschen Satzung. auch des Buchstabens, mit philosophischer, Sophistischer unrechten lehr, in der kirchen vermenget vertunckelt und mit mancherley falschem gottsdienst, abgötterey und gleissnerey, underm Antichrist verwüstet, widerümmb wirt zurecht brengen, besseren. Den Tempel Gottes messen, und seine Gemeinde Im heil: Geist erbawen, mehren und versamblen, das die kirche widerümb alsdan, durch den gnaden könig, Jesum Christum, zum heyligen Tempel Gottes wachsse, und Christus in den hertzen der gleubigen standhafftig wone, Das Er auch durch sie, in der liebe leuchte, und mit seiner herrligkeit und glorien recht erkant, und seine macht und Reich aller welt erkant werden. zu solchem Ampte, sprich Ich, do der herr Christus Im h: Geiste, alsdan mit mehr krafft wirt füren, Sollen Ihm die zwene propheten henoch und helias, Ja vil andere mehr, noch vor der Welt ende dienen. Damit dan auch der Menschen gewissen, nicht mehr auff den Sand, Sonder auff den grund, felss, und Eckstein Jesu Christum, seliglich sollen gegrundet und erbawet werden.

Citations from the same pages in *Three Kinds of Human Life* are also found scattered on 359, 369, and 373 of C in CS.

Caspar Schwenckfeld's Understanding of the Old Testament

Gottfried Seebass

In Selina Schultz's biography of Schwenckfeld,[1] which is useful but not always satisfactory in answering modern scholarly questions, various theological themes are noted as having priority in Schwenckfeld's thought during his Strassburg period (1529-1533). Among these are the questions regarding the Lord's Supper, baptism and infant baptism, the problem of the free will, the distinction between the Old and the New Testament and the question of the relationship between Christian authority and Christian freedom.[2] There is, however, little indication as to how these different subjects are related, and this is especially so in the case of the question regarding the relationship between the Old and New Testament. With only one exception—that of the very pointed discussion by William Klassen in his work on Pilgram Marpeck[3]—this topic is rarely dealt with in the literature of Schwenckfeld. Schwenckfeld himself, however, considered the relationship between the Old and New Testament as the most important topic[4] which he treated during his Strassburg period. In the first three sections of the paper which follows I want to make clear why the topic of the difference between the Old and the New Testament was of such interest for Schwenckfeld. In the final section I will sum up Schwenckfeld's position on this matter which is an important part of his understanding of the Holy Scripture.

1

The first and most important issue which caused Schwenckfeld to concern himself with the interpretation of the Old Testament was the controversy over the sacraments. Luther and Zwingli each used the Old Testament, though in a very different way, to support their distinctive teaching on the sacraments. Luther constantly insisted that in addition to his oral promises, God also gave external signs: The rainbow was an external sign of his bond with Noah and circumcision was the sign of the promise given to Abraham. Many other examples could be added. In Luther's opinion these signs were personally established by God. The same distinction is upheld in the New Testament as Luther indicated in his opposition to the scholastic differentiation between the sacraments in the Old Testament and in the New.[5] For Luther, God's promise of grace is revealed to men in words and signs, thus calling them to faith.

The situation is different in the case of Zwingli and the South German Reformers. Zwingli understood the sacraments primarily in a communal sense and saw them as signs for the faithful in their duty to follow Christ. For this reason he turns back to the Old Testament. For him the two New Testament sacraments, baptism and the Lord's Supper, correspond with those of the Old Testament—circumcision and Passover. Above all, Zwingli sees infant baptism as arising from the sign of the God-given covenant, the circumcision of Jewish children. His symbolic interpretation of the Supper as thanksgiving associates it with the Jewish passover.[6] More than Luther, Zwingli draws parallels between both sacraments of the Old and New Testament. Bucer likewise saw signs of the New Testament sacraments foreshadowed in those of the Old.[7]

Schwenckfeld disagreed with these doctrines and already in 1527 and 1528 he made a point to establish the fundamental differences between the Old and New Testament. There are two main arguments with which he opposed Luther's doctrine on the sacraments and his use of the Old Testament. Firstly, Schwenckfeld considers the whole New Testament as the fulfillment of the Old. To justify this, he refers primarily to John 5:46; Luke 24:27; Matthew 8:17, and Romans 3:21. He especially emphasizes what Paul says in Acts where he states that he 'says only what the prophets and Moses have said, that it should happen' (Acts 26:22). Although according to the context the passage is associated explicitly with the suffering and resurrection of Christ, Schwenckfeld understands it in a basic sense: Because in Moses and in the Prophets nothing concerning the second coming of Christ in the sacrament is prophesied, the presence of Christ in the bread is impossible.[8]

Secondly, Schwenckfeld rejects Luther's whole theory concerning the relationship between the promises (with external

signs) and faith. He deals with it comprehensively in reference
to the Old Testament in the fall of 1527 in his biblical appendix
to *De cursu verbi Dei* (*On the Course of the Word of God*). In
that work Schwenckfeld indicates that various promises were
made throughout the course of God's history among people
such as Adam (Gen. 3:15), Noah (Gen. 9), Abraham (Gen. 12),
and Moses. However, these promises were all lost and forgot-
ten. Indeed this was even true of the law of Moses. Although
Moses was the first to restore these promises, being urged by
the Spirit of God to write them down, they were lost and not
're-established' until they were rediscovered by Josiah (according to 2 Kings 22). Schwenckfeld is convinced that all these
various promises were spiritually oriented to Christ, the one
who is to come, the one promised *res promissa* as distinguished
from the promises (*promissio*). He concludes however that, according to the various words and their context, one must not
direct one's faith to the promise. Promises can serve as memories, doctrines, and confirmations but do not call forth belief.
Thus, circumcision is a seal of faith and assurance, nothing
more. Therefore, Abraham is the father of faith because he
was able to believe the true word of God without having heard
previous sermons or promises. Commitment to the external
promise is for Schwenckfeld a dead, worthless belief, which cannot alter the 'old man.' The same position is confirmed by the
cases of the believing pagans Abimelech, Hiob, Naeman, and
others in the Old Testament who indicate that man is made
a believer without outside influences or promises.[9] More than
the sacramental teachings of Luther, the external transmission
of faith as a whole is questioned. These ideas of Schwenckfeld
were probably also known to Bullinger since the latter (1534)
once stated that he wished to express his views on *de promis-
sionibus*.[10]

During his stay in Strassburg, Schwenckfeld stated (in his
third open letter to all Christians) that the sacraments of the
New Testament were independent of those in the Old Testament and must not be interpreted by referring to the latter
source. The attack against circumcision as a defence of infant baptism clearly indicates Schwenckfeld's opposition to the
South-German Reformers. He explicitly emphasizes that in
the classical reference to the parallels between baptism and
circumcision (Col. 2:11-13), there are three different phases

or levels of renewal. Circumcision is the first level and must
not be compared with the second or third levels, baptism as
a symbol of death and resurrection. The external circumcision of the Old Testament symbolizes the inner circumcision
of the heart which is followed by baptism, pointing also to the
previous, inner work of Christ. Baptism and circumcision are
neither externally nor internally equal.[11] But Schwenckfeld is
not hindered from using the Old Testament which he interprets christologically as well as employing figurative descriptions and prophecies from it concerning Christian baptism.
The following traditional topics thus become for him particularly meaningful—the flood (Gen. 9), the Red Sea (Exod. 14),
the cloud and fire column (Exod. 16:21), the crossing of the
Jordan, and the battle of Jericho (Josh. 3:14-17), the cleansing
of the priests (Exod. 29:4-21), and the cleansing of Naeman in
the Jordan (2 Kings 5:9-14).[12] From Ezekiel 36:25-27, 16:3-14,
and Isaiah 44:1-5, moreover, he extracts prophetic sayings concerning baptism and finds associations with baptismal water in
Genesis 1:1ff. and Psalms 65:9-11 and 147:18.[13] Schwenckfeld
therefore attacks those who claim that Christ merely changed
or reinstated other sacraments, namely, the practices of circumcision and Passover in the Old Testament. That would
be comparing pouring new wine into old skins (Matt. 9:17).
But such a position is for him merely an 'evangelical Judaism'
rather than a 'new Christianity.' Only those, such as the Jews,
who cling to the external can parallel baptism and circumcision. Schwenckfeld however notes only ironically, that infant
baptism and circumcision are rather similar: before God neither have any importance.[14]

   Schwenckfeld did not deal so explicitly with the issue of
the Supper in the Old and New Testament. Undoubtedly,
the reason that he did not is that in comparison with the
Passover, he did not feel that the parallel was as significant
for the reformers, as that of baptism and circumcision. But,
Schwenckfeld does indicate that he could have incorporated
the figurative descriptions and the prophecies into his theory, particularly figures such as Melchisedech (Gen. 14:18), the
Passover (Exod. 12), the Mannah (Exod. 16:1-23), the bread
of the priests (Lev. 24:5-9), the meal prepared by Joseph for
his brothers (Gen. 43:31-34), and the meal of King Ahasver
(Esth. 1:3). Moreover, he considers John 6:51 as the only

prophecy in this field.[15] It is worthy of note that Schwenckfeld interprets texts of the New Testament as well as 'figures' of the sacraments: Thus, the Lake of Siloah in which the blind man was cured (John 9:1-7), indicates baptism, and various references of Christ (Luke 12:36-43; Mark 13:32-37) foreshadow the Last Supper. Schwenckfeld thus finds spiritual references in the same manner in texts of the Old and the New Testament. This confirms his position that one ought to be attentive to the spiritual aspect of the sacraments. One must recognize their value before participating in them. Schwenckfeld therefore insists that spiritual circumcision must precede baptism since only the circumcised shared the Passover meal.[16] Participation in the sacraments is preceded by one's faith. In this regard, Schwenckfeld differs from Luther and the South German reformers. For him the Christians and their sacraments (and naturally also the outer word of promise which awakens faith) are comparable to the Jews and their sacrifices. In both cases he saw men falling away from God to creatures.[17] Therefore, the differences in theories between Schwenckfeld and the great reformers lies not in the figurative interpretation in reference to Christ, but rather in the fact that Schwenckfeld is totally guided by the spiritual and directs all externally related declarations of both Testaments toward spiritual healing in Christ.

2

We have thus already introduced the second question which was raised during Schwenckfeld's Strassburg period and accented his concern with the relationship between the Old and New Testament. This is the question of the meaning of externalities, of the sermon, of the sacraments, of church order, or in sum, the problem of Christian freedom. In his *Judicium on the Augsburg Confession*, which he compiled in December, 1530 at the request of various aristocratic friends and reformers Schwenckfeld explicitly discussed this issue. This was characteristically done in an introduction, followed by his views on the single articles. Thus, the significance the subject had for him is made clear.

Schwenckfeld uses the Pauline distinction between the dead letter and the living Spirit (2 Cor. 3:6). But whereas Luther

associates the dead letter with the law which convicts one of
his sins and the spirit with the awakening gospel of faith, the
Silesian nobleman associates these with the differences between
flesh and spirit, with the outer and inner state. In addition, he
emphasizes in a short classical formulation: 'In the Old Testament one finds the Jewish concept of externally influenced
faith, religion, and religious services, governed by time and by
people and upheld according to the law of Moses through the
sword.' Schwenckfeld quotes from men such as Erasmus and
other humanists when he asserts, 'The statues, laws and ceremonies of the Papists differed little from the rites of the Jews
and learned men who throughout time often criticized these
practices.'[18] With the coming of Christ, such rituals were no
longer valid (Heb. 9:9-11). From the point of view of the gospel,
mosaic and papal forms of worship are invalid. Christians are a
free, good-willed people thanks to the work of the Holy Spirit,
God, and Christ who are at complete liberty to work in them.
Schwenckfeld, however, does not wish to do away with the for-
malities of sermons, sacraments, church orders, and ministry.
They are necessary for the admonishment and encouragement
of men to learn and praise God and to thank him for what he
has worked inwardly in them. Schwenckfeld praises the fact
that freedom from ceremonies is noted in the twenty-eigth article of the Augsburg Confession, but he looks further for a
concept of freedom also in those issues without which salvation remains unattainable for the reformers. He desires freedom in the sermons and in worship just as in the reception of
the sacraments. By referring to Acts 5:15, 1 Corinthians 4:20,
and Romans 14:17, Schwenckfeld indicates that the Kingdom
of God is not attainable through speech, language, food, and
drink, although these texts could not be interpreted in this
way.[19] Otherwise, claims Schwenckfeld, no one who must live
under pagan or Turks could remain a Christian or be saved.
Freedom for baptism is justified in Mark 16:16 where lack of
faith is the sole reason for damnation, just as the words 'as
often as you do this' of the Last Supper support the issue of
liberty in the practice of this sacrament.

At the same time Schwenckfeld states his opposition on this
matter to the Anabaptists as well as to the churches of Rome,
Wittenberg, and Zurich. He denounces their externalism and
blames them all for their indirect regression to a new state of

Judaism when he claims in his treatment of the eighth article of the Augsburg Confession that only true believers belong to the church.[20] Schwenckfeld identifies the consequences of externalism with unrest, disharmony, and division which arise not from freedom but directly through force as is indicated in the case of the Anabaptists and elsewhere. Persecution of the faithful is continued in the Protestant churches, an activity compounding the tyranny of the Catholics.[21] Schwenckfeld thus associates the issue of Christian liberty with the question of force regarding faith by worldly authorities. Since 1530 this highly disputed use was taken up by preachers in various cities. In Strassburg, Wolfgang Schultheiss, Anton Engelbrecht, Pilgram Marpeck, and Schwenckfeld were among those who opposed the right of the authorities to establish church unity by external force, calling on the examples of the kings of Israel and Judah and the deuteronomic traditions of the Old Testament. The difference between him and Bucer became evident during the discussion of some articles that Bucer had written for the famous Strassburg Synod in the summer of 1533.[22] The right of the authorities in this issue of faith was also the starting point of the correspondence between Leo Jud and Schwenckfeld in the spring of 1533.[23] Also in regard to this matter the issue of the differences between the Old and New Testament remained controversial.

3

Naturally, Schwenckfeld heard of the debates in December, 1531 between the Anabaptist leader Pilgram Marpeck, whom he befriended, and Martin Bucer. He must have listened eagerly to the reports since, starting with the parallels between infant baptism and circumcision, the subjects with which they were concerned included the relationship between the Old and New Testament.[24] On the relationship between the two Testaments Marpeck and Schwenckfeld differed as did Schwenckfeld and other Strassburg Anabaptists including the Schweizer brothers and Melchior Hoffman.[25]

At the same time Schwenckfeld took up discussion of the relationship between the Testaments in a third area, namely in regard to the validity of Mosaic laws for Christians. The reason for this was a letter from Leonhard von Liechtenstein

to Capito and Schwenckfeld in which Schwenckfeld was asked
for his opinion of a book in which the Anabaptist leader Oswald Glait explicitly stated that even Christians must keep the
Sabbath. Unfortunately, despite the fundamental work of Gerhard F. Hasel, the beginnings of the Sabbatarians have been
insufficiently studied.[26] It was a legal biblicism which brought
Glait to his position, although perhaps he was influenced by
the traditions of the German mystics, traces of which we can
find in the early Luther and in a special manner in Carlstadt in
his discussion of the commandment regarding the Sabbath.[27]
Also the relationship of the Moravian Sabbatarians to the Jews
is still unclear, although it could be quite important for the interpretation of Luther's letter 'Against the Sabbatarians.'[28]

Since we are not concerned with the issue of the Sabbath
but rather with Schwenckfeld's understanding of the Old Testament. we will only note his answer to Leonhard von Liechtenstein in this matter. In his 'Summary.' Schwenckfeld compiles
eighteen arguments which reveal the differences between the
Old and New Testament. The Old Testament is declared to
consist of shadows. figures. and promises while the New Testament in Christ contains substance. truth. and fulfillment.
The essence of the Old Testament is external. carnal. tran-
sient. slavish. and timid. The opposite is the case in the New
Testament.[29] Schwenckfeld insists that the entire law including
that of the Decalogue as well as the ceremonial law and the cus-
toms handed over to the Israelites was valid (Rom. 2:28),[30] but
because it could not change man, it was completely destroyed
in Christ for Christians (Deut. 9:17: Heb. 7:18)[31] as is indicated by the violation of the Sabbath laws through Christ.[32]
Because the law of the Messiah, the grace of the Spirit, is implanted in the heart of all Christians, the law must for no reason
be reinstituted.[33] Every attempt made to accept the law—and
this means the entire law—is a renunciation of the grace of
Christ (Gal. 5:3).[34] All such attempts signify an establishment
of Judaism over Christian values which Schwenckfeld sees as
the result wherever formal ceremonies and 'means of grace' are
made obligatory.[35] Naturally. the issue of authoritative force
regarding faith is also a subject for discussion.[36]

At the same time Schwenckfeld freely insists that the two
seemingly contrasted Testaments are unified in regard to figure and fulfillment. In his figurative approach. the Israelites

represent all the God-less, sinners and non-Christians who live under the law, by which they should recognize their sins.[37] The Christians, however, fulfill the actual spiritual purpose of the law (Rom. 7:14). This was the case even during the Old Testament period when the literal law was never recognized literally by God, and the patriarchs were saved by faith in Christ.[38] In this context, Schwenckfeld treats the traditional spiritual interpretation of the Sabbath which stresses virtue and the fulfillment of the greatest commandment of faith.[39]

Schwenckfeld summed up his position against the Sabbatarians in a letter on January 18th, 1531 of which I discovered a fragment in the Archives of the Baron of Scheurl in Nürnberg.[40] This piece is particularly interesting because it, in contrast to the usual transmission of Schwenckfeld's letters which deal only with spiritual teachings,[41] contains information on daily matters. By it one can see how greatly the transmission of the remaining correspondence may deviate from its original form. The letter may have been sent to Johann Haner who was a clergyman in Nürnberg at that time and who was associated with Scheurl.[42]

A first impression makes Schwenckfeld's thesis concerning the complete rejection of the law and the decalogue appear similar to that of Luther. Indeed, in 1538, he actually published Luther's famous 'Instruction on how Christians ought to live by the Book of Moses'[43] with his own introduction and altered title. Here he disputes the fact that the Sabbatarians and other 'new Ebionites' desire the resurrection of Moses, associating themselves with the Old Testament where their fundamental teachings cannot be justified in the New Testament. In the context, Schwenckfeld refers to the 'Instruction' as a 'golden book'[44] and it is not surprising that Luther's idea concerning the rejection of Mosaic law was adopted by him. It differed, however, from his view of the law in the Old Testament. In 1531 Schwenckfeld denounced the 'new Ebionites' who follow Moses' law considering it Christ's law and who believe that they must come to Christ through the law even after grace has been revealed.[45] He is here referring to Luther and the other reformers who, convinced of the sinfulness of man, support the existence of the laws for believers to recognize their sin.

4

For Schwenckfeld. as we have seen. consideration of the relationship between the Old and New Testament in view of the
sacramental teaching of Christian freedom and church order
and of the understanding of the law, was necessary. As a result, after 1531/32 he occupied himself extensively with this
subject in two special compositions.[46] We may now examine
them and three significant later statements of Schwenckfeld's[47]
and briefly present his view of the Old Testament in the full
context of his 'heavenly philosophy.'[48]

In Schwenckfeld's opinion, God has revealed himself in two
ways; as creator in the works of mutable creation and as redeemer in the sending of Jesus Christ. This means the contents of the whole bible. However, proper knowledge of the
creation would actually suffice in bringing out man's gratitude
and obedience to God. In his reference to the preaching of
Paul in Acts 14:15-17 and 17:24-28 Schwenckfeld criticizes the
fact that the simple man is always confronted in the sermons
with the words of Scripture instead of. according to Christ and
Paul. being taught the Gospel in all creatures. He also refers to
Mark 16:15 and Colossians 1:23[49] but no longer recognizes the
earlier ideas of the Anabaptist Hans Hut. namely his 'Gospel
of all creatures.' Schwenckfeld may have been introduced to
this idea through students of Hut in Silesia or Strassburg. but
probably became acquainted with it in its form as altered by
Pilgram Marpeck.[50] Nevertheless, he associates it only with
the recognition of the creator in the work of creation, but not
with redemption as it was in the thought of Hans Hut.

The redemption is served by the Word of God which Jesus
himself is. Man attains it directly through the Spirit of God totally independent of the Bible and every mediation. Schwenckfeld employs Abraham as an example of this. Abraham, like
every believer. had heard directly from God the word of the
cross which kills the old man and is the comforting uplifting
word of life,[51] and thereby he was lead to believe. The word
of life is inner spiritual scripture which actually creates faith.
The external Holy Scripture—and Schwenckfeld understands
both the Old and New Testament as the 'letter' over against
the 'spirit' of the inner word—is necessary for man's remembrance. education, knowledge, and gratitude but does not contribute to building up faith. Faith is necessary before one can
understand the outer word of the Scripture.[52]

In Schwenckfeld's opinion the Old and New Testaments differ fundamentally in their spiritual aspects. He compares them according to the previously mentioned contrasting views. All the external aspects of the Old Testament (promises, mediator, covenantal people, covenantal signs, temple, ceremonies, priesthood, obedience) are internal in the New Testament.[53] For Schwenckfeld the external was from the beginning worthless in God's eyes; he strove only for the inner aspect, for Christ.[54]

In support of his non-literal, Christ-directed view of the Old Testament, Schwenckfeld uses three main groups of biblical texts: first, the various statements concerning sacrifices in the Old Testament made by Moses and the prophets, and to the words of Paul when he claimed that only inner circumcisions were valid (Rom. 2:28f);[55] second, the passages of the New Testament designating Christ as the fulfiller of the Old Testament (as Luke 24:47) or stating the purpose of Christ also for the fathers of the Old Testament (including John 5:46; Gal. 3:16; Heb. 13:8 and Apoc. 13:8);[56] and third the hard-sayings form the Sermon on the Mount.[57] In all its parts—law, history, and prophecy[58]—the Old Testament has to be associated with Christ and believers.

Therefore, Schwenckfeld makes use of allegory. He explicitly rejects the Jewish literal interpretation of the Old Testament and opposes Luther's rejection of allegory,[59] adopting this practice of interpretation himself wherever possible. The sacrifice of Isaac (Gen. 22) points to the sacrifice of Christ just as do the Paschal Lamb and all the other Old Testament offerings.[60] Christ's shed blood is represented by the blood shed in Exodus 24:6-8 and the sprinkling of the blood of the red cow in Numbers 19:2ff.[61] The appearance of Jesus in his suffering and resurrection according to Schwenckfeld, has a foreshadowing in the history of Joseph and of David as a potential king.[62] The story of Lot and his daughters reflects the redemption which Christ brought to the Jews and pagans, and the story of David and Bathseba is connected with the liberation of man, through Christ, from the law (Uriah). But Schwenckfeld realizes that these last allegorical interpretations would be the most difficult for his followers to accept.[63] Moreover, the Old Testament points to believers just as it does to Christ. The battles of the Israelites against the Canaanites represent the inner struggle

against Satan, original sin. and desire: and the conflicts between David and Goliath. and Saul and Absalom also point to
the battles of the Christians' fight against evil powers.[64]

The people of the Old Testament. signifying the old man,
did not understand any of this. Their life in Egypt, in the
desert, and under the law points to the imprisonment of man in
sin. death, and by Satan until the arrival of Christ.[65] Schwenckfeld claims the Jews had, from an external point of view, no
advantage over the pagans in whose hearts God had, from the
beginning, written his laws.[66]

Naturally. Schwenckfeld also recognizes the bliss which the
fathers of the Old Testament experienced. However, he found
therein an exception which stemmed from direct encounters
with God. But pagans also had similar experiences as indicated by the cases of Abimelech (Gen. 20:1-14) and Naeman
(2 Kings 5:1-19).[67] Therefore. Schwenckfeld spoke of a type
of dual revelation given to the believing fathers. Abraham is
the corporal founder of the Jewish nation and of God's people
but spiritually he is the father of the Christian faith. of the
Israel according to the spirit, and he forms an eternal bond
in Christ.[68] The faith of the Old Testament fathers points to
the Christ who is to come (John 5:46, 8:56).[69] They were protected in a state of purgatory until Christ suffered, rose from
the dead, and ascended to claim his kingdom. This very traditional idea is explicitly defended by Schwenckfeld against the
reformers for the sake of christology.[70] For him the story of
Jesus is the opening of salvation. indicating that man should
be ware lest that which is eternal and timeless in God's eyes,
passes before man as temporal.[71] This does not mean that
Schwenckfeld accepts in essence God's saving activity in the
Old Testament and an actual history of the acts of God among
men. Certainly he constantly renewed his accusation against
the reformers and others that they were not able to distinguish
truly between the two Testaments.[72] but nevertheless with his
spiritualism and religious allegorical interpretations he bound
the two Testaments together more closely than anyone had
previously done.

Notes

[1] See Selina Gerhard Schultz. *Caspar Schwenckfeld von Ossig (1489-1561)*. with an introduction by Peter C. Erb (Pennsburg. 1977).

[2] See ibid.. 180-204.

[3] See William Klassen, *Covenant and Community: The Life. Writings and Hermeneutics of Pilgram Marpeck* (Grand Rapids, 1968), 165-76.

[4] See CS 4:555.

[5] See Heinrich Bornkamm, *Luther und das Alte Testament* (Tübingen, 1948).

[6] See Gottfried W. Locher. *Huldrych Zwingli in neuer Sicht* (Zurich, 1969). 250-65 and Walther Köhler, *Zwingli und Luther*, vol. 1 (Leipzig, 1924), 110ff.

[7] See QGT 7: 353.31-33, No. 277.

[8] See CS 2:475-478. (Der erste grosse Sendbrief an alle christgläubigen Menschen. Febr. 1527).

[9] See CS 2:686-96.

[10] See CS 4:810.

[11] See CS 4:164-67 (Der dritte Sendbrief an alle Christen. Juni 1531) and 465. Likewise Schwenckfeld refuses to relate baptism to Jewish purification and to the baptism of John the Baptist (see ibid.. 158-60 and 155-58). The sharp distinction between the baptism of John and that of Christ is directed also against Zwingli and the South German reformers. Against the Anabaptists, Zwingli had drawn parallels between the baptisms of John and Christ.

[12] See CS 4:160-62.

[13] CS 4:168f: 170-74.

[14] CS 4:152f: 167f.

[15] See CS 4:174-76.

[16] CS 4:165 and 175.

[17] CS 2:688.

[18] CS 3:870.

[19] CS 3:876f.

[20] CS 3:880f: 911-17.

[21] CS 3:873: 880.

[22] See the acts of the Strassburg Synod (Summer. 1533) in QGT 8: 3-8. No. 356a-58: 21-32. No. 370f: 35-66. No. 373-77; 70-92. No. 384-87: see also the documents in *Martin Bucers deutsche Schriften 5: Strassburg und Münster im Kampf um den rechten Glauben 1532-1534*, ed. by Robert Stupperich (Gütersloh, 1978). 365-526. Cf. as well Werner Bellardi. *Wolfgang Schultheiss, Wege und Wandlungen eines Strassburger Spiritualisten und Zeitgenossen Martin Bucers* (Frankfurt. 1976) and his 'Anton Engelbrecht (1485-1558), Helfer. Mitarbeiter und Gegner Bucers,' in *Archiv für Reformationsgeschichte* 64 (1973). 183-206. In his discussion with Bucer on December 9. 1531 he charged that the preachers sought help and support from the political authorities. See QGT 7: 351-54. No. 277.

23 The four letters of Schwenckfeld to Leo Jud are in CS 4, Doc. 135; 141; 143; 5, Doc. 157.

24 See QGT 7: 351-61. No. 277 and 283: Klassen. 101-135. For Marpeck this was the opportunity to clarify his understanding of the Old Testament. (See *The Writings of Pilgram Marpeck*, trans. and ed. by William Klassen and Walter Klaassen, [Scottdale, 1978], 36). This occurred for the first time in his 'Bekenntnis' of Januar 1532 (See QGT 7: 416-518, No. 302, and 416-527. No. 303.

25 A full study of Schwenckfeld on this point is yet to be done. On Marpeck and Bucer see Klassen, 149-179.

26 See Gerhard F. Hasel, 'Capito, Schwenckfeld and Crautwald on Sabbatarian Anabaptist Theology,' in *Mennonite Quarterly Review* 46 (1972), 41-57.

27 For Luther see 'Von den guten Werken' 1520, in *Martin Luther, Studienausgabe*, ed. by Hans-Ulrich Delius, vol. 2 (Berlin, 1982), 12-88, especially 57-61; for Carlstadt see Ronald J. Sider, *Andreas Bodenstein von Karlstadt. The Development of his Thought 1517-1525*, (Leiden, 1974). 274 and 277-83.

28 WA 50:312-37. On judaising tendencies in the Christianity of eastern Europe since the late middle ages see George H. Williams. 'Protestants in the Ukraine During the Period of the Polish-Lithuanian Commonwealth.' *Harvard Ukrainian Studies* 2 (1978), 41-72.

29 See CS 4:470-79.

30 See CS 4:462.

31 See CS 4:480. 481, 483, 486-93.

32 See CS 4:461f; 507-10.

33 See CS 4:465, 481f, 488f, 510.

34 See CS 4:457f, 461.

35 See CS 4:464-66.

36 See CS 4:475f, 512.

37 See CS 4:484f.

38 See CS 4:464.

39 See CS 4:456f.,462f., 468f., 494ff., 497.

40 Freiherr von Scheurlsches Familienarchiv, Manuskriptband G, f. 132r-133v.

41 See CS 11:717.

42 A letter of Schwenckfeld to Johann Haner of 18.11.1544 indicates that he and Crautwald corresponded with Haner (see CS 9:151ff.).

43 See WA 16:363-93 and WA 24:2-16.

44 See CS 6:290-305. The preface and the quotations from the bible are also Schwenckfeld's.

45 CS 4:455.

46 See 'Unterschied des Alten und Neuen Testaments, der Figur und Wahrheit' (1531) and 'Sendschreiben an die Strassburger Brüder' (13.2.1532), in CS 4:414-43, Doc. 125, and 519-64. Doc. 127.

47 See 'Vom Alten und Neuen Testament. ein kleines Bedenken,' 1540. CS
    7:193-203. Doc. 331. This was taken up by Schwenckfeld in his new
    edition of his 1547 'Vom Gebet. Betrachtung und Auslegung des 25.
    Psalms' (original 1534) which the editors of the CS did not notice. See
    CS 5:15-96, Doc. 163, especially 16f. and 66-9. 'Von der heiligen Schrift'
    1551, CS 12:417-541, Doc. 780, and 'Summarium der Bibel' 1556, CS
    15:11-15, Doc. 987.
48 CS 11:13.
49 See CS 12:469-472. Schwenckfeld could accept the idea since he had
    earlier held the opinion that one could interpret daily experience by
    the allegorical method (see CS 2:318-323). But in 1526 he still did not
    have the idea of the Gospel of all creatures . The marginalia (CS 2:320)
    is either a later addition or is not his.
50 See Gottfried Seebass, *Müntzers Erbe. Werk, Leben und Theologie des
    Hans Hut*, (Theol. Habil., Erlangen, 1972), 432-47.
51 See CS 2:696f; note as well CS 2:690; 3:877; 4:132ff; 12:452-55.
52 See CS 2:687; 4:423; 12:431-35; 438-40; 461f; 496-98; 15:12.
53 See p. 63 and CS 2:476; 3:542; 4:151, 425. 476. 478. 757.
54 See CS 4:421f. Thus. Moses and Elijah stand as representatives of the
    Law and Prophets with Christ at the transfiguration. (see Matt. 17.
    1-13: CS 3:478f). In the incarnation Christ took all flesh up into the
    spirit (see CS 2:477; 3:480).
55 See CS 4:428f, 431.
56 See CS 2:476f; 3:156; 4:541.
57 CS 4:435f.
58 See CS 4:760.
59 See CS 4:762, 810; 12:462, 467f.
60 See CS 4:431, 533.
61 CS 3:540f.
62 CS 4:533f.
63 See CS 4:655f.
64 See CS 4:433ff. and 693ff.
65 See CS 4:151, 533f.. 535.
66 See CS 2:690.
67 See CS 4:809f.: 2:687. 689. 696-98.
68 See CS 4:427: 15:12.
69 See CS 2:476f.: 3:544; 12:465-68.
70 See CS 4:541-48.
71 On the distinction 'vor Gott'/'vor uns' see CS 4:442 and 758f. as well
    as 7:194.
72 See CS 4:439-42. 550-54 and 12:487-95 for a catalogue of Schwenckfeld's
    critique of those opposed to his view of the Old Testament.

Schwenckfeld on the Conscience

Fred A. Grater

When I was first approached about making a presentation at the Colloquium on Schwenckfeld and the Schwenkfelders, I was inclined to refuse on the ground that I am a librarian and not a research scholar. But on second thought I decided to accept the invitation, and to use the opportunity to say a few words about a subject I feel to be important in a Schwenkfeldian context—the development of the Christian conscience.

I believed then. and I believe now. that there would be in the Colloquium too much of a 'historical' nature, and too little dealing directly with what Schwenckfeld considered to be his most important contribution—the theological fruits of the gracious visitation of God which resulted in his own theological insights. But since we have almost nothing which bears directly on this visitation, I decided it would be appropriate to translate a text of Schwenckfeld's on the development of the Christian conscience. I had always wanted to read and to study this text and the Colloquium presented me with the perfect opportunity to do so.

The Christian conscience has been a major topic in Schwenckfeld's theology from its very beginning. The new man in Schwenckfeld's thought, had to be a totally new creation—a new being. To this end he had to have a new conscience, one which was spiritually directed, which arose from his relationship with Christ, and which was capable of further growth and development as the new relationship with Christ matured and developed.

Schwenckfeld sees the whole universe in terms of a duality: good/bad, God/devil, flesh/spirit, in short, everything in the spiritual (good) world has its direct counterpart in the fleshly (evil) world. This world view he inherited from the Greek church fathers and from the German mystics of the middle ages. It shaped his total concept of life, both Christian and pagan. It formed his outlook and shaped the whole of his philosophy (a word he came to despise because it smacked so much of the fleshly reason, which he saw as being in total opposition to the spiritual faith). For Schwenckfeld, in fact, philosophy stood in sharp contradistinction to theology, since the knowledge of the world was to be denigrated while the knowledge (or experience) of God was to be extolled.

This duality expressed itself in the distinction between the old (depraved, evil, corrupt) and the new (purified, good, whole) man. The old man was the result of the fall of man in the Garden of Eden. That fall was so complete, Schwenckfeld thought, that nothing of value was left after it in the physical world. But the fall was not the end of everything, even though it foredoomed all things not otherwise taken care of to utter and complete destruction.

This 'taking care of' was accomplished by the passion, death, and resurrection of Christ. Jesus Christ lived, died, and was raised up again so that the effects of the fall might be annulled. The creation had to be redeemed, lest God destroy it utterly. And, in fact, God did destroy it by making of the old creation a new creation, no longer under His divine condemnation. And Jesus Christ was the means by which this had to take place.

The essay I have translated (and which is printed in its entirety below) deals with these themes in some detail (some might say in too much detail, even though it is a short work by Schwenckfeld's standards). The conscience, Schwenckfeld asserts, is directly from God, is a part of the creation, and is given to all men. This is from Romans 1 and shows how Schwenckfeld adapted from St. Paul the 'philosophy' he needed. Paul cannot, nor does he try to, prove these assertions: for him they are statements of faith, and Schwenckfeld passes them on as such.

From this concept of the conscience as a 'given,' and from his own understanding of the 'progress' or development of the new life in faith, Schwenckfeld deduces the fact that the conscience, new in the new believer, must grow, be exercised, strengthened, and develop, even as the new man must grow and progress in his spiritual life. This development takes place by means of spiritual 'exercise,' even as the physical muscles are developed by a regular regimen of exercise.

The emphasis is on persistence, perseverance, and regularity of practice. Schwenckfeld suggests that one set aside a day for this practice, keep it regularly and faithfully, be punctual and prompt in the practice. What this practice should consist of, what its fruits can be, what one is to do when this exercise does not 'work'—these are the matters which round out this central section of the essay.

Schwenckfeld has built up this essay like an arch. The sections are:

1. Epistle Dedicatory.

2. The Development of the Conscience.

3. Daily Exercise and Examination of Conscience.

4. Conscience and Physical Things.

5. Aids (Topics) to Meditation.

The essay was written and in print by October 18, 1533. It was dedicated to Hans Conrad and Hans Friedrich Von Thumb, two brothers with whom Schwenckfeld had stayed on his way from Strassburg to Augsburg in the summer of 1533. He calls them his 'Schwäger,' brothers-in-law, which the editors of the *Corpus* take as a literal relationship. However the *Langenscheidts enzyklopädisches Wörterbuch*, ed. by E. Muret and D. Skanders (Berlin, 1963), lists as a possible definition, 'Comrade-in-arms, associate, companion,' so that it is at least possible that he was thinking of them as 'fellow-believers' rather than as relatives. He may even have had both terms in mind.

The longest section of the work is the part on the development of conscience (2 above). This section is a commentary on Romans 9 and 11 and deals religious—philosophically with the origin of the conscience, with the scriptural understanding of it, of the old and new man, and how the new man arises in faith within the old, until the old is totally done away with and the new is triumphant. Of especial interest is Schwenckfeld's discussion of the problems the rich have in entering God's

Kingdom. This is especially important since both Schwenck-feld and his two dedicatees fit into this category, so this is not an idle speculation on his part, but a serious admonition to the avoidance of the problems that wealth poses for the serious Christian believer.

The third section I have already discussed. It deals practically with what a person can *do* about his own spiritual growth. It shows in brief how the conscience may be strengthened by practical exercises.

The fourth section is the most typically Schwenkfeldian. It deals with the freedom of the conscience from the burdens imposed by physical things. Its emphasis is that spiritual development takes place apart from and beyond the confines of the physical. The importance of this lies in the fact that the ceremonies, rites, and rituals which the outward man may want, need, or think he wants and needs, have no power over ('cannot penetrate into') the things or conditions of the spirit. The spirit inspires when, where, and as He wills: physical things simply cannot effect any change at all in the spiritual realm. This is one of the basic tenets of Schwenckfeld's philosophical system. If it is understood, then most of his other philosophical thought will make its own kind of logical sense.

The last section is very short. It is typical of Schwenckfeld to include in a practical essay like this one a series of practical exercises. The conscience is developed and strengthened by exercise, and Schwenckfeld here presents a series of such exercises which have for their object the sharpening of spiritual awareness. Such things as the experience of Christ, the Kingdom of Christ, the promises of eternal life, the divine son-ship of God, and other topics are set up to be thought about, prayed about, meditated on, to the end that spiritual discrimination might be sharpened, spiritual judgment made more cogent, and spiritual knowledge and experience made more complete and deepened. In all that he does, says, and writes, these are Schwenckfeld's aims and ends. Not the knowledge of Christ, but the spiritual experience of Him is what counts.

I will close this introduction with a short story which exemplifies what I hope may result from this translation. While I was working on it, I was staying at the home of a good friend. She asked to see the work in progress, so I let her read it. The next morning after reading it overnight, she said that if she had had this material to read forty years ago she would be a better Christian person today. This epitomizes to me what Schwenckfeld wanted his readers to take from this essay, and what I, too, hope to impart to the modern English readers. If this happens—if the modern reader gets some sense of what Schwenckfeld was trying to convey of the importance, the desirability, and the necessity for spiritual growth and development, then this translation will have succeeded in being what I wanted it to be—a contribution to this Colloquium not simply as a scholarly presentation, but as a help in fostering the spiritual development of those modern-day descendants of the followers of the Apostle of the Middle Way.

On the Development of the Conscience

To the noble and best Hans Conradt, Hereditary Marshall, and Hans Friederich Thumb of Newenburg, etc., brothers, my especially beloved friends and brothers-in-law.

The grace of our Lord Jesus Christ, and my willing service [I offer you] before all else, friendly, dear, and beloved brothers-in-law. Since at the request of several of my good friends I have journeyed from Strassburg through Speyer and thence to Augsburg, and on the way have been sheltered in your homes, I have been importuned by your people there to write something in brief on the development of the conscience, as well as about how a simple person who is not yet well instructed in the Scriptures might in these most dangerous times, as much as he is able, attain to a knowledge of the foundation of true faith, and to the beginning of a God-pleasing life and Christian existence with the help of the grace of God. This [essay] I desire herewith to send to you, not that in this way I might repay your love and friendship towards me, but rather, that you might thus be enabled to recognize and receive in some measure my heart and goodwill. In the same way I hope that you might be able to perceive in it something with no denial. That I should be accepted by anyone else in any manner other than as a peaceable Christian, or should be held to be unfriendly or that it should be held that such a disposition on my account should be proper before God or as increasing His honor—these things I deny categorically, and I urge that such malice might be put aside.

This instruction is quite simple, easy. and unpretentious, so
much so that on this account it might easily be deplored by
some people as being a new set of laws. These people would
be such as see in the Gospel more of a fleshly security than
a spiritual practice for their lives, or those who look more for
the appearance of faith than for the power, nature, and true
appearance of faith than for the power, nature, and true characteristics of it. Such people are also those who always say
'Grace and Peace,' but who really give little heed to the office,
work, and disciplining of the grace of God which has appeared
in flesh. Although, I say, this essay will not count for much with
such people, I hope nevertheless that it will not be completely
in vain for those who make use of it.

I do not desire with this [essay] to turn anyone away from
something better (which he might be doing), nor to bind anyone to my opinion either in this or in anything else. It is not,
however, so simple a task for an inexperienced person to attain to the true grace which makes one pious, to understand
this grace, or to accept properly the Gospel of Christ with
the heart, as perhaps many people imagine. Saint Paul says
that faith is a gift of God and not everyone's thing. Then the
Tempter, the Evil Spirit comes along into the bargain, so that
he might soon, when one is not paying proper attention, blow
out the just enkindled light, and cause the newly-begun work,
because it is still so new and weak within us, to be destroyed.
For this reason it is necessary for us to be awake and to pray,
even as Our Lord Christ Himself admonishes us, so that a man
might thoroughly examine himself, develop his conscience in
the Word of God, and be constant in the study of that Word.
He must also be careful to observe, so that he holds not the
appearance to be the reality, the image to be the truth, or the
letter to be the spirit, and thus thinks that he has enough and
to spare of the Gospel and of faith, when in truth before God
he has neither begun to believe nor to have even made a good
beginning.

In short, wherever the works, fruits, and powers of faith or
of the Gospel, together with the improvement of life, are not
yet present, do not let anyone suppose that there is present
within a man's heart any faith which has value before God.
In this way many people have misunderstood the matter, and
many more have abused it, as one so often reads that they have

dealt thoughtlessly and ignorantly, when they say that 'Faith alone makes one righteous and holy,' and therin they have not properly considered the manner, nature, and characteristics of saving faith. Because of this little 'Faith' in the spiritual dealings of the Kingdom of Christ by Paul [Romans 3:24, 28; 4:5; 5:1; 10:4; Galatians 2:16; 3:24; Ephesians 2:8; Philippians 3:9], and by the Lord Christ Himself [Mark 16:16; Luke 8:12; John 3:15-16; 6:47; 11:25-26] are ascribed salvation and eternal life, the word [Faith] has quite a different connotation and understanding than it does in worldly, figurative, and literal dealings. In these [physical dealings] it has nothing but the character of an understanding convincement, opinion, or persuasion that something which has been said or demonstrated is true and certain, and that the mind may depend upon it with strong trust, and that a man may then depend upon it, in which he may rely and hold it to be true, etc. This is the only way that many people can understand it when it is said 'Works are good for nothing, only faith saves,' as if it were enough that a person, without love or [good] works, but only with strong, manly thoughts (as is the way of the flesh in other matters as well) should throw himself upon God or Christ, hold them to be his Savior, and believe that His Word, indeed also the Holy Scriptures, is true, which indeed every natural man easily can do with only his own powers.

Christian faith, however, desires to be judged according to a higher standard with regard to its spiritual characteristics, rather than simply according to the standard of the rhetorical name or human convincement. It is, rather, the perceived power of God and of the Resurrection of Jesus Christ [Ephesians 2:8; Colossians 2:12]. In it the heart is cleansed, the conscience is developed, and the mind is changed, and the person is converted to God. As Saint John says, Faith in Jesus Christ is the victory which overcomes the world, the remorse and sorrow for sins, as well as the forgiveness of them, which brings a new God-pleasing life and the Holy Spirit with it. Only to such a faith can salvation be ascribed. But without works faith is like water without wetness or like fire without heat. Concerning such faith Paul also writes when he declares that man is saved by faith, without the addition of the works of the law (Romans 3:28). Here, however, one must understand what Paul means by 'works of the law,' concerning which he also writes in Titus 3:4-8. It is as if he said, 'Only Christ makes us pious and righteous before God with His Gospel (if we accept Him by means of true faith, so that henceforth we might live in the obedience of faith), and not Moses with his law nor with the works of his law. In this regard, let one look at the Eleventh Chapter of the Epistle to the Hebrews [11:1], for Paul there describes faith, and he will then know easily how to distinguish saving, living faith from the dead, history-believing faith, and will also thus learn to interpret properly the words of the Lord, when he says, 'Whoever believes in me has eternal life [John 6:47].

This is what I wished to show in this [essay], so that the little word 'Faith' and its salvation might be more deeply considered. This is the kind of understanding and experience of the Christian faith, God be praised, that I have spread among you, so that you should no longer persist in the above-mentioned opinion as do so many others, but that you might recognize that more belongs to the salvation of the soul and to our blessedness than that [small amount] which so many suppose in a purely historical manner to believe concerning Christ, and to recognize much of value about Him, etc., yet at the same time to remain still in the old sinful existence, and to refuse to imitate Christ in the obedience of faith. You may well hold with Paul [Galatians 5:6; Ephesians 3:17] that only that faith in Christ is good for anything which works powerfully through love, and by which Christ dwells in our hearts. Of what more I have seen, heard, and experienced during the short time I was in your homes and in your company, I will say nothing further. But I praise God the Lord who even now by His gracious visitation reveals Himself in so many places, so that much of value is still to be expected from Him. I pray that He may further strengthen and increase the already begun work of his grace still more among you and in your hearts, and that He might graciously lead you on to your souls' salvation and to His own praise. Amen.

Saint Paul writes that not many noble, not many powerful, not many wise persons according to the flesh are called into the Kingdom of God, but, rather, that which is foolishness according to the world, that is what God has chosen, so that He might humble the proud; and that which is weak before the world, God has chosen to humble what is strong; and that which is ignoble before the world and that which is despised. God has chosen; and that which is nothing, He has chosen, to destroy that which is something, so that no flesh should boast before Him [1 Corinthians 1:26-29]. Because this is so, it is not proper for a person to look to his neighbor [to see what he is doing], but, rather, each person should look to himself to see to it that he is following after Christ, that he may become a partaker of His Heavenly calling. The noble, rich, powerful, learned, and wise men who are called to the Kingdom of God should expect nothing else than that their high-ness must fall, so that they set neither fame, comfort, nor hope in it. God desires to have their hearts: therefore, they must dismiss from their worldliness all their pomp, arrogance, pride, tyranny, and rich appearance with their whole hearts. From now on they must become newborns in Christ the Crucified (and to this world lowly and despised) with their mode of life, each according to the measure of faith, conformably as a member of His Body—that is, if they desire to inherit the Kingdom of God [John 3:3]. They will still embody their own persons and stations in life, as well as the other gifts of God, but they will soon come into another appearance, usage, practise, meditation, consideration, association, heartily to be commended to you all by God the Lord. Augsburg, October 18, 1533. Caspar Schwenckfeld von Ossig.

The Development of the Conscience in the Beginning and Growth of Faith and of a Good God-pleasing Christian Life

God the Almighty Creator of Heaven and Earth created man among the other created things by His word, to be the most glorious and His only image and representation. He also foresaw that in man He would dwell, live, and exist in the future, as in a living temple. To him accordingly God depicted and revealed these things in His creation. In the same way He gave him, to understand this by an implanted law of nature, so that, indeed, even today no one might be able to excuse himself as if he knew nothing of God, or that God did not exist. Concerning this, see Romans 1:19-20, 2:14-15. For this reason God the Lord displayed at the very beginning His goodness, love, and benefit to men in that for five days, day after day, He

created all creatures before man, prepared them for him, and
subjected them to him, so that man might have dominion over
them and might make use of them in his need [Genesis 1:1-31].
He does not permit Himself even today to be unrecognized, in
that He lets the sun shine upon the just and on the unjust: He
sends rain from heaven, fruitful seasons of harvest [Matthew
5:45 Acts 14:17], habitation, food, drink, health, strength, en-
durance, and gives to everyone the breath of life, etc.

For this same reason all men are by nature and in all their
powers obligated to seek for God that they might feel Him to
find Him [Acts 17:27], that they might sometime hear His voice,
that they might not harden their hearts, but that, rather, without any hindrance they might permit Him to come in to them,
and that they might honor Him as God. For this same reason
they will wish to shun everything which is contrary to Him as
the Highest Good, praise Him with their lips and their hearts,
do Him honor with their manner of life and conduct, and thus
thank Him for every received benefit generally and severally,
fear Him as their Lord, learn to love Him from the heart, take
counsel from Him in every contingency, and always and forever
keep Him before their eyes. To do such things, I say, are all
men obligated before God. This is why he made them and why
He has done so much good for them, and continues even today
to do so much for them, so that they might always stand ready
at His command, and hold Him to be their Lord and God,
even as the above-mentioned work of creation has, according
to its own measure, a love and fear of God which includes
the law of nature. The work of Creation teaches us fearfully
to avoid the works of death, that is the gross external vices
against God and our neighbors both because of their natural
inheritability and also because of the consequent punishment
for them. On the contrary, for the love of virtue and its reward
this same work of Creation teaches us to do good works, which
both human righteousness and the Law of Moses require of us.
Everyone, indeed, even all the heathens, are required to live
within these natural guidelines, as they are obligated and convinced in their natural consciences, and insofar as they do not
desire to be punished by God in the end. Indeed, every man is
by nature obligated to do everything that God will have him
do, and not to do that which He does not want done: this is
indeed the sum of all the Law and the Prophets.

This is now the beginning of faith in God the Almighty Creator of heaven and earth. The fear of the Lord is the beginning of divine wisdom: this is with the Lord's Prayer and the Ten Commandments what people are accustomed to teach their children in the Catechism, even as Paul also taught the heathens, after which he converted them to the faith in Jesus Christ, after he, by using the visible work of the creation of God as an example, brought them to a knowledge of his invisible power, essence, and glory [Romans 1:20] and made the presence of God as plain as day before them. In this way he instilled in them the divine fear. For God is also as Creator with His power and strength present to all created things, for which He preserves their life, and provides them with strength, nourishment, and growth. Thus, among us, for in Him we live, (in Him) we move, and (in Him) we have our existence. This is what some of the poets have said, for we are His people.

Now therefore because God the Lord desires that his created beings should show forth and manifest their obedient service and fear to the praise of God, which otherwise appear naturally in all the unreasoning created things, for each one praises God in its own way, glorifies its Creator, and stands ready to hand before Him (and blessed is he who recognizes, understands, and who is improved by this understanding). For this reason one should be all the more ready to turn himself to God, to abstain from all unrighteousness. He should keep God firmly in mind, and try to get to know Him with all the might and power of his flesh from the very beginning. A man should accustom himself to being thankful to God from his very depths for all His benefits, for food, drink, and His care in all his difficulties, and that He distributes in all the works of love and mercy, the gifts of God, mildly, and stretches forth His hand to the needy. For whoever is unfaithful and thankless in these smallest matters, how may greater and important things be entrusted to him? Concerning these things the Lord Christ speaks (Luke 16: 10-12) as he says further: If you are not faithful in strangers' (that is, of the goods and riches of this world) things, who will give you the things which are your own, which are the spiritual heavenly things procured for us by Christ, which we are eternally to enjoy? In sum, whoever does not show himself to be faithful, proper, and thankful to God on account of his natural gifts—how will he then attain to the gifts of the Kingdom of God and of eternal life? But whoever is faithful to God and seeks Him properly will certainly find Him.

If one were now to ask how one attains to such saving faith, in which a man may live and be pleasing to God, I answer: True faith is given by grace in the word of truth which proceeds out of the mouth of God. For this reason a man should occupy himself with hearing of the Gospel of Christ and the Word of God; indeed, he should pay attention with the inner ears to what the Lord will speak to him of how He awakens him from spiritual death and proclaims in his heart the words of grace and life. For faith comes by hearing, and hearing comes by the Word of God (Romans 10:17). If the Word of God is heard, it must then be considered properly with spiritual understanding, accepted, and received by the heart, so that a man might willingly surrender himself to it, repent in all humility before God, and properly learn to experience Christ. Then indeed the Word of God will grow up with love and truth, with sweetness, power, and strength (just as a bitten mustard seed) in his heart. For it is not yet enough, and you do not become so soon a Christian before God as you believe and accept the Gospel of Christ according to its simply literal sense, or as soon as you delight to hear it that way, or indeed speak gladly about it and thus confess Christ. You must, rather, progress still further and employ yourself so that by God's grace it may truly be laid upon you and might become for you a true Good News, the proper, joyful tidings, so that the comfort of Christ might be in your heart. Then a good conscience will result in you, as the beginning and growth of a Christian divine life and confession.

This is also the word of faith, concerning which Paul writes, that is, if you confess Christ with your mouth, that He is the Lord, and if you believe in your heart that God awakened Him from death, then you will be saved. For it is with the heart that one believes unto righteousness, and with the mouth that one confesses unto salvation [Romans 10:9-10]. In short, mouth and heart, the outward confession and the inward power or truth must be together with each other. Thus, everything that the mouth speaks concerning Christ and whatever a man works of goodness, indeed, what he believes concerning God, proceeds out of the whole heart and stands powerfully delineated therin, if that faith is truly genuine. That is, moreover, an important matter which St. Paul speaks concerning this, namely, To hold Jesus (the Crucified) to be the Lord, to believe in Him and to confess Him; therin indeed is encompassed the whole of the experience of Christ. For this reason Jesus is Lord without being in the Holy Spirit. [1 Corinthians 12:3] But who considers today what Paul intends with these words? Because today almost everyone calls Him Lord and yet so few of them have the Holy Spirit. But whoever busies himself with dealing from the heart with God and loves Jesus Christ most warmly, and also concerns himself about the mystery of His heavenly Kingdom, and prays with consideration—these and other matters will not remain hidden to him.

In sum, if you desire to become a Christian, that is one anointed of the Lord, and desire to be accounted faithful by God, you must (as mentioned above) not only hear God's Word, but must properly understand it, receive it with you heart, turn yourself repentantly to God, and come to experience Christ spiritually and properly. This is how the pious disciples of Christ acted; concerning this He speaks in John to the Father, saying, The words which You, O Father, have given to me, I have given to them, and they have received them and have truly known that I have come from you, and they believe that You have sent me (John 17:8). Behold there you have the hearing of the word, the reception of it, the experience, and faith, one after the other, as they should proceed in all faithful Christians.

What the experience of Christ encompasses, how and why Jesus is called Lord, God will make manifest in some other place so that it may there be more fully explained, for it is almost the most necessary point of our Christian faith, from which flows all blessedness, all love and true piety. For it is in this experience [of Christ] that our sins are forgiven to us, God is appeased, and you are made more righteous, as it is written in Isaiah 53:11, if this is comprehended in true faith.

By such experience and faith the naturally good pharisaical conscience which is solely founded on fleshly righteousness is changed into a God-pleasing, Christian, new conscience, one which is founded in the Spirit, in the pure desires of the heart, and in Christ. Just as has been said previously concerning the stages of faith and of the experience of God, and to which I add my own personal testimony, a man must thoroughly examine himself; his pharisaism and hypocrisy must be cast aside if he still continues in them, and he must know how to build up and establish his conscience in Christ Jesus and in His righteousness, so that he might become certain and assured of his Christian faith, that he might be born anew, and that Christ might dwell in his heart.

For the naturally good conscience does not suffice unto eternal life, even so little as does a pharisaical conscience which arises out of the Law, which is formed by doing and by not doing and which puts its confidence in its works. This is so because all flesh is by nature evil, worthless, and full of its own self-love before God, be it ever so honorable, just, and pious before men as it will. One says well concerning such a person that he is a pious worldly person, an upright citizen, a just man, and such things may even be said of a pious heathen or of a Jew, but he does not therefore become all at once a pious Christian person, for more is required to attain to that distinction, which is the New Birth, the Spirit of Christ, and righteousness of the heart, together with true faith.

Hence it is that the Lord speaks to His disciples, and, indeed, to all of us: Unless your righteousness (this also applies to the conscience) exceeds that of the scribes and pharisees, you will not enter into the Kingdom of heaven [Matthew 5:20]. Only from such divine righteousness, by which the heart is made pious, can a constant, good conscience come forth, one which is blameless before God and man, through our Lord Jesus Christ. Paul boasts about this in 2 Corinthians 1:12 and 2:15-16. In the same way he speaks before the governor (Acts 24:16). We should also occupy ourselves with this, so that at all times we might have an untroubled conscience before God and men.

This is why the Lord admonished us, when in Matthew He distinguished His righteousness from human righteousness, His doctrine from the Mosaic doctrine, as the Gospel from the Law, and the Kingdom of the World with its Mammon from the Kingdom of God. This is what He says (Matthew 6:33): Seek first (that is chiefly and before all other things) for the Kingdom of God and for its righteousness, and all these other things (which men look after and use to take care of their bodies) will be given to you. That means that we are to erect our consciences, all our doings, deeds, and manner of living only upon Jesus Christ, as upon the only Rock, Cornerstone, and Foundation of God, and upon His Spirit and doctrine, that we might become citizens of His Kingdom, pious and proper Christians from the heart. From now on we are to shun all bad companions, to stand aside from all godless existence, flee from all unrighteousness, practice true repentance, and strive against all evil desires. In sum we are to surrender and open our hearts to Christ the Son of God who daily knocks, so that He might circumcise them and by His grace reign, live, and dwell in them, to the praise of God His heavenly Father. This is the chief necessary thing, to which a man should give serious consideration, that is, everyone who desires to be a Christian and who hopes to inherit the Kingdom of God; he must grasp for this and strive to understand it properly. Then the rest, that is, the other necessities of the body and whatever else is external, will simply be added and may in the Name of the Lord be well and properly used.

Now because all this might appear to unpracticed persons in the first newness of their conversion to be rather difficult, or indeed too high and as good as impossible, especially if the flesh is still flesh and frisky, and also if a man has become accustomed to the ways of the world, physical honors, and all its pleasures, or else if he is otherwise burdened with many cares and much business, yet nevertheless, this all becomes easy and bearable in Christ Jesus if we keep Him before our eyes and if we take advantage of His grace in all our necessities. By His grace, I say, everything becomes pleasant (no matter how harsh it may appear) as soon as one surrenders oneself with fixed purpose to becoming a Christian and to living from now on, as much as possible, a life pleasing to God.

Therefore, no man, of whatever condition he may be, should harbor any doubts in this matter, as if it were too high, too incomprehensible, or too difficult. Let him but try to make a beginning in faith, to focus his attention on the level [he has attained] and on the work of the grace of God; then the increase and the growth together with the development of the conscience will ensue with power. This is also the righteousness which is valid before God, which is revealed in the Gospel, and which arises from faith to faith. The Lord Christ encourages us to this by a comforting promise, when He says: Ask, and to you will be given; seek, and you will find; knock, and it will be opened to you. For whoever asks, will receive; whoever seeks, will find, and to whomever knocks, it will be opened (Luke 11:9). Ah! What shall our pious Lord do more? He has even poured out His Blood for this reason, so that we might attain to these things and become heirs of His kingdom.

He says in another place [Mark 9:22] that to the faithful person (that is, one who seeks God with full intention and receives Christ with his heart) all things are possible. And for our comforting he has also invited the weak and heavily burdened to come to Him, those who would like to be rid of their sins' unrighteousness and their work-weary existence— these especially He calls (Matthew 11:28). Come to me all of you who are weary and heavily burdened, and I will refresh you. I, says the Lord, I will refresh you, and no one else will. He wants to do it, and does it through and through for all who really desire it. He cannot ever deny the faithfulness and love which He has for men even to all eternity, for His Name is Faithful and Truth (Revelation 19:11). Take my yoke upon you and learn from me, says Christ further, for I am gentle and humble of heart, and you will find peace for your souls, for my yoke is easy, and my burden is light (Matthew 11:29-30).

Behold, my brother, [this Christian existence is] like a precious reading, that is, something which deserves to be constantly considered and which ought to be inscribed upon the innermost part of the heart, and in which we ought daily to spiritually exercise ourselves if we are really serious about the Kingdom of God, when we have begun to long for the joy of eternal life. These two virtues, gentleness (which is true goodness or patience) and humility of heart, are the chief points which go to make up a proper Christian. They are the true test of the beginning and growth of faith and of a Christian life.

Thus, we have now heard that no one (who has not become pious of heart) may excuse himself from this obligation, for God desires to assist all men in it, even as in grace He invites all men to partake of this life in grace. He desires that all men should be healed and should come to a knowledge of the truth (1 Timothy 2:4). It is really not difficult for anyone to become a Christian, except for the nobles, the powerful, and the rich in this world. For this reason the Lord says, How hard it is for the rich to enter the Kingdom of God. It is easier for a camel to go through the eye of a needle than for a rich man to enter the Kingdom of God. But when the disciples were appalled at this saying they said, Alas, who can then be saved? Thereupon the Lord responded with a most comforting saying: With men this is impossible, but with God all things are possible (Matthew 19:24-26; Mark 10:25-27; Luke 18:25-27).

How is it possible with God that the rich, noble, and powerful persons come into the Kingdom of God? Answer. [This happens] when God touches their hearts, gives them over to the experience of Christ, converts them to Him, and by divine power graciously pulls them away from the thorns, thisles, and cares of this world with which the heart is entwined and the Word of God is entwisted. Then they no longer wish to ride so high, but rather, they turn their thoughts from riches, set no more faith in wealth, desire to help those in need, leave behind their vain display, concern themselves more with God than with the world, and, in short, hold fast to the points described above, let them suffice for their needs, and no longer desire to be rich nor to collect for themselves earthly treasures. Those who desire to be rich fall into temptations and snares and into many insane and harmful desires which sink men into destruction and damnation (1 Timothy 6:9). They should rather concern themselves as to how they might become rich in God and gather together such treasures which would endure into eternal life, as related in Luke 12:21, 33.

This is also what St. Paul desires to say, when he writes to the Corinthians and says: Dear brother, the time is very short; this means that those who have wives should be as if they did not have them, and that those who mourn should be as if they did not mourn, and that those who rejoice should be as if they did not rejoice, and that those who buy should be as if they owned nothing, and that those who make use of this world should not misuse it, for the existence of this world is passing away (1 Corinthians 7:29-31). The same he writes as well to Timothy [1 Timothy 6:17-19] It does not become the rich of this world to think too highly of themselves (nor to be too proud), nor to put their hope into uncertain wealth; they should, rather, put their hope and trust in the Living God, who gives us every good thing for our refreshment (that is for proper use in our need). Thus, (it behooves them) to do good, to become humanitarians, so that they might gather up for themselves treasures as a solid foundation for the future (these are eternal, spiritual treasures. concerning which the Lord speaks in the Gospel [Matthew 6:19-20; Luke 12:33]—so that they might at last attain to eternal life.

Behold therefore the rich, noble, and powerful persons should be so disposed as to pursue righteousness, blessedness, faith, love, patience, gentleness, etc. [1 Timothy 6:11], if they wish to be saved. How hard this appears viewed from the point of view of the flesh I will let everyone judge for himself. But by the grace of God it all becomes easy if one simply takes the task in hand, and sets the heart to thinking more on the heavenly riches and eternally-abiding joy (promised to all men) than about temporal, pride-filled things, and about this poor, miserable life. He should direct his thoughts, courage, and reason to the Lord Jesus Christ. Then that which is temporal will have its true usage and progress, when God will deal with him, who is our gracious Lord, so that everything takes place according to His will and in the consciousness of God. For the earth is the Lord's and all that is in it, the world and all that dwells upon it (Psalm 24:1).

On the Exercise and Daily Examination of the Conscience

But so that the simple people might have instruction as to how they should practice and become aware of themselves at the beginning of their Christian life, I will share with them, and especially with those who are weighted down with temporal cares or who are still somewhat immersed with their hearts in this world, (but who would like to escape from it) my advice. Let everyone test it, and let us all pray to God that He might come to aid all who desire this with the power of his grace. Amen. In brief, therefore.

Every man who desires to enter heaven and desires to be saved is obligated to see to it on a daily basis, for the sake of his soul's salvation, for the sake of his life and existence, his doing, and refraining, that he live in divine fear, that he grow up in the grace of Christ to become a New Man, that he frequently test and consider in his conscience whether he is serving God, is pleasing to Him, whether he loves Christ and His people, and is not shamed of the poor of Christ, etc. On the contrary, he is also obligated daily to consider in what ways he still angers God, in what ways he offends his conscience, wherein he still practices unrighteousness, whether he still puts his neighbor to the test, wherein he still is not acting according to love, etc. He should put away these things one after the other; he should strive against the still adhering sin and still rising evil thoughts, and he should hate all vices. If this does not take place at first as zealously as it should on a daily basis, a man should at least once a week make an accounting within himself, so that what is still evil in him might be improved, and whatever is good might be further strengthened by the grace of God. This should take place chiefly on Sunday (whence some people call it the day of reconciliation) or on some other specified day in a most simple manner, which will be described below.

When a man arises in the morning and gives thanks to God the Lord for his shelter, rest, and the other benefits of the previous night, he should also consider seriously the mystery, use, and value of the Resurrection of Jesus Christ from among the dead; how our Lord on that day after he had suffered for our sins, etc., resurrected joyfully from death and entered into a new, heavenly completely divine life, so that we might also rise up with Him by His power from the death of sin, from the evil conscience, and from the sleep of the heart, and might follow Christ the King of Honor with a new divine mode of life into the Kingdom of God by the assistance of His grace. This means that we are to put to death our Old Man (who seeks, loves, and admires this world and all that is in it) willingly with Christ's help, and to offer ourselves up to God as a living sacrifice. In this way we will present ourselves through the suffering of Christ to the killing off of our old self in all patience under the Cross, and thus come forth with Him to the joyful resurrection of the New Man, here [on earth] experientially and truly according to the truth of faith, and there [in heaven] according to the perfection, according to our present understanding (2 Corinthians 5:7-17).

This is also the association of the good conscience which is struck with God by means of the Resurrection of Christ (1 Peter 3:21). The New Testament in the Blood of Christ is founded on this, which, by His Spirit is written in our hearts. All this takes place when God the Lord calls us to Himself,

touches us, and makes us alive in faith. For, before God, all
men are dead who are not alive in Christ, as even the faith in
Jesus Christ is nothing else than the power of God by which
He awakened Christ from death. This takes place, I say, when
we see to it that we are born anew by the Spirit of Christ,
sanctified and renewed in the reason of our hearts. On this
one may read further in Romans 12:2; Philippians 3:10; and
Colossians 3:10 [Ephesians 4:23].

Thus, may a man meditate with good thoughts at night
when he cannot sleep but yet does not wish to get up. He
should drive out all evil thoughts and should converse with
Christ in his bed, even as the Prophet David admonished
[Psalm 4:1-2]. When he arises he should let nothing hinder
him from kneeling in a secret place and thanking God the Lord
for His holy bitter passion which He underwent for the sake of
our sins, and also to render Him praise and honor for His joyful
resurrection which took place for the sake of our righteousness.
He should also pray that the Lord would make him to be more
and more a partaker of this mystery, together with his merits
and all other benefits in the truth, that all this might occur
with divine power, and that he might be sealed to eternal life
in his heart.

In preparation for this, however, he should put aside completely all hatred, envy, anger, and contempt which he has for
any other person. In this way he may call upon God with a
peaceful and free mind, for, as has been explained above, such
calling must take place from the heart with sighs, desires, and
hopes and in true faith so that in this way our Christ may
be gracious to us, for all of what Christ has suffered, done,
and acted has taken place on account of poor sinners, that is,
because of such sinners who desire to improve themselves and
not to harden their hearts, but rather to have true remorse
and sorrow for their sins and daily to depart from them and to
dwell in the fear of the Lord. For God the Lord neither desires
nor is able to deny or cut off His grace from those who seek
it earnestly and pray constantly for it. If then the evil spirit
disturbs one, or causes one to go astray in prayer or in one's
spiritual meditation, that person should always begin anew,
and, as much as possible, control his thoughts and guard himself from wandering thoughts, so that the Spirit of God might
perfect His work in him.

Then he should make a general confession to God the Lord through Jesus Christ, so that he might say with the prophet David: I will confess my transgressions to the Lord and he will forgive me the misdeeds of my sin [Psalm 32:5]. For the Lord is good and kind; therefore He will instruct the sinners, and lead them onto the path which is right (Psalm 25:8-9). Therein he ought to consider as much as he is able how he has lived in the preceding week, wherein he has sinned or dealt contrary to the Commandments of God, whether by anger, swearing, greed, pride, impatience, deception of his neighbor, suspicion, hatred, envy, gluttony, seeking one's own will, and such other works of the flesh.

Also he should consider whether he has given proper attention to his soul's salvation, whether he has become cold in this consideration, whether he has little of Christian love; he should also look to see whether he has served God spiritually with meditation and prayer, or whether he has let temporal considerations hinder him too much in the way of God, and let them lead him astray from God's spiritual gifts, whether he has in the preceding week depended, followed, and hoped more in vain upon God and His Word, whether in thoughts, words, or deeds, this should cause him real sorrow. He should pray God for forgiveness, cleanse his conscience in the outpouring of the Blood of Christ, wash away his sins in the grace of God. In this way he may prepare to do better in the week to come, and to break away even more and more from the party of sin, so that his conscience might be strengthened, his faith increased, and the powerful works of grace might be better recognized and experienced in us more comfortingly.

On the contrary a man should also consider what God the Lord has done for good for him in the preceding week, physical or spiritual, internal or external. He should lift these things all up to God as the only Giver of all good things, with hearty thanksgiving. He should also pray for an increase of grace and for eternal life so that his heart might be turned from the gifts to the Giver of them, and from the created things to their Creator Himself, so that he might accustom himself to have in God and in Jesus Christ His Word alone all his pleasure, joy, comfort, and satisfaction.

This meditation does not need many words, fearfulness, or reasons, as much as it needs sighs, meditations, hearty thanksgivings, desires for grace and love to God, together with an earnest intention. In short the heart and conscience are to be turned constantly toward God through Jesus Christ, so that they might be surrendered and willingly offered to Him. For wherever the treasure is, says the Lord, there is the heart, and contrariwise, wherever the heart is, there will be the treasure as well, [Matthew 6:21]. And because the treasure which Christ has gained for us is laid up for us wholly in heaven, we must direct, guide, and aim our hearts there as well. Even if riches, honor, favor of men, or such other physical things were to be present, then the heart, as the Prophet David reminds us [Psalm 62:11], should still not be turned towards them, but they should be used with all disinterestedness, to the honor of God and from a good conscience.

This is enough concerning the testing of the conscience in brief. It is highly necessary to know for any beginning or growing Christian. Now for some people this might occur without any difficulty or any especial effort, even as the same confession, discovery, and knowledge progress so easily and so often in hypocrisy. Yet this will most often occur with difficulty, because it involves the whole heart, in which man now recognizes his sin and his wounded conscience. For this reason also after the above-mentioned offering up of oneself, or surrender to the will of God, or bowing under the yoke of Christ, everything which disturbs the conscience must be put aside. Then a man must pay attention to how he deals and from what knowledge he deals with God, with himself, and with all created things, so that in the future he might day by day become more aware, in the future weeks of his existence, of every word and deed more than before. In this way he will try to keep God before his eyes every day, every hour, indeed every moment (so to speak). He will thus pay more attention that he causes Him to be angry less and less, that he sins less and less frequently, and that he strives more effectively against the rising evil desires of the heart, overcomes temptation better, and does not let it get into his works. By this means also a man will reach the goal set up for him; he will know and become certain that God has called him from this wretched world into His heavenly Kingdom, and that Christ dwells in his heart. Then a great deal of diligence, effort, and watchfulness will be necessary, until one attains to a proper exercise in Christ, so that the evil spirit (who will seek to thwart this undertaking with much cunning, many strategems, and frequent deception) can no longer tear out, disturb, or destroy this work of grace. They that look to the Lord will be enlightened, and their face will not be put to shame (Psalm 34:6).

This is then a true repentance, that is, the serious conversion in the Name of Christ and the turning away of the heart from the world and from everything that is harmful to it, and toward God in heaven. Thus, I have said that the God-fearing person should look to this with all diligence, so that the work, the value, and the fruit of the Resurrection of Jesus Christ might be applied to his heart, and, indeed, to his whole mode of life. By the Cross of Christ he is obligated to take up his own cross, and in all humility, patience, and resignation, to follow his Lord Christ into the Kingdom of Heaven, in the same manner as Christ also as the Head had to suffer, and by suffering had to enter into the glory of God (Luke 24:26). In this same way His Christians, as the members of His Body, each according to the measure of his own faith, through His power and effect, must follow Him in conformity, so that the impudence of the flesh might be rooted out and its evil nature controlled, if the Spirit of Christ is truly to dwell in us and to rule our consciences powerfully in God's grace.

A man must look upwards so that he is more and more separated from this world, from all its crowds and godless existence, so that in future he is no longer conformable to the world in his life, nor lives to please it, as Paul writes (Romans 12:2). Rather, he is to become transformed in the image of Jesus Christ the Son of God so that he might, as has been said now on several occasions, enter into a new spiritual, holy life by the power of His Resurrection, which life will be blameless before God and man. Above all else, one should leave no room for greed, which St. Paul calls idolatry and the root of all evil, which hinders in the present, together with self-will much more than all the other vices the growth in the Gospel; it disturbs much that is good, and, by the especial working of Satan takes a disproportionate control and reign.

It is also necessary for one who desires to grow in faith, in his conscience, and in divine life that he associate himself with pious, virtuous, and God-fearing persons: by them he will be continually improved in their speech, doctrine, and way of life. Bad conversation, St. Paul says [in 1 Corinthians

15:31] destroys good habits, and evil men go from bad to worse;
they lead men astray and are themselves led astray (2 Timothy 3:13). O, blessed is the man who does not live according
to the counsel of the godless nor stands in the way of sinners,
nor sits in the seats of scorners. But his delight is in the Law
of the Lord, and he speaks of His Law day and night, as King
David says (Psalm 1:1-2). Again, he always shows his love for
his neighbor and for all men in need, and especially for the
brothers and comrades in faith, as St. Paul teaches (Galatians
6:10). In this way he will gain more and more love in himself
for Jesus Christ, who so willingly gave Himself up to death for
us; he will pray for the increase of His Spirit within himself,
and will rejoice in the Lord with spiritual joy that he might
dwell and live eternally in His Kingdom.

When then Sunday or some other especially designated day
comes around again, then the God-pleasing person will hold
an accounting within himself to examine his conscience so that
as before he might consider whether he had in any way departed from the way of God, whether God through Christ had
increased his power and works in him by grace, so that now
he trusts Him more, loves Him more steadfastly, prays more
earnestly, strives more diligently against his misdeeds, etc. If
something good has been received or applied by the grace of
God so that the spirit of God effects it, and in his conscience in
Christ a good testimony is given concerning it, then he has a
good hope soon for further increase, to love God, and to thank
him joyfully for such received benefits as well as for the effect-
ing of his salvation. In this way a new Christian person grows
up in grace, from faith to faith, from love to love, from clarity
to clarity, from one virtue to another so that he rushes forth
into complete perfection (Philippians 3:15) which we shall first
receive only in Heaven.

But if after this prescribed examination of his conscience
before God nothing of substance is found, but the heart is still
cold in the love of God, the meditation still cramped, faith still
weak, and the fear of God still imperfectly realized, then he has
even more reason to come before the Mercy Seat, Jesus Christ,
to pray diligently to Him, and to remind Him with more sighs
of the love and goodness which He has obtained for the whole
race of men by His sufferings, to watch still more diligently over
his soul, and to be daily more perceptive of the calling of God

through Christ. If he will do this even for a short time and will take up the matter with diligence and seriousness by the grace of God, he will certainly become aware of the effects of the grace of God in his heart with thanksgiving, and he will be able to build upon an eternally enduring foundation. Let others say what they will and each believe as he has experienced, etc. For in short there must soon be a surrender (I mean a willing surrender in Christ) in our weak flesh if it is not to forget the dealings it had with God.

Even so little as the sun can fail in its shining when the air is clear, just so little, in fact even less, may God hold back from enlightening with His grace when we earnestly ask Him and desire it from the heart, even as it is written in Psalm 145:18: The Lord is near to all who call upon Him in truth. He casts away all our sins, and as soon as a man sighs in faith from his heart, He will no longer remember any of his misdeeds. For just as a Father takes pity on his children, so also does the Lord take pity on those who fear Him (Psalm 103:13). Let a man only see to it that he flees from sin, improves his life, and avoids or puts away whatever burdens the soul or disturbs the life pleasing to God.

How the Conscience is Affected by External Things

In conclusion I should also speak, regarding the development of the conscience, further of external things, whether the conscience is built up by them, founded on them, or may indeed be hindered by them, and how one is to deal with them—but this cannot all be covered here. In this connection, one should certainly not forget the Christian Freedom which the Son of God has procured for us by the shedding of His Blood, concerning which see Galatians 5:1-2, 13-14; 1 Peter 2:16. For by this [Freedom] all Christians are made free of created things and may use them properly as the gifts of God, as Paul says: To the clean, all things are clean (Titus 1:15). All things are cleansed for them through prayer and through the Word of God (1 Timothy 4:5), goods or money, houses or lands, food or drink, products, or whatever else they might be. They know, however, (note that 'they' are Christians) how they are to deal with these things according to the true knowledge of the saints, for [knowledge] deals properly in all things, looks to God whence all things come and whither all things are to return. Thus, the external is ruled, driven, and led by the internal with a good conscience, as God will have it.

Secondly as regards the public worship of God in the New Testament or of the Kingdom of Christ, the Lord Christ has also released the conscience from the Law and from all external things, so that it might be directed towards Him alone, and might pray unburdened to the Father freely in Spirit and in truth. For the Kingdom of God comes not with external signs; one cannot say Behold here it is, or there, for, lo, the Kingdom of God is within you. It is righteousness and peace and joy in the Holy Spirit; whoever serves in it is pleasing to God and valuable to man. Therefore, a man should not let his conscience be bound in any way at all by human laws, ceremonies, or with the things of this world as necessary to salvation, nor let himself be carried captive away from Christ by [misguided] preachers. But he must see to it carefully that he is dealing from within outwardly in the freedom of the spirit, and not from without inwardly in the service of the things of this world, and thus learn to build up his conscience. Just as no external thing may cleanse, pacify, strengthen, or help the conscience before God, indeed it may not even penetrate to it, so also [the conscience] neither can nor may be burdened, driven, or held captive by any external thing (be it what it may). It must, rather, be founded and erected solely on the rock which is Jesus Christ. For they who are driven by the Spirit of God are the Children of God (Romans 8:14).

In the Old Testament and among the Jews the consciences were heavily burdened, held captive, and ruled by external things because of the old, disobedient flesh. This situation lasted only to the time of the perfect completion (Hebrews 9:1-10). That means, until Christ came in the flesh and a new Spirit, the Spirit of love and freedom. Therefore, now in Christ everything which might have burdened the conscience outwardly is set aside. That handwriting which had accused us has been erased. The old has passed away; by His Flesh He has taken away the enmity, that is, the Law which was presented in the Commandments, so that of two [natures] He might create for Himself one New Man. In sum, in Christ everything has become unchangeable, eternal, and new (2 Corinthians 2:14). He is now the only Ruler of our hearts, the only Duke of our faith, the only Head of His Church, and the only Lord and King of our conscience. In Him neither circumcision nor foreskin is of any value (neither this nor that); only the New Creation and the faith which is made powerful by love (Galatians 5:5; 6:15) are of any account with Him.

For this reason Paul admonishes us (Galatians 5:1-5): Let us stand fast in the freedom (of conscience, spirit, and faith) with which Christ has freed us, and not let ourselves become again entangled in the yoke of bondage; since we take hold of righteousness not by means of external things, by letters or by the flesh, but in the spirit through faith, as we all hope. As Paul says in Colossians 2:20-23: If you have now died in Christ to the elements of this world, why do you now let yourselves become ensnared in legalism, as if you still lived in the world? They who say, Thou shalt not handle this; Thou shalt not taste that; Thou shalt not touch something else which things are all consumed under your hands—they are teaching human law and doctrine which has only the appearance of wisdom, etc.

Paul does not intend this simply of the Jewish regulations, in which men made consciences, but he means it to be understood of all other doctrines and burdens to the conscience as well, as the words, 'died with Christ' and 'no longer alive to the world' sufficiently show. He has truly warned us before with regard to philosophy (which according to the testimony of all the Church Fathers has been the deception and foundation of all the heretics). Hence simple men are not to let themselves to be robbed by it of Christ, but are to hold fast to their Head in this as in all other things; in Him they will find all things which His Body (which is the Christian Church) will need for its growth and sustenance from His own Hand. This will also help them to hold together and to grow (that is, in conscience, spirit, faith, love, and life), for the greatness of God (Colossians 2:8, 19).

Because, then, as you have heard, Christians are given grace, privileged, and as newly born men freed by Christ by His sufferings, must not let themselves with their consciences be bound to any external thing in any way at all as necessary to salvation, they must let their hearts be raised up above all external things. They have been killed to the Law and to all ceremonies by the Body of Christ, so that they now belong to another, that is to Him who has been raised up from death, so that they might bring forth fruit to God (Romans 7:4). They whom the Son frees are free indeed (John 8:36), free that is in conscience and faith, from death and sin. They who have Christ, moreover, who is Lord over the Sabbath and of everything else, have a most important part of the Kingdom of God. Their conscience is above nature and heavenly; how then could it be subject to earthly ceremonies or physical elements? Why after their Knowledge of God, would they wish to return to weak and poor elements, to serve them again? (Galatians 4:9)

But with this, the external worship of God, the Sacraments, and the proclamation of the Word of God established by Christ and the Holy Spirit are not to be despised, belittled, or cast aside. Rather, as everything is ordained in the free way of the grace of God, the conscience also should always be directed towards Christ the Lord. In this way the faithful person will also come to experience the inward mastery of His Kingdom in an external way, even as the worship service represents and brings to mind the internal presence of grace in an outward way, the working of the Holy Spirit, and the presentation in the heart of the benefits of Christ. In this way the whole Christian man, spirit and flesh, body and soul, can praise God and glorify Him for Christ's sake. For everything connected with the worship of God in the New Testament which is external has not necessarily been instituted by Christ Himself; it is also not ordained therefore that it should bind the conscience, or can even reach in to it, or can grant salvation. Rather, external things like these point from the letters higher in faith to the present Christ, to the mystery of His Kingdom, and to the divine power which is presented to itself only in Christ and in His words; in Him alone is all its foundation, life, salvation, and blessedness. He desires to remain with His own people to the end of the world (Matthew 28:20).

On this account the rulers of this World are further obligated to obedience because of this above-mentioned Christian freedom of conscience, not simply not to take it away, but to permit it to become even more active and more firmly established, as Paul says: A Christian should be subservient, not simply on account of punishment but also for the sake of his conscience, not simply because of worldly authorities, but because of God who ordains all worldly authority (Romans 13:1-2,5). Because he knows that God has entrusted the authorities with much responsibility so that men should show them honor and render them obedience and subservience as His truly ordained people, and that they [authorities] are to rule with justice. In sum, a Christian conscience gives to everything its value and knows, to the praise of God, how to discriminate among them.

Summation

This is written about the beginning and growth of faith, of Christian practice and life, as also concerning the freedom and development of the conscience for all pious and concerned persons, to be of service to them. These matters herin considered are inseparable and must in the proper knowledge of God proceed together. Paul calls this the having of the mystery of faith in a pure (good) conscience. So soon as the good conscience is cut off from these things, faith and all blessedness must fall away. and it must suffer terrible shipwreck and deprivation (1 Timothy 1:19).

Because in Christ a good conscience is such a great treasure, because it comes to our aid in all our troubles, sufferings, and temptations, and stands steadfastly with a man if he will pray to God with all seriousness and look to Christ so that in Him he might receive such a good, pure, and clean conscience, this cannot take place unless we have previously recognized our evil conscience. Thus, the beginning of the good conscience is the revelation of the evil knowledge and conscience which adheres in the old man, so that a man after taking cognizance of himself, of God, of Christ, and of using created things, will desire to have a good knowledge of them, so that he might be inwardly driven to examine the Word and will of God and to live according to them. that he might earnestly desire to become a Christian. Then a new knowledge and conscience are founded in his heart by the influx of the grace of God. Then he must look sharply to guard himself from the robbers (the evil spirits), be firmly established in grace, and as soon as it is threatened or attacked, he must build it up again in Christ and establish it in His Blood through faith, cleanse it and anoint it therewith. In this way may we live and proceed in a Christian manner. Amen.

Points Regarding Which a Christian Should Make his Meditation

1. On Christ and on the true experience of Him according to the Spirit, for therin is eternal life; from that all blessedness flows forth, and in this mystery are hidden all the treasures of divine wisdom and knowledge. [John 17:3; Colossians 2:3; 2 Corinthians 5:16]

2. On the Kingdom of God and what it is, of what it consists, when it was established and how it may be recognized. [Luke 17:20-21; Romans 14:17]

3. On the promises of eternal life, to whom they are applicable, how they may be received and accepted. [Galatians 3:5-29]

4. On the Childship of God, who are called children of God in the Scriptures, and how we might attain to being Children of God. [John 1:12-13; Romans 9:7-8; Galatians 3:26; 1 Peter 1:14-23]

5. On the New Christian Man, whence he has his origin, what his life, existence, and growth are like, and how he may be chiefly recognized. [Ephesians 4:23-32; Colossians 3:1-17]

6. On divine righteousness, what it is, how it differs from human pharisaical righteousness, and what it can do. [Matthew 6:33; 5:20-48; Philippians 3:9-10]

7. On the Spirit of Christ, what its Nature, Manner, and Characteristics are, also what is gifts are, how it may properly be tested and how we may attain to it. Also how it differs from the spirit of the Mosaical Law. [Matthew 11; Romans 8:14-17; 2 Timothy 7:7]

8. On a good Christian conscience, what it is, whence it comes, what sort of peace, joy, and assurance it brings with it, and how it differs from a good, pious, pharisaical conscience. [1 Timothy 1:5,19; 2 Corinthians 1:12]

Printed at Augsburg by Philipp Ulhart. 1533.

[translated from CS 4, Doc. 149, 859-82]

Schwenkfelders
and Sabbatarian Anabaptists:
A Tragedy of the Early Reformation

Daniel Liechty

No period of church history has been devoid of 'heresy' and dissent. Nevertheless, it was the genius of the Roman Church in the middle ages that it was able to incorporate, via the various religious orders, ideas and concerns which on the surface appear to be mutually exclusive.[1] By the time of the Reformation, however, with the rise of national sentiments on the continent and elsewhere in Europe, the church had largely lost this ability. The Reformation literally tore the church apart. The spirit of exclusiveness was deeply rooted in the Protestant experience and bitter disputes concerning 'the one true faith' have characterized much of that history until quite recently, when secularism has placed all faith traditions equally on the defensive.

The present ecumenical pluralism within the church makes it very difficult for us to understand what was at stake in these early disputes. In terms of his toleration and ecumenism, Caspar Schwenckfeld stands in marked contrast to most of his contemporaries. This makes the episode of the falling out between Schwenckfeld and Pilgram Marpeck only all the more surprising and unintelligible.[2] Schwenckfeld was one of the few in his day who actually seems to have given the writings of his opponents a fair and careful reading. He took it as a point of honor not to distort the views of others simply to make debating points. Yet despite Marpeck's protestations, Schwenckfeld persisted in attributing views to him which he did not teach.

Scholars have generally turned to Strassburg in their investigations of Schwenckfeld's view of Anabaptism. It is the thesis of this essay, however, that by the time Schwenckfeld arrived in Strassburg, he already had behind him an encounter with Anabaptists which formed in his mind a decidedly negative view of the movement, a view which stayed with him throughout his life. In order to gain a better perspective on Schwenckfeld's view of Anabaptism, and therefore the better to understand his sharp exchange with Pilgram Marpeck, we must take a closer look at a lesser studied debate which took place in Silesia some fifteen years earlier, in 1528.[3] This was, in all probability, Schwenckfeld's first encounter with Anabaptists.

1

In the latter half of the 1520s, Anabaptists began to appear in Silesia, where the 'Lutheran' Caspar Schwenckfeld had been gathering a distinguished following for the Reformation cause since the earliest part of that decade.[4] The first Anabaptists seem to have been from the indigenous population, but the atmosphere of toleration which Schwenckfeld carefully nurtured soon attracted many refugees from other lands.[5] The largest, or certainly the most vocal, of these Anabaptists was the cluster of congregations set up around the leadership of Oswald Glaidt in Liegnitz.

Glaidt was originally a monk or priest, but was converted to the Reformation cause by 1523 at the latest. He appears in Nicolsburg that year as a leader of the Lutheran faction there.[6] In the next several years, Glaidt became increasingly radicalized. He was won for Anabaptism by Balthasar Hubmaier soon after his arrival in Nicolsburg. He became one of Hubmaier's closest associates, only to reject Hubmaier and follow after the chiliastic Hans Hut. After the Nicolsburg debate[7] he left with Hut for Vienna. Hut made his last missionary journey up the Danube toward South Germany, and although Glaidt did not travel with him, he followed the same route a few weeks later.

Glaidt appears soon after this missionary trip in the Liegnitz area of Silesia as leader of the Anabaptist group there. This group was most likely a mixture of indigenous and refugee people. By this time, late 1527 or early 1528, Glaidt was teaching not only a Hutian-influenced version of Anabaptism, but also Sabbatarianism, the practice of Saturday worship.[8] Thus, the stage was set for Schwenckfeld's first encounter with Anabaptists.

Of the personal exchanges and written debate which followed, only the documents from the Schwenckfeld side are extant.[9] We can thank the spirit of exactness and fairness on the part of Schwenckfeld and his co-worker Valentine Crautwald, however, for the fact that there is enough direct quotation and argument with their opponents that we can reconstruct a comprehensive account of the Sabbatarian side of the issue.[10]

It is not necessary here to give a detailed account of Schwenkfeldian theology. It is sufficient to note that Schwenckfeld and Crautwald had developed a theology of the true 'evangelical' faith, based on inner personal experience. This inner experience of Christ made superfluous the ceremonies and external trappings of Roman Catholicism. Schwenckfeld had quite rightly seen a similar emphasis in the early writings of Martin Luther, and had eagerly joined the ranks of the Reformantion as a 'Lutheran.' He and Crautwald could not have been other than perplexed, disappointed and perhaps angered by Luther's violent rejection of their interpretation of the Lord's Supper, an interpretation which unquestionably was more in line with consistent 'spiritual' presuppositions than what was being taught at the time in Wittenberg.[11]

As noted above, Oswald Glaidt arrived in Liegnitz in late 1527 or early 1528, and along with his co-worker from Upper Austria, Andreas Fischer,[12] began to teach not only adult baptism (an issue on which they may well have found common ground with the Schwenkfelders), but also a new stress on the Jewish law, the Decalogue, and the keeping of Saturday as the proper day of worship.

The origin of this teaching among the Glaidt/Fischer group is not entirely clear. It cannot have come from Hubmaier's influence on Glaidt. Hubmaier, even if he rejected his earlier position of rabid anti-Judaism,[13] certainly taught until the end of his days that Sunday was the Christian 'Sabbath.'[14] We also have no evidence that Hans Hut taught anything directly concerning a Saturday Sabbath. But we do know that Hut's teachings were a paradoxical mixture of extremes, and that the 'legacy' Hut left behind was that of many disciples, each laying hold to one or more of the diverse elements in Hut's theology.[15] One of the options Hut left behind was that of an extreme biblical literalism. It is most probable that Glaidt, picking up on that aspect of Hut's teaching, developed the Sabbatarian ideology before or just after his arrival in Liegnitz.

The other possibility, of course, is that Glaidt learned the
teaching from Andreas Fischer. In spite of the fact that Crautwald clearly considers Glaidt to be the leader of the two, it must
be said that the pattern of Glaidt's life had been to follow after strong and charismatic figures. Fischer also exhibits a more
enduring commitment to the Sabbatarian ideology. Whereas
Glaidt left the doctrine behind in the 1530s, Fischer went on
to propagate the teaching among the Moravian Anabaptists
through to his death in circa 1540.[16] But if the Sabbatarian
ideology originated with Fischer, it can only be argued from
silence. We know practically nothing of Fischer's intellectual
development,[17] and he first arrives on the historical scene as
one of the participants in the discussion with the Schwenckfeld
circle in Liegnitz.

There is, however, a bit more evidence that points back
to Glaidt. Writing on Hans Hut, Packull reports: 'Curiously,
Hut's concordance of the seven judgments makes reference under the very first heading of the "covenant of God" to those
who will "hold the Lord's Sabbath." '[18] Exactly what Hut had
in mind here is obscure, but it is all a part of his confused
apocalyptic vision. From what we know through Schwenckfeld
of Glaidt's defense of the Sabbath practice,[19] Glaidt employs
not less than seven clearly chiliastic arguments.

1. Holding to the belief in the thousand year kingdom,
Glaidt does not see the law of the Messiah fully in effect.
He is looking for a second coming where the law of the
Messiah will go out from Jerusalem.

2. The Sabbath will be spiritual only when human beings are spiritual, that is, after the resurrection of the
dead in Christ's coming kingdom.

3. Because the eternal rest is postponed, we must continue to keep the Sabbath.

4. Just as the Sabbath was a sign to the Jews of old
of the coming rest in the Kingdom of God, so it is to
Christians also, because they still await that kingdom.

5. Paul speaks of this future rest (Heb. 4:3) as having
come to us already only in hope.

6. After death and resurrection, the Sabbath will no
longer be a sign. But until then it remains a sign.

7. The Sabbath is not a sign of the first coming of Christ
but of his second coming.

Andreas Fischer, on the other hand, does not use overtly eschatological arguments to make his case for Saturday Sabbath.[20] Significantly, Glaidt's opening shot in this discussion, his book *Vom Sabbath*, was written in early 1528. Fischer's *Scepastes Decalogi* was written in late 1528. We do not have to look far to understand why the eschatological arguments were deleted in the book by Andreas Fischer, who then defended the Sabbath ideology on the basis of a non-chiliastic, covenantal theology. It obviously has directly to do with the failure of Hans Hut's predictions on the second coming, scheduled for Pentecost 1528, to materialize.

What we see emerging therefore is a pattern that has been repeated over and over in the history of religions. A practice which originally has to do directly with eschatological fervor is retained and justified on a non-eschatological basis after the original hopes of an immediate end to history have been disappointed.[21]

2

It seems that the early discussions between Glaidt and Schwenckfeld were friendly enough.[22] Apparently there was an agreement to exchange booklets on the subject.[23] Oswald opened with his lost *Vom Sabbath*, to which Crautwald replied with a booklet also lost. Some months later, Fischer replied to this with his *Scepastes Decalogi*. To this, Crautwald penned his *Bericht vnd anzaigen*.[24] At some point, however, the friendly discussion had soured[25] and by the time Fischer entered the debate, his book was full of invectives and personal attacks against Crautwald. His most serious charge against Crautwald was that he had many well-to-do friends and sat in idle riches because of his work as a theologian.[26] Crautwald responded to these invectives in kind, calling Fischer such names as 'donkey-preacher' and 'Jew-lover.'[27] By the end of this exchange, we can assume that neither Schwenkfelders nor the Anabaptists could see in each other Christian brothers, much less potential allies.

The Sabbatarian Anabaptist encounter with the Schwenckfeld circle could not have come at a more inopportune time. Schwenckfeld had only recently received a decided rejection from Martin Luther concerning his interpretation of the Lord's

Supper. To the Schwenckfeld circle, it looked as if the 'external trappings' of religion were creeping back into the Reformation movement from the top on down, obscuring the true 'evangelical' faith based on the inward experience of Christ. Furthermore, there was trouble in the newly-established University of Liegnitz over the sacrament issue, and the duke, Friedrich II, was beginning to shift away from Schwenckfeld and towards the Lutherans. By 1528, the fight against externals must surely have seemed to the Schwenkfelders to be a fight for the survival of the gospel itself!

At that moment, Glaidt and Fischer arrived on the scene with their Sabbath teaching. Like the Schwenkfelders, these men were reformers and turned to the Bible for an answer to the question of where the church went wrong. But there they found not only a teaching about the need for inner conversion. They probably assumed this already. They were instead looking for answers to concrete questions of ethics and practice. They agreed with the Schwenkfelders that the priestly law (the laws of ceremony) was superceded by Christ, and that the New Testament commandment of love fulfills the demands of the law. Yet they had had repeated experience (not the least among the Moravian Anabaptists) that to teach that the law is no longer in effect can be a recipe for trouble. They therefore insisted that the moral law, the ethical law, is still in effect: it is 'fulfilled' by Christ, but certainly not abolished. Yet whatever else the moral law may include, the bottom line has to be the Decalogue. Here they found the teaching to hold the seventh day, Saturday, as holy. And if you break one Commandment, you break them all (Mt. 5:19; James 2:10). They therefore located the 'fall' of the church, that is, when the church ceased to follow the moral law, at that point when the church forsook Sabbath/Saturday worship.[28] Any program of renewal would have to, in their view, include the reinstitution of the Sabbath.

In hindsight, this is all very easy to understand. But given the deteriorating position of Schwenckfeld and Crautwald at the time (Schwenckfeld went into voluntary/forced exile within a matter of months), how could it have looked otherwise to them than that the floodgates of externals had been opened wide[29] and that the very foundations of evangelical Christianity were being directly threatened? That no agreement or understanding could be reached, and that the attacks became nasty and personal, is not only not surprising, but inevitable.

This small episode in the early Reformation period is truly a tragedy in the dramatic sense of the word. Not so only because sincere men on both sides talked past each other. Given their starting points, this was predictable. It is much more a dramatic tragedy because this first encounter with Anabaptists, happening as it did just before his exile, colored Schwenckfeld's view of Anabaptists for the coming decades and made understanding and unity between Caspar Schwenckfeld and Pilgram Marpeck, which by all measures could have been a very productive combination indeed, impossible.

Notes

1 See K. Davis, *Anabaptism and Asceticism* (Scottdale, 1974), 36-64.

2 The best secondary sources are J. Loserth, 'Marbeck und Schwenckfeld' in *Gedenkschrift zum 400 jährigen Jubiläum der Mennoniten oder Taufgesinnten* (Ludwigshafen, 1925), 144-47; T. Bergsten, 'Pilgram Marbeck und seine Auseinandersetzung mit Caspar Schwenckfeld' in *Kyrkohistorisk Arsskrift* (1957/1958), 39-135.

3 Horst Weigelt (see his *Spiritualistische Tradition im Protestantismus* [Berlin, 1973], 115) dates this exchange as having taken place in 1530. This is because Weigelt followed too closely the theories of Petr Ratkos and Waclaw Urban concerning the Slovakian origins of Andreas Fischer, and therefore assumed that the arrival of Fischer in Silesia did not take place until after his first missionary effort in Slovakia in 1529. As I have shown elsewhere, however, these theories are wrong. See my article 'Andreas Fischer: A Case of Mistaken Identity' in *Archiv für Reformationsgeschichte* 76 (1985).

4 See G. Koffmane, 'Die Wiedertaufer in Schlesien' in *Correspondenzblatt des Vereins für Geschichte der evangelischen Kirche Schlesiens* 3 (1887), 37-55.

5 See H. Schubert, *Bilder aus der Geschichte der Stadt Schweidnitz* (Schweidnitz, 1911), 241-43.

6 J. Loserth, 'Bilder aus der Reformationszeit in Mahren, 2. Teil, Oswalt Glayt' in *Zeitschrift des deutschen Vereins für die Geschichte Mahrens und Schlesiens* 1 (1897), 65-73.

7 See R. Friedmann, 'Die Nikolsburg Artikel von 1527' in *Jahrbuch der Gesellschaft für die Geschichte des Protestantismus in Oesterreich* 82 (1966), 15-29.

8 *Mennonite Encyclopedia* 4, 396.

9 Schwenckfeld's reply to Oswald Glaidt's *Vom Sabbath* is published in CS 4:445-518, and is titled *Wider den Alten vnnd Newen Ebionitischen Jrthumb*. Crautwald's booklet against Andreas Fischer's *Scepastes Decalogi* is as yet unpublished. It is titled *Bericht vnd anzaigen wie gar one kunst vnd guother verstandt, Andreas Fischer, Vomm Sabbat*

geschriben. auch das er Jn wider alles rechten sucht, noch als nothig fur Christenthumb zuohalten mogen schutzen. The original of this booklet is in the Staatsbibliothek Preussischer Kulturbesitz in Berlin, MS. Germ. 527. A complete transcription of the document by the present writer can be found in both the Mennonite Historical Library in Goshen and in the Schwenkfelder Library in Pennsburg.

[10] I have treated the Sabbatarian side of the debate extensively in my article 'The Origins of Sabbatarianism Among the East-Central European Anabaptists in the Sixteenth Century,' a paper delivered at the July 1984 Sixteenth Century Colloquium held in Strassburg.

[11] Schultz, 73ff.

[12] On Andreas Fischer see D. Liechty, *Andreas Fischer: Leader of the Sabbatarian Anabaptists in Silesia, Slovakia and Moravia* (diss. University of Vienna, 1982). The relationship between Fischer and Glaidt is not entirely clear, but Crautwald definitely thinks of Glaidt as the leader, calling Fischer one 'aus seiner (Glaidt's) gesellschaft' (*Bericht*, 2, line 4).

[13] See H. Vedder, *Balthasar Hubmaier* (New York, 1905), 38-44. Also H. A. Oberman, *Wurzeln des Antisemitismus* (Berlin, 1981), 99-104.

[14] See Hubmaier's final statement on the subject in *Balthasar Hubmaier: Schriften* (Gütersloh, 1962), 482f.

[15] See W. Packull, *Mysticism and the Early South German-Austrian Anabaptist Movement* (Scottdale, 1976).

[16] Glaidt soon gave up his Sabbatarianism and joined the Hutterites. For my reconstruction of Fischer's activities from 1532 until his death, see my article 'Andreas Fischer: A Brief Biographical Sketch' in *Mennonite Quarterly Review* 58 (1984), 125-132.

[17] All we know is that Fischer attended the University of Vienna between 1498 and 1505, and that he earned the Magister Artium title. See my article above.

[18] Packull, 78.

[19] For what follows, consult Schwenckfeld's *Wider den Alten*, 500-04.

[20] Horst Weigelt (117ff.) noticed that the chiliastic eschatological arguments are missing in Fischer's defense, but imputed them to Fischer anyway. I see no justification in the sources for this whatsoever.

[21] There is no direct continuity between Fischer and Glaidt and the present-day Seventh Day Baptists or Seventh Day Adventists. Nevertheless, a study of the history of these later Sabbatarian groups would reveal the same pattern. Compare, for example, the writings of Ellen G. White with those of the present-day Seventh Day Adventists' most able spokesman, Samuele Bacchiocchi.

[22] Schwenckfeld writes: '/Oswald/ mit welchem ich etwan zur Liegnitz jnn Schlesien fruntlich gesprech gehalten...' (454, lines 24f.)

[23] *Bericht*, 1f.

[24] Schwenckfeld's own part in the written debate actually was written in 1532 in Strassburg. During his final months in Silesia he was too busy

with other more pressing matters to write books. But there is no doubt that he personally turned this task over to Crautwald, that he kept abreast of the exchange, and that he counselled Crautwald concerning the matter.

25 The Sabbatarian Anabaptist community, while under the leadership of Glaidt, was very enthusiastic and charismatic. There are dark hints in Crautwald's *Bericht* to the group's excesses and public displays which had brought shame on the whole Reformation cause in Liegnitz.

26 *Bericht*, 36, lines 29ff. This seems to be characteristic of Fischer. Elsewhere, he calls another opponent a 'belly-servant' (*pauchknecht*)! See *Egyhaztortenelmi emlekek* II, 377.

27 *Bericht* 10, line 30; 28, line 34.

28 This is a very interesting point since it is one example of Anabaptists going back even before Constantine to locate the 'fall' of the church. It would be wrong to modernize Fischer's thinking too much in terms of the present-day Jewish/Christian dialogue. But it must be said that at least Fischer had a very open mind concerning Judaism. He says: 'We believe with the Jews that there is one God, and that salvation has through the Jews.... Why should we not then keep the Sabbath with them?' (*Bericht*, 20, lines 24ff.) Considering the time, this is quite remarkable, and shows that there is in fact a history of concern for closer relations between Jews and Christians. At the very least, it demonstrates that not all of the attitude towards Jews within Protestantism must be characterized by the venomous invectives of Dr. Luther!

29 Interestingly enough, it was Fischer who demanded that the icons, which he called *gotzen*, be removed from the church in Liegnitz. Crautwald's attitude is more relaxed—we didn't put them there and we will not put any more there, but we are not so concerned that they be removed. He places Fischer's demand for their removal in the context of 'works righteousness.' (*Bericht*, 37, lines 9ff.)

Schwenckfeld and the Schwenkfelders of South Germany

R. Emmet McLaughlin

The Schwenkfelder movement was composed of two parts, one in Schwenckfeld's homeland, Silesia, and one in South Germany where he lived from his exile in 1529 until his death. Horst Weigelt has written a masterful study of the Silesian Schwenkfelders.[1] In this article I will review what we know about the Schwenkfelders in South Germany.

Unlike the Silesian branch of the sect, which was a mass movement comprising whole communities from peasants to ruling princes, the Schwenkfelders in the South were normally small groups either attached to individual Schwenkfelder ministers or composed of members of several interrelated families. In my survey I will follow Schwenckfeld as he travelled about during 1533-1536 laying the groundwork for his network of friends, patrons, and disciples in South Germany.

He had become known to many of these people already through his publications and letters, through mutual friends, and personal visits. Such was the case with Johann Bader, pastor of Landau.[2] Schwenckfeld had corresponded with Bader in 1530-1531 on baptism and eventually weaned Bader away from his Zwinglian understanding of the sacrament.[3] An attempt by Bucer in early 1533 to use Bader to scout Schwenckfeld's real opinions and intentions preparatory to the Strassburg Synod had backfired. Bader accompanied Schwenckfeld to the March Frankfurt *Messe* and on the return trip Schwenckfeld stopped over in Landau for a short visit.[4] If prior to the trip Bader was anxious to be an honest broker between Bucer and Schwenckfeld, afterwards he was concerned to prevent Bucer from making the mistake of 'misunderstanding' Schwenckfeld.[5] Bader's neighbor Nicolaus Thomae of Bergzabern had also been impressed by Schwenckfeld's *Catechism* in 1531 despite the warnings of Bucer's amanuensis Konrad Hubert.[6] Strassburg's hostility toward Schwenckfeld had the effect in Bergzabern, Landau, and elsewhere of loosening the bonds of trust and cooperation with Strassburg. Schwenckfeld's arguments against infant baptism impressed Bader, and his more general criticism of the equation of the Old and New Testaments found a welcome reception.[7] By 1534 he had been convinced of the accuracy of Schwenckfeld's views on the church and his complaints against the various reformed churches. In that year he translated Crautwald's Latin treatise *Of the Church, its Ministers, Keys and Sacraments* into German for publication.[8] It was a full exposition of the Schwenkfeldian ecclesiology.

The year 1538 marked a further step in his adherence to Schwenckfeld's views. Following a lengthy illness he began openly to argue Schwenckfeld's positions, much to Bucer's dismay.[9] In 1541 Bader instituted a *Stillstand* on the eucharist and on baptism of the 'impious' which lasted till his death in 1545.[10] In 1542 he defended Schwenckfeld's christology, with which Thomae of Bergzabern also sympathized.[11] Another Schwenckfeld visit in 1543 (there may have been others in the meantime) was followed by the publication in 1544 of a catechism for Landau that was redolent with Schwenckfeld's views.[12] In May 1544 Bucer held a colloquy with Bader, but to no avail.[13]

The attractions of Schwenckfeld's theology for Bader were manifold. From as early as 1526 Bader was deeply concerned with general moral improvement and the worthy reception of the eucharist. In an apology published that year he based his interpretation of the eucharist on 1 Corinthians 11:25 and John 6:48-60, Schwenckfeld's proof texts.[14] Bader never ceased to cling to the early Strassburg spiritualistic consensus.[15] His disappointment with the lax standards and lack of concrete improvement in the Protestant world in general and his congregation in particular convinced him that Schwenckfeld was right, that the new Christian church had not yet arrived, and that God's intervention, not human church building, was the answer.[16]

Bader took care to insure the continuation of his course after his death. He arranged for the hiring of Johann Liebmann as preacher in 1545 with the understanding that Liebmann would eventually succeed as pastor.[17] Liebmann had been preacher in Pfuhl just outside Ulm until forced to leave

because of his Schwenkfeldian views and opposition to the
Wittenberg Concord.[18] His succession to Bader at the latter's
death in September 1545 came at the price of reinstituting the
eucharist, a demand which the Strassburg *Rat* had impressed
upon Landau.[19] At Liebmann's death in 1553 Leonhart Brun-
ner, Schwenckfeld's antagonist from Worms, became pastor,[20]
and pressure was brought to bear on the Schwenkfelder community for the first time.[21] How effective these measures were
is difficult to determine, but there were Schwenkfelders in the
area well into the seventeenth century.[22]

Schwenckfeld may have visited Landau on his way to nearby
Speyer in September 1533. It was in Speyer that he wrote his
third letter to Jud (Sept. 10).[23] Schwenckfeld developed a circle of friends among the judges and lawyers of the imperial
court, in particular Dr. Hieronymus zum Lamb, the scion of
a patrician family important in Frankfurt a. M. and elsewhere
along the Rhine.[24] The family zum Lamb remained prominent
in legal circles for at least three generations. Between Bader in
Landau and the lawyers in Speyer there was the basis for a continuing Schwenkfelder group. How extensive that group was is
impossible to determine. The high point of the movement's influence was achieved under Bishop Marquand of Speyer (1560-
1581), who was himself a Schwenkfelder.[25] He may have become interested already as a young cathedral canon, but by
1572 he was one of the three important Schwenkfelder leaders
in South Germany. Most of the members of his court (drawn
from the lower nobility as was he), his personal physician, and
his mistress were all Schwenkfelders. The bishop maintained
close ties with the Schwenkfelder community in Ulm, and may
have opened doors for Schwenckfeld's teachings at the courts
of the emperor, the bishop of Strassburg, and the archbishop of
Cologne.[26] More importantly, Marquand established a printing
press in the imperial city of Wimpfen for Schwenkfelder use.
The unerring ability of Schwenckfeld and his followers to get
access to the presses remains one of the distinctive features of
the movement.

The next stop on Schwenckfeld's journey was the imperial
city of Esslingen. After initially winning over Jakob Otter,
the leading pastor of the city, and being drawn into a nasty
squabble among the clergy, Schwenckfeld eventually lost the
friendship of Otter and the other clerics.[27] Nonetheless he was

often in the city and took refuge there both in the early 1540s and again after the Smalcaldic War. His friend and patron there was the Burgermeister, Hans Sachs.

From Esslingen Schwenckfeld went to nearby Koengen, the Schloss and village of Hans Friedrich Thumb von Neuburg,[28] and Stetten in Remstal, the home of Hans Konrad Thumb and his sister Ursula.[29] From there he travelled to Ulm[30] and then finally to Augsburg where he arrived late on Thursday October 2, 1533.[31] He took up residence with Bonifatius Wolfhart, one of Augsburg's pastors with whom Schwenckfeld had become acquainted in Strassburg. Wolfhart had invited Schwenckfeld to the city and Schwenckfeld hoped to continue his study of Hebrew with him there.[32] Wolfhart consistently preached a Schwenkfelder doctrine of the sacraments. There were other clerics who were also considered Schwenckfeld's partisans.[33] Hans Heinrich Held, like Wolfhart originally from Strassburg, was a very quiet figure, but firmly attached to Schwenckfeld.[34] Bartholomaeus Fontius, a Venetian refugee who had taught Old Testament in Strassburg before leaving for Augsburg, defended Schwenckfeld in response to Bucer's charges.[35] Jakob Dachser, a reconverted Anabaptist, also formed part of the Schwenkfelder clergy.[36] One of the earliest reformers of Augsburg, Michael Keller, often allied himself with the Schwenkfelders, though he himself would more accurately be described as a Zwinglian.[37]

Through Wolfhart, who enjoyed socializing with the upper classes in Augsburg, Schwenckfeld got to know many of the leading political figures.[38] Most important was Wolfgang Rehlinger, Burgermeister during Augsburg's Reformation year 1534. His son Jakob, who would arrange the printing of Sebastian Franck's *Güldene Arche* in 1538, was also counted a Schwenkfelder. So was Georg Regel, a patrician and former Anabaptist whose wife Anna had had an affair with Ludwig Haetzer. Regel and his wife had only been readmitted to the city in 1531. These names make their appearance in correspondence during Schwenckfeld's stay in Augsburg. From later records other names can be determined: Ulrich Welser of the banking family, Wilhelm Vetter, Jorg von Stetten (who married into the Fugger family), and Jorg's brother Laux (who married the widow of Ulrich Fugger). Most of these people were patricians, claimed patrician status, or achieved it in the 1538 'promotion' of families to the patriciate. From the very beginning

Schwenckfeld had many sympathizers among the ruling class
of the city. Of a lower rank were Hans Zoll, a bookkeeper,
and his wife Anna. The tailor Bernhard Unsinn, one Hans
Oesterreicher (a 'Papierer'), the rope maker Leonhard Seiler,
and the clockmaker and gunsmith Balthasar Marquand. More
characteristic of Schwenckfeld's circle of friends and supporters were the professional men: jurists Dr. Marcus Zimmer-
man and Dr. Georg Tradel, the physician Dr. Thalhauser, the
grammarian Valentine Ickelsamer and the poet and translator
of ancient literature Johann Spreng. Throughout the history
of the Schwenckfeld movement doctors, lawyers, and scholars
would play an important role.[39]

The Augsburg Schwenkfelder community began building
before Schwenckfeld's arrival, and even before Wolfhart's arrival in 1531.[40] It grew unopposed until 1553 when an effort was
finally made to control it.[41] What the resulting investigation
uncovered is revealing. Leonhard Hieber divulged the names of
fifty citizens to whom he had given, lent or sold Schwenckfeld's
works in the preceding three or four years. The names were
those of the leading families of Augsburg and the surrounding
countryside: Fugger, Welser, Rehlinger, Manlich, Hoerwart,
Walther, Hang, Gienger, and Königsberg. Claus-Peter Clasen
has tabulated sixteen families in the next lower level of society,
the upper bourgeosie, and thirteen families with less property
or none at all. When one considers that the upper classes are
usually more successful in avoiding the glare of public scrutiny
and certainly in escaping public prosecution, these figures show
that Schwenckfeld's ideas found broad interest and sympathy
among Augsburg's upper classes.

Schwenckfeld's teaching satisfied the political and social
elite in two ways. On the one hand, his theology of the sacraments and in particular his opposition to the Lutheran real
presence made him many friends in Zwinglian Augsburg. On
the other, his refusal to countenance the forcible imposition of a
rigorous state church order appealed to Augsburg's leadership
who found the Zwinglian ecclesiology threatening to the general peace and order of the city and their own pre-eminence in
it.[42] And there was always the Emperor to consider. He might
intervene directly if the Zwinglian party proceeded to over-
throw the remains of Catholic worship and to confiscate the
wealth of the Catholic church. Schwenckfeld was thus able to

offer sacramental purity without the Zwinglian political price-tag.

The Anabaptists in Augsburg also found Schwenckfeld's teachings attractive. With his low-key opposition to infant baptism and his spiritualizing attitude to the entire visible church, Anabaptists who were weary of suspicion and persecution felt that they could once again return to the church of Augsburg. Conventicles flourished alongside the more public services.[43] Indeed, a *de facto* religious toleration was practiced in Augsburg at least until 1553. Despite Augsburg's official political acceptance of the Wittenberg Concord (1536), the religion of the mass of the population was a Schwenkfeldian/Zwinglian mix.[44] The city was also a center of Schwenckfeld publication in the 1530s and early 1540s.[45] For a while Wolfhart was in control of censorship, and during the entire period members of the *Rat* helped finance publications by Schwenckfeld, Sebastian Franck, and others.[46]

During his Augsburg stay Schwenckfeld made a quick visit to Memmingen and Mindelheim.[47] Two of his close friends lived in the latter, Adam Reissner and Wilhelm von Zell.[48] At Memmingen he was welcomed by the two *Bürgermeister*, Eberhard Zangmeister and Hans Ehinger, and the city clerk Georg Mauer, and he was asked to preach in public and in private.[49] Schwenckfeld had made the journey in order to counter the charges emanating from Bucer in Strassburg and Blaurer in Constance. This he achieved and a period of coolness in the relations between Memmingen and those two reformers ensued. Schwenckfeld may also have visited Kempten, with the same results.[50]

Schwenckfeld's impact in the Allgäu was both significant and long-lasting. It is also almost impossible to quantify or even sketch with real accuracy. In Memmingen there was a strong Schwenkfelder party among the patricians and rich burgers. Perhaps daunted by their strength Gervasius Schuler, the leading pastor in Memmingen, seems not to have made any efforts against them until 1545.[51] In that year his attacks on Schwenckfeld from the pulpit persuaded the Memminger Schwenkfelders to protest and to appeal for help from Hans Wilhelm von Laubenberg zu Wagegg,[52] a local nobleman and staunch Schwenkfelder, and Jakob Held von Tieffenau,

Schwenckfeld's closest lieutenant. They presented a written defense to the *Rat* and requested the opportunity to publicly debate the issues. Schuler was reluctant and the *Rat* backed him, citing the dangerous times and the need for unity. Nonetheless, the *Rat* was very careful in its dealings with Laubenberg, who was an imperial counsellor and imperial governor (*Landvogt*) of the region around Ravensburg until August 1545.[53] Negotiations dragged on into the new year. Laubenberg even attempted to have a Schwenckfeld catechism accepted by the city. The *Rat* made no effort to proceed against the Schwenkfelders. Rather it was a purely defensive action in support of Schuler. Isolated incidents in 1568, 1571, 1573, and 1585 revealed the continuing presence of Schwenkfelders in the city and countryside. At no time did the *Rat* attempt to suppress them, a fact which embittered the preachers.[54]

Laubenberg was also busy elsewhere in the Allgäu. He had vindicated Schwenckfeld before the *Rat* of Lindau as well. A letter from the Lindau *Rat* expressing their thanks for Schwenckfeld's books contained the information that the Lindau preachers had examined and approved them. This letter formed part of Laubenberg's brief to the Memmingers.[55] Laubenberg's role in the Ravensburg Reformation was even more important.[56] As imperial *Landvogt* for the region Laubenberg was able to provide protection and encouragement for the Protestant faction within the city during 1542-1545.[57] This eventually led to his dismissal from office, but by then the Reformation was too far advanced to be halted. The city joined the Smalcaldic League in 1546 just in time to share in its defeat. The imposition of a Catholic *Hasenrat* prevented the installation of a Protestant church order, a fact which crippled the Lutherans' chances in the city. Despite a Lutheran victory in a local eucharistic controversy (1555-1557), the population remained Zwinglian. As in most of the cities of the region a practical tolerance produced a remarkable religious diversity under the appearance of state church conformity. Because there was no effort to root out the Schwenkfelders, they do not often appear in the documents. Those that do were from the more prominent families.[58]

Kempten remained a welcome place for Schwenckfeld. It was in the Benedictine Abbey in Kempten, as a guest of Abbot Wolfgang von Gruenstein that he wrote his *Great Confession*(1541).[59] People from Kempten sought him out whenever he visited Laubenberg in nearby Wagegg. Kaufbeuren also welcomed him for a visit in 1545 in an almost festive way. Isny had Schwenkfelders of prominent families.[60] With such strong support among the nobles of the countryside and the urban ruling classes Schwenckfeld and his followers were not merely tolerated. They were an accepted part of the religious landscape.

Schwenckfeld left Augsburg in early June 1534 and returned to Strassburg by way of Memmingen, Ulm, and Koengen.[61] The exact extent of Schwenckfeld's following in Strassburg is difficult to determine, but its leaders are known from Schwenckfeld's voluminous correspondence.[62] For the most part they were drawn from the various elites and privileged classes within the city. Among the clergy, the preacher Matthaeus Zell was sympathetic toward Schwenckfeld, and Katherina Zell, Matthaeus' wife, was one of the leading figures in the Schwenkfelder circle.[63] Wolfgang Schultheiss, one of those whom Bucer called 'Epicureans' for their opposition to his efforts to establish church discipline, can be considered a Schwenkfelder ally, at least for a time.[64] Paul Volz, preacher at St. Nicholai and the only Strassburg cleric to refuse to sign the Wittenberg Concord, was probably a full member of the group.[65] Alexander Berner, a bookbinder and city official in charge of Strassburg's exemplary poor relief system, was expelled from the city in 1535, but eventually gained readmission.[66] Another city official, the *Gerichtsschreiber* Johann Schweintzer, was a Schwenkfelder for a quarter of a century before the *Rat* took action against him.[67]

Another early follower and one with whom Schwenckfeld maintained warm and close ties was Margareta Engelmann, in whose house he lived for a time. It is not clear who she was, although the suggestion that she was a half-sister to the three daughters of the noble Peter Scher von Schwarzenberg has some plausibility.[68] Scher, an imperial counselor, was originally from Alsace but held an imperial fief near Basel.[69] By 1543 he was a 'Schirmburger' of Strassburg. His three daughters were important figures in the second generation of Schwenkfelders. Felicitas was married first to Franz Frosch, the Strassburg city advocate whose legal arguments were crucial for the introduction of the Reformation in Strassburg.[70] Her second husband, whom she probably married in 1543, was the famed Doctor Johann Winther von Andernach, former physician to Francis I.

They and their house became the center of Schwenkfelder activity in Strassburg.[71] The second daughter, Elisabeth, was married to Doctor Hans Christoph Hecklin, also of Strassburg.[72] When both sisters died within three months of each other in 1562, Katharina Zell performed the burial services because the preachers of Strassburg had refused.[73] Zell's own death anticipated proceedings against her. The third daughter of Peter Scher was Margareta, the wife of Klaus von Grafeneck, an official of the duke of Württemberg.[74] Klaus was *Obervogt* of Blaubeuren just outside Ulm from 1538 to 1543, during which time Margareta and Katharina Streicher, a leading figure among Ulm's Schwenkfelders, became fast friends. Klaus also served as *Obervogt* of Kirchheim unter Teck (1543-1547) another center of Schwenkfelder activity.[75]

Perhaps Schwenckfeld's closest friend and follower from his Strassburg years was Jakob Held von Tieffenau, the brother of Johann Heinrich Held the preacher in Augsburg. Of the nobility, though of uncertain provenance, Held was expelled from Strassburg in 1535 for refusing to baptize his child,[76] but he was eventually allowed to return. Held was often in Schwenckfeld's company throughout the decades that followed.[77] He served as Schwenckfeld's confidential messenger to opponents and helped to bind together Schwenckfeld's far-flung network of correspondents and followers. At Schwenckfeld's death in 1561 Held was chosen his literary executor.

In most of the rest of Schwenckfeld's correspondence with his followers in Strassburg later editors carefully deleted the names of the addressees, with two exceptions: Elizabeth Pfersfelder, the companion of the executed Claus Frey, and one Hans Christmann. They are representative of a larger group of people whom Schwenckfeld 'influenced.' Though nominally under Schwenckfeld's tutelage, Elizabeth was probably a member of the Hoffmannite community in Strassburg.[78] A letter to her shows that Schwenckfeld continued to fish in the troubled waters of post-Münster Anabaptism. The two letters to Christmann were consolatory and held little theology or polemic.[79] Throughout his career Schwenckfeld was to remain for many a simple and pious man of God and doctor of souls.

Schwenkfelders were also found at a later date across the Rhine in Baden. In the 1540s Schwenckfeld made the acquaintance of Markgraf Ernst von Baden whom he visited and supplied with books.[80] Decades later (1572) Markgrafin Anna of

Baden-Durlach and her children travelled with the Schwenkfelder physician Samuel Eisenmenger to Ulm in order to be
treated by Agatha Streicher.[81] The extent of Schwenkfelder
influence at the various courts of Baden is difficult to gauge. It
also spread among less exalted ranks. In the 1560s and 1570s
the government of Baden became increasingly concerned by the
appearance of Schwenkfelder preachers and communities.[82] In
1578 two hundred Schwenkfelders were uncovered and ordered
to attend sermons and receive the eucharist.[83] The evidence
from the period is sketchy and does not allow a fuller picture
of Baden's sectarian communities, but it is clear that radiating
from Strassburg, the entire course of the upper Rhine became
an important center of Schwenkfeldianism.

After leaving Strassburg Schwenckfeld returned to Württemberg. There he became involved in the maneuvering at the
newly re-established court of Duke Ulrich. Backed by a powerful party headed by the *Erbmarschall*, Hans Conrad Thumb
von Neuburg, Schwenckfeld was able to silence his opponents
in the duchy at the Tübingen Colloquy in May 1535.[84] Despite an earlier unfavorable report to Ulrich from his Council
in April 1535 and the resulting decrees against Anabaptists,
sectarians, and unauthorized preachers, very little action was
taken and none of it against Schwenckfeld or his followers.[85]
A visitation decree in 1536 mentioned the Schwenkfelders, but
thereafter they were not singled out.[86] Behind the scenes there
must have been competition and intrigue at court between the
various factions. The Thumbs' ascendency may be read in
the absence of the Schwenckfeld name in later decrees. Still,
the legal status of the Schwenkfelders was unclear. Were they
or were they not sectarians or Anabaptists? In this regard,
however, they were not much worse off than the Zwinglians
and other 'Sacramentarians' who were banned by the treaties
of Kaaden and Vienna. Even the Anabaptists were not suppressed with rigor or efficiency. Under the guise of a uniform
and unified state church, Württemberg harbored a profusion
of beliefs.[87] As far as the Schwenkfelders were concerned, there
is no record of any action taken against a Schwenkfelder before
1544.

The Thumb family formed the core of the Schwenkfelder
movement in Württemberg[88]: Hans Konrad and Hans Friedrich, Hans Friedrich's wife Margaret von Vellberg, their sister Ursula the widow of Hans von Hutten, the two daughters

of Hans Konrad, Margaret von Liebenstein and Sybilla, and
Sybilla's husband Hans von Sperberseck. Von Sperberseck was
one of Schwenckfeld's close companions and often served as
messenger and intermediary.[89] Von Sperberseck was also one
of the Duke's most loyal and trusted subjects during Ulrich's
exile. He would be another voice at court for Schwenckfeld.
But the most important Schwenckfeld supporter at court after
the Thumbs was Nicolaus Maior.[90] Maior had been a counsellor to Philip of Hesse since 1522. In 1535 he took service
with Ulrich and replaced Dr. Johann Knoder as chancellor of
the chancellary in Stuttgart. His main area of activity was the
administration of the church. His appointment was effected by
Hans Konrad Thumb.[91] Among other things this removed the
chancellary as a source of difficulties for Schwenckfeld. Other
figures who belonged to the court nobility were Margareta the
wife of Klaus von Grafeneck. Hans von Gültingen the brother
of Balthasar the *Landhofmeister* to both Ulrich and his successor Christoph. and Graf Ulrich XVI von Helfenstein.[92] The
Schwenkfelders were a compact and powerful group at court
and they were able to block any actions against Schwenckfeld
or his followers.

The fate of the Schwenkfelders was closely tied to that of
the Thumb faction. When the *Erbmarschall* fell from favor in
December 1544 the Schwenkfelders in Württemberg suffered
the consequences.[93] A collection of charges prepared by Georg
von Ow, another leading figure at Court, was preferred against
Thumb in February 1545.[94] It included highway robbery, col-
lusion with the Austrian administration during Ulrich's exile,
harboring of Anabaptist and Schwenkfelder sectarians, adultery. and helping Ulrich's enemies to acquire the best offices
in the land.[95] Though it has been suggested that the *Erbmarschall's* ties to Schwenckfeld were the cause of his downfall,
this is hardly likely.[96] Ulrich, unlike his son and heir Christoph,
would not break with his most powerful noble merely over religion. The ferocity of the proceedings against Hans Konrad
Thumb, his supporters at court, and the Schwenkfelders under his protection can only be explained by Ulrich's fear that
Thumb was once again' preparing to switch his allegiance to
the Bavarians and Austrians.[97] In any event, Thumb left the
court, many of his allies in the bureaucracy were cashiered or
arrested, and he himself was stripped of his marshall's title.

Though Ulrich may not have been moved by religious concerns, the court faction which had brought about Thumb's downfall and the dismissal of his allies was committed to Lutheran reform. Led by Georg von Ow, the Lutherans had probably brought about the abrupt departures of Ambrosius Blaurer (1538) and Nicolaus Maior (1543).[98] Beginning in June 1544 the Schwenkfelder communities which had grown up under Thumb's patronage also came under attack.[99] The *Erb-marshall* had installed Schwenkfelder ministers on his properties at Mühlhausen an der Enz and Stetten im Remstal. From Stetten the Schwenkfelders missionized in Stuttgart, Schorndorf, Kirchheim unter Teck, and Cannstatt with great success. The Schwenkfelder communities were in constant communication with the Schwenkfelders in Ulm and with Schwenckfeld himself.[100] When the authorities in Stuttgart finally intervened at Cannstatt they discovered that the sect had a broad popular base and that at least five members of the town Rat were involved.[101] These were dismissed from office and the leader of the Schwenkfelders in Cannstatt, a bookseller named Andreas Neff, was arrested and held in prison for two years.[102] The Schwenkfelder minister in Stetten, Burckhard Schilling, was dismissed. He took a post in Kaufbeuren but died soon thereafter.[103] Alexander Hoeldt, the pastor of Mühlhausen held on until 1548 when he appears as an eye doctor at Landau, another Schwenkfelder outpost.[104]

The Thumb family eventually recovered from its disgrace. Hans Konrad's son was awarded the *marschall's* office in 1553 and received Stetten as a fief after his father's death in 1555, but at the price of expelling all Jews and sectarians from his lands.[105] This deprived the Schwenkfelders of their main refuge in the duchy. Large scale gatherings or congregations were not uncovered by the church authorities in later years.[106] Only individual Schwenkfelders were discovered by the visitation. They tended to be found in or near Cannstatt and Schorndorf. Schwenckfeld himself seemed to have no direct contact with these individuals, but his books were still to be found, read, and feared in Württemberg to the end of the century. *Schwenck-feldisch* became a generic term for anyone who avoided the eucharist, did not listen to sermons, and did not think well of the state church and its clergy. What the status of the movement was among the upper classes is difficult to decipher because even at its most powerful the church's bureaucracy was never in a position to police the nobility. But in at least one case there is evidence that Schwenckfeld's message was passed on from one generation to another.[107] Württemberg was still trying to root out the Schwenkfelders in the middle of the seventeenth century.[108]

Despite the campaign against his followers and supporters in 1544-1545, Schwenckfeld himself was not banned by Ulrich. Under Ulrich he was officially tolerated.[109] Ulrich's successor Duke Christoph repaired this oversight. In 1554 and again in 1558 he forbade Schwenckfeld to enter the duchy and threatened him with arrest should he do so.[110] This was the first official governmental action against Schwenckfeld, and it only came after twenty-five year of activity in South Germany.

From Württemberg Schwenckfeld went to Ulm where he stayed with Bernhard Besserer, Ulm's *Bürgermeister*.[111] Into the seventeenth century Ulm and surrounding areas could boast one of the most numerous and public Schwenkfelder movements.[112] As in Augsburg and Württemberg, the key to Schwenckfeld's success was the toleration and sympathy of the patrician ruling circles. The Besserers, both Bernhard and Bernhard's son Georg, and Hans Walther Ehinger, Bernhard Besserer's son-in-law, formed the core of Schwenckfeld's patrician support.[113] Both the Besserers and the Ehingers were among the most influential patrician families in South Germany, with branches in all the major cities.[114] The Schwenkfelders and other dissidents enjoyed their patronage throughout the century.[115] Another noble, Peter Loew, was considered to be a leader among them.[116] To what extent we would be justified in labelling these patricians Schwenkfelders is a difficult matter to decide. They certainly agreed with Schwenckfeld on the eucharist, and in fact shared a generally spiritualistic interpretation of baptism as well.[117] They may have participated in conventicle meetings, but since the *Rat* was concerned to maintain at least the appearance of order and uniformity, they would have been very discreet. In any event, any indiscretion on the part of one of the *Herren* was unlikely to make its way into official-records. It is more likely that they limited themselves to family prayer and informal dinner discussion.[118] Certainly they could be called Schwenkfelders with as much justice as their colleagues in other cities were deemed Lutherans or Zwinglians or Calvinists. Perhaps one difference is important. These men agreed with Schwenckfeld because he agreed with them. That is, Schwenckfeld's message was a variation on the early Reformation consensus in Ulm's ruling class. Pastor Martin Frecht and his allies were the real dissidents.

Schwenckfeld also found followers among what might be termed civil servants.   Sebastian Aitinger, son of Konrad Aitinger the city's principal secretary, and himself secretary to the powerful Committee of Five, was a convinced Schwenkfelder.   A female relative, either his mother or his wife, was also a follower.[119] Hans Negelin, the head of poor relief for the city, was identified with the sect by the pastors.[120]

Though Frecht was able to maintain discipline for the most part among his fellow ministers, over the years Schwenckfeld found clerical allies and admirers in the city and surrounding countryside: Johann Liebmann, pastor of Pfuhl; Konrad Schaffner, pastor of Mähringen; Martin Karter, pastor of Böhringen and then Altheim before moving to the Palatinate; Georg Keller, preacher in Ulm and then pastor in Oepfingen; Johann Willing, preacher in Ulm; Salomo Mileus, preacher in the city hospital.[121] Liebmann and Keller led the opposition among the clergy to the Wittenberg Concord. Liebmann would eventually (1545) join Johann Bader in Landau.[122] Keller was forced out of Ulm in 1536 because he could not get along with Frecht, but he was given a post in Oepfingen by Ludwig von Freyberg, host and friend of Schwenckfeld.[123] While the *Rat* was quite willing to accept an open Schwenkfelder presence among the laity, it would not tolerate the divisions which Schwenkfelder ministers brought to the clerical corps.

The heart of the Schwenkfelder movement in Ulm was found among the middle levels of society. The Streicher household provided its headquarters. Helena Streicher was a widow with five daughters and one son.[124] Schwenckfeld developed a particularly close relationship with the family. He became a warm personal friend of Helena and something of a guardian or 'uncle' to the young Streichers.[125] One of the daughters, Katharina, was an outspoken advocate of Schwenckfeld's views and was the leader of the growing group of Schwenkfelders. The son, Hans Augustin, was also a convinced Schwenkfelder. He studied at Tübingen and became a physician. The youngest child, Agatha, also became a physician and ministered to the

Schwenkfelder bishop of Speyer and Emperor Maximilian.[126] Their aunt, the sister of Helena, Juliana Roggeburger was also an initiate.[127] In addition Schwenckfeld corresponded with a Barbara Kurenbach and a Barbara Roellin, both of unknown backgrounds.[128] This Schwenkfelder cell was well-known to both the preachers and the authorities.

In 1544 and 1545, probably in coordination with events in Württemberg, Frecht moved against the Schwenkfelders. At Frecht's insistence Johann Liebmann of Pfuhl was dismissed because he did not mention the eucharist in his sermons nor support Frecht's campaign against Schwenckfeld's christology.[129] Five of the laity were cited as Schwenkfelders: Hans Augustin Streicher, Katharina Streicher, Juliana Roggeburger, one Hans Kishaber, and one Frau Ott (Oetin). Frecht was disturbed that many others, including the patrician Peter Loew, were not summoned.[130] Katharina Streicher spoke for the rest.[131] She denied separating from the church. She did admit to avoiding the clergy, having come to the realization that they were a hindrance to salvation. They preached one thing today, another tomorrow. They wanted to make Christ a creature (a reference to Schwenckfeld's christological controversy with Frecht) and they wanted to bind salvation to external things and ceremonies. Therefore, she and her friends remained at home and placed their trust in Christ alone in accordance with Scripture. The *Rat* limited itself to ordering the Schwenkfelders to hold no conventicles and to remain silent. Such mild treatment did little to discourage them.

Thirty years later, impelled by the Lutheran Superintendent Ludwig Rabus, the *Rat* took more vigorous action.[132] Agatha Streicher's maid, Susanna Hornung, was accused of recruiting other working women, a David Pflaum and his wife, the daughter of Hans Pfitzenmayer, the daughter of the Apothecary Gaudenz Leschenbrand, the wife of Wolf Unfeld and her maid. Susanna, was expelled in 1578. Helena Arnoldt, whose maiden name was Kishaber (Kifhaber) was expelled along with her children. Agatha Streicher and others were warned not to hold meetings or indoctrinate others. The *Rat* thought it had cleared it all up.

But in 1580 they were once again investigating the sect.[133] One of the city gate-keepers was found to possess and distribute

Schwenkfelder books. Others involved were a barber, a mason, a goldsmith, and two men of undetermined occupation. In 1581 conventicles were being held in the house of Martin Kalhart. The goldsmith Bartholomew Holtz, shoemaker Samuel Reitzin, and Anna Steter, the younger Helena Streicher's maid, all took part. The maid was expelled. Ulm also complained to Michael Ludwig von Freyberg about his schoolmaster, Daniel Friedrich. Friedrich often conducted the conventicles in the city. With the death of the prestigious Agatha Streicher, the Schwenkfelders lost the protection which her name ensured. On December 7, 1582 the *Rat* ordered all unrepentant Schwenkfelders to leave. Eight obeyed: Helena Streicher and her two maids, Anna the wife of Daniel Pflaum, the three sisters Maria, Katherine, and Rosina Altenstaig along with their maid. Others recanted, but Martin Kalhart and Samuel Reitzin later left the city. Those who needed help were received by the von Freyberg family at Justingen. To demonstrate his displeasure Ferdinand von Freyberg gave up his *Bürgerrecht* in Ulm the following year. Though these actions were a blow to the Schwenkfelders in Ulm, it by no means marked the end of their presence there. Schwenkfelder books were always being discovered. Just outside the city, Justingen remained Schwenkfelder till 1630 and Oepfingen till 1660.[134]

As elsewhere, so in Ulm Schwenckfeld had access both to the printing press and to the distribution system. Hans Varnier, Ulm's leading printer, published many of Schwenckfeld's works in the 1530s and 1540s.[135] And in the 1560s the bookseller Sebald Trautner was repeatedly warned, to little effect.[136] The spate of publications, along with the presence of Schwenckfeld-influenced clergy, explains to a large extent the spread of Schwenckfeld's views outside the city into the towns and villages surrounding Ulm. At about the same time as the expulsions from the city five married couples, three men, and a woman were forced to leave Leipheim.[137] Already in 1560 Geislingen, the home of Hans Augustine Streicher, was considered a trouble spot by the authorities.[138] In Söflingen another Streicher daughter and her husband were warned in 1584.[139]

The von Freyberg family and its holdings at Justingen and Oepfingen outside Ulm remained the center of Schwenkfelder activity around the city well into the seventeenth century.[140] Schwenkfeldianism became a family tradition, perhaps even determining marriage alliances.[141] The von Freybergs were of the class of 'Free Lords' who were directly responsible to the emperor alone. They possessed most of the privileges of their more important neighbors like the dukes of Württemberg.[142] In theory they were independent. In practice they were vulnerable to political pressure or armed intervention. Following the lead of Württemberg Ludwig (Lux) von Freyberg introduced the Reformation in Justingen in 1534.[143] In the same year he concluded an alliance with Ulm which gave him the rights of citzenship in the city and its protection.[144] He also bought a house. It may have been there that he met Schwenckfeld. In any event, after Schwenckfeld's departure from Ulm, Justingen was his favorite residence up until the Smalcaldic War. The preacher Georg Keller was made pastor in Oepfingen in 1536 after his dismissal by the city.[145] Keller conducted his campaign against the Wittenberg Concord from there. Ludwig von Freyberg was a forceful, one might say violent and headstrong supporter of the Reformation. Given his choice of preachers and his invitation to Schwenckfeld, he seems to have been another of the Zwinglian lords. His son Georg Ludwig was a convinced Schwenkfelder.[146] Georg Ludwig's wife Katharina was the sister of Hans Wilhelm von Laubenberg whom we have already discussed.[147] Their two children, Michael Ludwig and Ferdinand, were given to Schwenckfeld to educate.[148] Michael Ludwig married Felicitas Landschad von Steinach. Her mother Anna Elizabeth was a Schwenkfelder, and Felicitas may well have been too.[149] The Landschad family served in Württemberg and the Palatinate.[150] Georg Ludwig was himself born in the Schloss in Stuttgart while his father was serving there.[151] The von Freyberg ties to the Württemberg nobility were extensive. The other son of Georg Ludwig, Ferdinand, married Veronika von Pappenheim of Groenenbach near Memmingen and Kempfen.[152] Veronika was a convinced Schwenkfelder. Whether the brothers chose their wives for their religious convictions, or whether the women only entered Schwenckfeld's sphere of influence with their marriages, it is clear that marriage ties and blood lines were often the route by which Schwenkfeldianism spread.

Their adherence cost the von Freybergs dearly during the Smalcaldic War. Their estates were seized by imperial troops

hunting for Schwenckfeld, and it took two years for them to re-
gain possession.[153] They were required to leave the Catholic religion undisturbed.[154] Schwenckfeld was less often at Justingen
thereafter, but the Schwenkfelders remained a discreet presence
there until a Catholic branch of the von Freyberg family inherited during the Thirty Years War. The two brothers provided
much of the money to publish Schwenckfeld's collected works
(1564-1570).

There was one other major center of Schwenkfeldianism in South Germany whose contact with Schwenckfeld
seems totally to have depended on printed works and written
correspondence—Nürnberg.[155] Though he wrote to the City
Council there and sent them a copy of his *Confession* in 1542,
there is no evidence that he ever visited the city.[156] Despite the
fact that the conservative Lutheran Nürnberg was the first city
in South Germany to seek to prevent publication and to suppress distribution of Schwenckfeld's works (1534), it remained
an important center of Schwenkfelder publishing.[157] The first
Schwenkfelder in the city was the *Kriegsschreiber* Eukarius
Ulrich.[158] He probably came to know of Schwenckfeld through
Elisabeth Pfersfelder whom Ulrich had helped leave Nürnberg
in 1532. It was Ulrich who carried Schwenckfeld's letter and
Confession to the City Council in 1542. Perhaps as a result of
this action, but at his own request, he was transferred out of
the city to Velden as a *Pfleger*.

The extent of Schwenckfeld's small following was revealed
to the City Council when they ordered the arrest and interro-
gation of Hermann Rigel, Schwenckfeld's messenger to Luther
in 1543.[159] Rigel was soon released, but he gave the Council
the names of two prominent Schwenkfelders: Jörg Lang and
Georg Schechner. Schechner was a mainstay of the Schwenkfelder group. He came of a well-to-do family of craftsmen in
Munich, had seen Müntzer in Wittenberg in 1522, had joined
Hans Hut's Anabaptists back in Munich, and had finally helped
dissolve the Augsburg Anabaptist movement in 1528. Schechner had been accepted as a citizen in Nürnberg in 1530 and
was a very successful dyer. He was one of the many who grew
disillusioned by Anabaptism, and he worked diligently to win
Anabaptists over to Schwenckfeld's views. One of his converts
was another leader of the Schwenkfelders, Hans Weichner.

Because they were very circumspect (in part because Schwenckfeld advised them to be) the Nürnberger Schwenkfelders

went unmolested for a decade and a half.[160] In 1558 the City Council was finally moved to arrest the movement when church officials of Karl of Baden asked the Council to examine the book distributor Bernhard Fischer concerning his involvement in the publication of Johann Sigismund Werner's Postils.[161] They discovered that Weichner, who was apparently a bookseller, had been the receiver of the work in Nürnberg. Weichner, Schechner, Lang, Fischer, a tailor named Wolf Ulrich, and an innkeeper named Linhart Amman were called before the Council and ordered to hand over their books. In addition Lang and Ulrich abjured Schwenckfeld's teachings. The others were ordered to consult with the Nürnberg preachers. Nothing further was done.

In 1563 a new Schwenkfelder, Paulus Grassmann, a very successful watch maker with patrons at the imperial court, was investigated, this time at the request of Duke Christoph of Württemberg.[162] This began a legal tussle with an ever prudent Council fearful of angering Grassmann's friends at Maximilians's court. In the process a numerous Schwenckfeld following was uncovered.[163] Among the new names were Schechner's son-in-law Lienhard Nürnberger, the furrier Hewart Geschwinat, the innkeeper Martin Pregel, one Wolf Geuss, the cobbler Hans Strauch, the wife of one Veit Seng, and Hans Meilendorfer. In the next four years the Council warned, threatened, cajoled, and enticed the Nürnberg Schwenkfelders. All finally made their peace with the city by *(pro forma?)* acceptance of the Augsburg Confession. Compared to the treatment meted out to the Anabaptists, that afforded the Schwenkfelders was marked by forbearance, patience, and a desire to avoid bringing down upon the city the ill-repute of religious persecution. That those involved were drawn primarily from the ranks of the well-to-do craftsmen in part explains the Council's tolerant attitude. More important, however, was the recognition that the Schwenkfelders posed absolutely no political or social threat. They were a purely religious issue.[164]

The social composition, recruitment pattern, and organization of Schwenckfeld's following are explainable in large measure by the means through which his message was propagated.[165] In the years covered by this study the movement was built by word of mouth. Personal friends and acquaintances formed the first points in Schwenckfeld's network. These, be they ministers or laypeople, would recruit others. This explains the importance of blood lines and the initial top-heaviness in social terms of the movement. Schwenckfeld was of the upper class and associated for the most part with his peers. Where the minister was a Schwenkfelder, however, the movement quickly spread among all classes. Reliance upon personal contact and word of mouth was necessary in the 1520s and 1530s because Schwenckfeld's printed works, though fairly numerous, were mostly non-polemical in nature. For example, *Christian Warfare and the Knighthood of God,* (1533) went through eleven editions all told.[166] His polemical writings were rarely published, and those that were were directed against the Catholics and Lutherans. He was therefore indistinguishable from the rest of the South German theologians. The letters and treatises which would have given him his own peculiar theological profile were circulated in manuscript among his followers only.

Schwenckfeld's procedure changed in the 1540s and 15-50s.[167] Alongside his non-controversial works he began printing doctrinal and polemical treatises. The numbers and geographical spread (from Riga to Dublin) of Schwenckfeld's extant printed corpus suggests the wide distribution and easy availability which these works had in the sixteenth century.[168] As a result isolated individual Schwenkfelders crop up more and more in the visitation records. Schwenckfeld books replace Schwenkfelders as the source of contagion. And in fact, one starts to find the adjective 'Schwenckfeldisch' more than the noun 'Schwenkfelder.' By the second half of the sixteenth century Schwenkfeldianism had become a recognized body of beliefs no longer necessarily associated with membership in a body of fellow believers.

But even for the 1520s and 1530s the term Schwenkfelder covered a variety of degrees of commitment and self-conscious identification with Schwenckfeld and his teachings. The Streichers in Ulm, Jakob Held von Tieffenau, Margareta Engelmann, the Scher family, the Thumbs, the preachers in Stetten and Muehlhausen, and the members of the Schwenkfelder conventicles in Augsburg all publicly identified with Schwenckfeld and spread his doctrine. Johann Bader, Bonifatius Wolfhart, and Katharina Zell were close confidants of Schwenckfeld and agreed with him on most issues, but maintained a certain autonomy. With them Schwenckfeld discussed but did not instruct. It may be that their clerical (or in the case of Katharina Zell, quasi-clerical) status prevented a more domineering role for Schwenckfeld. Schwenckfeld's relationship with political figures such as Bernhard Besserer and Wolfgang Rehlinger is more difficult to define. They valued Schwenckfeld's advice and companionship. They agreed with him on most issues. They were his patrons and protectors. On the other hand, they were rulers of the churches in their cities. They could not or would not break with their churches, nor with the clergy which they employed. They did not seek to mold the church along Schwenkfelder lines and they maintained an outward uniformity. Their relationship to the church was similar to that with the city as a whole. Though they ruled the city/church, they were not themselves fully a part of the community. While imposing order upon the city/church they remained largely free and independent. Within the sphere of religion that was reflected in their refusal to countenance the rigorous methods suggested by the clergy to establish true doctrinal uniformity among the population. Besserer's attitude in this matter may well have been the bond between him and Schwenckfeld, since Schwenckfeld too refused to join any of the competing 'sects.'

The general appeal of Schwenckfeld's teachings, it is safe to say, was in many ways that of the Reformation as a whole in its early phases. The spiritualistic tenor of the early Luther and Zwingli continued unabated, if not intensified, in Schwenckfeld. Later developments in the theologies of Luther, Zwingli, and the movements they fostered were viewed by many as a betrayal. The pervasive anti-clericalism which had provided much of the Reformation's initial impetus reappeared as the reformers tried to consolidate their hold on the church. Schwenckfeld played upon both these positive (spiritualism) and negative (anti-clericalism) strains of early Protestantism. The fact that he was able to recruit ministers as well shows the continued power and attraction of the ideal which many readers found in Luther's *Freedom of a Christian*.

Schwenckfeld was not the only one to offer an alternative to the increasingly clericalized Protestant churches. The Anabaptists had also capitalized on lay discontent, and Schwenckfeld was to recruit many of his followers from among the Anabaptists. He was able to offer a warm personal piety and

a sense of commitment and rigor without requiring a break
with the world in a political or social sense. This was especially attractive after the debacle of Münster. Schwenckfeld
offered a religious dissidence shorn of its political and social
corollaries.[169] Schwenckfeld was not unaware of this appeal of
his teaching. His treatise *On the Edification of the Conscience*,
written at the request of the Thumb brothers in 1533,[170] was in
essence an explanation of Christ's saying 'Truly, I say to you,
it will be hard for a rich man to enter the Kingdom of Heaven,'
(Mt. 19:24-26; Mark 10:25-27; Luke 18: 25-27). Schwenckfeld's
treatment robs the passage of any social significance and con-
centrates on Christ's answer to his disciples' dismay: 'With
men this is impossible, but with God all things are possible.'
Salvation for the 'noble, the powerful, and the rich,' is merely
another occasion of God's omnipotence and sole-sufficiency.[171]
The powerful of the world are admonished not to set their
hearts on the things of this world. But Schwenckfeld does not
suggest that they divest themselves of these millstones or even
that they be selflessly dedicated to the service of the neighbor. Schwenckfeld's spiritualism safely insulated the upper
class Christian from the demands of a social gospel. Christianity is an interior thing, a matter of personal ethics not
societal reform. *On the Edification of the Conscience* went
through three editions in Augsburg, one in Strassburg, and
was translated into Czech. Schwenckfeld presented an auto-
graphed copy to the presidents of the Strassburg Synod. It
even found a grudging welcome with Ambrosius Blaurer.[172]

The presence of doctors, lawyers, and humanist city clerks
in the ranks of Schwenckfeld's followers may owe something
to the inherent professional jealousies which these groups felt
toward ministers and theologians. Humility and sheep-like devotion did not sit well upon their shoulders. Self-assertion and
self-esteem demanded a more independent role in religion.[173]
Such men did not support the reform in order to erect a new
Papacy.

The preponderance of women among Schwenckfeld's followers was remarked at the time and ever since. The usual explanation has been the attractiveness of Schwenckfeld's personality: his courtliness, his nobility.[174] No doubt this played a
role with both male and female followers. Other personality
traits, however, were more important. Schwenckfeld betrays

no sign of the pervasive misogyny of the age. He genuinely
liked and respected the women with whom he corresponded.
For the most part he treated them as equals with whom he
discussed important theological issues.[175] There is none of the
heavy-handed paternalism that one associates with the Reformation era. He solicited their opinions and exhorted them to
study on their own. He took them seriously. But the spiritualism and anti-clericalism of his teachings were in themselves
attractive. The early Reformation had offered women a measure of autonomy and importance which the later Protestant
churches revoked.[176] Among the South German Schwenkfelders
women retained positions of leadership. The desire for independence was also reflected in the fact that many of Schwenckfeld's
women followers were either widows who had not remarried or
women who had never married. Schwenckfeld approved.[177]

The focus of Schwenkfelder piety was the home. This too
helped promote the role of the women. There were a few instances where Schwenkfeldianism divided families.[178] But for
the most part entire households were Schwenkfelder. Conventicles were held in private homes, and religion was discussed
over meals. Preparatory fasting, Bible study, prophesying, and
the use of the *Confession of Sins* (all of which could easily be
done at home) characterized the Schwenkfelder gatherings in
Strassburg.[179] It is not unlikely that this was the case in Ulm
and Augsburg as well. What took place in the *Schlösser* Koengen, Stetten, or Justingen we do not know.

The relationship of the conventicles to the larger church
was strained. Schwenkfelders often absented themselves from
services altogether, or if they attended they refused to participate in the eucharist. If the minister was a Schwenkfelder the
eucharist was usually neglected, but there were no hard and
fast rules. Schwenckfeld even advised attendance at services
for prudential reasons.[180] In any event, there seems to have
been no mechanism for disciplining the straying. There was no
Schwenkfelder ban. The exact relationship between the conventicles and church was usually determined by the attitude
of the clergy. If the ministers were tolerant or perhaps even
favorable a conventicle might become an *ecclesiola in ecclesia*.
Where the clergy showed more zeal the battlelines were quickly
drawn.

The organization of the Schwenkfelders seems to have developed ad hoc in default of any guidelines from Schwenckfeld.

In some ways it seems to answer to the hopes of Luther during the early years of the Reformation.[181] But the lack of a developed ecclesiology and *Ordnung* left the Schwenkfelders more vulnerable to the allures of Pietism at the beginning of the seventeenth century. Just as Schwenckfeld had presented an attractive alternative to the dangers of Anabaptism, so Pietism offered a way to address most of the concerns of the Schwenkfelders, while allowing them to remain within the church.[182] This proved more dangerous for the movement than the Thirty Years War.

Notes

[1] *Spiritualistische Tradition im Protestantismus—Die Geschichte des Schwenckfeldertums in Schlesien* (Berlin, 1973).

[2] On Bader see J. B. Gelbert, *Magister Johann Baders Leben und Schriften, Nicolaus Thomae und seine Briefe* (Neustadt, 1868).

[3] See CS 4:1-49. 240-61. See also Joh. Martin Usteri, 'Weitere Beiträge zur Geschichte der Tauflehre der reformierten Kirche: Joh. Bader ein wenig bekannter Verteidiger der Kirchentaufe,' *Theologische Studien & Kritiken*, 56 (1883), 610-16.

[4] Bader to Bucer (Jan. 24, 1533), Thesaurus Baumianus, 26 vols., Ms. Strassburg BNU (henceforth Th.B.) 6.

[5] Bader to Bucer (July 31, 1533), Th.B. 6.

[6] Gelbert, 128; *QGT* 4:250.20-33. The work referred to is *Catechismus von ettlichen Hauptartickeln des Christlichen Glaubens* (CS 4: 208-38).

[7] Bader's later views on baptism combine a spiritualistic distinction of inner and outer to the disadvantage of the latter, with a refusal to baptize the impious. See Gelbert, 246, 248, 255-56; Schiess (ed.), *Briefwechsel der Brüder Ambrosius und Thomas Blaurer 1509-1548* (Freiburg, 1908-10), 2:272-73. Bader advised Bucer to get Schwenckfeld's works on the two Testaments from Leo Jud and read them before criticizing them (Bader to Bucer, July 31, 1533, Th.B. 6). See Gottfried Seebass' paper in this volume on Schwenckfeld's use of the Old and New Testaments. On Schwenckfeld's treatment of baptism see my *Caspar Schwenckfeld, Reluctant Radical: His Life to 1540* (New Haven, 1986), 83-84, 134-38.

[8] CS 6:193-230. On the publishing history of this work see 193-97. Bader had obtained it from the Strassburg printer Schweintzer, a pupil of Crautwald's and publisher of his works.

[9] As reported to Hubert by Thomae (Gelbert, 229-30).

[10] Gelbert, 248; Schiess 2:272-73.

[11] Schiess 2:134; Gelbert, 245-47, 265-66.

[12] On Schwenckfeld's visit see Gelbert, 246-47; on the catechism see 255-56.

13 Gelbert, 259-64; Schiess 2:272-73.

14 Gelbert, 115-16, 123, 207-08.

15 It shows up again in his 1544 catechism (Gelbert, 255-56). There were differences between Schwenckfeld and Bader over the eucharist, but that was occasioned by what Schwenckfeld thought was a Zwinglian interpretation of the words of institution (Gelbert, 257-58). Gelbert (220) wrongly interprets a Blaurer letter to say that Bader accepted the Wittenberg Concord. The letter only says that Blaurer wanted to read a 1533 Bader treatise on the eucharist (Schiess 1:838). It may well be that Bader signed the Concord, but there is no evidence. On the early Strassburg consensus see my article, 'Schwenckfeld and the South German eucharistic Controversy 1526-1529,' in this volume.

16 Bader's decision to halt the celebration of the eucharist was a direct result of the perceived immorality and godlessness in Landau (Gelbert, 246, 248).

17 CS 8:602.

18 CS 8:601-02.

19 Gelbert, 270-74. Bucer was sent by Strassburg to oversee its implementation.

20 QGT 4:433 fn 3.

21 QGT 4:433-44; 'Ratsbeschlüsse ... über Bernhard Herxheimer,' March 27 to April 11, 1554. Herxheimer had published his own work containing Schwenckfeld's teachings. After his expulsion he was pastor at Edenkoben until he was found out and expelled in 1559. On later actions (1556) against Schwenkfelders see QGT 4: 435.

22 In 1556 a visitation discovered that Neustadt and surrounding areas in the Palatinate were pretty much under the control of the Schwenkfelders and Anabaptists, due in large part to Herxheimer's efforts (QGT 4:149-50). Despite concerted efforts Schwenkfelders were still found in the area in 1563 and 1607 (QGT 4:161, 237). A 1558 visitation revealed the same situation in and around Neukastel (QGT 4:270-78). A Schwenkfelder was reported at Meisenheim in 1585 (QGT 4:287). And two pastors were found to have Schwenckfeld's books in 1605 and 1609 (QGT 4:288-89).

23 CS 4:843.22. CS conjectures that Schwenckfeld visited his printers in Hagenau and Bader in Landau on the way (CS 4:824).

24 Schwenckfeld returned to Speyer in September 1534 where, according to Martin Frecht's letter to Capito (Sept. 30, 1534, Th.B. 7), he had been entertained at a dinner given by lawyers. Schwenckfeld probably visited again in 1538, after which he wrote a letter to his host, Hieronymus zum Lamb (Jan. 1539), CS 6:428-44. On the zum Lamb family see CS 6:428-29. During October 1547 he made another risky journey there (Franz Michael Weber, *Kaspar Schwenckfeld und seiner Anhänger in den freybergischen Herrschaften Justingen und Oepfingen* [Stuttgart, 1962], 42). One wonders if we do not see some influence in R. W Scribner, 'Memorandum on the Appointment of a Preacher in Speyer 1538,' *Bulletin of the Institute of Historical Research*, 48 (1975) 248-55.

25 On this fascinating chapter of Schwenkfelder history see Hans-Peter
    Mielke, 'Schwenckfeldianer im Hofstaat Bischof Marquands von Speyer
    (1560-1581),' *Archiv für mittelrhenische Kirchengeschichte*, 28 (1976),
    77-82, and his *Die Niederadligen von Hattstein, Ihre politische Rolle
    und soziale Stellung*, 312-15.
26 The means would have been Samuel Eisenmenger, court physician and
    the second leader of the Schwenkfelders. Agatha Streicher of Ulm was
    the third. Eisenmenger studied at Wittenberg under Melanchthon and
    continued his studies at Tübingen where he got his doctorate in 1564. He
    lost his professorship at Tübingen in 1567 and his position as personal
    physician to Markgraf Karl of Baden in 1572 because of his religious
    opinions. Bishop Marquand recommended him to the bishops of Strass-
    burg and Cologne (Mielke, 'Schwenckfeldianer,' 79-80). Marquand also
    arranged for Agatha Streicher's appointment to tend the dying Em-
    peror Maximilian II (Mielke, *Die Niederadligen*, 315). The extent of
    Schwenkfelder influence at the imperial courts has not yet been investi-
    gated, but given the emperor's religious predilections a Schwenkfelder
    presence is not unlikely. Another figure associated with the Imperial
    courts at Speyer who became a Schwenkfelder was Aggaeus van Al-
    bada, about whom consult Wiebe Bergsma's paper in this volume.
27 On this episode and Schwenckfeld's ties to Esslingen see my *Caspar
    Schwenckfeld*, 162-63.
28 Blaurer is our source for this; see Blaurer to Machtolf (Oct. 19, 1533),
    Schiess 1:428-29; Blaurer to Bucer (Oct. 19, 1533), Schiess 1:434.
29 CS 4:850, 859.1-25.
30 On this our only source is Frecht to Bucer (Oct. 30, 1533, Th.B. 6).
    QGT 8:202.31-203.13 is only an excerpt.
31 QGT 8:132.26-29.
32 CS 4:847; Karl Wolfart, 'Beiträge zur Augsburger Reformationsge-
    schichte III. Caspar Schwenckfeld und Bonifacius Wolfhart,' *Beiträge
    zur bayerischen Kirchengeschichte*, 8 (1902), 102.
33 Friedrich Roth, *Augsburgs Reformationsgeschichte, Zweiter Bd. 1531-
    1537, bzw. 1540* (Munich, 1904), 56-57, 94-96; Wolfart, 'Beiträge... III,'
    passim; J. V. Pollet, *Martin Bucer. Etudes sur la correspondance avec
    de nombreux textes inedits* (Paris, 1958, 1962) 1:80-105, 2:254-64.
34 Roth, 46; Claus Peter Clasen, 'Schwenckfeld's friends: A social study,'
    Mennonite Quarterly Review, 46 (1972), 65; Pollet 2:227 fn. 9
35 QGT 8:210-12 (Nov. 25, 1533); K. Wolfart, 'Beiträge... III,' 105-06. For
    Bucer's comment on this letter see QGT 8:231.4-8.
36 Clasen, 'Schwenckfeld's friends,' 65-66, Roth, 60.
37 Roth, 14-15, 60, 70; Pollet 2:241 fn. 6; QGT 8: 344.15-20; Walther
    Kohler, *Zwingli und Luther* (Leipzig, 1924, 1953), 1:265, 719-21; Dr. W.
    Germann, *D. Johann Forster der Hennebergische Reformator* (1894),
    126-27, 167-69, 225-26.
38 See Roth, 59-61, for the following patrician or upper class supporters.
    On the Schwenkfelder movement in Augsburg as a whole see Clasen,
    'Schwenckfeld's friends,' 62-66.

[39] Others were Adam Reissner who will be discussed a little further on; Daniel Sudermann in Strassburg at the end of the century; Nicolaus Maior jurist and vice-chancellor to the duke of Württemberg; the physicians Samuel Eisenmann, Agatha Streicher, and Johann Winther von Andernach.

[40] Geryon Sailer reported to Bucer (Jan. 25, 1531) that Burgermeister Rehlinger was 'addicted' to Schwenckfeld as was Regel, though both were concerned that Schwenckfeld may have been rebaptized. From what Sailer wrote, it seems that Schwenckfeld's earlier publications had been sufficient to win him a following, (QGT 7:300.8-20).

[41] On this incident and the information which it produced see Clasen, 'Schwenckfeld's friends,' 62-66.

[42] This is especially clear from Johann Forster's account: see W. Germann, 129-30, 147-50, 152-59, 177-78, 241, 245, 248, 254; Karl Wolfart, *Die Augsburger Reformation in den Jahren 1533/34* (Leipzig, 1901), 91, 104.

[43] Roth, 60-61.

[44] Gottfried W. Locher, *Die Zwinglische Reformation im Rahmen der europäischen Kirchengeschichte* (Zurich, 1979), 468-69.

[45] W. Germann, 162-65, 220-21, 243-44, 255-56; Roth, 412-14.

[46] K. Wolfart, 'Beiträge... III,' 150; W. Germann, 166, 255-56.

[47] CS 5:10.13.

[48] On Reissner see Peter C. Erb, 'Adam Reissner, his learning and influence on Schwenckfeld,' *Mennonite Quarterly Review*, 54, 32-41; Karl Schottenloher, 'Jakob Ziegler und Adam Reissner' (Diss., Munich, 1908); Otto Bucher, 'Adam Reissner: Ein Beitrag zur Geschichte der deutschen Reformation,' (Diss., Erlangen, 1950). For a biographical sketch of von Zell see CR 96, 327, fn. 1.

[49] CS 5:12. See Blaurer's description to Bucer (March 11, 1534, Schiess 1:477-78, and April 7, 1534, Schiess 1:484).

[50] Frecht to Blaurer (April 5, 1534, Schiess 1:452); Blaurer to Bucer (April 7, 1534, 454); Bucer to Blaurer (April 30, 1534, 497). The Kempteners delayed sending a copy of Schwenckfeld's 'Apology' to Blaurer (Schiess 1:484).

[51] On this episode see Döllinger, 'Memminger Sektenbewegungen im 16. und 17. Jahrhundert,' *Zeitschrift für bayerischen Kirchengeschichte*, 12 (1937), 139-43.

[52] On Laubenberg see Weber, 13.

[53] Hans-Georg Hofacker, 'Die Reformation in der Reichstadt Ravensburg,' *Zeitschrift für württembergische Landesgeschichte*, 29 (1970), 93.

[54] Döllinger, 143-47.

[55] Döllinger, 145.

[56] See Hans-Georg Hofacker, 'Die Reformation in der Reichstadt Ravensburg.'

[57] Among the leaders was the *Stadtschreiber* and later *Burgermeister* Krottlin, to whom Schwenckfeld wrote (June 25, 1545; CS 9:349-53).

58 Hofacker, 119-20; Döllinger, 146-47.

59 CS 7:451-884.

60 On Kempten, Kaufbeuren, and Isny see Weber, 16.

61 Schuler to Bucer (June 25, 1534, Th.B. 7); Frecht to Bucer (June 26, 1534, Th.B. 7); Frecht to Blaurer (June 28, 1534, Schiess 1:504-06); See also Hans Konrad Thumb to Jakob Sturm (June 26, 1534, QGT 8:363.6-364.2). Bucer complained to Blaurer of Schwenckfeld's presence in the city (July 10, 1534; Schiess 1: 508).

62 For an analysis of the Strassburg group see Daniel Husser, 'Caspar Schwenckfeld et ses adeptes entre l'église et les sectes a Strassburg,' *Strasbourg au coeur religieux du XVIe siècle* (Strassburg, 1977), 521-24.

63 On Katharina Zell see Roland Bainton, *Women of the Reformation in Germany and Italy* (Minneapolis, 1971), 55-76. On both her and her husband see William H. Klaustermeyer, 'The Role of Matthew and Catherine Zell in the Strassburg Reformation' (unpubl. Ph.D, Stanford, 1965).

64 On Schultheiss see Werner Bellardi, *Wege und Wandlungen eines Strassburger Spiritualisten und Zeitgenossen Martin Bucers*, (Frankfurt a. M., 1976).

65 CS 5:527.

66 QGT 7:337-38.

67 QGT 7:123; CS 4:642-43. Schweintzer, a Silesian, had printed Schwenckfeld's second *Apology* (1530) and other works before giving up publishing and entering governmental service. He was discharged in 1556.

68 CS (4:846-48), and Schultz, (172), speculate that she was the wife of one Jakob Engelmann. But the brothers Christoph and Caspar Engelmann both married women named Margareta (Thomas Brady, *Ruling Class, Regime and Reformation in Strassburg 1520-1555* [Leiden, 1978], 179n, 312, 326-27, 378, 384, 388). Caspar was a goldsmith and his wife was the daughter of Klaus Kniebis, leader of the evangelical faction in the 1520s. She herself had been a novice at St. Margarethe. Christoph was a cloth merchant. His wife's maiden name was Surgant. Husser (523) claims Margaret as a half-sister to Margarete von Grafeneck, but gives no proof. If true it would provide the initial contact point between the Scher family and Schwenckfeld.

69 On Scher see J. Bernays, 'Zur Biographie Johann Winthers von Andernach,' *Zeitschrift für die Geschichte des Oberrheins*, 55 (1901), 35-38; Walther Bernhardt, *Die Zentralbehörden des Herzogtums Württemberg und ihre Beamten 1520-1629* (Stuttgart, 1972), 1:323. Scher was related (by marriage?) to Ambrosius Blaurer, and thus shows up in Schiess (*passim*). The family name is variously spelled: Scher, Schaer, and Schoer.

70 On Felicitas see Bernays, 28-58; CS 8:621-23.

71 Bernays, 47-52.

72 Dr. Hecklin is variously identified as 'von Steineck' (Bernays, 38, 57) and 'von Bertringen' (CS 8:621). The family name is variously spelled

Hoecklin, Heglini, and Hecklin. Whether he was a doctor of Laws or Medicine is not specified. There is a family Hoecklin von Steineck (Bernhardt, 380-81) from a slightly later period whose progenitor, Dr. Apollinaris Hoecklin von Steineck, was a jurist in Basel. Since professions tended to run in families, Hans Christoph may well have been a lawyer.

73 Bernays, 45-52; Bainton, *Women of the Reformation*, 73.

74 CS 9:18-20; Bernhardt, 322-23.

75 Hans Friedrich Thumb was *Obervogt* of Kirchheim u. T. in the mid-1530s when the Reformation was being imposed in that part of the duchy. Schwenckfeld was often a guest there (Ernst Boger, *Geschichte der freiherrlichen Familie Thumb von Neuburg* [Stuttgart, 1885], 108-09).

76 On Held in Strassburg see QGT 8:438, 457, 466, 473, 493. QGT's (438) identification of Held as the individual who achieved *Burgerrecht* in the *Tucherzunff* in 1528 may or may not be correct.

77 Husser (527) lists some of these activities. Held also accompanied Schwenckfeld on the latter's visit with Philip of Hesse (Schultz, 238).

78 Schwenckfeld's letter to Elizabeth Pfersfelder (Aug. 1540?; CS 7:99-104) attempted to woo her away from the Hoffmannite christology. On November 14, 1540, Crautwald also wrote her (Cod. Aug. 37. 27. 2., 109-17).

79 On the two letters to Hans Christmann, the second dated February 4, 1537 see CS 5:632-37, 638-41.

80 See Schwenckfeld to Ernst von Baden, April 17, 1543, (cs 8:482-96); and before April 13, 1544 (CS 9:26-28).

81 QGT 4:54.20-29.

82 QGT 4:24.1-19, 46.5-18.

83 QGT 4:64.24-35.

84 Consult my *Caspar Schwenckfeld*, 178-90 on these developments.

85 There is only one case concerning an Anabaptist in Schorndorf in 1535 (QGT 1:44). Schorndorf remained a hotbed of Anabaptism throughout the century.

86 QGT 1:61. See also Julius Rauscher, *Württembergische Reformationsgeschichte* (Stuttgart, 1934), 151.

87 See Ludwig Friedrich Heyd. *Ulrich, Hertzog zu Württemberg* (Tübingen, 1841-1844), 3:160-62.

88 On the Schwenkfelders in Württemberg see QGT 1, *passim*; Gustav Bossert d. A., 'Die Schwenckfelder in Cannstatt und ihre Freunde,' *Schwäbische Merkur* (1921), Nr. 160; Gustav Bossert d. J., 'Aus der nebenkirchlichen religiöser Bewegung der Reformationszeit in Württemberg (Wiedertäufer und Schwenckfelder),' *Blätter für Württembergische Kirchengeschichte*, 33 (1929), 1-41; Julius Rauscher, *Württembergische Reformationsgeschichte*, 153-55; Ernst Boger, *Geschichte der freiherrlichen Familie Thumb von Neuburg*, 1-117; Weber, 6-8, 11-18, 23, 44-45.

89 QGT 1:97n; CS 8:24; Clasen, 'Schwenckfeld's Friends,' 672-78.

90 Also known as Mueller genannt Mayer (Walter Bernhardt, *Die Zentral-behorden des Herzogtums Württemberg und ihre Beamten 1520-1629*, 1:571). They corresponded in 1538 (Nicolaus Maior to Schwenckfeld, Sept. 1, 1538, Cod. Aug. 33. 27. 2., 555-56; and Schwenckfeld to Maior, Sept. 16, 1538, CS 6, 176-92). Most of both letters concerned Schwenckfeld's opinions of legal and religious issues relating to marriage. Maior was a licentiate in both laws.

91 Rauscher, 154-55; Gustav Bossert, 'Der Beamtenwechsel in Württemberg um 1544,' *Zeitschrift für Württembergische Landesgeschichte*, 8 (1944-1948), 281.

92 Margareta was one of the Scher daughters already discussed. Hans von Gültingen was a patrician in Strassburg (QGT 8:492.28) and may well have been one of the nobles that Bucer complained of (QGT 8:450.20-24). On him and his brother see CS 14:40-42. Balthasar had no sympathy for Schwenckfeld. On his career see Bernhardt 1:332-33. On Helfenstein's involvement with Schwenckfeld in the 1550s see Weber, 11-18.

93 Bossert, 'Beamtenwechsel,' 280-97.

94 On von Ow see Bernhardt 1:25; 2:532-33.

95 QGT 1:1009.16-1013.20.

96 Bossert, 'Beamtenwechsel,' 293-94.

97 Two of Thumb's allies, Martin Nuettel and Hans Hafenberg, were arrested in 1543. Both had served in the Austrian administration and both faced charges on that account. Neither was a Schwenkfelder. Nuettel, if anything, was a Catholic. And Nuettel was also implicated in a plot of Catholic Bavaria against Ulrich (Bossert, 'Beamtenwechsel,' 285-93; Bernhardt 1, 337-40, 524-25).

98 Rauscher (154-55), suspects the Thumbs of engineering Blaurer's dismissal. He probably relied on Bossert ('Beamtenwechsel,' 280-81), for this explanation. Bucer's misleading letter to Margaret Blaurer (June 12, 1538, Schiess 2: 835) is the source of this view. Although it is not impossible that there was bad blood between Blaurer and Thumb, Thumb would hardly have had Blaurer dismissed because of religious differences. Blaurer was the closest thing Thumb had to a clerical ally at court. Bucer's letter provides a hint at the real reason. He complains that the split between Schnepf and Blaurer allowed these things to happen. Blaurer's steadfast opposition to the Lutherans and Philip Melanchthon's efforts to have him replaced by Johannes Brenz were the most probable causes of Blaurer's dismissal: see James Martin Estes, *Christian Magistrate and State Church. The Reforming Career of Johannes Brenz* (Toronto, 1982) 12-13; Martin Brecht, 'Ambrosius Blarers Wirksamkeit in Schwaben,' in Berndt Moeller (ed.), *Der Konstanzer Reformator Ambrosius Blaurer 1492-1564 Gedenkschrift zu seinem Todestag* (Constance and Stuttgart, 1964), 165-67. Nicolaus Maior left Ulrich's service after he was charged with spending too much money on an embassy to Spain (Bernhardt I, 512).

99 Gustav Bossert d. A., 'Die Schwenckfelder in Cannstatt und ihre
    Freunde,' *Schwäbische Merkur* (1921), nr. 160; and his, 'Aus der
    nebenkirchlichen religiösen Bewegung der Reformationszeit in Würt-
    temberg (Wiedertäufer und Schwenckfelder),' *Blätter für Württem-
    bergische Kirchengeschichte*, 33 (1929), 20-21.
100 Cf. QGT 1:73.33-74.5, 75.14-88.21.
101 QGT 1:88.22-96.19. It was reported that over fifty people were members
    of the sect.
102 On Neff's ordeal see QGT 1:98.33-101.38, 102.16-114.8, 114.20-118.10,
    118.23-119.30, 120.10-122.27, 124.14-125.22.
103 Bossert, 'Nebenkirchlichen Bewegung,' 37. Schwenckfeld was busy in the
    area around Kaufbeuren at the time and probably arranged Schilling's
    appointment (Weber, 16).
104 Alexander Hoeldt to Andreas Neff, March 16, 1548, QGT 1: 120.30-
    122.28.
105 Boger, 118; QGT 1:1018.6-1020.26.
106 QGT 1:*passim*. Consult the index under 'Schwenckfelder.'
107 In the 1570s Susanna von Grafeneck was cited as a Schwenkfelder and in
    1590 Juliana von Grafeneck. They were the daughters of Klaus and Mar-
    garet von Grafeneck (QGT 1:647.3-20; Clasen, 'Schwenckfeld's Friends,'
    61). It is also possible that the von Thalheims and the Witterhausens
    were involved (Clasen, 'Schwenckfeld's Friends,' 61).
108 Action against Schwenkfelder Matthaeus Felber (May 11, 1549), QGT
    1:911.6-10. QGT's collection only goes to 1652.
109 Heyd, *Ulrich*, 3:74-75. On the toleration of Schwenckfeld see QGT
    1:100.3-9.
110 QGT 1:129.32-39, 1036.22-37.
111 Johannes Zwick to Vadian, Sept. 16, 1535, Vad. Br. 5, 250; Schwenckfeld
    to Philip of Hesse, Sept. 26, 1535, CS 5: 401-03, esp. 402.7-11. Cf. CS
    5:404-05.
112 On the Ulm Schwenkfelders see F. Fritz, *Ulmische Kirchengeschichte
    vom Interim bis zum dreissigjährigen Krieg (1548-1612)* (Ulm, 1934),
    145-46, 185-86, 192-209; Carl Theodor Keim, *Die Reformation der Re-
    ichstadt Ulm* (Stuttgart, 1851), 271-72, 280, 307-10; Weber, 9, 13, 26-27.
113 On Bernhard Besserer see Max Ernst, 'Bernhard Besserer, Burgermeis-
    ter in Ulm (1471-1542),' *Zeitschrift für Württembergische Landesge-
    schichte*, 5 (1941), 88-113; Heinrich Walther, *Bernhard Besserer und die
    Politik der Reichstadt Ulm während der Reformationszeit* (Ulm, 1929).
    Schwenckfeld had first met Bernhard Besserer while the Burgermeister
    was visiting Augsburg in January 1534 (Wolfhart, 'Beiträge... III,' 104-
    05; Frecht to Bucer, Jan. 8, 1534, Th.B. 7; Frecht to Blaurer, Jan 14,
    1534, Schiess 1:462-63). Wolfhart mistakenly believed that Schwenck-
    feld had visited Besserer in Ulm in January.
114 Albrecht Rieber, 'Das Patriziat von Ulm, Augsburg, Ravensburg, Mem-
    mingen, Biberach,' in Hellmuth Roessler (ed.), *Deutsches Patriziat
    1430-1740* (Limburg/Lahn, 1968), especially 305-06, 311-12, 317.

115   The Besserers provided Johann Liebmann with a position in their vil-
      lage of Schuerpflingen after he was dismissed in 1544 (Fritz, 194). Was
      this before or after he served in Landau (Gelbert, 270-74)? In 1573 the
      Burgermeister, another Hans Ehinger, complained of the inquisitorial
      methods of the visitation (Fritz, 200). Only in the late 1570s was an
      earnest attempt made to combat the Schwenkfelders.

116   Keim, *Ulm*, 307.

117   In the period 1527-1528 a spiritualistic outlook dominated Ulm's Ref-
      ormation. It was left up to each parent when and whether a child would
      be baptized (Keim, *Ulm*, 119-21). The first successful reformer of Ulm,
      Konrad Sam, offered a particularly spiritualistic form of Zwinglianism,
      denying the real presence, rejecting the idea of sacraments as media
      of grace, and even de-emphasising the role of the word in the elicit-
      ing of faith (Keim, *Ulm*, 189-91). These views were enshrined in the
      1531 Church Order and Liturgy (Keim, *Ulm*, 243, 247). Cf. Julius En-
      driss, *Das Ulmer Reformationsjahr in seinen entscheidenden Vorgangen*
      (Ulm, 1931), 74, 85.

118   Schwenckfeld claimed this as the limit of his activities (CS 5:536.7-17,
      541.9-13).

119   Schwenckfeld to Sebastian Aitinger, February 10, 1539 (CS 18:208-20).
      Both Sebastian and his father Konrad were also supporters of Sebastian
      Franck (Walther, 47). Schwenckfeld's letter to Sebastian Aitinger dis-
      cusses Schwenckfeld's theological disagreements with Franck. Because
      of the close ties with the *Fünferschreiber*, Schwenckfeld was actually
      able to arrange the revision of the minutes of his last hearing before the
      Rat in 1539 (Schwenckfeld to Sebastian Aitinger, Sept. 12, 1539; CS
      6:549-55). See also the letter to Anna Aitinger, February 2, 1540 (CS
      7:3-9). Anna was probably the wife of Konrad and mother of Sebastian.

120   Keim, *Ulm*, 307.

121   Keim, *Ulm*, 307-10; Fritz, 193-94.

122   Gelbert, 270-74; Fritz, 186.

123   Keim, *Ulm*, 348-53.

124   Julius Endriss *(Kaspar Schwenckfelds Ulmer Kampfe*, 19) corrects CS
      5:477 by asserting five daughters, not four. In fact CS lists the names
      of five daughters there.

125   The series of letters to Helena Streicher and her children have a special
      tone not found in Schwenckfeld's other correspondence. There is per-
      haps a hint that Schwenckfeld's relationship to the widow bordered on
      intimacy, but was consciously restrained: 'Ihr wisset mein fürgeliebte/
      ja hertzgeliebte/ wie es denn in aller reinigkeit und zucht bey den
      christen sein sol/ welcher in Christo ein hertz und ein seele ist/...,'
      CS 5:48.37-39. His fifth letter to the family (after December 25, 1536;
      CS 5:546-49), shows his concern for the children. CS 5:549.6-25 reads
      like a parent or close relative sending endearing little messages to the
      individual children. In the sixth letter (ca. March 1537) he admonishes
      the children not to fight or quarrel among themselves, to accept their

punishment well, and to read the *Imitatio Christi* after dinner (CS 5: 657-60). Schwenckfeld was also concerned for Hans Augustin Streicher's education and moral training at the University of Tübingen (Sept. 21, 1536; CS 5:529.11-530.15).

126 See Lore Sporhan-Krempet, 'Agatha Streicher, die Ärtzin von Ulm,' *Ulm und Overschwaben*, 35 (1958), 174-80.

127 Endriss, *Schwenckfelds Ulmer Kampfe*, 19. She was taken before the *Rat* in 1544 (Fritz, 186).

128 Schwenckfeld to Barbara Roellin, May 5, 1537 (CS 5: 685-89). Schwenckfeld to Barbara Kurenbach, ca. January 1535 (CS 5:266-69).

129 Fritz, 186.

130 Ibid.

131 Fritz, 186; Keim, *Ulm*, 310.

132 Fritz, 202-03.

133 Ibid., 202-03.

134 Ibid., 208-09.

135 Ibid., 185. In 1547, fearful of the emperor's wrath, Ulm confiscated Schwenckfeld's works still in press at Varnier's (Weber, 43).

136 Fritz, 199.

137 Ibid., 203-09.

138 Ibid., 203-09. Upon refusing to swear an oath as physician in Ulm, Hans Augustin Streicher moved to Geislingen (196).

139 Ibid., 203-09.

140 On the von Freybergs and Justingen see Weber; A. Schilling, *Die Reichsherrschaft Justingen. Ein Beitrag zur Geschichte von Alb und Oberschwaben* (Stuttgart, 1880).

141 Weber, 49-50.

142 Schilling, 38, 47, 49.

143 Weber, 24-25.

144 Weber, 12.

145 Weber, 25-26.

146 Weber, 24-25.

147 Weber, 13.

148 Weber, 24.

149 Weber, 49-50; Schultz, 358.

150 Bernhardt, *passim*; and Robert Irschlinger, 'Die Aufzeichnungen des Hans Ulrich Landschad von Steinach über sein Geschlecht,' *Zeitschrift für die Geschichte des Oberrheins*, 47 (1934), 205-59.

151 Weber, 14.

152 Weber, 49-50.

153 Weber, 38-41.

154 There were Catholic priests in Justingen (1556), and Oepfingen (1575), at the same time as there were Schwenkfelders (Weber, 45-46).

155 See Hans-Dieter Schmid, 'Nürnberg, Schwenckfeld und die Schwenkfelder,' in Horst Rabe, Hans-Georg Molitor, Hans-Christoph Rublack

(eds.), *Festgabe für Ernst Walter Zeeden zum 60 Geburtstag am 14. Mai 1976*, (Münster, 1976), 215-47.

[156] Letters to the Council (CS 8:125-30) and Preachers (CS 8:131-34) of Nürnberg, July 18, 1542. On the possibility of a visit by Schwenckfeld to the city in 1529 see Schmid (216) versus Weigelt, *Spiritualistische Tradition*, 105.

[157] Schmid, 216-28.

[158] Ibid., 233-34.

[159] On this episode see Ibid., 226-27.

[160] On Schwenckfeld's advice to continue attending the local church see CS 11:802.

[161] See Karl Schottenloher, 'Der Pforzheimer Buchdrucker Georg Rab und die beschlagnahmte Postille des Schwenckfeldjungers Johann Werner 1558,' *Zeitschrift für die Geschichte des Oberrheins*, 42 (1928), 400-11. On the events in Nürnberg see Schmid, 228.

[162] Schmid, 228-36.

[163] One jurist complained, 'so weren doch derselben secten laider vil hie, also do mans alle hinaujagen wolt, das meine herren ein grosses loch in die stat machen müsten' (cited by Schmid, 233-34). In 1565, the preacher Johann Schelhamer had complained that there were a great number of burgers participating in the conventicles (Schmid, 236). Neither gave precise figures, but it is probable that we are talking about dozens, but not hundreds of followers.

[164] Schmid (247) emphasizes the class and wealth of the Schwenkfelders as the cause of their gentle handling. But had they threatened the order and peace of the city they would not have been so treated. See the Council's 'Abschied' for Schechner, where his exemplary behavior as a citizen is cited (Schmid, 242, fn. 163). To be sure, one of the major attractions of Schwenkfeldianism was its ability to offer religious radicalism while maintaining a conservative social and political outlook.

[165] That is not to say that Clasen's speculations, 'Schwenckfeld's Friends,' 66-69, would not also be accurate.

[166] CS 4:658-746.

[167] Schwenckfeld's involvement in the christological controversies and his departure from Ulm made him more intransigent and inclined to publish his more polemical works.

[168] For the information on the locations and numbers of Schwenckfeld's extant works consult the 'Bibliography' to the individual works in CS. Schultz (309) refers to the period 1544-1558 as 'An Era of Publications.' Fifty works were published in 1544-1550 alone.

[169] The authorities in Stuttgart were cognizant of this aspect of Schwenkfeldianism. See 'Ordnung der Widerteufer und anderer sectarien usser der manuduction gezogen,' after July 25, 1558, QGT 1:1022-1047. Especially 1034.34-41:'Als gleichwol die personen, so mit solcher secten behaft, esserlich mit irem leben in politia gemeinlich nit ein bösen schein füren, aber doch eusserlich mit ir mainung und opinion, reden und ler wider die rainen sacramenten und des ministerii blasphemieren.'

170 CS 4:850-87.

171 CS 4:869.39-871.17.

172 On the various editions and Schwenckfeld's gift to the presidents of the
Synod see CS 4:850-53. On Blaurer's reaction see his letter to Bucer
(Dec. 23, 1533, Schiess 1:452).

173 See Lucian Febvre 'Une question mal posée, Les origines de la réforme
français,' *Au coeur du XVIe siècle* (Paris, 1957), 1-70, for a discussion
of the motives of the middle class in accepting the Reform. See also
Natalie Davis, 'Strikes and Salvation at Lyons,' *Archiv für Reformationsgeschichte* 56 (1965), 45-64, on the printers of Lyon for much the
same appraisal.

174 For an example see Schultz, 176.

175 This is especially clear in his correspondence with Katharina Streicher,
e.g., May 24, 1538 (CS 6:68-78). See also Joyce Irwin, *Womanhood in
Radical Protestantism 1525-1675* (New York, 1979), 27-28, 136-39.

176 See Natalie Davis, 'City Women and Religious Change in Sixteenth Century France,' in Dorothy G. McGuigan (ed.), *A Sampler of Women's
Studies*, 18-45; Miriam Chrisman Usher, 'Women and the Reformation
in Strassburg 1490-1530,' ARG 63 (1972). 143-68; Nancy L. Roelker,
'The Appeal of Calvinism to French Noblewomen in the Sixteenth Century.' *Journal of Interdisciplinary History* (1972), 391-413.

177 Note, for example, the widows: Katharina Zell, Helena Streicher the Elder, Ursula Thumb; 'Jungfrauen': Katharina Streicher, Helena Streicher
the Younger, Agatha Streicher. Schwenckfeld seemed to get along well
with nuns as well: see Gottfried Maron, *Individualismus und Gemeinschaft bei Caspar Schwenckfeld* (Stuttgart, 1961), 94-95. In a letter to
Sibilla Eisler (April 1547) he writes: 'Es ist den leuten seltzam/ das
die junckfrawen alle unverheuerat bleiben/ welchs die welt/ die auch
sonst aller unzucht ausser dem Ehstande vol steckt/ gar uebel kan lei-
den/ wir wellen aber noch erleben/ das vil frommer junckfrawen und
witwen/ sich dem herrn werden auffopffern und ergeben' (CS 11:13.9-
12). The margin has 'Vom keueschen ledigen Stannde etc.: Von witwen
und junckfrawen stand/ und vom stillstande beim heueratten.'

178 Jakob Held had problems with his wife (CS 11:516), and Georg Schechner with his (Schmid, 226-27).

179 On the use of the *Bekanntnuss der Sünden* see CS 17: 59.30-60.1. On
fasting, prayer meetings and revelations see CS 4: 78.14-29.

180 Karl Ecke, *Schwenckfeld, Luther und der Gedanke einer apostolischen
Reformation* (Berlin, 1911), 228-29; Schmid, 228.

181 Especially in Luther's early emphasis on the home as the school of piety
(Gerald Strauss, *Luther's House of Learning* [Baltimore and London,
1978], 4-5.

182 An excellent study is Peter C. Erb, 'Christian Hoburg und Schwenckfeldische Würzeln des Pietismus, einige bisher unveröffentliche Briefe,'
Jahrbuch für schlesische Kirchengeschichte, 56 (1977), 92-126. But the

exact relationship between Schwenkfeldianism and Pietism has yet to be established. Cf. Egon W. Gerdes, 'Pietistisches bei Kaspar von Schwenckfeld,' *Miscellanea Historiae Ecclesiasticae. Bibliotheque de la Revue d'Histoire Ecclesiastique*, fasc. 44 (Louvain 1967), 105-37.

Schwenckfeld and the South German Eucharistic Controversy, 1526-1529

R. Emmet McLaughlin

In a letter dated December 31, 1525 Martin Luther bewailed the spreading controversy over the eucharist.

> This error concerning the sacrament has three sects agreeing in one understanding (*in uno sensu*). Zwingli proceeds with other arguments than Carstadt's. With yet other arguments the Silesian Valentine [disagrees] with both of them and everyone else.[1]

A few days later, in his letter to Reutlingen, Luther explained: 'This sect already has three heads, for they agree that in the sacrament there is mere bread and wine, but they disagree as to the reason why and as to the proof that it must be so.'[2] The Wittenberg reformer wrote under the immediate impact of a visit (Nov. 30 to Dec. 4) from the Silesian nobleman Caspar Schwenckfeld von Ossig (1489-1561), whose friend and colleague, Valentine Crautwald (1490-1545), was Luther's 'third head.'[3] Though Luther would add other 'heads' to his list, he never lost sight of the Silesians. They would be prominent in all his eucharistic writings from the 1526 'Forward' to the *Schwabischen Syngramma*, to the 1528 *Confession*.[4] His last word on the matter, and on Schwenckfeld personally, came at the end of 1543.[5] Still later in the century the authors of the *Formula of Concord* felt compelled to single out Schwenckfeld and his teachings for condemnation.[6] Despite this, and despite the obvious importance (as we shall see) which the leaders of the Swiss and South German churches placed upon the Silesians and their views, the role of Schwenckfeld and his eucharistic position in the controversies of the later 1520s has generally been ignored. The sole exception is Walther Koehler's massive, *Zwingli und Luther*. Koehler was impressed again and again by Schwenckfeld's acumen, and his ability to anticipate later issues.[7] But even Koehler's treatment is marred by his faulty

understanding of the nature and development of Schwenckfeld's eucharistic teaching. In correcting that misperception
new light is cast on the course of the controversy, the nature
and composition of the competing parties, and the place which
Schwenckfeld himself held in the early Reformation movement.

Through June 1524 Caspar Schwenckfeld had been a loyal
and enthusiastic follower of Martin Luther.[8] Beginning in 1519
after a personal religious crisis (*Heimsuchung*), Schwenckfeld
had been instrumental in the reform movement's successes in
his native Silesia. A member of a long-established noble family,
from his position at the court of Friedrich II of Liegnitz (1480-
1547) and through his own personal preaching and evangeliz-
ing, Schwenckfeld had played a central role in the Protestant
triumph during 1524. By the summer of 1525, however, he
was clearly dissatisfied with the moral fruits of that victory.
Immorality was rife in Protestant Silesia. At first Schwenckfeld thought that this was but a passing phenomenon, that
the reform had not yet had time to take effect, reasoning that
even Christ had not been able to mend men's lives in his three-
year ministry.[9] But then Schwenckfeld became convinced that
there was something in the Protestant message itself that was
producing these untoward results.[10] The controversy between
Luther on the one side and Carlstadt and Zwingli on the other
focussed Schwenckfeld's attention on the eucharist.

In July or August 1525 Schwenckfeld produced a document
which marks the beginning of Schwenckfeld's own doctrine of
the eucharist.[11] Composed of twelve 'Questiones,' it was based
on John 6:54-56: 'He who eats my flesh and drinks my blood
has eternal life, and I will raise him up at the last day. For
my flesh is food indeed, and my blood is drink indeed. He who
eats my flesh and drinks my blood abides in me and I in him.'
If these words were applied to the eucharist, Schwenckfeld argued, then anyone who received the bread and wine would be
saved. And in point of fact, Schwenckfeld had found that many
Lutherans did believe that their sins were forgiven by partaking
of the eucharist. Here was a source of the immorality and lack
of religious fervor. For if these words concerning the life-giving
flesh and blood had actually applied to the bread and wine of
the eucharist, too many anomalies would have resulted. It was
clear that many who received the bread and wine showed no
visible improvement, and this would have been impossible if

they had abided in Christ and he in them. The clearest example of the untenability of the real physical presence (and that is what Schwenckfeld was arguing against), was to be found in the case of Judas. He had shared the bread and wine, but it was the devil and not Christ who had entered into him. And one can scarcely believe that he obtained eternal life. All those who partake of Christ's body and blood in any fashion must be saved, for otherwise one must assume that the body was in some way separable from the Word, the living Word of God, the Logos. This last point was directed at the 'Impanationists' like Luther who distinguished two eatings in the sacrament, one for the unworthy and one for the faithful.

Schwenckfeld makes no use of the classic Zwinglian proof-text John 6:63, 'It is the spirit that gives life, the flesh is of no avail.' On the contrary, Schwenckfeld argues from the indispensability of the flesh, Christ's flesh. The entire economy of salvation is bound to that flesh and blood, and the Christian's participation in it constitutes salvation. Luther's theology of justification owes much to the theology and practice of the Catholic sacrament of penance. Schwenckfeld's is based upon the eucharistic experience.

Given the power of Christ's glorified body and blood, it could not be contained in the bread and wine. Instead, it must be given directly to believers in a spiritual manner through faith. In a sense, participation in Christ's body and blood is the objective basis for the subjective experience of faith. This inner spiritual eucharist is the true sacrament. The eating of the bread and wine is but an external adumbration of the inward experience. Although in the twelve 'Questiones' Schwenckfeld assumes that by and large the inner eucharist is coordinated with the outward ceremony, it is clear that the bond is tenuous.[12]

At the heart of Schwenckfeld's attack on the real presence is a strong positive theology of the eucharist. It is clear that it does not derive from Zwingli or Carlstadt, though Schwenckfeld knew the works of both and often used their arguments. In many ways it is closer to Luther's own thought on the matter, especially in its christology. Without assuming a single specific source, it is still safe to say that Schwenckfeld's teaching on the eucharist arose out of late medieval eucharistic piety, the piety of a Thomas a Kempis, a Wessel Gansfort, an Erasmus, or the early Luther.[13] Luther's own insistence on a real presence, however defined, owes more than a little to that same tradition.

But having solved to his own satisfaction the question of what the eucharist was Schwenckfeld had still to deal with the words of institution, 'Hoc est corpus meum.' From the beginning he rejected both Carlstadt's and Zwingli's treatments.[14] He himself was not greatly concerned with that phase of the controversy.

> I didn't let the words: 'Hoc est corpus meum,' trouble me. I was fortified beforehand with the... reasons from the sixth chapter of John.... The little word in the supper [must be] judged by all of Scripture, and not the whole of Scripture... by that little word.[15]

Schwenckfeld turned to Valentine Crautwald, a tri-lingual humanist, in order to dispose of this technical problem. Though Crautwald was still Lutheran with regard to the eucharist, he was persuaded by Schwenckfeld's arguments. In turn, in the process of pondering the applicable texts, he was granted a revelation as to their proper interpretation.[16]

> II. The words of the Lord's Supper ought to be studied in conjunction and compared with those words of Christ in John VI.[:56], 'My flesh is truly a food.'
> III. 'This is my body [Lk. 22:19]' is the same as 'My flesh is truly a food.' And 'This cup is the New Testament etc.' [Lk. 22:20] is the same as 'My blood is truly a drink [John 6:56].'
> IIII. Therefore, 'This is my body which is given for you [Lk. 22:29]' must be understood in this way: 'My body which is given for you is this, a bread.' What sort of bread it is, is shown by the words 'given for you.' It is the body of Christ.... If you invert the words the problem is explained. 'The bread which I will give is my flesh [John 6:52].'[17]

Crautwald had provided a exegetical counterpart to Schwenckfeld's theology of the eucharist. And it was this exegesis which Luther would seize upon to describe the new sect. Hence Crautwald was cited as its head. Interestingly, Schwenckfeld was not fully convinced of the validity of Crautwald's interpretation at the time of the Wittenberg visit.[18] His 'conversion' only came sometime in the first half of 1526.[19]

These then were the bare bones of the Schwenckfeld position: emphasis on John 6:54-56 and the centrality of Christ's glorified flesh; the problem of the unworthy recipient and the case of Judas; the clear distinction between a real inner eucharist and the outward bread and wine; and Crautwald's exegesis. In his emphasis on the real, though spiritual participation in Christ's body and blood, in his concern for the problem of the unworthy recipient,[20] and his clear distinction between the inner and the outer eucharists, Schwenckfeld clearly belonged to the developing Reformed tradition, much of which he anticipated, though his emphasis on distinguishing inner and outer would push him over the line into spiritualism.[21] On the other hand, his devotion to the glorified Christ placed him closer to both the Catholics and the Lutherans, and would eventuate in a christology which alienated the Swiss and South Germans alike.[22]

Koehler's treatment of Schwenckfeld's eucharistic position is flawed by his failure to recognize a 1529 publication as the original 1525 'Questiones.'[23] Instead of placing them at the beginning of Schwenckfeld's development he places them at the end.[24] As a result Koehler, like Luther, places more emphasis upon Crautwald's exegesis than upon the positive theology which underlay it. He also misses some evidence of Schwenckfeld's impact in Switzerland and South Germany.[25] More importantly, Schwenckfeld's relationship to the South Germans, the development of a middle way position,[26] and the configuration of the parties to the eucharistic controversy, are all altered in a subtle yet significant way.

When Schwenckfeld left Wittenberg in December 1525 he had promised to forward further explanations of the Silesian position. Though, as we have seen, Luther was already condemning them in letters to third parties at the end of December, it was not till the following April that the Wittenbergers notified Schwenckfeld and Crautwald of their disapproval.[27] But already before that date the Liegnitz reformers were reaching out to the rest of Silesia and the South by means of letters and messengers. One of these letters to the South has survived. It is from Crautwald to Dominicus Schleupner (before

April 8, 1526), a personal friend now a preacher in Nürnberg.[28]
From its contents it is clear that there had been an ongoing exchange of letters and treatises, and that Nürnberg and Liegnitz
were well-informed concerning each other's thought. The Silesians were particularly pleased by the Nürnberger 'Ratschlag'
(1525) which had been forwarded by Schleupner.[29] Composed
primarily by Osiander, and published without the permission
of the Nürnberg Rat, the 'Ratschlag,' does show striking resemblances to the Liegnitz position. Osiander emphasized the
importance of Christ's indwelling in the faithful man by means
of the Holy Spirit. Citing John 6:35 and John 6:56, Osiander
sees faith as the sole and sufficient means of partaking Christ's
body and blood. The bread and the wine are mere symbols
and reminders.[30]

Schwenckfeld and Crautwald were so impressed by the
Nürnberg pamphlet that they placed themselves at the orders
of their southern colleagues. They all agreed on the disas-
trous nature of the schism and the need to bind the church together through use of the eucharist, the ban, and rigorous cate-
chization of the faithful.[31] Interestingly, neither Crautwald nor
Schwenckfeld seemed disturbed by Osiander's forceful if confused attack on the spiritualism of Müntzer and Carlstadt.[32]
Though Osiander was later (1527) to deny his adherence to
the anti-Lutheran position, doubts concerning his reliability
called forth a Lutheran reaction.[33] In 1526 Pastor Andreas
Flam of Stoeckelsberg near Nürnberg published an attack on
those who denied the real presence, and a prominent place
was reserved for the Liegnitz position.[34] Though Osiander re-
entered the Lutheran fold, Schwenckfeld would continue to cite
the 'Ratschlag' with approval.[35]

What should we make of all this? The 'Ratschlag' was written sometime before December 10, 1524, that is, before the eucharistic controversy and the various parties had really taken
shape. Osiander himself would not really address the issues until 1527.[36] In the interim, Osiander might attack Zwingli in unpublished sermons and Zwingli's works might be banned, but
if the 'Ratschlag' is any indication, the Nürnberg reformer was
not yet really Lutheran either.[37] He and some of his colleagues
held a middle position, one emphasizing real participation, but
one not yet bound to the bread. No wonder that as late as 1528

Crautwald could only be suspiciously unsure of Nürnberg's position, and could still count some of its preachers as friends.[38] One could perhaps be clear about where a Zwingli or perhaps a Luther stood, but for the confused mass of theologians in between, it was a very difficult matter. Even the participants were uncertain where to draw the lines at that early stage.

The attempt to link up with the Nürnberger reformers must in any event be termed abortive. The Silesians had considerably more success, however, in their other efforts to make contact with the South.[39] The Silesian Matthias Winkler (Wickler) travelled to Zurich over Strassburg and Basel in April 1526.[40] Winkler probably came from Silesia by way of Wittenberg, since he brought the southern reformers the news that their books were now banned in Saxony.[41] Winkler also brought news of developments at Liegnitz, and the news delighted Zwingli. In a letter dated April 17, 1526, Zwingli welcomed Crautwald and Schwenckfeld, 'Bishops of Liegnitz and in Ossig,' to the alliance against the real presence.[42] Winkler had made him well aware that they differed on the exegesis of the words of institution, but that was of no importance. The various explanations, Zwingli argued, were merely designed to make clear the nature of the eucharist.[43] What was important was that the real presence in the bread be denied. That was where the dividing line must be drawn. Zwingli, Luther, and Schwenckfeld all agreed on that.[44] And it was Zwingli's and Schwenckfeld's steadfast refusal to acknowledge that real presence which bound them together despite their differences. Zwingli's relations with Oecolampadius and Strassburg were also governed by that principle.

Unfortunately, what divided Zurich and Liegnitz was the positive content of the sacrament. Schwenckfeld confessed a real spiritual participation in the glorified body of Christ. This was the objective substantive form which faith, justification, and sanctification took in the Christian. But Zwingli in the process of breaking with Erasmus, and in combatting Catholic opposition in Zurich, had rejected the notion of Christ's glorified body in the eucharist. Any sort of real spiritual presence or mystical union with Christ was also denied.[45] In so doing Zwingli clearly, if unknowingly, distanced himself not only from Schwenckfeld, but also from Bucer and Capito in Strassburg, and Oecolampadius in Basel. And if Koehler is correct, it was

by turning his back on this sort of thought, with the help of
Cornelius Hoen, that the distinctively Zwinglian position was
developed.[46]

The real diffe.ences dividing Schwenckfeld and Zwingli
could not remain hidden for long, however. Both Koehler and
Weigelt see an effort on Schwenckfeld's part either to close the
gap or at least to paper it over during the rest of 1526 and
1527. Such an effort, had it occurred, would have presupposed
an awareness of the problem. But, in fact, what changes there
were, were directed at the Lutherans, not the Zwinglians.[47]

When the important divergence of their ways of conceiving
of the eucharist finally became apparent to Schwenckfeld in
1528, however, it still did not lead to an open break. In a letter
to Duke Albrecht of Prussia dated March 22, 1528, Schwenckfeld touted a 'middle way' between the errors of Luther and
of those of Zwingli. While Luther had ascribed too much to
the words of institution, Zwingli had ascribed too little. The
sacrament was not mere symbol. There was a positive content,
a spiritual eating of the glorified body of Christ, which, however, was not in the bread and wine.[48] But while Schwenckfeld
was cognizant of his disagreement with Zwingli on this point,
it still did not constitute cause for breaking with the Swiss.
Even after this letter to Duke Albrecht, Schwenckfeld maintained a common front with Zwingli against Luther.[49] Like
Zwingli, Schwenckfeld was caught between the Lutherans and
the Catholics. Agreement on the denial of a real physical presence was enough common ground for both to stand united.
Such was the condition of Zwingli's relationship, in some measure, with Oecolampadius, and in larger measure with Bucer
and Capito. And it is significant that in the months following
the letter to Duke Albrecht Schwenckfeld and Crautwald took
the initiative in establishing closer ties with all three men.

In 1528 Zwingli arranged the publication of Schwenckfeld's
Anwysung unbeknownst to the author.[50] The manuscript,
a shortened version of an earlier treatise, had gotten into
Luther's hands, and had formed the basis of attack on the
unnamed Silesian in Luther's *Vom Abendmahl Christi, Bekenntnis* (1528).[51] In defense, Schwenckfeld sent it to Strassburg
in April 1528. It was sent to Basel and forwarded to Zurich.
Zwingli had it published in August. In a preface provided by
Zwingli, he re-affirmed the united front against the Lutheran

real presence and praised the Silesian emphasis on the role of
faith and the spiritual nature of the eucharist. Even the exegetical differences were described as disagreements in appearance
only.[52] Elsewhere, referring to the *Anwysung*, Zwingli praised
the Silesian's treatment of spirit and flesh.[53] As viewed from
Zurich, Schwenckfeld and Crautwald were still close and valued
allies.

The real break came in September 1529 during a face to
face discussion between Schwenckfeld and Zwingli in Strassburg, where the Swiss reformer stopped over on his way to the
Marburg Colloquy.[54] The point of discord, however, was not
the eucharist per se, but Schwenckfeld's incipient christology
of the glorified humanity of Christ. Though Schwenckfeld's
christology and eucharistic theology were intimately related,
neither man thought it necessary to extend their disagreement
to the sacrament. Interestingly. Martin Bucer showed no disapproval of Schwenckfeld's christology until 1535, when it was
again made a bone of contention by Martin Frecht of Ulm.[55]

The conversation in Strassburg led also to discord between
Schwenckfeld and Oecolampadius, with whom the Silesians had
developed a close relationship. This had begun in April 1526
when Matthias Winkler stopped at Basel on the way from
Strassburg to Zurich. One immediate effect of Winkler's visit
was that Jakob Imeli from Basel used the argument from John
6:54-56 and Judas a month later at the Baden Disputation.[56]
Again in April 1527 a messenger from Liegnitz made his way
to Strassburg, Basel, and Zurich.[57] Fabian Goppert, formerly
a teacher at the famed Goldberg Gymnasium and now the
city secretary (*Stadtschreiber*) of Liegnitz, had been sent by
Friedrich II of Liegnitz to hire professors for his new university. Matthias Winkler's reports of the year before had
greatly impressed the Liegnitz reformers.[58] Because there was
no one available in Basel at the moment, Goppert was sent on
to Zurich where with Zwingli's approval he obtained the services of young Theodore Bibliander.[59] Bibliander would teach
rhetoric for two years at Liegnitz before returning to Zurich to
take Zwingli's place lecturing on the Old Testament.

Goppert had brought along some works of Crautwald and
Schwenckfeld to while away the hours during his long journey.[60]
One of Schwenckfeld's writings. *De cursu verbi dei*, was put
into print by Oecolampadius, again without Schwenckfeld's

knowledge or permission.[61] One of Schwenckfeld's finest treatises, *De cursu verbi dei* is a clear and sustained attack on the Lutheran use of the word. Schwenckfeld distinguished the outward word of Scripture and preaching from inner faith and spirit. God's direct intervention must occur before any external ministrations. Internal must precede external. The external never mediates the spirit. That was not to say that Scripture and preaching were to be abandoned. They were gifts of God. But they were meant for the flesh, and then only after the prevenient grace of God had remade the reborn Christian. The treatment of Scripture and preaching found in *De cursu verbi dei* was a perfect counterpart to Schwenckfeld's eucharistic thought. And it was because of its applicability to the Lutheran teaching on the Word in the sacrament that Oecolampadius had had it published.[62] In the preface which he provided, Oecolampadius hastened to deny any intention on the part of the 'learned and pious' Schwenckfeld to denigrate the external word, which the Holy Spirit uses more specially and effectively than almost anything else. He also hoped that many passages of Scripture would now be made clearer, leading to faith and peace.[63] In fact there was nothing in Schwenckfeld's treatise with which Oecolampadius could disagree.[64]

Though Oecolampadius found no occasion in his preface to discuss the eucharist, he and Schwenckfeld stood very close on that score as well. It was always clear that Oecolampadius differed from Zwingli with regard to the positive content of the eucharist.[65] Oecolampadius steadfastly maintained some form of a mystical union or presence. The eucharist was never merely a memorial. And while he would deny, along with Luther and Zwingli, the applicability of John 6:54-56 to a real presence in the sacrament when he was arguing with the Catholics, when he discussed his own views John 6:54-56 figured prominently. According to Oecolampadius those passages could not be used legitimately to prove transubstantiation or consubstantiation, but they did support a spiritual participation.[66] As Ernst Staehelin has described Oecolampadius's 1528 position:

> Therefore, for Oecolampadius the eating of the body was not only faith in Christ's act of reconcilation, but was rather at the same time a participation in the ascended (*erhöhten*) Christ. The participation is first of

all a participation in the spirit; but because divinity and humanity cannot be separated, it is at the same time a participation in the body. At the same time, however, the elements of the Lord's Supper remain mere sacraments, mere symbols of the fact. Also according to Oecolampadius, the celebration of the Lord's Supper appears to give nothing more of the act of reconciliation or the spiritual-bodily participation in the ascended Christ than the 'verbum audibile,' although for many the 'verbum visibile' is a clearer proclamation. The special significance of the celebration of the Lord's Supper lies rather in the community of thanksgiving, in the 'professio' to one's neighbor of being forgiven, and in the strengthening of the bonds of love between the members of the mystical body of Christ.[67]

With the exception of the last sentence, this describes fairly well Schwenckfeld's own position. But the emphasis on the visible community, and the role of the sacraments in maintaining that community, is one that was foreign to Schwenckfeld.[68] Schwenckfeld viewed even the visible sacraments as having a more individualistic and private value than Oecolampadius, Zwingli and, as we shall see, Bucer would have welcomed. In this Schwenckfeld was still closer to Luther than to his erstwhile allies.

This basic agreement on the eucharist, and the growing divergence in ecclesiology, are both evident in 1528. In Schwenckfeld's letter to Duke Albrecht of Prussia Zwingli is criticized, as is Carlstadt.[69] Neither Oecolampadius nor the Strassburgers are mentioned, though Schwenckfeld and Crautwald were maintaining an extensive correspondence with both.[70] And in that correspondence the topic of the eucharist recurred. Oecolampadius was exhorted to restrain Zwingli in his response to Luther.[71] The united front against Luther clearly still stood. Oecolampadius was also asked to exert a moderating influence on Bucer, who had begun his campaign against Anabaptism.[72] Thus, appeared the first tremors signalling the breakdown of fellowship between the Liegnitz reformers and those of Basel and Strassburg. Bucer's and Oecolampadius' concern for a united and disciplined Christian congregation, which was a factor in their efforts to establish Protestant concord over the eucharist, caused them to see in the Anabaptists or any other autonomous group a threat to the health of the church. This was

the earliest and most enduring stone of offense in the estrange-
ment of Schwenckfeld and Bucer which began with Schwenckfeld's arrival in Strassburg in 1529. Oecolampadius' early death
and Schwenckfeld's distance from Basel forstalled the deterio-
ration of their relationship.

Schwenckfeld's involvement with Strassburg began as early
as his visit to Wittenberg, where he defended Bucer's and
Capito's motives for getting involved in the controversy.[73] The
Strassburg reformers had written Luther in December 1524
and followed it up by sending a messenger, the young lecturer
in Hebrew, Gregor Casel, to Wittenberg in October-November
1525.[74] A month later Schwenckfeld arrived. Both Strassburg
and Liegnitz were only interested in saving the simple, ending
division and teaching the truth, Schwenckfeld argued. It was
not out of malice or envy that they had been caught up in the
controversy.

Schwenckfeld's indirect contact with the Strassburg reformers may well have decided the Silesians to add Strassburg to
Matthias Winkler's 1526 itinerary. He was well-received and
in the following year (1527) Fabian Goppert also stopped over
in Strassburg, perhaps to use Bucer's and Capito's good offices
for enlisting professors.[75] It was probably at this time that a
correspondence between Strassburg and Liegnitz began.[76] As
we have seen, this visit also resulted in the publication of the
De cursu verbi dei. The year 1528 saw further contact, exchange of books, the beginnings of disagreement, and plans for
refuge in Strassburg should Liegnitz become too dangerous.[77]
As matters turned out, only Schwenckfeld had to take advantage of this arrangement. But why Strassburg, and not Basel
or Zurich? Because the Liegnitz reformers felt themselves to
be in thorough agreement with Bucer and Capito concerning
the eucharist.[78] And they were right.

Though there has been much disagreement concerning the
sources of Bucer's eucharistic position, there is a consensus that
it was a tertium quid, neither Lutheran nor truly Zwinglian.[79]
The arrival of Cornelius Hoen with Hinne Rode's letter in
1524, coupled with the persuasions of Bucer's colleague Capito,
forced Bucer to crystalize his own objections to a physical real
presence in the bread.[80] Capito claimed him for the Zwinglian
camp in December 1524.[81] But already in December 1525

Bucer was de-emphasizing the Zwinglian 'est=significat' exegesis of the words of institution, and at the same time began to emphasize a spiritual eating of the real body of Christ.[82] This shift in Bucer's approach at the exact time that Schwenckfeld was explaining his views to Wittenberg could simply be coincidence, but there is the intriguing possibility that the Strassburg reformers had learned of Schwenckfeld's twelve 'Questiones' through Casel. Schwenckfeld seems to have sent a copy to Luther the preceding summer.[83]

In any event, by the time Matthias Winkler arrived in Strassburg at the beginning of April 1526, Bucer had clearly developed his own position on the eucharist. The *Apologia* (March 1526) is neither Lutheran nor Zwinglian.[84] Despite the opinion of certain 'great men' that the sixth chapter of the Gospel of John had nothing to do with the eucharist, Bucer accepted it as normative for understanding the sacrament.[85] And that understanding included a spiritual participation in the real body of Christ.[86] This positive treatment of the content of the eucharist is immediately followed by a denial that the unworthy participate, though he does not discuss the case of Judas.[87] The bread and wine remained mere symbols and their relationship to the real spiritual eating was left unclear. This was Bucer's position until 1528.[88]

In that year Bucer published two major works which dealt with the eucharist. The first was his commentary on the Gospel of John. His treatment of the sixth chapter could have been written by Schwenckfeld so close is it to the Silesian's own position.[89] Based upon John 6:54-56, if Luther's eucharistic theology were correct, everyone who received the bread and wine would be saved.[90] There is a two-fold eating, and just as bread feeds the body, so does Christ's body and blood feed the soul. It is the nourishment of the spiritual inner man. This inner bread must precede the outer meal. The inner bread cannot be conveyed by the outer, nor can it be offered by the word, as the Lutherans asserted.[91] But God can co-operate or work in parallel with the outward action, so that the body of Christ or the Word of God is poured into the Christian as the sacrament is performed or the sermon preached.[92] It was this 'cooperatio' in Bucer's thought that made possible a significant shift.

As we have seen, the appearance of Luther's *Vom Abendmahl Christi, Bekenntnis* caused great concern in both Silesia

and South Germany. Schwenckfeld's *Anwysung* was circulated
in response. Bucer's *Vergleichung D. Luthers und sein gegen-
theyls vom Abentmal Christi* (Aug.   1528) was his reply to
Luther's onslaught.[93] At one and the same time it shows Bucer
to have been in full agreement with Schwenckfeld on the eucharist, while anticipating the issues which would eventually
separate them. This time Bucer even used the case of Judas
when discussing the unworthy.[94] He went further by explicitly
defending the Silesians, and in the process borrowed extensively from the *Anwysung*.[95] He explained the Silesian exegesis
of the words of institution in a way which Schwenckfeld would
have approved, and which properly played down the importance of that part of the controversy for Schwenckfeld.[96]

But while tightening the bonds uniting him to the opponents of the Lutheran real presence, Bucer also extended an
olive branch to Luther. In the *Vom Abendmahl Christi, Bekenntnis* Luther had developed his concept of a 'unio sacramentalis,' in part as an effort at concord.[97] Bucer had immediately
seized upon it and made his own effort to narrow the gap.[98]
In the 'unio sacramentalis' he saw his own idea of 'cooperatio.'
Though this was a misunderstanding of Luther's position, it
became the foundation for Bucer's efforts at concord.[99] There
were strong forces at work here for Bucer. He, and Capito along
with him, had always looked upon the eucharist as a communal
event, a visible bond of charity uniting the congregation.[100]
That, instead, it should shatter Protestant unity had been
a constant scandal to the Strassburgers. This community-
building aspect of the sacrament was foreign to both Luther
and Schwenckfeld, and it now began to mold Bucer's entire
outlook.[101] Ominous in this regard was the work's ending,
where the Anabaptists were mentioned. With the eucharistic
controversy over, Bucer argued, the Protestant leaders could
turn their attention to the Anabaptists.[102] Bucer's interest
in both intra- and inter-congregational unity, and the threat
which the Anabaptists posed to it, were the real motives for
Bucer's departure from the common eucharistic position which
he shared with Schwenckfeld and the Silesians from 1525 to
1528.

The correspondence between Strassburg and Liegnitz in
1528 reflects these issues: agreement on the eucharist and disagreement on baptism and the Anabaptists. By applying the

same logic to one sacrament as to the other, the Silesians felt that infant baptism was incomprehensible.[103] They did not approve of re-baptizing, primarily because baptism as such was of secondary importance.[104] They were truly appalled that the Anabaptists were being executed by the Catholics, and were greatly disturbed by the intransigent attitude of Bucer.[105] They were made very uneasy by Bucer's reliance on Old Testament precedents and rabbinic interpretations.[106]

But when Schwenckfeld arrived in Strassburg in May 1529 he was still warmly welcomed, especially by Capito, who proceeded to publish an apology by Schwenckfeld and provided it with a long preface glowing with praise.[107] Schwenckfeld had been forced to leave Silesia because of the publication of the *Anwysung*. King Ferdinand, overlord of Silesia, and his advisor, Johannes Faber, were incensed both by its contents and its association with the arch-heretic Zwingli. Schwenckfeld took advantage of his friendship with Bucer and Capito and found refuge in Strassburg. He would spend the rest of his remaining thirty-two years in South Germany. In the *Apology*, directed at Friedrich of Liegnitz and Ferdinand, he excused the publication which had been done without his permission, but he did not recant any of its contents.[108]

Capito's preface claimed Schwenckfeld as one of Strassburg's own. Schwenckfeld, according to Capito, had only written what they preached in Strassburg.[109]

> Our brothers here have never ceased to proclaim exactly such a true, living (*lebhaffige*) eating of the body of Christ. And therefore [they] have collated the sixth chapter of John with the Supper and thereby have made clear the intentions of their writings: that Christ alone is known as a spiritual food which nourishes, guides and strengthens the true believers to all good things whenever his death and what followed therefrom are remembered in the breaking of the bread.[110]

· The Silesians differed with Zwingli and Oecolampadius on the explanation of the words of institution, but, Capito argued, they agreed on the positive content of the eucharist and the denial of the real presence.[111] Since Schwenckfeld had had no occasion to discuss baptism in his treatise, Capito did not bring it up. It was a painful subject since both Capito and Schwenckfeld were at odds with Bucer about it at the moment.[112] The agreement on the eucharist was all the more pleasurable for the Strassburg reformer.

Having discussed the Silesian reformer's interaction with the Swiss and South German leaders, what conclusions should be drawn? Schwenckfeld and Crautwald clearly and rightfully belonged in the South German-Swiss camp in opposition to Luther on the issue of the real presence, and they were perceived as belonging to it by both friend and foe alike. But within that camp there were two major groups: those who followed Zwingli in denying any real content for the sacrament, be it a physical eating or a spiritual presence; and those like Schwenckfeld, Crautwald, Oecolampadius, Bucer, and Capito who confessed a real, if often not clearly defined spiritual presence and participation. This latter position was not a by-product of Zwingli's. It was autonomous, substantive, having its own roots in a late medieval spiritualizing conception of the eucharist found in people like Thomas a Kempis, Wessel Gansfort, Erasmus, and the early Luther. It was so prevalent among those caught up in the eucharistic controversy that even some of Zwingli's early Catholic opponents held it.[113] It was perhaps the majority party in the South. It is therefore a mistake to view the competing parties to the eucharistic struggle as basically only two, with Zwingli and Luther at the poles and everyone else strung out between them in various stages of indecision. The third, middle, party was not the product of vacillation, though the pull of the competing Lutheran and Zwinglian position did affect individual formulations.[114] On the other hand, both Zwingli and, to a lesser extent, Luther also experienced the tidal tug of the middle position. Even in Bucer's case the desire for concord did not play a role in the formation of his middle way. But his place in the middle did make attempts at concord more tempting because seemingly more possible. And here I think Koehler, in his desire to trace the roots of the Wittenberg Concord (1536), misinterprets Bucer's development by placing too much emphasis on his irenic tendencies. Bucer pursued an agreement with Luther because he thought that agreement was possible, because they both really did believe in a real participation. Zwingli, though hoping for a settlement, was always less sanguine because he did not believe in that sort of real participation. That Bucer could come to an agreement at Wittenberg, but have that agreement eventually fail, are clues to his distinctive theological position. And it is from this middle group that Calvin's eucharistic teaching would arise. Calvin was not Zwingli's heir.

Schwenckfeld's role in all of this is also clear. Having developed his own position in collaboration with Crautwald, he presented it to the Swiss and South Germans who accepted it as agreeing with their own on the important points. Schwenckfeld was always closer to Bucer, Capito, and Oecolampadius than to Zwingli. His relationship to Zwingli on the eucharist was much the same as the Strassburgers' and even Oecolampadius' to the Zurich reformer. Schwenckfeld's discovery of his differences from Zwingli in 1528 occurred at a time of closer ties to Basel and Strassburg. Owing to the distance separating Silesia from the South these ties could never be as tight as among the Swiss and South Germans themselves, but even so they were remarkably well-maintained. It was only natural that Schwenckfeld should come to Strassburg when driven out of Silesia. His problems with his erstwhile allies would arise from questions of christology and church discipline, not the eucharist.

During 1526-1529 there was a constant exchange of letters, books, and ideas. It is probably impossible to credit one or the other of the theologians with originating their common position, though the use of the case of Judas seems distinctively Schwenkfeldian. What has often been called vacillation in some of the South Germans should rather be seen as a developing precision, a clearer understanding and formulation of an undefined but strong sense of Christ's presence in the eucharist, in may ways like Luther's own search for clarification. Urbanus Rhegius, reformer in Augsburg, was one such theologian. He too was contacted by the Silesians.[115] And by applying our conclusions to his case we may shed some light on his development. Almost all of the secondary literature on Rhegius has been hard put to define Rhegius' place in the eucharistic controversy during his years in Augsburg.[116] He is either portrayed as shifting between Luther and Zwingli, or combining the two in a confused and self-contradictory way. If, however, we take the middle position seriously as a third viable and concrete option, then Rhegius' behavior, though still vacillating, is more coherent and believable.

Already on the eve of the controversy Rhegius held an unclear position, probably influenced more by Erasmus than by

Luther. An emphasis on the grace-dispensing but not-to-be-defined presence of the glorified Christ combined with the need for faith and the consoling function of the eucharist produced an Erasmian/Lutheran hybrid (1521).[117] This was followed by a few years in which Rhegius polemicized against those who would speculate about the nature of Christ's presence in the sacrament, and those who would adore the elements (1523).[118] With the appearance of Carlstadt's tracts on the eucharist, Rhegius was drawn into the fray willy-nilly. Rhegius attacked Carlstadt's denial of a real presence by positing a two-fold parallel working of the spirit and the external symbols, not the Lutheran consubstantiation.[119] It is clear that he was hoping to maintain both halves of the sacrament, though the external symbols seem tenuous at best. In the next year he drew the attention of the Swiss and South Germans who applied pressure and watched his wavering with great interest.[120] In September 1526 he assured Zwingli that the truth about the eucharist was triumphing in Augsburg.[121] That truth was clearly not Zwingli's version, but rather something akin to Bucer's and Schwenckfeld's. In *Nova doctrina* (1526) Rhegius builds his view of the sacrament on the basis of John 6:35-59, not John 6:63.[122] We eat though faith, partaking of the body and the salvation which it offers. In his 1526 response to Billicanus, Rhegius expressly denied the applicability of John 6:63 to Christ's flesh, which bears divinity in it.[123] Rhegius did not now, or ever, accept Zwingli's exegesis of the words of institution as his own.

Rhegius' middle position recurred in the 1527 *Adhortacio*.[124] He was at that time attempting to re-establish unity among the warring Protestant factions in Augsburg.[125] The *Adhortacio* sought to encompass all sides on the basis of the unclearly defined real spiritual presence as discovered in John 6. It was at this point in time that Fabian Goppert arrived in Augsburg. Rhegius, seizing the opportunity, wrote to Liegnitz urging silence as a means to damping the fires of controversy.[126] This was advice which they would follow for a year until Luther's *Vom Abendmahl Christi, Bekenntnis* re-opened the battle in 1528. When Crautwald wrote back in April 1528 it was to someone still deemed a safe ally, and with good reason.[127] The *Prob zu des herrn nachtmal* (1528) maintained the middle position of spiritual eating.[128] In a letter to

Ambrosius Blaurer (Dec. 21. 1528). Rhegius declared himself at odds with Zwingli, probably over the words of institution.[129] He also vehemently rejected a spiritualistic trend in Augsburg which emphasized the inner spiritual eucharist to the exclusion of the visible sacrament. In reaction to this spiritualism Rhegius praised the value of the symbols as pedagogical devices for the 'sleepy' congregation, not as means of grace.[130] At the end of 1528 and the beginning of 1529 Rhegius re-emphasized the positive content of the eucharist, the spiritual eating of the real body of Christ.[131] In his formulation of all this Rhegius was increasingly influenced by the writings of Hilary, one of Schwenckfeld's favorite authors.[132] And these later works read like Schwenckfeld's own heavily christological eucharistic writings. It would only be after Rhegius' move to Lutheran Celle (1530) that he would truly enter the Lutheran ranks.[133]

Rhegius was not alone in Augsburg. Michael Keller spoke much the same language in 1528.[134] And Johann Landtsperger, a Carmelite monk and early protagonist of the Augsburg reform, outlined a real spiritual presence while denying a physical presence in the bread in works from 1524, 1526, and 1527. All of this was based on John 6.[135] It comes as no surprise, then, that in the decades to come Augsburg would be one of the centers of Schwenckfeld's support.[136]

There has been some speculation about the social factors which might have fueled enthusiasm for Schwenckfeld and his message in South Germany. Though he did have a disproportionate following among the upper and upper middle classes, there were people from all stations of life who looked to Schwenckfeld for guidance.[137] While not denying a social factor, there is something else involved. When preparatory to and consequent upon the Wittenberg Concord (1536) Bucer and his South German allies moved toward the Lutheran formulation of the eucharist, there was a large and vociferous opposition.[138] Zwinglian, or perhaps more accurately anti-Lutheran, sentiment was widespread. Schwenckfeld fell heir to this discontent. And the latent spiritualism of the Swiss and South German theologies was easily exploited by Schwenckfeld. He would find enduring support in most every city of South Germany, and rightly so, since he, more than the signers of the Wittenberg Concord, had kept the common faith on the eucharist.

Notes

1 Luther to Michael Stifel (Dec. 31, 1525). WA Br 3:653.

2 Luther to Reutlingen (Jan. 4, 1526) WA 19:120.25-30. By February Luther would recognize five heads (WA Br 4:42.4-11) and in March six (WA Br 4:42.34-48).

3 On Schwenckfeld's visit to Wittenberg, Reinhold Pietz, *Die Gestalt der zukünftigen Kirche, Schwenckfelds Gespräch mit Luther* (Wittenberg, 1525), 1959; R. Emmet McLaughlin, *Caspar Schwenckfeld von Ossig (1489-1561): Nobility and Religious Commitment—Crisis and Decision in the Early Reformation,* (Unpubl. Ph.D.; Yale University, 1980), 147-54; Walther Koehler, *Zwingli und Luther,* 1:197-201. Our sources for Schwenckfeld's interviews, primarily with Bugenhagen, is a Schwenckfeld letter to a relative, Friedrich von Walden, dated May 8, 1540. It is clear that his report must have been based on some sort of diary written at the time of the visit. The text is found in CS 2:235-82. It has been translated in part by Schultz, 75-96. On Crautwald see Horst Weigelt, *Spiritualistische Tradition im Protestantismus* (Berlin, 1975), 64-65; Ferdinand Bahlow,'Die Kirchenbibliothek von St. Peter und Paul in Liegnitz,' *Mitteilungen des Geschichts- und Altertumsvereins für die Stadt und das Fürstentum Liegnitz* 2 (1908), 140-75; Gerhard Eberlein, 'Die Kirchliche Volksunterricht nach den Anschauungen der Schwenckfeldischen Kreise in Schlesien im ersten Drittel des 16. Jahrhunderts. Zugleich ein Beitrag zur Würdigung des Valentin Krautwald,' *Correspondenzblatt des Vereins für Geschichte der Evangelischen Kirche Schlesiens* 7, 1. (1900), 6-16; 'Zur Würdigung des Valentin Krautwald,' *Correspondenzblatt,* 8 (1903), 268-86.

4 'Erste Vorrede zum Schwabischen Syngramma,' WA 19:459.3. 'Vom Abendmahl Christi, Bekenntnis,' WA 26:433.1-437.29.

5 Luther to Schwenckfeld's messenger (Dec. 6, 1543), *Martin Luthers Briefwechsel* ed. by Enders and Kawerau, 15, 275-77.

6 *Book of Concord.* trans. and ed. by Theodore G. Tappert (Philadelphia, 1959), 499-500, 635.

7 See note 3. Throughout the work Koehler weaves Schwenckfeld's development and influence into the main events of the eucharistic controversy. His remarks are invariably appreciative of Schwenckfeld's mental and verbal prowess. For example, in describing Schwenckfeld's conversations with Bugenhagen at Wittenberg Koehler makes such comments: 'Der Schlesier hat Bugenhagen richtig verstanden...' (197); 'Schwenckfeld replizierte treffend...' (198); 'Aber Schwenckfeld treibt ihn hier in die Enge.' (198); 'Hier bohrt Schwenckfeld weiter, und Bugenhagen weiss sich nur durch den Rückzug auf "das Wort" zu behaupten.' (198); 'Diese Lücke hat Schwenckfeld wiederum geschickt erspäht.' (200). In general, in Koehler's eyes, Bugenhagen was no match for Schwenckfeld. Schwenckfeld had homed in on central problems of the Lutheran position; problems which until then had escaped the notice of its proponents (201).

8 For Schwenckfeld's participation in the Lutheran movement 1519-1524, see my *Caspar Schwenckfeld, Reluctant Radical: His Life to 1540* (New Haven, 1986), 22-56.

9 'Ermanung des Missbrauchs,' (June 1524), CS 2:100.8-27.

10 This is most clearly stated during Schwenckfeld's visit to Wittenberg (CS 2:270.37-271.6) and in a circular letter sent out by the Liegnitz reformers (April 21, 1526), CS 2:330.7-25.

11 On the genesis of Schwenckfeld's teaching on the eucharist and its relationship to Crautwald's contribution, see R. Emmet McLaughlin, 'The Genesis of Schwenckfeld's Eucharistic Doctrine,' *Archiv für Reformationsgeschichte*, 74 (1983), 94-121. The document in question is found in CS 3:492-507.

12 CS 3:504.16-26.

13 On Luther see Koehler, 58-59; on Erasmus see Koehler, 49-58, and Friedrich Krueger, *Bucer und Erasmus. Eine Untersuchung zum Einfluss des Erasmus auf die Theologie Martin Bucers* (Wiesbaden, 1970), 202-04. Book 4 of the *Imitatio Christi* is particularly interesting in this regard. While in Strassburg Schwenckfeld may have taken part in publishing the first Protestant edition of the *Imitatio*, though Book 4 was not included (CS 4, Doc. 123). Schwenckfeld may have been directly influenced by Gansfort. In particular Gansfort's *De sacramento eucharistiae et audienda missa*, in Wessel Gansfort, *Opera* (Groningen, 1614), 655-708, bears some striking resemblances to the twelve 'Questiones.'

14 During his visit to Wittenberg in December 1525 Schwenckfeld clearly agreed with Carlstadt and Zwingli in denying the real presence. He also plainly disagreed with their exegesis of the words of institution (CS 2:243.14-16).

15 CS 3:370.14-18.

16 Crautwald described the experience in a letter (Oct. 1526), CS 2:173-209.

17 CS 2:204.9-3

18 CS 2:280.6-13.

19 It is from Crautwald's correspondence that we first learn that Schwenckfeld had finally and decisively accepted Crautwald's exegesis (Crautwald to Moibanus [June 24, 1526], Munich, Bayerische Staatsbibliothek, CLM 718, 384v).

20 Koehler (436-38) credits Mattheus Alber with introducing this theme in 1527. In the passage which he cites (Christoph M. Pfaff, *Acta und Scripta publica ecclesiae* [Wirtembergiae, 1719], 31-35), Albers argues the case of unworthy recipients on the basis of John 6:54-56 and the case of Judas. But that was not its first appearance in South Germany and Switzerland. Jakob Imeli from Basel used the exact same combination of arguments, John 6:54-56 and Judas, at the Baden Disputation (May 29, 1526), *Die disputacion vor den xij orten einer loblichen eidtgnoschafft... zu Baden im ergow irer stattgehalten unnd vollendet* (Lutzern, 1527),

fol. Qiiiir-Qiiiiv. Konrad Sam in Ulm also used the case of Judas in a June 1526 sermon, republished as *Einfeltiger warer und Christlicher Verstand des Heiligen Nachtmals...* (Heidelberg. 1569), 12 or fol. Biiiv. Cf. Zwingli, *Werke*, CR 95:632. Koehler (332, 425, 438) does not perceive their relationship to Schwenckfeld. Both of these appeared after the visit of the Silesian Matthias Winkler to Strassburg, Basel, and Zurich, on which see below.

[21] Schwenckfeld's slide into spiritualism owes much to Crautwald's influence and Schwenckfeld's experience of persecution and exile (See my *Caspar Schwenckfeld, Reluctant Radical*, 57-119).

[22] Schwenckfeld's initial break with Zwingli occurred during a 1529 interview during which the two men clashed over the issue of the glorified Christ (CS 14:99).

[23] The main body of the text is the original document. Both the introduction (CS 3:498) and the final two pages (CS 3:506-07) are later additions (McLaughlin, 'Caspar Schwenckfeld,' 123).

[24] Koehler, 271-73, 760-61.

[25] See note 20.

[26] Koehler (702) on Schwenckfeld and the 'Middle Way' of concord; Urbanus Rhegius and the 'Middle Way,' (712-17); Capito and 'Middle Way' (735-36). Koehler places Schwenckfeld, Rhegius, and Capito in a camp with a growing consensus on the need for concord on the basis of a spiritual real presence. Bucer, as we shall see, was a leading light of the movement.

[27] Luther to Crautwald (April 14, 1526), WA Br 4:53; Luther to Schwenckfeld (April 14, 1526), WA Br 4:52-53; Bugenhagen to Crautwald and Schwenckfeld (April 13, 1526), in *Dr. Johannes Bugenhagens Briefwechsel*, ed. by Otto Vogt (1966), 61-62. Luther's letters were an excommunication of the Silesians. Bugenhagen's letter was a sorrowful and moderate parting of the ways.

[28] CLM 718, 289r-298v. This letter is mentioned in Crautwald's letter to Michael Wittiger (April 8, 1526), CLM 718, 306v.

[29] Andreas Osiander, *Gesamtausgabe* (Gütersloh, 1975), 1:319-45. Crautwald admitted not having read the entire 'Ratschlag,' but Schwenckfeld had and was enthusiastic about it. It agreed thoroughly with Schwenckfeld's latest—unspecified—work, CLM 718, 290r-290v. Cf. Crautwald's letter to Johannes Hess of Breslau, CLM 718, 273r-273v. The work was probably completed in December 1524, and published in early 1525. Osiander (*Gesamtausgabe*, 1, 319). Concerning the exchange of books, CLM 718, 289r-289v.

[30] Osiander, *Gesamtausgabe*, 1:340.34-341.11, 344.18-29, 345.8-13.

[31] CLM 718, 290v, 292v.

[32] Osiander, *Gesamtausgabe*, 1:320.22-322.3, 332.1-27, 334.8-14. This reveals how far the Silesians were from developing their own spiritualistic tendencies. Osiander was probably reacting to the activities of Hans Denck, who was driven from the city, January 21, 1525 (Friedrich Roth,

Die Einführung der Reformation in Nürnberg 1517-1528 (Würzburg, 1885), 248-49).

33 The editors of Osiander, *Gesamtausgabe* 2:547-48, n. 62, 539.31f., identify Crautwald as the person whom Osiander accused of defaming him by placing him in the Swiss camp. He had already written Bucer in 1526 making deprecatory remarks about Crautwald's views (Gottfried Seebass, *Das reformatorische Werk des Andreas Osiander* (Nürnberg, 1967), 132).

34 Koehler, 243-44; Friedrich Roth, 231. Flam stole much of his material from Luther's *Buchlin vom Sacrament wider die hymelischen propheten*, Bugenhagen, Billicanus, and the *Syngramma*. He may also have had an independent knowledge of the Silesian position.

35 CS 13:778; 15:146.

36 Seebass, 118.

37 Seebass, 117.

38 Crautwald to Capito (June 29, 1528), QGT 7:165.

39 On Silesian contacts with the South, Weigelt, 77-93.

40 Winkler/Wickler (both names appear in the correspondence) carried a letter from Capito dated April 4, 1526 (CR 95, no. 465) and one from Oecolampadius dated April 9, 1526 (CR 95, no. 466). Weigelt (78) seems to have overlooked the Capito letter.

41 Oecolampadius to Zwingli, CR 95:559.8-14. Winkler was also travelling in the company of Erhard Hegenwald, a Swiss who was returning from from Wittenberg with a new doctorate. Might Winkler have been the messenger who carried Schwenckfeld's and Crautwald's works to Wittenberg (Weigelt, 71)? That could explain why the Wittenberg theologians only wrote to Liegnitz in April.

42 CR 95:567-70, no. 470.

43 CR 95:568.17-569.9.

44 WA 19:25.3 and Koehler:181-82. For Schwenckfeld, CS 2: 249.16-25.

45 In 'Ein klare underrichtung vom Nachtmal Christi,' (1526), Zwingli rejects both the glorified body and any idea of eating the real body 'modo quodam ineffabili' (Zwingli, *Werke* (Schuler and Schulthess (Zurich, 1828-1842) 2,1:454). In his letter to Theobaldus Billicanus (1526) Zwingli distinguished three real presences which were to be rejected: Catholic transsubstantiation, Lutheran consubstantiation, and participation in Christ's glorified body (*Werke*, 3:652).

46 Koehler, 66.

47 Koehler (457-58) perceived a de-emphasis of the peculiar Crautwaldian interpretation of the words of institution, and a general accommodation to Zwingli. Weigelt (86) pointed to a subtle shift in which instead of referring to a 'geistige Niessung des Leibs und Bluts des erhöhten Christus,' Schwenckfeld spoke of a spiritual eating of the body and blood of the Logos. As for the exegetical shift, I do not find it. But it would not be worrisome if it did exist. For Schwenckfeld the exegesis was a very secondary issue, a hurdle to be overcome, not a central issue in

itself. The use of the Logos terminology must be seen in conjunction with the *De cursu verbi dei* (1527), CS 2:581-99. Both were directed at the Lutheran position that the Word was in the sacrament. By using the Logos Schwenckfeld brought the matter back from the written or preached word to the substantial word, the Logos, Christ himself as opposed to his message. And that word could not be in the eucharist for all the reasons which Schwenckfeld and enumerated in the twelve 'Questiones.'

48 CS 3:35-60. See especially 36.6-21, 41.34-37, 44.5-22. Schwenckfeld was a personal acquaintance of Duke Albrecht. Weigelt (99) is probably correct in seeing Luther's writings as the cause of the new perception of disagreement between Zwingli and Schwenckfeld.

49 Schwenckfeld to Martin Bucer (July 3 and 7, 1528), CS 3: 77.27-28, 78.10-41. In this letter Schwenckfeld still limits the differences to the exegesis of the words of institution.

50 CS 3:1-23.

51 WA 26:433.1-437.29. On the provenance and history of the *Anwysung*, Weigelt, 93-97.

52 CS 3:4.5-26.

53 'Uber doctor Martin Luthers buch bekenntnuss gennant, antwurt Zwinglis,' '(June-July 1528), *Werke*, 2,2:201.

54 Described by Schwenckfeld in 1554 in 'Ein christlicher sendbrieff vom span und rechten Mittel zwischen der Lutherischen und Zwinglischen opinion imm Artikel des Herren Nachtmals und von vil anderen Christlichen puncten' (CS 14:99). Schwenckfeld rightly pointed out that his views were contained in the *Anwysung* which Zwingli had published.

55 Weigelt, 165.

56 See note 22.

57 Weigelt, 82. Weigelt seems unaware of Goppert's itinerary over Strassburg. Crautwald to Bucer (April 28, 1528), QGT 7: 155, where Crautwald mentions it. Goppert also went to Augsburg, Crautwald to Urbanus Rhegius (April 28, 1528), CLM 718, 396r-396v.

58 Oecolampadius to Zwingli (April 24, 1527), CR 96:100.

59 Weigelt, 82-3. Interestingly, the Strassburgers had also found someone, Bonifacius Wolfhardt, to teach theology. For some reason it fell through (CR 96:170, 224). Wolfhardt was a student of Oecolampadius, and it may have been the Basel reformer who sponsored his nomination. Wolfhardt also became one of Schwenckfeld's closest friends and supporters later in Augsburg. On the short-lived university, Gerhard Eberlein, 'Die erste evangelische Universität,' *Evangelische Kirchenblatt für Schlesien*, 4 (1901), 281-82, 289-90, 297-98.

60 Crautwald to Oecolampadius (April 28, 1528), CLM 718, 391v-392r.

61 CS 2:581-99, originally a letter to the Liegnitz professor and staunch Lutheran, Conrad Cordatus (March 4, 1527). On Schwenckfeld's views concerning Scripture and preaching, R. Emmet McLaughlin, 'Spiritualism and the Bible. The Case of Caspar Schwenckfeld,' *Mennonite Quarterly Review*, 53 (1979), 282-98.

62 Ernst Staehelin, *Das theologische Lebenswerk Johannes Oekolampads* (Leipzig 1939), 394-95.

63 *Briefe und Akten zum Leben Oekolampads*, ed. by E. Staehelin, 2:69.

64 Staehelin, 295.

65 Staehelin, 271-73; Koehler, 124-25, 459, 540-41, 614-16, 682-83. For example, 'Panem quidem panem fateor, sed iam non communem, si quidem consecratus fuerit. Scio, quae sit vis verbi mysterii. Numquam negavi in mysterio adesse corpus Christi; et certus sum veteres doctores in nostra sententia fuisse' (Oecolampadius to Pirkheimer [April 22, 1525], *Briefe und Akten*, 1:364-65. Cf. Ibid., 373).

66 'Das der leyb Christi uns geistlich zu einer speysz, und sein blut zu einem tranck verordnet sye, da er sein fleisch ein brot unnd speysz nennet unnd sein blut ein tranck. Disz brot ist ein zeytland sovil als beschlossen gewesen, und was ein brot der engel, den menschen unerkannt. Aber also sich Christus für uns in den Tod hat geben, da ist er uns zu einer speysz worden, da ist das brot gebrochen worden, damit es, wie es vom vatter in ewigkeit versehen, auseteylt wurde uns zu einer speysz,' in 'Uber d. Martin Luthers buch 'Bekenntnusz' genant, zwo antworten Joannis Ecolampadii und Huldrychen Zwinglis,' (1528), fol. 126.

67 Staehelin, 329. This was not the same thing as Schwenckfeld's participation in the body of the glorified Christ, but it was as close as one could get without actually having Schwenckfeld's christology. Cf. Staehelin, 322, 328; Koehler, 576.

68 For Schwenckfeld's ecclesiology see Gottfried Maron, *Individualismus und Gemeinschaft bei Caspar von Schwenckfeld* (Stuttgart 1961).

69 On Carlstadt, CS 3:60.3-15.

70 Schwenckfeld apologized to Oecolampadius for the delay in answering his letter and cited the distance separating them (Schwenckfeld to Oecolampadius [May 3, 1528], CS 3:62.2-5).

71 Crautwald to Oecolampadius (April 28, 1528), CLM 718, 394v, and *Briefe und Akten*, 2:179.

72 CLM 718, 393v-394r; *Briefe und Akten*, 2:178-79.

73 CS 3:251.20-252.18; 260.5-261.10.

74 Robert Stupperich, 'Strassburgs Stellung im Beginn des Sakramentsstreits,' *Archiv für Reformationsgeschichte*, 38 (1941), 257-61, 267-70.

75 See notes 39 and 58. Interestingly, Matthaeus Zell and the other Strassburg reformers told Osiander (July 8, 1526) that they had not read anything by Crautwald, though they clearly knew of his peculiar exegesis of the words of institution (Osiander, *Gesamtwerke*, 2:331). Did Winkler carry a written work of Schwenckfeld's? Zwingli certainly knew both men from Winkler's oral(?) report.

76 QGT 7:155-56 (Crautwald to Bucer, April 28, 1528).

77 The surviving letters are: Crautwald to Bucer (April 28, 1528), QGT 7:155-60; Crautwald to Capito (June 29, 1528), QGT 7:165-73; Crautwald to Bucer (July 5, 1528), QGT 7:174-78; Schwenckfeld to Bucer

(July 3 and 7, 1528), CS 3:74-82. On the plans for a Strassburg refuge, QGT 7:171.32-36.

[78] In the same letter in which Crautwald sounded out the possibility of exile in Strassburg, he states: 'Benedicimus deum et patrem eiusdem domini nostri, qui gratia sua efficit, ut ea omnia, quae Schwenckfeldius atque ego fraternitatis vestrae miserimus et scripserimus, grata vobis fuerint, apudque vos locum invenerint' (QGT 7:165.3-7).

[79] On Bucer and the eucharist see Hastings Eells, 'The Genesis of Martin Bucer's Doctrine of the Lord's Supper,' *Princeton Theological Review* 24 (1926), 225-51; W. Ian P. Hazlett, 'Zur Auslegung von Johannes 6 bei Bucer während der Abendmahlskontroverse,' in *Bucer und seine Zeit. Forschungsbeiträge und Bibliographie*, (hrsg.) Marijn De Kroon und Friedhelm Krueger (Wiesbaden, 1976), 74-87: James M. Kittelson, 'Martin Bucer and the Sacramentarian Controversy: The Origins of his Policy of Concord,' *Archiv für Reformationsgeschichte*, 64 (1973) 166-83; Koehler, passim ; Friedhelm Krueger, *Bucer und Erasmus*, (Wiesbaden 1970). A. Lang, *Der Evangelienkommentar Martin Butzers und die Grundzüge seiner Theologie*, (Leipzig, 1900); Robert Stupperich,'Strassburgs Stellung im Beginn des Sacramentsstreits (1524-25),' *Archiv für Reformationsgeschichte*, 38 (1941) 249-72. Krueger (3-27) reviews the various attempts to categorize Bucer. He himself sees Erasmus as the source for Bucer's position.

[80] Krueger, 152-53. James M. Kittelson, *Wolfgang Capito: From Humanist to Reformer*, (Leiden, 1975) 147-48, points out Capito's own claim to have convinced Bucer.

[81] Capito to Zwingli (Dec. 21, 1524), CR 95:279-80.

[82] Strassburg preachers to the Herren von Gemmingen, in Johannes Brenz, *Frühschriften*, Teil. 2, (ed.) C. M. Brecht, G. Schaefer, und F. Wolf (Tübingen, 1974), 375-84. Cf. W. Ian P. Hazlett, 83, and Koehler, 217-18. Krueger (206-07) sees it already in his translation of Bugenhagen's commentary on the Psalms (Oct. 1526).

[83] Schultz, 66.

[84] *Apologia Martini Buceri qua fidei suae atque doctrine, circa Christi caenam...*; Cf. Koehler, 289-92.

[85] Apologia, fol. Cv or 18v. These 'great men' (*magnis*) must certainly be Luther and Zwingli since the Catholics did accept the chapter's applicability to the sacrament (Hazlett, 75-77).

[86] *Apologia*, fols. C-C4 or 18r-20r; Hazlett, 81-83; Krueger, 208; Koehler, 290-91.

[87] *Apologia*, fols. C4-C4v or 20r-20v.

[88] Koehler, 517-18; Krueger, 209-13.

[89] *Enarratio in evangelion Johannis, praefatio summum Disputationis & Reformationis Bern. complectans... M.D.XXVIII*. The applicable pages (fol. 131b-150a) are also reprinted in A. Lang, 446-63. Cf. Koehler, 733-34; Krueger, 213-15.

90 'Si enim panis Eucharistiae, est vere. realiter et corporaliter, corpus Christi. aut est in pane illo, corpus Christi realiter et corporaliter, omnino consequens est, ut qui edit panem Eucharistiae, quisquis sit, pius ve impius, vere et realiter atque corporaliter edat corpus Christi bibatque eius sanguinem, si iam hoc dederint, sequitur huiusmodi aeternam habere vitam, et in die novissimo resuscitandum in beatam immortalitatem, a qua felicitate nemo nescit plurimos, qui Eucharistiae panem edunt esse alienissimos' (*Enarratio*, fol. 135b).

91 Ibid., fols. 138b-140b.

92 Ibid., fols. 141a-141b.

93 *Martin Bucers Deutsche Schriften*, Bd. 2, (ed.) Robert Stupperich (Paris and Gütersloh, 1962), 295-83.

94 Ibid., 358-59.

95 Ibid., 300-01, 363-71.

96 Ibid., 363-64. Bucer distinguishes between Zwingli and Schwenckfeld on Christ's intention in instituting the eucharist, and places himself on Zwingli's side (Ibid., 371). Koehler (786) sees this as politically motivated, since according to Koehler, Bucer actually agreed with Schwenckfeld.

97 WA 26:442.23-28.

98 *Deutsche Schriften*, 2:312.

99 Koehler, 737, 773-74; Hazlett, 83-84; Krueger, 218-22.

100 Kittelson, 'Martin Bucer,' 175, 178; Kittelson, *Wolfgang Capito*, 148-53.

101 As Kittelson, 'Martin Bucer,' 182, points out, Luther viewed the sacrament as a communion with Christ, Bucer as a communion among Christians. Schwenckfeld would have agreed with Luther.

102 *Deutsche Schriften*, 383. Cf. Koehler, 791.

103 Crautwald to Bucer (July 5, 1528), QGT 7:175.35-176.16; Schwenckfeld to Bucer (July 3 and 7, 1528), CS 3:80.19-81.15. Crautwald also applauded Martin Cellarius's 'De operibus dei,' for which Capito had provided a preface. Crautwald to Capito (June 29, 1528), QGT 7:170.10-14, 171.36-172.2. Cellarius's work created tension between Capito, on the one hand, and Bucer and Zwingli, on the other (Staehelin, 390-91). Cellarius had also argued from the eucharist to baptism.

104 QGT 7:167.14-38, 168.13-24. In Liegnitz they were trying to postpone baptism until the children could at least be instructed (QGT 7:159.30-160.16). But they were unsuccessful in postponing it too long. There was no idea of individual conversion experiences or of an *ecclesiola in ecclesiam*.

105 QGT 7:167.14-21, 168.1-11, 175.25-34. CS 3:79.19-33, 81.34-82.2.

106 QGT 7:170.15-171.23.

107 Capito to Zwingli (May 18, 1529), QGT 7:237. announced the arrival of Schwenckfeld, 'vir vere nobilis. Totus Christum spirat' (*The Apology*, CS 3:291-431).

108 CS 3:408.3-14.

109 CS 3:394.27-395.25.

208   Schwenckfeld and Early Schwenkfeldianism

110 CS 3:395.29-396.2.

111 Capito's treatment of Zwingli and Oecolampadius makes both sound like Bucer and Schwenckfeld (CS 3:396.2-15). His description of Schwenckfeld is quite accurate (396.15-34).

112 See note 103.

113 Note, for example, Joachim von Gruedt (Koehler, 310-14).

114 Koehler's (760-61) placement of Schwenckfeld's twelve 'Questiones' in 1529 rather than in 1525 serves to heighten this impression in Schwenckfeld's case. Why Koehler chose to ignore the *Corpus Schwenckfeldianorum*'s suggested dating is not explained. Koehler (272-73, 457-61) also tends to portray Schwenckfeld's position as either arising from or being dependent upon Zwingli's. Had he given the 'Questiones' their due he would not have done so. Koehler also brings up the idea of a 'middle way' in 1528 (see note 26), while Schwenckfeld had used it, usually referring to a middle way between Luther and the Catholics, since 1524 (CS 2: 621.13-17; 649.4-650.19; 654.4-12). Koehler also tends to view the formation of the middle way as directed toward seeking concord. Yet for both Schwenckfeld and Capito clarity, not concord, was at stake (Kittelson, Wolfgang Capito, 152).

115 Crautwald to Rhegius (April 28, 1528), CLM 718, 396r-398v.

116 Otto Seitz, 'Die Stellung des Urbanus Rhegius im Abendmahlsstreite,' *Zeitschrift für Kirchengeschichte*, Gotha, 19 (1899), 309, 314, argues for Rhegius' thoroughgoing Zwinglianism until turning Lutheran in 1528. Gerhard Ulhorn, 'Urbanus Rhegius im Abendmahlsstreite,' *Jahrbücher für Deutsche Theologie* 5 (1860), 3-34, sees a mix of Zwingli and Luther. Maximilliam Liebmann, *Urbanus Rhegius und die Anfänge der Reformation* (1980), 188, see a mix as well.

117 Ulhorn, 4-6.

118 Ulhorn, 7-8; Seitz, 302-04.

119 'Wider den newen irrsal Doctor Andres von Carlstadt, des Sacraments halb warnung. D. Urbani Rhegii,' (Nov.-Dec. 1524), Ulhorn, 9-13; Seitz, 299-300.

120 Zwingli's 'Ad Theobaldi Billicani et Urbani Rhegii epistolas responsio,' (March 1, 1526), CR 91, no. 77. Cf. CR 95, no. 426 (Zwingli to Vadian, Dec. 23, 1526), no. 438 (Oecolampadius to Zwingli, Jan. 12, 1526); *Briefe und Akten*, 1, no. 327 (Capito to Oecolampadius, Jan. 23, 1526); CR 95, no. 454 (Oecolampadius to Zwingli, Feb. 1526); no. 459 (Zwingli to Vadian, March 7, 1526).

121 'Quod ad eucharistiam attinet, Auguste nihil est periculi. Veritas triumphat, mussantibus nonnullis, sed nihil efficientibus, quippe egregie ineptientibus in re non intellecta,' CR 95: 727.25-28 (Rhegius to Zwingli, Sept. 28, 1526.)

122 *Nova doctrina. per Urbanum Rhegium. MDXXVI*, 34-35. Seitz (309) argues that Rhegius has an almost pure Zwinglian position here. But Koehler (323) correctly emphasizes that for Rhegius something concrete is given in the sacrament. Cf. Liebmann, 188-89.

123 'Quid quod ne his quidem verbis tuto nituntur. caro mea nihil prodest, si patrum patrocinia quesierunt? hec enim sic tracta Cyrillus, Quoniam cum vivificante verbo, caro coniuncta est, tota est effecta vivifica, quamvis natura carnis, ut caro est, vivificare nequeat. facit tamen hoc, quia totam verbi operation suscepit. Corpus enim est non cuiusvis hominis, cuius caro prodesse quicquam potest (non enim Pauli aut Petri aut caeterorum) sed ipsius vitae et salvatoris nostri Jhesu Christi corpus, in que deitatis plenitudo corporaliter habitat, facere hoc potest,' in 'De verbis coenae Dominicae et opinionum varietate, Theobaldi Billicani ad Urbanum Rhegium Epistola. Responsio Urbani Regii ad eundem.' (1526) fol. Cvar. This is surprisingly close to what Schwenckfeld had to say.

124 'Adhortacio ad fratres cenee domini participes fieri volentes. Ain ermanung zu den brudern, die des herrn nachtmahl tailhafftig wellen werden,' (April 15, 1982), CR 96:136-37; Koehler, 564-65. Seitz (315) felt the formula was too Zwinglian to be accepted by the Lutherans.

125 Koehler, 448-51; Liebmann, 199-200. It is not clear whether Rhegius sought to include the Anabaptists, or was using concord to exclude and isolate the Anabaptists as Bucer would later do.

126 Crautwald to Rhegius (April 28, 1528), CLM 718, 396v-397r.

127 Rhegius had given his opinions the year before 'minime nobis gravatim communicaveris' (CLM 718, 396v-397r).

128 Prob zu herrn nachtmal für die eynfeltigen Durch Urbanum Rhegium, (1528) fols. Aiiiiv-Avr (Koehler, 710).

129 *Briefwechsel der Brüder Ambrosius und Thomas Blaurer*, ed. by T. Schiess (Freiburg i. B., 1908, 1910), 1:174-76. Soleo et iam de coena sic loqui publice et privatim, ut synaxeos vim et fructus perdiscant simplices citra iacturam evangelicae veritatis, ommittant autem contentiones inutiles, eisi ipse non sentiam cum Zwingli' (174).

130 *Briefwechsel*, 175. Koehler (710-11) is correct in pointing out that Rhegius had never been a Zwinglian, so this represents no great shift. Both Seitz (316) and Ulhorn (41-43) are mistaken in seeing a Lutheran idea of 'Gnadenmittel' here.

131 'Materia cogitandi de toto missae negocio.' (Dec. 1528), Koehler, 712-17. 'Responsio Urbani Rhegii ad Duos libros primum et tertium de missa Joannis Eccii,...' (Feb. 16, 1528), Koehler, 717-19. Ulhorn (44-45) errs in seeing a 'Gnadenmittel' teaching here.

132 McLaughlin, 'Caspar Schwenckfeld,' 216-19.

133 Even at the Augsburg Reichstag (1530) Rhegius tried to mediate the dispute. His change of environment to Lutheran Celle was decisive (Liebmann, 251-56).

134 Koehler, 719-21. But here again I think Koehler's emphasis on the desire for concord tends to overshadow the positive content of Keller's statement.

135 Koehler, 390-94, 606-07. Max Martin. *Johann Landsperger* (Augsburg, 1902), esp. 49-41, 66, 70-74. Landsperger's views are so similar to

Schwenckfeld's and Crautwald's that he has often been credited with writing Crautwald's 'Von der gnaden Gottes. irem ordentlichen gang und schnellen lauff' (CS 3: 86-98): Cf. Martin. 104. Landtsperger left Augsburg in the Fall of 1527, perhaps because of his association with the Anabaptists, and moved to Bern where he died in 1529 or 1530 (Martin, 76-77, 110-11).

[136] Claus-Peter Clasen, 'Schwenckfeld's Friends: A Social Study,' *Mennonite Quarterly Review*, 46 (1972), 58-69.

[137] Clasen emphasizes the patricians, nobles, and professional people in Augsburg (64), but at Cannstatt (60) it seems that the entire village was Schwenkfelder.

[138] Carl Theodor Keim, *Die Reformation der Reichstadt Ulm* (Stuttgart, 1851), 335-36. When a renewed battle broke out in 1543, the leading Zwinglian, Georg Keller, was accused of following Schwenckfeld and Carlstadt, a charge which he did not deny (350-51).

Schwenckfeld and Leo Jud on the Advantages and Disadvantages of the State Church

Klaus Deppermann

Caspar Schwenckfeld's four letters written in 1533 and 1534 to Leo Jud, the second most important member of the Zurich church, are among the most significant sixteenth century pleas for religious tolerance known to us. Yet, as so often before, Schwenckfeld's engagement for liberty of conscience and a free church was greatly disappointed. On Christmas Day 1533, Leo Jud, who initially accepted Schwenckfeld's position whole-heartedly, discontinued the correspondence and indulged in a totally undeserved abuse and disparagement of Schwenckfeld. He no longer responded to the last of Schwenckfeld's letters sent on March 2. 1534. Schwenckfeld's four letters are pre-served and though Jud's letters have been lost, we are able to reconstruct his thought by examining the correspondence between himself, Bucer, Blarer and Bullinger, as well as by referring to the letters exchanged by Bullinger, Bucer, Capito, Ambrosius Blarer, and Vadian which deal with Jud's disturb-ing development.[+]

The correspondence between Schwenckfeld and Jud dealt mainly with the essence of a true church, with the dangers to which the church was exposed through its association with the state, and finally with the question whether the 'corpus Christianum,' that is, the unity of church, state, and society was justified by the New Testament, or if it belonged to the period of the Old Testament which was fulfilled and overtaken by Christ. This was a burning issue because between 1530 and 1535 church ordinances were enacted by the state every-where in Switzerland and in South-West Germany, especially in Ulm and Constance in 1531, in Bern. Esslingen, Heilbronn and Memmingen in 1532, and in Strassburg in 1534.

In the following, I will attempt to answer two questions:

(1) How was it possible that Leo Jud who participated along with Zwingli in the establishment of the Zurich state church began to doubt the Christian nature of the Zurich position and sympathized instead with Schwenckfeld's notion of the independent church and of religious tolerance?

(2) What influences and arguments caused Leo Jud to reject these concepts and eventually to break with Schwenckfeld?

The Crisis between Church and State in Zurich following the Second Cappel War (1531)

Following the surprising military defeat in the Second Cappel War, the city of Zurich found itself forced to comply with the Second Cappel Peace Treaty and to promise to the five conservative Catholic cantons of Schwyz, Uri, Unterwalden, Zug, and Lucerne to 'allow them to continue in their true, unquestionable Christian faith' and to halt the abuse against the Catholic faith on the part of the Protestant clergy of the city. Furthermore, they were to permit the penalization of the free districts (*Freie Aemter*) of Bremgarten and Mellingen, territories governed in common by both parties which had not remained neutral but which had unlawfully joined with Protestant forces during the war. Eventually, the inhabitants of the Common Dominions (*Gemeine Herrschaften*) were to be guaranteed the right to return to the old Catholic faith according to majority decision.[1]

The city, however, was not only oppressed by the former opponents of the war but also by its own vassals. The inhabitants of the countryside of Zurich, that is, the peasants in the villages round the Lake of Zurich, had disapproved of the war against the Catholics from the start, because they had to carry the main burden. They placed the responsibility for the defeat on the 'foreign clerics and demagogues' (*die hergelaufenen Pfaffen und Schreier*). The villages belonging to Zurich made four demands on the city authorities during their assembly at Meilen on November 16, 1531:

> (1) Their right to veto declarations of war, proposed by the city council; (2) The abolishment of the 'secret councils' (*Geheimen Räte*) and the displacement of important political decisions from the Great Council (*Grosser Rat*) to the Small Council (*Kleiner Rat*), which was more

inclined to conservative and peace-loving attitudes; (3) The dismissal of 'brawlers and agitators' (*Schreier und Hetzer*) from their offices; (4) Rigid controls imposed on clergymen, forbidding their involvement in political affairs and their public condemnation of individuals from the pulpit. The appointment of peace-loving clergymen was requested for the future.

The city was compelled to comply with these demands as stated in the 'Cappel Brief' of December 9, 1531.[2]

The Second Cappel Peace Treaty and the Meilen Articles (or rather, the Cappel Letter of 1531) are certainly indicative of a change of course taken by the magistrates of Zurich. The expansion of the Protestant faith was no longer a political priority; instead, the emphasis was placed on the preservation of peace and on the unity of the Swiss Confederacy. As a result, the expansion of Protestantism in Eastern Switzerland was interrupted, the final denominational schism of Switzerland and a definite neutralization, if not a secularization of this Confederacy came about. This was actualized during the Smalcaldic War when Zurich, despite Blarer's cries for assistance, forsook the south-west German Protestant cities, in particular Constance with which it was closely associated. Within the government, the clergy lost a considerable amount of authority and influence. The anti-clerical trends in the city and countryside which formerly had opposed the Catholic priests now turned against the political Protestant preachers. Nevertheless, through the intelligence and steadfastness of Heinrich Bullinger, the Zurich clergy did not become mere puppets of the council even though the suggestions of the theologians—as in the time of Zwingli—were no longer considered in political discussions. Bullinger's suggestion to dissolve the Swiss Confederacy and to divide the Common Dominions (*Gemeine Herrschaften*) among the Protestant and Catholic cantons was dismissed without delay by the council.[3] Like the Strassburg magistrate following the defeat of the Smalcaldic War, the Zurich council considered the exigencies of the raison d'état to be of a greater significance than religious desiderata.

Naturally, this new change in attitude led soon after to a breach of trust between the municipal council and the clerics. Already in November 1531, it became evident when the

countryside (*Landschaft*) instituted a change in the manage-
ment of the military. Zwingli's friends Lavater and Göldi were
dismissed by their opponents on the grounds of their military incompetence and cowardice and the anti-clerical opponent of Zwingli, Hans 'Klotz' Escher who had rejected any
earlier confrontation with the Catholic cantons, became the
chief commander. Escher swore that at his next opportunity
he would massacre Leo Jud, the war-monger. The severely
shaken preacher hid at the home of friends for a number of
days to allow the anger of the maniac to subside.[4] Like Leo
Jud, Heinrich Bullinger also felt that the peace treaty with the
Catholic cantons was a betrayal of God and the people. At
the end of January 1532, he wrote in a letter to Bucer that
it had been concluded secretly and unscrupulously—without
knowledge of the Protestant clergy—by their 'superiors,' that
is, 'hypocrites and enemies of the gospel.' The devout Protestants were reduced in power and, because of the bloodshed and
the years of starvation, the people wanted peace at any cost
though they gradually realized that they had been trapped.[5]

Bullinger disagreed with the 'Cappel Letter' for the countryside (*Landschaft*) as he did with the Second Cappel Peace
Treaty. On the same day, namely, December 12, 1531, on which
the magistrate of the Zurich clergy announced the appointment of Bullinger as the successor to Zwingli, the Councillors
also addressed the astonished clergy, telling them to abide by
the Meilen Articles which meant that they must not denounce
Catholicism, become involved in worldly affairs, or make public
attacks on individuals. Following four days of consideration,
the preachers explained that they would abide by the laws of
moderation during their sermons but would have to insist on
being allowed to use their own discretion in proclaiming the
gospel, even if it displeased their opponents.[6]

On January 28, 1532, Bullinger held his commemorative
lecture on Zwingli under the theme 'De prophetae officio' and
directed it to the clergy and academics. Here, as well, he condemned the restrictions of the authorities made on the free
speech of the clergy. The divine commission of the preacher
was to correct vices—with moderation, patience, and forbearance, to be sure. Likewise, it was the preacher's duty to
make the world aware of biblical laws and standards. Eventually, Bullinger criticized the meaning assigned to the defeat of

Zurich which was wrongly considered a divine judgment condemning false faith and 'false prophets.'[7] In those first weeks
of 1532. rumours were already being spread in south-west Germany and in Bern that the mass would be reinstated in Zurich
and that people were returning to the Catholic faith.[8]

The existence of the Protestant faith was, however, never
endangered at any point in the canton of Zurich. Despite the
defeat, there had never been a majority consensus in the council which seriously considered allowing masses to be held in the
city again or the reopening of convents. The peasants' demand
for the expulsion of militant followers of Zwingli from the Great
and Small Councils had no sweeping effect. As a result, the
conservative, partly still Catholic-oriented Konstaffel (the urban nobility) strengthened its representation at both councils
but the Protestants still held a clear majority.[9] To the relief of
many of Zwingli's followers, on May 29, 1532, the council rati-
fied the Great Mandate of March 26, 1530 by which all citizens
became obliged to accept Protestantism; to reject this decree
would be to jeopardize one's right to hold an office, one's membership in a guild, and one's rights to the commons.[10] In view
of this development, Bullinger's doubts concerning the Christian nature of the politicians in Zurich were quickly removed.

However, Escher's threat to kill the main 'war-monger,' the
upsurge of anti-clerical feelings in the rural districts, the imposition of restrictions on sermons by the magistrate, the return
of several villages in the 'Common Dominions' to the Catholic
faith by majority vote, above all the expulsion of some radical
Zwinglians from the Council, all greatly shocked Leo Jud. He
questioned whether or not the reformed city of Zurich was really a Christian town and if the majority of the people would
ever become true followers of Christ. Simon Grynäus, a professor in Basel, taught him that the church of Christ could not be
established by the decision of a majority.[11] At the same time,
the Confession of the Moravian Brethren (Unitas Fratrum) was
published in Zurich by Froschauer, the ideas of which concerning true Christian community deeply impressed Jud. The
notion of an independent minority church based on voluntary
association and good church discipline became gradually more
appealing to him. The first indication of this is evident in
his lengthy letter sent to Bullinger at the beginning of March
1532.[12]

In this hysterical exclamation of hatred, Leo Jud condemns the Zurich aldermen, calling them 'pigs, dogs, enemies of the name of Christ, of piety, of justice, community, of the Word of God, and of his disciples.'[13] The church of Zurich is said to be occupied by papists, profligates, persecutors of the gospel who are both secretly and publicly concentrating all their efforts on the destruction of the kingdom of God. Neither the government nor the church teach moral ethics or punish offenders. The righteous and the sensible are driven out of the council daily by 'windbags.'[14] All is confused and in chaos.[15] The church, he stated, was being ruined by the state because the magistrates appointed unworthy persons as preachers; they betrayed the poor and protected rich offenders.

In an effort to produce radical changes, Jud recommended the separation of church and state and the enforcement of excommunication by elected church elders. The duties of state and church are fundamentally different. The state must focus on goods and chattels while the church must concentrate on the mind and soul. Both institutions are divinely appointed and in contrast to the false views of the Anabaptists, a Christian may accept a government position. But the powers of excommunication must rest with the church alone and with its elected leaders. The Church, too, is obligated to punish sinners for offences which may appear trivial to magistrates, as for example, adultery and usury. Excommunicated persons should be forbidden to receive Communion.

Consequently, excommunication ought not to affect a person's civil position according to Jud. The excommunicated should not be ejected from the council, from guilds, or from civil associations.

He also protested against the reproach of perfectionism. A pure church could not be established on this basis, he admitted. Hypocrites are to be tolerated since it is difficult to discover them. But the hardened, unrepentant open sinner must be driven out of the church.

The Jewish practice of unifying the religious community, the people, and the state proves no example for the Christian church since the members of the first Christian community have been ejected from the synagogue and a new voluntary church for Christians has been established through the association of Jews and Gentiles.[16]

Jud was fully aware that his proposals violated the traditions of Zurich and Bullinger's church politics. At the end he did reassure his friend and colleague that he would sooner leave Zurich than conspire against him.[17]

In his letter of March 15, 1532, Bullinger opposed his elder colleague on all essential issues. Unperturbed by Jud's arguments, he upheld the unity of state and church and the idea of a closed 'corpus Christianum.'[18] Church and state are not entirely different; rather both are obliged to enforce the will of God on earth—the magistrate mainly by protecting the good and by punishing the wicked, the church by teaching the mind and by comforting the soul. According to Scripture only God-fearing men in possession of the truth and of the Holy Spirit are fit for the office of the magistrate.[19] The power of excommunication must not necessarily lie with the magistrates, but it is no mistake if they use it. Excommunication does not affect the soul which is the main concern of the parson's office but only the body. According to St. Paul, excommunication is not more than a public reprimand given to discipline the body for having given public offence.[20]

Bullinger then describes the advantages arising out of the unification of church and state for the public mandate of the Christian faith. If the church laws were enforced by church elders without any authoritative power, the church would be weak. No one would consider its disciplinary actions as serious. In contrast, powerful excommunicated villains would create divisions in the church and establish their own pseudo-church. Even if the magistrate would not apply disciplinary methods as severely as desired, offenders could still be accused of having violated public law over which pastors and the righteous could watch.

The struggle for a perfect church was ultimately hopeless. Even among the twelve apostles there was a traitor. 'We cannot change the world from what it was in the beginning.'[21] Bullinger also reminded Jud of the advantages which were obtained by the church through its association with governmental authorities during the Reformation: the gospel could now be freely proclaimed and the true Christian faith could be openly confessed. One must fear that through a change in the articles concerning excommunication 'the Godless who had been forced to comply with the law would be granted liberty to the extent that eventually our freedom of speech, acting, and worship would be jeopardized.'[22] Bullinger persisted in adhering to the old program of Zwingli which proposed to proclaim Christ's teachings in public, to remind the magistrates of their duties, to persecute public offenders and defectors according to the example of the Old Testament prophets, and to warn the pious and summon sinners—especially before Communion—to engage in self-examination.

As indicated by the response in his letter, Jud was not persuaded by these arguments.[23] The transference of 'the power of the keys' to the magistrate should not have happened without the consent of the whole church. He did not demand the perfection of the church but wanted to witness efforts made toward it. He felt that Bullinger's pessimistic philosophy that the gospel could not change the world was a false attitude which contradicted the teaching of Christ who expected his disciples to work as new-borns toward the renewal of the world.

Criticism of the Zurich council was not confined simply to the private complaints of Leo Jud. On June 24, 1532, the feast day of John the Baptist, Jud, as Johannes Redivivus, openly attacked the Zurich authorities from the pulpit. He fervently protested against the Second Cappel Peace Treaty which recognized the false papist religion as a true Christian faith. He condemned the idleness of the city in view of the reinstatement of Catholicism in the Common Dominions (*Gemeine Herrschaften*). Eventually, he expressed his disapproval of the ejection of the militant followers of Zwingli from the council. In the place of these faithful servants of the Word of God, adulterers and criminals were appointed to the council.[24]

Luckily, the Zurich council was better than Jud thought. His criticism did not endanger his life as it did in the case of his New Testament model but only evoked a strong reprimand on the part of the council which criticized him for his 'greatly inexcusable, rebellious words from the pulpit.'[25] Jud's criticism of the council's politics was in fact based on a poor assessment of the political situation, thus indicating the blindness of a religious zealot. In view of the superior military standing of the five Catholic cantons and the threat of opposition from the Zurich countryside, the Zurich council even with the best intentions could have done little other than accept the ultimately quite lenient Second Cappel Peace Treaty and the Meilen Articles. It tried to help the Protestants in the Common Dominions with all its might, but this was greatly diminished after the military defeat.

In the fall of 1532, Jud again made an attempt to convince Bullinger of his ideal of an independent church. The clergy ought not to participate in the establishment of the new school and church ordinance of the 'heathen' council.[26] Bullinger paid no attention to this admonition and Jud himself authorized this new church ordinance on October 22, 1532.[27] Probably it was the only choice open to him if he hoped to remain in the city any longer.

This authorization did not mean a change in attitude. Jud occupied himself with the Anabaptists, publishing the documents of the disputation of Zofingen, and in the winter of 1532-33, he read Schwenckfeld's 1531 treatise *Vom Unterschied des Alten und Neuen Testaments (On the Difference between the Old and New Testament)*.

He planned to write a book in which he would outline the reasons why the magistrate had no authority over ecclesiastical affairs and was forbidden to intervene in church matters, to interpret the Bible or to persecute heretics.[28] Now he opened correspondence with Schwenckfeld in order to learn of additional reasons for the separation of church and state.

In his response of March 3, 1533, Schwenckfeld assured Jud, who was known to him only through their correspondence, that he was completely in agreement with him concerning the hunting of heretics and the censoring of sermons by the government.[29] He supported this claim by referring to the fundamental differences between state and church. According to Schwenckfeld only the chosen people to whom eternal life is granted belong to the church. 'No one comes to Christ if the Father does not draw him.' Therefore, worldly, contrived faith is useless. The Christian church is founded on freedom from worldly influences and on the equality of all its members. The criteria for eternal life is 'the new creation and the faith which are put into effect through love.'[30]

Schwenckfeld places the main responsibility for the mingling of church and state and the consequent corruption of Christianity on the bishops who already at the time of Arius called for the persecution of heretics. The theological error which maintains that the two Testaments form a unit, is responsible, according to Schwenckfeld, for the imposition of religion by the power of the magistrate. However, there is a fundamental difference between the Old and New Testaments. The Old Testament defines the will of God only in terms of the law while the New Testament writes God's will directly into the heart of the believer through the Holy Spirit, which means that the believer partakes of the divine nature.[31]

In spite of the declaration in Luther's *Von weltlicher Obrigkeit* (1523) on freedom of worship, the Reformation did not make any significant progress towards religious tolerance as is clear from the persecution of heretics in Lutheran terrorities. The insistence that there is a close relationship between heresy and social revolution as Luther and Melanchthon maintained since 1531 is plainly rejected by Schwenckfeld. Schwenckfeld does assert an association between the persecution of heretics and the Lutheran teaching on Communion. They both make an attempt to externalize the spiritual kingdom of Christ.[32]

As for the rest, Schwenckfeld states a complete agreement between Jud's opinions and his own ecclesiastical views: neither reformer has an intention of founding the perfect church of visible saints but rather desires only to bar the openly unrepentant sinners from Communion.[33] Both reject the view of the Anabaptists who claim that a Christian can never hold a public office.[34] Both also agree with the notion that even a Christian magistrate must confine himself to the concerns of the world.[35]

Schwenckfeld's hope to have discovered in Leo Jud a friend and ally was soon greatly disappointed. Already on July 5, 1533, only four months later, Schwenckfeld was compelled to account for Leo Jud's complete change of mind as shown in his second letter. Jud had returned to his earlier conception of the inseparable unity of state and church. He admitted that worldly officials had extensive authority in religious matters, a position, he had rejected in his first letter to Schwenckfeld. It also seemed that he reaffirmed the idea stating the unity of the two Testaments. Above all else, he criticized Schwenckfeld's 'separation' from the existing Protestant church. This position of Schwenckfeld was destroying the church according to Jud. Schwenckfeld replied evasively, saying that he never separated himself from any person (he referred specifically to 'person' and not to 'church') who earnestly sought God and loved Christ.[36]

Influences on Jud's Change of Mind

Without doubt Schwenckfeld's embittered opponent Martin Bucer played an important initial role in Jud's change of mind. Bucer remained in Zurich from May 6-8, 1533 in order to persuade the Zurich theologians that they should approximate Luther's position in the eucharist controversy.[37] It is very likely that Bucer spent these May days urgently warning Jud about Schwenckfeld. Bucer saw in Schwenckfeld the cause of all division and regarded him as a creator of sects which had been associated with the Protestant church since the 1520s.[38] The dissension between the two men was already apparent in 1528 when Schwenckfeld warned the Strassburg reformer to suppress the Anabaptists with state authority. This alienation grew to open hatred when Schwenckfeld hesitated to acknowledge that the church of Strassburg belonged to the true Christian community. Schwenckfeld accused the preachers of obtaining more success through the destruction of the papacy than in the moral reform of their congregations. Though Bucer could to a certain extent appreciate Schwenckfeld's position on the *Stillstand* (i.e., on his staying away from the Lord's Supper), as long as there was no church discipline being enforced in Strassburg, he viewed this extreme spiritualism, this indifferent attitude towards the sacraments and the 'literal word,' as a threat to all south-west German Protestant churches. In his opinion it was probable that Schwenckfeld's propagated indifference to the institution of the church would one day result in an obvious contempt for the priesthood and in a separation from the church.[39]

In the meantime, Capito, in whose home Schwenckfeld had lived as a guest from 1529-31, also made an abrupt change of attitude. Because of great misfortunes—in 1531 he had lost his wife and two friends, Zwingli and Oecolampadius, and he was greatly in debt—Capito was no longer sure that his recent spiritualist convictions were right and, at the end of 1531, he again committed himself to the course of church politics developed by Martin Bucer which he had considered with mistrust for four years.[40] Like Bucer, he foresaw the fall of the true church if it

was not admitted that Christ was present in the literal word
of the sermon and with the sacraments. He also disapproved
of religious freedom because it led to the slandering of God's
name and the revolt of the common man. Along with Bucer
and Bullinger, he accepted the unity of the two Testaments.[41]
Beginning in 1532, Capito and Bucer endeavoured to free Jud
from his liberal conceptions of the church and to lead him away
from Schwenckfeld.

In spite of his letter or retraction addressed to Schwenckfeld, Leo Jud appears to have wavered in his views concerning
the establishment of the true church of Christ until the winter of 1533. Still in September 1533, Bucer considered Jud,
his colleague in Zurich, as being an unreliable, untrustworthy
pillar of the church which was made unstable by the corruptive influences of Schwenckfeld. Therefore, both Bucer and
Capito recommended against Jud being given a position as the
head of the church in Ulm or Memmingen.[42] At the end of
August or beginning of September, Jud turned for the third
time to Schwenckfeld for the answers to two matters: (1) did
the Strassburg Anabaptist leader Melchior Hoffman deserve
the death sentence for his heresies; and (2) for what reason did
Schwenckfeld refuse to associate himself with any church. Jud
himself expressed the opinion that Hoffman must be executed
for the heretical views in his christology.[43] Since the end of May
1533, Hoffman was imprisoned in Strassburg and in June of the
same year, his teachings were all condemned by the Strassburg
council which also found fault with Schwenckfeld.[44] In spite of
Jud's change of mind, Schwenckfeld patiently, and with a clear
conscience responded to the questions of the Zurich theologian
at some length, thereby showing that he had not yet dropped
him for good.

The arrest of Melchior Hoffman represented for Schwenckfeld one of the most explicit examples of injustice provoked by
class-hatred: oppressing the defenceless poor while 'the educated only engaged in written combat' without the threat of
any real penal consequences.[45] Leo Jud's accusation that the
Anabaptist leader had denied Christ's humanity and therefore
deserved to be severely punished for his slander appeared totally unjust to Schwenckfeld. Hoffman glorified Christ to a
much greater degree if he attributed the act of the redemption not to our own crude nature but to the divine essence of

Christ.[46] He regarded Hoffman as a peace-loving Anabaptist like the Swiss Brethren who had to this point not stirred up rebellion or disturbed private property.[47] In order to justify his refusal to commit himself to any Protestant church, Schwenckfeld gave the following explanations:

(1) Because of the tie with the state the meek spirit of Christ had disappeared from the church, and church members treated one another in the spirit of Moses, according to the rule: 'An eye for an eye, and a tooth for a tooth.'[48] (2) Receiving Communion presupposes that through the practice of moral ethics and the enforcement of excommunication, an 'obedient body of Christians' will be assembled. Because that was not the case he refrained from approaching the altar of Christ.[49] (3) Luther's teaching on Communion which made the body of Christ a food for the impious is false. In spite of that, Bucer, an opportunist, endeavoured against his better judgment to make friends with Luther.[50] (4) The true baptism of Christ which is an experience of the Spirit through fire and suffering is disrupted by infant baptism.[51] (5) Finally, no one need be a member of an established church for 'the church of Christ is not confined to a location. God is within you.'[52] The church is found anywhere the spirit of Christ guides the people and they are led through pain and suffering to conformity with Christ.

In conclusion, Schwenckfeld again turned to the common problem concerning freedom of worship. In opposition to Leo Jud's argument that religious tolerance disrupts both church and civil law, Schwenckfeld noted that Christianity had developed in the Roman Empire without the support of the state. For examples of societies with multiple co-existing religious convictions, Schwenckfeld referred to the Eastern Roman Empire at the time of Chrysostom, to Bohemia following the Hussite War, and to Poland in the sixteenth century. Common faiths are not at all necessary for the preservation of the people's peace, law, and order. Only when a certain group desires to impose its views by force on others, must the authorities resort to suppression.[53]

Schwenckfeld's long third letter to Leo Jud made an obvious impression on its recipient for the question concerning the legitimacy of persecuting heretics remained a great concern for

him as is apparent in a letter which he sent to Bullinger in
mid-December, 1533. Jud still regarded Schwenckfeld at that
point as 'a man who strove to increase God's honour and who
was uprightly and fervidly zealous.'[54]

The increasing hatred of Bucer, Bullinger, and Ambrosius
Blarer toward Schwenckfeld became evident in the fall of 1533.
To their horror they discovered the extent to which his theology affected their close friends and colleagues. In Strassburg,
the deacon Alexander Berner[55] and Bucer's Venetian assistant, Bartholomeo Fonzio, in Augsburg the pastor Bonifatius
Wolfhardt,[56] and in Esslingen the Reverend Jakob Otter[57] all
committed themselves to Schwenckfeld's party. The influential
minister of legal affairs in Württemberg, Hans Konrad Thumb
of Neuburg, the Lords of Freiburg, the Duchess Margarete of
Grafeneck were among his friends. In Ulm, Cannstatt, Esslingen, Stuttgart, and Memmingen there were small communities
which associated themselves with Schwenckfeld.[58]

When Schwenckfeld refused in his 'Schutzschrift' (apology
against Bucer) to acknowledge that the church of Strassburg
was a true Christian community established according to the
decree of the apostles, Bucer's long suppressed hatred for him
was brought into the open. In a letter to Ambrosius Blarer, he
presented a devastating portrait of Schwenckfeld's character.
He called him a 'timid man who flees the cross, who insinuates
himself into the preachers' favour most disgustingly, abuses
their friendship and authority in order to subvert their spiritual office, who inflates all consent which he obtains from the
preachers, whereas he declines to admit that they preach the
true gospel.'[59]

In October 1533, Bullinger, who was very attached to his
homeland, made the only trip of his life outside his country; he
travelled to Constance to visit Ambrosius Blarer. Both wished
to confer regarding Schwenckfeld's influence in south Germany
and in Switzerland and its containment.[60] This discussion resulted in the 1533 composition and September 1534 publication
of Bullinger's treatise *De Testamento seu Foedere Dei unico et
aeterno brevis expositio*. In his work Bullinger attempts to refute Schwenckfeld on the highest theological level and directs
his criticism against Schwenckfeld's 1531 *Unterschied des Alten und Neuen Testaments/ der Figur und der Waarheit*.[61]
Underlying the abstract question concerning the conformity of

the New and Old Testaments was the issue which considered whether the Old Testament's unification of church, state, and society corresponded with the notion of a Christian community in the New Testament.[62]

According to Schwenckfeld, the promises of God in the Old Testament are associated only with worldly goods and with physical welfare. They were made to the Jews under the condition that they keep the law. The few individual personages of the Old Testament who through their faith were sanctified discretely and secretly attained their blessed state outside the general rule. New Testament ethics are fundamentally different from those of the Old Testament. The Old Testament justifies the annihilation of the heathen with the term 'holy war' while the New Testament emphasizes love of enemies. Those who still associate the extermination of the godless with the establishment of the Kingdom of God are confusing the Old and New Testaments.[63]

By contrast, in the New Testament, eternal life and various kinds of spiritual qualities are promised. The notion of retaliation in the Old Testament is incompatible with the emphasis on love in the New. The covenant of the Old Testament is misunderstood if one attributes the idea of retaliation solely to the corruptive influence of the Pharisees.

Not until after his death and resurrection did Christ gain control over all powers in heaven and on earth, and thereafter believers received the Holy Spirit who causes the will of God to control man to the extent that no outside constraint is required. In this respect, Christ replaces the law. He who insists on the unity of the two Testaments understates the importance of Christ's death and resurrection.

Schwenckfeld, however, was not as radical in his approach as Marcion who concluded from the differing ethics of the Old and New Testaments that the creator and God of the Old Testament was completely different from the God who revealed himself to us in Christ. In contrast, he continues to find in the Old Testament a veiled example, a 'figure' of the New Testament. However, a constant, complete, and clear teaching about the definitive will of God is, according to Schwenckfeld, not contained in the Old Testament.[64]

On the other hand, Bullinger maintained that the Old Testament, like the New, was a covenant of grace, not of works

or law. At the beginning of the Old Testament, we find undeserved promises made by God rather than references to the
law or to the obedience of man. Abraham was declared to be
righteous only because of his faith in God's promises before the
rite of circumcision, without ceremonies, before the law. It was
one and the same faith which was exercised by Abel, Enoch,
Abraham, Moses, the prophets, apostles, and pious Christians
and which bound them all to the true church. The patriarchs
and prophets of the Old Testament honoured God through
their faith and through a pure life, not through their perfect
fulfillment of the law.[65] The formal laws are not the essence of
the Old Testament but serve only as guidelines in faith for the
weak.[66]

This covenant of grace is strengthened and illuminated through Christ but remained essentially unchanged. In Christ,
the Creator of all gives himself completely to the people,
presents them with all they require and frees them from sin
and eternal death. In return, he expects that the people will
call him alone for assistance, that they will keep his commandments, will fear him, and lovingly and obediently honour him.
The statement 'I am God the omnisufficient' applies to both
Testaments.[67]

The divine laws have also remained virtually unchanged in
the New Testament. Christ reinterpreted them and made their
actual purposes relevant after they had been corrupted by the
Pharisees. He did not come to destroy the law of the Old Testament but rather to fulfill it.[68] In both Testaments, there are
sacraments, visible signs of invisible grace, which are important because man does not consist simply of a mind and soul
but requires bodily and sensual fulfillment as well. The circumcision and the Passover of the Old Testament correspond
with baptism and Communion in the New, whereby the circumcision of the foreskin is a prefiguration of Christ's death
and of the circumcision of the heart.[69]

Since in both Testaments, the undeserved grace of God
forms the basis for the covenant of which man is made a part
through faith and obedience, Bullinger came to the conclusion
that the two Testaments form a substantial unit.[70] Yet unmen-
tioned is the notion—which diametrically opposed Schwenckfeld's conviction—to which Bullinger committed himself, stating that the people, the state, and the church form one insep-

arable unit and that it is the duty of the civil authorities to carry out the will of God on earth as interpreted by the church.

As expected, Martin Bucer also committed himself to the proceedings which were intended ultimately to break Jud's tie with Schwenckfeld. On November 30, 1533, he composed a long letter for Leo Jud in which he lay the responsibility for the coming catastrophe in Münster on Schwenckfeld.[71] In Münster all the city churches except Rothmann's were closed and the opponents to infant baptism, namely the preachers from Wassenberg, Roll, Vinne, and Klopriss, had nearly destroyed the church. 'We attribute that to Schwenckfeld and Hoffman,' he wrote, 'of whom that fellow [Schwenckfeld] appointed this one [Rothmann] to the office of Bishop of Münster here [in Strassburg] and the disciples of Hoffman sent him over there.' These suppositions of Bucer were not grounded in truth. Thereafter, Bucer once again considered the notions which Jud had put forward since the Second Cappel War against the state church of Zurich. He acknowledged to him that he would prefer to have the openly unrepentant sinners banned from the church. The shortcomings of the Protestant church in terms of church discipline was the basis for the rise of the Anabaptists. Nevertheless, one could not maintain that without the enforcement of excommunication a true church of Christ on earth could not exist. Considering majority decisions which became problematic for Leo Jud when a number of communities in the Common Dominions decided to return to the Catholic faith, Bucer observed that in democratic societies decisions were brought about by the consensus of the majority. Though the correctness of a decision could not be guaranteed by a majority vote, it was impossible to maintain that truth and reason are usually to be found with the minority. He who considers the majority decision to be false ought to flee from the consensus of the wicked, in the worst case, by moving out of the town. Concerning the main issue, the union of church and state and the legitimacy of persecuting heretics, Bucer reiterates his constantly defended viewpoint: the civil authorities are justified in persecuting those who mock the true teachings. For this purpose, one must firstly establish a public confession of faith to serve as a binding precept for the city. Whoever opposes it should be initially warned and admonished orally. Should that prove ineffective, the erring heretics must be censured humanely but

the unrepentant must be severely punished in order that other
people may not be corrupted. One must sympathize with but
not tolerate an erring conscience, for 'though a murderer be
insane, he is still a murderer.'[72]

Pressured by Bucer, Leo Jud sent his correspondence with
Capito, Bucer, and Schwenckfeld to Heinrich Bullinger in the
middle of December 1533, in order to get his advice for a final
decision. Nevertheless, he begged him not to pass Schwenckfeld's letters on for he did not wish Schwenckfeld to suffer any
inconveniences on his account.[73]

Heinrich Bullinger responded unhesitantly in a letter in
which his dislike for Schwenckfeld was evident. His hatred was
by no means less intense than Martin Bucer's.[74] Bullinger explained that according to the contents of Schwenckfeld's letters,
the author was corrupt, vain, and verbose. His arguments were
weak, tumultuous, cranky, unbalanced, and dull. He obscured
all and put everything into confusion. He only revived the false
teachings of the Donatists (concerning the pure church) which
were not only denounced by the Catholic church but by all
true Christians for more than a thousand years. Bullinger condemned Schwenckfeld above all on two grounds; First because
he (Schwenckfeld) made the declaration ('with unaccustomed
insolence') that the gospel had not yet been proclaimed just as
the true church of Christ had not yet been established. The
second reason was based on the sympathy he had shown to the
Anabaptists through his pleading for religious tolerance; this
man, 'a true god of change, a juggler, and great performer' simultaneously distanced himself from the Anabaptists' theology
though he insisted that infant baptism was incompatible with
true baptism. The fact that in the margins of his third letter to Leo Jud Schwenckfeld had written out biblical passages
which upheld Hoffman's monophysitic christology so infuriated
Bullinger that he would gladly have destroyed Schwenckfeld's
letter had he not, upon further consideration, remembered his
promise to Jud to preserve it. Hoffman who had been assisted
by Schwenckfeld, was no naive saint who went astray out of
ignorance but was a false prophet who through his denial of
the incarnation of Christ destroyed many souls and slandered
the name of God. Schwenckfeld's defence of Hoffman through
subtle, cunning arguments proved that he was not pious in the
least. Jud was advised to break away from this association

with the source of all division and heresy. His good nature was being confused and frightened by it. Any attempt to change Schwenckfeld's attitudes would be in vain since Schwenckfeld was only willing to teach but not to be taught.

After being warned about Schwenckfeld from all sides by Bucer, Bullinger, Capito, and Ambrosius Blarer, Jud finally broke his ties with the patron of religious tolerance on Christmas Day, 1533. Following much mockery of Schwenckfeld, Jud finally added to the conclusion of the letter: 'Because I now realize that it is the spirit of Satan which moves you, I am sending you a last farewell.'[75]

By now accustomed to suffering, Schwenckfeld responded in a quiet tone and in a distinguished and composed manner to Jud's unanticipated abuse.[76] He claimed to be astonished by Jud's breach of trust for he had passed letters on to Bullinger which were intended for him alone. He also had provided no evidence to support the accusation that he—Schwenckfeld—was under the influence of Satan. He also stated that he did not associate with the Anabaptists and only protected them out of Christian kindness. The actual conflict between himself and Jud was based on the fact that he—Schwenckfeld—considered it unchristian to persecute a person of a different faith. Schwenckfeld even concluded his letter with a reconciliatory comment in which he drew attention to the fact that he considered Leo Jud and his friends more 'pious, educated, and God-fearing' than the papists. However, this testimony did not suffice for his enemies. Shortly thereafter Ambrosius Blarer exclaimed to his good friends 'that Leo is [again] totally committed to us.'[77] The reformers had again agreed to engage in a common battle against the Anabaptists and spiritualists.

Because of Leo Jud's short-time association with Schwenckfeld, he was no longer considered a candidate for the position as head of a large Protestant church in a main city of Germany. In his exaggerated assaults on the Zurich council—assaults which ended in an unconditional surrender and in his being attracted to Schwenckfeld whom he later condemned—Jud proved himself to be fickle, irresponsible and inclined toward the irrational. Even his friends could not forget these aspects of his character.[78]

Jud's sympathy for Schwenckfeld's ideas caused this Silesian spiritualist to be regarded as a dangerous opponent who disrupted their own ranks in the eyes of Bucer, Capito, Ambrosius Blarer, and Bullinger. Thereby their hatred for Schwenckfeld became more intense and caused his opponents to agree to a 'concentrated action' which would lead Leo Jud back to orthodoxy.

The permanent results of this debate were Schwenckfeld's famous third letter to Jud on September 10, 1533, which was one of the most noteworthy defences of religious liberty in the sixteenth century, and Bullinger's *Treatise on the Unity of the Old and New Testaments* from which the Protestant federal theology developed.

It is not easy to distinguish truth from error in the two positions. Certainly Schwenckfeld was mistaken when he defended his idea of religious toleration by the contention that there was no connection between heresy and social revolution, and that all Anabaptists—without exception—belonged to the peaceful followers of Christ. At Waldshut and in eastern Switzerland the early Swiss Anabaptists had been involved in the Peasants' War;[79] the followers of Hans Hut had tried to achieve Thomas Müntzer's aims by different means,[80] and in 1534/35 the Melchiorites at Münster and in the Netherlands again proved the revolutionary powers of Anabaptism.[81] Here Bucer and Bullinger estimated the potential for social upheaval inherent in Anabaptism much more accurately than did Schwenckfeld.

They certainly did Schwenckfeld an injustice by defaming him as the patron of the Anabaptists and by declaring that he had appointed Rothmann to the position of 'Bishop' of Münster. Schwenckfeld had in fact seen Rothmann in Strassburg in 1531, but otherwise had had no contact with him, neither spoken nor written.[82] Nothing was further from Schwenckfeld's mind than the extermination of the godless as proposed by Hoffman and Rothmann. In spite of his rejection of infant baptism, Schwenckfeld was not an Anabaptist in disguise. He who rejects infant baptism is not necessarily a supporter of adult baptism. It is also doubtful whether Bucer or Bullinger ever recognized that Schwenckfeld's spiritualism was incompatible with the Anabaptist idea of making the true Christian church appear as a tangible, well-ordered community of visible saints.

Schwenckfeld made an erroneous estimation of the political situation of the sixteenth century when he was asserting the necessity of an independent church separated from the state. In view of the military threats coming from the Pope, the Emperor, and the Catholic princes, the Protestant church undoubtedly required armed protection. Without the assistance of the Protestant princes and magistrates, united in the Smalcaldic League, it would have been wiped out very soon. Perhaps Schwenckfeld would even have put up with this consequence, because he was convinced that martyrdom ennobles man and that the martyr strengthens the persuasive power of his faith through steadfastness in suffering.

One might also doubt whether Schwenckfeld's retreat into small private circles of personal friends was an adequate response to the public mission of Christianity. Due to their connection with the state, the Protestant churches obtained many possibilities of influencing public life, especially in the areas of social welfare and education.

Finally it is an open question whether Schwenckfeld's spiritualism and his disparagement of the literal word and the sacraments (including the office of the clergy) would in the long run have disrupted not only the church but Christian faith as well, because, as a rule, the 'inner word' is transmitted through the 'outer word'—as taught by Luther.[83]

After all, which indispensible truth did Schwenckfeld want to drive home in this debate? It is the precept that the church of the New Testament should be something completely different from the state. As a voluntary, universal community it includes all nations, races, and states, but it cannot be identified with a single nation, state, or political party. The basis of its ethics is the demand to love all men, even one's enemies, whereas the state cannot do without the ethics of retaliation. This love for one's enemies requires that the church should tolerate the nonconformist who differs from the official creed. In consideration of this Schwenckfeld could not acknowledge one of the existing churches of his time as a true church of Christ because they all persecuted each other in mortal hatred. Indeed, nothing impaired the credibility of Christianity in the following centuries more than the attempts of both Catholics and Protestants to expand their own confession at the cost of the other by every means, and ultimately by the use of sword and fire. In these affairs Schwenckfeld was more far-sighted than the official reformers.

Schwenckfeld also realized that extending the definition of 'blasphemy'—which was considered to be a capital crime— would destroy all attempts at religious tolerance in the Protestant church. Hoffman's monophysitic christology was correctly classified by him as heresy, not as blasphemy. The persecution of heretics was, indeed, increasingly justified in Protestant territories by the claim that nonconformists were 'blasphemers.'

Schwenckfeld ardently desired a church to come which was a free brotherly community of reborn Christians spontaneously enlightened by the Holy Ghost. He anticipated the ecumenical ideals of Jane Leade, William Penn, and the German Pietists. In horror he realized that even the Protestant church was being divided, and that in the Protestant state churches faith was giving way to an obsession with dogmas and ceremonies. Undoubtedly, union with the territorial states has hastened and increased this tendency in Protestantism for division, stricter control, and dogmatization of the faith.

Eventually Schwenckfeld recognized in the murky mingling of believers and unbelievers, of frivolous sinners and sincere repenters the main, deep-rooted evil of the new Protestant state churches, paralyzing their life. It was certainly more than a regrettable deficiency as Bullinger thought. Because the preachers 'wanted to drive more people into heaven than God wished to have there'–as Schwenckfeld ironically commented in his third letter to Jud[84] the Protestant churches of Germany could not resist the temptation to comply with the wishes state and society had, even if they were totally unchristian.

Under the difficult conditions of the sixteenth and seventeenth centuries, in the face of the permanent military threat of the Catholics, both the state church and the free church concept of Protestantism was realized at great cost. The Protestant state churches had to pay for the necessary protection of the secular arm with acceptance of the state's intervention in their inner life, the regimentation of their creeds, the wars of confession, and, eventually, with a loss of credibility and moral substance. The Protestant free churches could maintain themselves on the European continent only at the cost of separating from society, by renouncing public influence, and restricting themselves to small circles of the 'quiet in the land,' and very often this withdrawal from society into a 'pure' spirituality had to be paid for by a kind of inner stagnation.

Notes

† Jean Rott offers a report on the correspondence between the Zurich and Strassburg preachers in 'Die Ueberlieferung des Briefwechsels von Bullinger und den Zürchern mit Martin Bucer und den Strassburgern,' in *Heinrich Bullinger 1504-1575. Gesammelte Aufsätze zum 400. Todestag* (Zurich, 1975), 2:257-86.

1 See also Helmut Meyer, *Der Zweite Kappeler Krieg. Die Krise der Schweizerischen Nation* (Zurich, 1976); and 'Krisenmanagement in Zürich nach dem Zweiten Kappeler Krieg,' in *Zwingliana* 14 (1977), 349f.

2 Kurt Maeder, 'Die Unruhe der Zürcher Landschaft nach Kappel (1531/32) oder Aspekte einer Herrschaftskrise,' in *Zwingliana* 14, (1974-1978), 109-44; Helmut Meyer, 'Stadt und Landschaft Zürich nach dem Zweiten Kappeler Krieg,' in *Heinrich Bullinger*, 1:251-67.

3 See Hans-Ulrich Bächtold, 'Bullinger und die Krise der Zürcher Reformation im Jahre 1532,' in *Heinrich Bullinger* 1: 269-89, esp. 278f.

4 See Carl Pestalozzi, *Leo Jud. Nach handschriftlichen und gleichzeitigen Quellen* (Elberfeld, 1860), 34f.

5 'Bullinger to Bucer, Ende Januar—Anfang Februar 1532,' in *Heinrich Bullinger: Briefwechsel* II: 'Briefe des Jahres 1532,' ed. by Ulrich Gäbler (Zurich, 1982), No. 62, 42-45.

6 See Heinrich Bullinger, *Reformationsgeschichte* (Frauenfeld, 1840), 3:293.

7 See Fritz Büsser, 'De prophetae officio. Eine Gedenkrede Bullingers auf Zwingli,' in *Festgabe Leonhard von Muralt* (Zurich, 1970), 245-57.

8 Bullinger, 'Berchtold Haller an Bullinger vom 17. 3. 1532,' in *Briefwechsel*, No. 76, 2:80.

9 See Helmut Meyer, 'Krisenmanagement in Zürich,' in *Zwingliana* 14, (1977), 349f.

10 See Emil Egli (ed.), *Actensammlung zur Geschichte der Zürcher Reformation in den Jahren 1519-1533* (Zurich, 1879) No. 1853, 797-99.

11 See Heinold Fast, *Heinrich Bullinger und die Täufer* (Weierhof, 1959), 32-34.

12 Bullinger, 'Jud an Bullinger,' in *Briefwechsel*, No. 70, 2: 57-64.

13 Ibid., 2:59.56-58.

14 Ibid., 2:62.179-80.

15 Ibid., 2:61.129-30; 'Jam confusa et perturbata sunt omnia.'

16 Ibid., 2:61.139-47.

17 Ibid., 2:64.251-54.

18 Ibid., 2:71.70-79.

19 Ibid., 2:71.20-39.

20 Ibid., 2:71.40; 72.34.

21 Ibid., 2:75.150-51.

22 Ibid., 2:74.122-24.

23 'Leo Jud an Bullinger, bald nach dem 15. März 1532' in Ibid. No. 75, 2:76-78.

24 Jud's sermon is repeated in Heinrich Bullinger's *Reformationsgeschichte*, 3:320-22.

25 See Emil Egli, *Actensammlung*, 'Mandat vom 27. 6. 1532' No. 1864, 805.

26 'Jud an Bullinger,' undated in Bullinger, *Briefwechsel* No. 139, 2:245.

27 Printed in Egli, *Actensammlung*, No. 1899, 825-37.

28 We know of this plan by Jud from Schwenckfeld's second letter to him on July 5, 1533 (CS 4:803).

29 Schwenckfeld, '1. Brief an Leo Jud vom 3. 3. 1533' (CS 4: 747-71).

30 CS 4:753-54.

31 CS 4:762.

32 CS 4:764.

33 CS 4:768.

34 CS 4:770.

35 CS 4:752. See also Schwenckfeld's response to the article on the magistrate which Bucer drew up for the Strassburg synod of 1533; 'Artikel XIV-XVI,' in CS 4:800.

36 See 'Zweiter Brief Schwenckfelds an Leo Jud, 5. 7. 1533 (CS 4:801-11).

37 See 'Der Brief Bullingers und sämtlicher Zürcher Pfarrer an Martin Bucer vom 8. 5. 1533,' in Bullinger, *Briefwechsel*, ed. by Endre Zsindely und Matthias Senn (Zurich, 1983), No. 219, 3:119-20.

38 'Schwenckfeld an Bucer, 3. und 7. 7. 1582,' in CS 3:74-82.

39 See Bucer, 'Scriptum Schwenckfeldio, Ende August 1533,' printed in QGT 7, No. 418, 2:124-29.

40 Concerning Capito's conversion to an apocalyptic spiritualism between 1527 and 1531 and his eventual acceptance of the theology of Martin Bucer, see Klaus Deppermann, *Melchior Hoffman. Soziale Unruhen und apokalyptische Visionen im Zeitalter der Reformation* (Göttingen, 1979), 169-74; 247-48.

41 Capito's conversion is already evident during the Bern Synod of 1532; see Simone Sulzero (ed.), *Acta Synodi Bernensis*, 1532; Otto Erich Strasser, *Capitos Beziehungen zu Bern* (Leipzig, 1928). A precise summary of Capito's world of ideas following his period of indecision is contained in his letter to Jacob Truchsess of Rheinfelden on May 21, 1534, printed in Christian Friedrich Sattler, *Geschichte des Herzogthums Württemberg* (Tübingen, 1771), Supplement No. 12, 3:107-12.

42 'Bucer an Ambrosius Blarer, 22. 9. 1533,' in Schiess No. 361, 1:423.

43 See CS 4:835.

44 See Deppermann, *Melchior Hoffman*, 253-58.

45 CS 4:836. By this statement, Schwenckfeld was referring to the bitter dispute over Communion between Bucer and Luther during which both accused the other of having denounced God.

46 CS 4:835. In fact, Schwenckfeld was inclined to the monophysitic chris-
    tology of Hoffman. It is true that he rejected the Melchioritic dogma of
    the incarnation, stating that Christ did not take on a human body; how-
    ever, when we consider Schwenckfeld's teaching on the divinization of
    Christ's human nature following his ascension, which he supplemented
    by the speculation (after 1539) that Christ's flesh was not created, it
    is clear that he was not very distant from the theory of Hoffman. See
    Emanuel Hirsch, 'Zum Verständnis Schwenckfelds,' in *Festgabe für Karl
    Müller* (Tübingen, 1922), 145-70; Horst Weigelt, *Spiritualistische Tra-
    dition im Protestantismus* (Berlin and New York, 1973), 163-67; Dep-
    permann, *Melchior Hoffman*, 186-91.

47 CS 4:831-32.

48 CS 4:830.

49 CS 4:830.

50 CS 4:841-42.

51 CS 4:839.

52 CS 4:830f.

53 CS 4:837-38.

54 'Jud an Bullinger, Mitte Dezember 1533,' in Bullinger, *Briefwechsel* No.
    300, 3:254.

55 See QGT 8, No. 660; also, Deppermann, *Melchior Hoffman*, 240, 258.

56 See Johann Wilhelm Baum, *Capito und Bucer* (Nieuwkoop, 1967), 495.

57 Schiess, I. No. 366.

58 See Martin Brecht und Hermann Ehmer, *Südwestdeutsche Reformat-
    ionsgeschichte* (Stuttgart, 1984), 239-41. Also see Schiess, I, No. 365.

59 'Bucer an A. Blarer, 19. 10. 1533,' in Schiess I, No. 370. Also see Brief
    No. 374; Blarer repeated Bucer's accusations almost literally in 'Brief
    an Bullinger vom 30. 10. 1533,' in Schiess, I, No. 372.

60 'Bullinger an Vadian, 3. 1. 1534,' in *Vadianische Briefsammlung*
    (St. Gallen, 1903), No. 752, 5:143-44.

61 CS 4:417-43.

62 From the start, Schwenckfeld never wavered on this matter: 'Was be-
    wegt dann die Jhenige/ so nur *ain* Testament machen wollen... [als]
    das sie/ Ihren kirchen ein *unordentlich gemenge aines volcks* haben'
    (CS 4:437, marginalia).

63 CS 4:434.

64 CS 4:429. As regards the early 1530s, Gottfried Maron's assertion
    that Schwenckfeld had conceived of a Christian church hidden in all
    faiths and religions for all times 'wodurch die Geschichtlichkeit der
    Offenbarung Gottes in Christus völlig entleert wurde' is inaccurate
    (See Gottfried Maron, *Individualismus und Gemeinschaft bei Caspar
    von Schwenckfeld* (Stuttgart, 1961), 124-29). His assertion that 'es für
    Schwenckfeld keine Heilsgeschichte gibt' (66) is just as incorrect. The
    difference between the time of the Old and New Testament forms the
    basis for Schwenckfeld's notions of history. Schwenckfeld turned against

a non-historical mysticism, not based on the historical Christ, but developed from the teaching of the 'divine seed' and 'free will' in man as was upheld by Hans Denck. His controversy with Denck can be found already in Schwenckfeld's letter from 1530 (see CS 3:830-34).

[65] Bullinger, *De testamento seu foedere Dei unico*, 6, 25, 34.

[66] Ibid., 28f.

[67] Ibid., 14-15.

[68] Ibid., 36.

[69] Ibid., 43.

[70] Ibid., 28; 'ex his omnibus liquere puto unam esse dumtaxat ecclesiam, testamentum unum veterum et nostrum.... Oboedientia sive ipsa fide qua sanctos probari constat, non legalibus.'

[71] Printed from QGT 7, No. 463, 2:215-17.

[72] QGT 7, No. 463, 2:217.6f.

[73] 'Jud an Bullinger, Mitte Dezember 1533,' in Bullinger, *Briefwechsel* No. 300, 3:254.

[74] 'Jud an Bullinger, Mitte Dezember 1533,' in Ibid., No. 310, 3:255-57.

[75] 'Bullinger an Vadian, 3. 1. 1534,' in *Vadianische Briefsammlung* No. 752, 5:143-44.

[76] See Schwenckfeld's fourth letter to Leo Jud, March 2, 1534 (CS 5:6-10).

[77] 'Ambrosius Blarer an Bullinger, 11. 3. 1534,' Schiess, I, No. 403.

[78] See 'Bucer an Blarer,' Schiess, No. 361, 1:423. Wolfgang Capito experienced a development similar to that of Jud between 1527 and 1531 when he—under the influence of Cellarius and Schwenckfeld—sympathized with the Anabaptists and the concept of a voluntary church. Even Capito had to pay for this transgression as Martin Bucer rose to the position of leader of the Strassburg church during that time.

[79] James M. Stayer, 'Reublin and Brötli, the revolutionary beginnings of Swiss Anabaptism,' in Marc Lienhard (ed.), *The Origins and Characteristics of Anabaptism* (The Hague, 1977), 83-104; also Stayer, *The Anabaptists and the Sword* (Lawrence, Kans., 1976).

[80] See Gottfried Seebass, 'Müntzers Erbe. Werk, Leben und Theologie Hans Huts.' (Erlangen Habil., 1972) [unpublished].

[81] A. F. Mellink, *De Wederdopers in de Noordelijke Nederlanden. 1531-1534* (Groningen, 1953); Gerhard Brendler, *Das Täuferreich von Münster 1534/35* (Ost-Berlin, 1966).

[82] See 'Schwenckfelds Brief aus dem Jahr 1534 an den Erbmarschall Hans Konrad Thumb von Neuburg,' in CS 5:323.

[83] Luther, 'Wider die himmlischen Propheten,' Weimarer Publication, 17:136-37.

[84] CS 4:834.

The Schwenckfeld-Vadian Debate

R. Emmet McLaughlin

The sixteenth century saw a rehashing of issues which had dominated the christological debates of the Fathers and scholastics. For the most part christological speculation was peripheral to reformers like Luther, Zwingli, and Calvin. They delved into its murky waters with hesitation and some distaste. The terminology and conceptual tools were not biblical, and the guiding principles were disturbingly remote from the immediate concerns of the Protestant movement. Nonetheless, they were drawn into its depths by recurrent controversies about the eucharist, controversies which threatened the immediate prospects of the Reform as a whole. But on balance, while some of the christological polemic showed real skill and inventiveness, it remained an alien body in the Protestant theological corpus. There were exceptions, however. For Caspar Schwenckfeld, issues concerning the metaphysical composition of the God/Man Jesus Christ and his relationship to the Trinity were of vital concern.[1] Not only did they provide the basis of his eucharistic teachings and form the underpinning of his spiritualistic critique of the visible church, they also touched the heart of Schwenckfeld's own religious experience—a direct personal encounter with the glorified Christ.

Schwenckfeld began his reforming career as a zealous follower of Martin Luther around 1519, and played a major role in the successes of the Reformation in Silesia through 1524.[2] Thereafter, he became increasingly critical of the Reform and its failure, as he saw it, to effect meaningful change in the lives of individual believers. The eucharistic controversies between Luther and Carlstadt, and then Luther and Zwingli, drew his attention to that sacrament. He was soon convinced that the Lutheran retention of a real presence had injected an 'externality' into the Protestant religious experience that vitiated its transformative effect upon individual believers. During the summer and fall of 1525 he and his close friend and colleague Valentine Crautwald developed their own doctrine of the eucharist. While denying a real presence in the bread and wine they insisted on a real participation in the glorified flesh of Christ. The liturgical eucharist served as a reminder, a symbol, a recapitulation of the inner eucharist; its chronological and causal relationship to the 'real' eucharist were to remain problematic.

But it was clear from the beginning that for Schwenckfeld (less so for Crautwald) the inner eucharist constituted the core of the soteriological process. Christ's divine flesh was the cause, the instrument, and the goal of man's salvation. The atonement had served to fashion a new spiritual flesh which was conveyed to man in the inner eucharist and which served as the seed from which would grow a new spiritual and heavenly race of Christians. The transformation began in this life (making visible improvement among believers both possible and necessary) but was only completed in the next. The fundament which provided the objective footing and the subjective consolatory guarantee of salvation was the closest possible union of the two natures in Christ. Schwenckfeld's earliest writings on the eucharist emphasize it already, and criticize the Lutherans for attempting to separate the Logos from Christ's humanity.[3]

In defending their position against Lutheran criticism, Schwenckfeld and Crautwald developed a dualistic theology which emphasized the chasm separating Christ's glorified flesh from the fallen flesh of the Old Adam. The poles of that dualism—spiritual/material, spiritual/fleshly, heavenly/earthly—braced all of Christian experience, and through their opposing attractions separated out the internal and external elements of Christianity. Schwenckfeld's spiritualism had a solid christological base.

This is how matters stood when Schwenckfeld was forced to leave Silesia in 1529. He fled to Strassburg, at that time the refuge of many of the leading figures of the Radical Reformation. There he met Michael Servetus, whose christological speculations had a profound impact upon Schwenckfeld's own formulations. As a result in 1531 Schwenckfeld introduced a new polarity—non-creaturely/creaturely.[4] Christ's humanity, through its life, suffering, and glorification had shed all of its earthly, material, carnal, and creaturely attributes. Christ according to his humanity had ceased to be a creature after his resurrection and glorification. Martin Frecht, the leading pastor of Ulm, was the first reformer to seize upon this development. As a result of the controversy which followed, Schwenckfeld was driven in 1538 to the conclusion that Christ had in fact never been a creature, that he was the son of God even according to his humanity, begotten, not made.[5]

Though Frecht was eventually able to force Schwenckfeld out of Ulm itself (Sept. 11, 1539), he could not prevent Schwenckfeld's publication of his views. Frecht himself was forbidden to publish by the Ulm city counsel which had many Schwenckfeld supporters and was fearful of becoming involved in a public dispute.[6] Casting about for allies, Frecht decided upon Joachim von Watt (1484-1551), better known as Vadianus, humanist, historian, physician, Bürgermeister and Reformer of St. Gall.[7] Using the good offices of Johannes Zwick of Constance and Heinrich Bullinger of Zurich, Frecht would flatter and bully Vadian into a long and increasingly distasteful battle with Schwenckfeld. The clash between the historically well-versed, if unimaginative Vadianus, and the speculatively creative Schwenckfeld became a set piece in which the issues which had dominated the formulation of orthodox christology through the centuries were addressed in a straightforward and sophisticated manner.[8] Terms such as 'Arian,' 'Nestorian,' 'Monophysite,' and 'Monothelite' were used with a measure of precision not usually found in the sixteenth century. As a result it is possible to define Schwenckfeld's own position with an accuracy which has eluded many other figures from the era of the Reformation. Vadian, for his part, provided a formulation of the Swiss christology which impresses by its clarity.

Vadian's attraction for Frecht and Zwick rested no doubt on his reputation as a humanist and his position as *Bürgermeister*. That he was not a cleric, but rather a layman, and a member of the patrician elite of St. Gall made him the perfect foil. Schwenckfeld's support in southern Germany was particularly strong among the landed nobility and urban ruling elite; he counted at least four *Bürgermeister* among his admirers.[9] Furthermore, and in part relating to his popularity among these groups, was Schwenckfeld's low-keyed if thoroughgoing anticlericalism. For him the opposition were always 'pastors' and 'preachers,' no matter what the confessional stripe. He was a firm believer in clerical conspiracy theories. Vadian had the advantage of being a lay reformer, not a member of the clerical guild.[10]

Frecht's interest in Vadian was initially piqued by the knowledge that Vadian had already addressed some of the christological problems at issue in a scholarly/polemical work. At Bullinger's request, Vadian had prepared his *Orthodoxa et erudita... Epistola* (Aug./Sept. 1536) to address the Lutheran teaching on Christ's ubiquity.[11] In form the *Epistola* was an historical review of the ancient christological controversies and a polemical treatise addressing the question which Bullinger had posed: Whether Christ's body, through its inseparable union with the Word, puts on conditions which are alien to a body? Although Vadian had already been informed concerning Schwenckfeld's christology by Zwick, in the *Epistola* he did not criticize it.[12] Nonetheless, since it did address many issues with a bearing on Frecht's disagreements with Schwenckfeld, Frecht set out to have it published, approaching Vadian directly and encouraging Bullinger to support his plea.[13] It is not clear whether Vadian gave prior approval, but in any event it was published in Zurich in August/September 1539 and provided with a prefatory letter by Bullinger attacking the new 'pneumatici.'[14] Vadian's first shot, however, failed to provoke a response. It may have been because it nowhere mentioned Schwenckfeld by name, nor for that matter did it really come to grips with any of Schwenckfeld's key concerns or peculiar formulations. In any event, Schwenckfeld never considered the *Epistola* part of his argument with Vadian.[15]

But neither Vadian nor Zwick would let matters rest there. Already on October 8, 1539 Zwick knew that Vadian planned a new work directed specifically at Schwenckfeld.[16] In order to be better informed about Schwenckfeld's teachings, the two men conspired to get copies of Schwenckfeld's works. A close friend of Schwenckfeld's, Wilhelm von Zell, had retired to Constance in the Summer of 1539 and was staying with Zwick. Pretending interest, Zwick borrowed two works from von Zell which he forwarded to Vadian.[17] The two men pretended that Zwick was favorably inclined towards Schwenckfeld's position and had sought Vadian's advice.[18] A third work of Schwenckfeld's was later also passed on to Vadian.[19] On the basis of the

information received, Vadian was able to revise an earlier letter to Zwick and to produce the *Antilogia*, which he published
together with the Zwick letter at the end of August 1540.[20]

This time Vadian did catch Schwenckfeld's attention. Sometime in November, Zwick, still playing the 'honest' mediator,
passed a copy of the *Antilogia* on to von Zell so that in turn
he might give it to Schwenckfeld.[21] Schwenckfeld's initial response, a brief letter to von Zell (Dec. 6, 1540) expressed some
dismay that Vadian had placed him in the company of notorious heretics, but Schwenckfeld was heartened by what he perceived to be the candor, gentility and Christian charity of both
Zwick and Vadian. The fact that the *Apologia* was in Latin disturbed him, since this limited the audience. His own response,
as he explained, was delayed by ill-health and the difficulties
placed in the way of publication by the 'clerical conspiracy.'[22]
Schwenckfeld eventually wrote directly to Vadian (before July
26, 1541) requesting a personal meeting to discuss matters.
Vadian did not reply until January 14, 1542, and then only to
suggest that a written correspondence would suit him better.[23]

The occasion of Vadian's tardy reply was the visit of
Schwenckfeld's close friend and ambassador, Jakob Held von
Tieffenau. Held came bearing Schwenckfeld's long awaited reply to the *Antilogia*, the massive *Confession*.[24] The long delay
was occasioned by the nature of the attacks which had been
brought to bear on Schwenckfeld. Both the *Antilogia* and the
condemnation of Smalcald (Mar. 1540) had been careful to
place Schwenckfeld's teachings in the context of ancient christological heresies.[25] In order to respond, Schwenckfeld had to
immerse himself in the writings of the Fathers, not an easy task
for someone barred from most urban centers and libraries. But
he seems to have found what he needed at Kempten, a city in
which he was quite welcome, in the Benedictine Abbey, whose
abbot was a good friend and supporter. He was at work on it
throughout the autumn of 1541.[26] In January 1542 Schwenckfeld sent a short synopsis of the *Confession*, the *Confession*
itself, and letters to Philip of Hesse and Philip Melanchthon.

Schwenckfeld's messenger, Hans von Sperberseck, went first
to Hesse and then to Wittenberg. Philip of Hesse eventually
wrote a criticism of the *Confession*, but urged Melanchthon
to enter into consultation with Schwenckfeld. Melanchthon, in

turn, promised to write a critique of Schwenckfeld's christology. Though his friends in southern Germany would press him to redeem his promise, Melanchthon never did write against Schwenckfeld.[27] Schwenckfeld also sent copies of the *Confession* to the churches of Nürnberg, Ulm, Strassburg, and perhaps Augsburg. Through his other messenger, Jakob Held von Tieffenau, Schwenckfeld got in direct contact with Vadian at St. Gall and the theologians of Zurich. Held also carried copies of the *Confession* for them.[28]

Held's embassy to Switzerland had been designed, in part, to arrange for a personal meeting between Schwenckfeld and Vadian. This the latter refused and offered instead to conduct a correspondence to discuss the issues involved. Vadian also promised not to publish further until they had discussed the matter further. This was a major concession on his part since he already had another work in manuscript, the *Pro veritate carnis*.[29] Vadian's offer of a truce came as a shock to Zwick and, especially, Frecht. The Ulm preacher immediately embarked on a letter campaign to persuade Vadian that Schwenckfeld was not to be trusted to maintain his end of the agreement. The pressure proved successful. The *Pro veritate carnis* was in circulation less than two months after Held's visit.[30] But before Schwenckfeld could reply, another work appeared in Autumn 1542 attacking his christology—the German language *Grüntlicher Bericht*.[31] Produced by Bullinger and the Zurich clergy, the *Grüntlicher Bericht* was composed primarily of passages drawn from the works of Vadian. But there were some additions, including a diagram composed of circles which purported to explain the relationship of the persons of the Trinity to each other and to the human nature of Christ. Because of the diagram Schwenckfeld always referred to it as the 'Circle booklet.' And although it was published anonymously, Schwenckfeld soon knew who was behind it.[32] In response Schwenckfeld produced *Von der Anbettunge Christi* around the New Year 1543, and it was printed by April 17, 1543. By May 11, 1543 five hundred copies had already been sold.[33] But even before Schwenckfeld's reply to the *Gründtlicher Bericht* was ready, Vadian had produced his final contribution to the controversy. The *Dreyzehen namhaffter irrthumb* was Vadian's one German language attack on Schwenckfeld and his teachings. Frecht in Ulm had seen manuscript versions of the new

work in November 1542, but it did not appear in print until
the following spring, arriving in Ulm in April.[34] Schwenckfeld
closed the public controversy with his answer to the *Dreyzehen namhaffter irrthumb*—the *Verantwortung unnd Defension*
probably written in May 1543, but not published until 1591.[35]
In this work Schwenckfeld reviewed the course of argument
with Vadian and addressed once again all the major questions
at issue. Both he and Vadian seemed to realize that there was
nothing to be gained by further discussion. Schwenckfeld was
already caught up in a new battle with the Lutherans, and Vadian was clearly sick and tired of the endless war of words and
the fanaticism which he detected in his ally Frecht. Perhaps
too the death of Zwick removed some of the impetus. In any
event, though there was some further communication between
the two men, their christological battle was at an end.[36]

In the course of the controversy, Vadian accused Schwenckfeld of Theopassionism, Monophysitism, Valentinianism, and
Monothelitism. In return, Schwenckfeld charged Vadian with
Arianism and Nestorianism. In many ways their arguments
represented a reprise of the battle of Alexandria and Antioch, Wittenberg and Zurich. Schwenckfeld always placed the
emphasis on the unity of the two natures in Christ, while Vadian was forever pointing up their continuing distinctiveness.
But as Schwenckfeld made clear right at the beginning, it was
the nature and significance of Christ's humanity that was at
issue.[37] How does one define 'humanity'? In what ways does
the union of Christ's humanity with his divinity affect that humanity? What changes did the resurrection usher in? What
role did/does Christ's humanity play in the economy of salvation? As a general guideline it is safe to say that Schwenckfeld
ascribed greater importance and power to Christ's human nature, and as a result was ready to define that nature in a less
restrictive manner than Vadian. Vadian for his part was concerned to uphold a narrower definition of human nature and
its potential, and was thus forced to deny Christ's humanity
as extensive a role as Schwenckfeld felt necessary.

Their differing tendencies became immediately apparent
when they discussed Schwenckfeld's distinctive christological
contribution—his denial that Christ's humanity was a 'creature.' As has been noted, initially Schwenckfeld had argued
that as a result of the passion, resurrection, and glorification

Christ's humanity had shed its creaturely characteristics, and had formed a more perfect union with his divinity.[38] But as it became clear that such a position was logically untenable, Schwenckfeld extended Christ's non-creaturely status back to his conception.[39] Schwenckfeld argued that Christ according to his humanity was the natural son of God. As such he could not be considered a 'creature.' 'Creaturehood' and 'sonship' were mutually exclusive terms. Both terms described the relationship existing between God and other beings; in the first instance that of creation, in the second of procreation.[40] To claims that denial of the creaturehood of Christ's humanity abrogated the authenticity of his human nature, Schwenckfeld responded by emphasizing the difference between a thing's substance and its mode of origination. Christ's human nature was complete and completely human—body, soul, and spirit. How it came into being was certainly of interest and important, but in no way affected what it 'was'.[41] Nor was 'creatureliness' part of the essence or definition of human nature.[42] To be sure, no man before Christ had not been a creature. But then no one could deny that Christ was unique.

Vadian, while rejecting Schwenckfeld's claims, was immediately placed in an uncomfortable position. For one thing, there was no precedent for this issue in the patristic christological debates.[43] He was eventually forced to draw upon the despised scholastics for support.[44] For another, Vadian was not eager to declare Christ simply a 'creature'. In point of fact, Vadian juggled terms like 'natural son,' 'adopted son,' and 'homo assumptus' in an attempt to come to grips with the problem.

For those who are acquainted with Schwenckfeld's theology it may come as a surprise that it was Vadian who introduced a stern dualism into the discussion. He accused Schwenckfeld of introducing a *tertium quid* between 'creature' and 'creator' where none existed.[45] Either Christ according to his humanity was a creature or he was the creator. Since Christ's human nature was clearly not the creator (if for no other reason than that it came to exist in time itself), then it must be a creature. The elements of the body were drawn from Mary, herself a creature descended through a long line of creatures from Adam, who in turn had been made from dust. The dust itself had been created *ex nihilo*. Vadian, who at times was unclear about Schwenckfeld's own position on the matter (or perhaps only feigned it), charged that if Schwenckfeld denied Christ's creaturehood he must also deny Mary's contribution to Christ's human nature.[46] This would be to revive the heresies of Apelles and Valentinian, and would make Schwenckfeld participant in the errors of Melchior Hoffman and Michael Servetus, all of whom had portrayed a 'heavenly flesh' which had come down from heaven and which had merely passed through Mary as if through a pipe.[47]

Schwenckfeld, whose christology had developed in competition with Hoffman's, was quick to deny Vadian's allegations. According to Schwenckfeld Mary provided what every other mother did.[48] And therein lay a problem. In the early sixteenth century there were two basic competing explanations of the mechanics of human reproduction.[49] The Aristotelian model posited a single 'seed' from the male which was nourished and nurtured in the female's womb. According to the Galenic model there were two 'seeds,' one from each parent. Unfortunately, neither Schwenckfeld nor Vadian made explicit which model they employed. Indirectly, however, it is possible to determine that both were working from an Aristotelian perspective.[50] This played into Schwenckfeld's hands beautifully. He argued quite simply that in Christ's conception God the Father, working through the Holy Spirit, had played the paternal role providing the initial impetus.[51] Though he never described God's contribution as a 'seed,' it is clear that the divine intervention took the place of the male 'seed' and that Mary provided the 'flesh' of the human nature as did other human mothers, through nourishment and nurture. For Schwenckfeld, then, Christ according to humanity was the natural son of both God and Mary. And though the elements of his body were derived from creaturely sources, his direct filial relationship to God took precedence.[52] He was not a creature.

Vadian took a defensive position based upon the 'homo assumptus' doctrine popular among the Fathers.[53] He argued that Christ's humanity had been created in Mary's womb at the moment of conception, and that immediately thereafter it had been assumed by the Word in the hypostatic union.[54] Though the Galenic two-'seed' model would have suited his argument better, Vadian held to the Aristotelian explanation. He simply denied that there was any male 'seed' or its equivalent. God had formed Christ from Mary's flesh just as he had

formed Adam from the dust of the earth.[55] His explanation
of how Christ could be truly human if he was not conceived
in a human manner echoed Schwenckfeld's: method of origination must be distinguished from the essence or substance of the
thing itself.[56] But the end result was quite different. Christ's
two natures were utterly divided by their origins. Christ according to his divinity had a father and no mother, and according to his humanity a mother and no father.[57] Confronted
by Schwenckfeld's effort to join the two natures more closely
by 'equalizing' them, Vadian responded by drawing the lines
of distinction more sharply and clearly. This was to be the
way the entire controversy unfolded. Schwenckfeld rejected
the 'homo assumptus' position as both Arian and Nestorian.[58]

Perhaps sensing that his original definition of 'creature'
failed to provide a secure base from which to attack Schwenckfeld, Vadian extended it by equating creature with the temporal and creator with the eternal. Anything which had not
existed from eternity was a creature.[59] Christ's humanity had
begun to exist in time, hence it was a creature. Schwenckfeld
found this argument disturbingly like that of Nestorianism and
branded it as such.[60] In response he pointed to his own distinction between those works of the six days of creation, and those
new things which came into being with Christ.[61] Only the first
were creatures. The latter were a *tertium quid*, engendered by
God in time, but eternal (that is, everlasting into the future),[62]
divine, and spiritual. It was this new type of being, which included the reborn Christian, that was the goal and purpose of
the incarnation. It made of the man Christ and the saints in
heaven true literal sons of God (though the latter were only
such by adoption).

Vadian recognized the roots of Schwenckfeld's dissatisfac-
tion with the idea that Christ could be a creature. It was
the infirmities, the 'vanities' as Vadian would term them, that
adhered to creatures and which seemed inappropiate to the
Messiah.[63] Sinfulness, for instance, was a product not of creatureliness *per se*, but of the sexual act in which the creature was
conceived. The need for food and drink, the physical vulner-
ability and mortality of all earthly creatures, these are things
which do not pertain to the essence of being a creature. Christ
was free from sin at conception and shed the other weaknesses

in heaven.[64] According to Vadian there was no need to go further and deny Christ's essential creaturehood. To do so threatened to place the Fall not in the Garden with Adam and Eve, but with God at the creation.[65] For Vadian it was essential to maintain the integrity of Christ's humanity, and creaturehood was an important element of that integrity. But even he was aware that the rigor with which he defended it threatened to undermine the unity and dignity of the person Christ. Therefore, he thought it better to refer to Christ simply as the natural son of God, while understanding of course that the term referred to the divine nature and the hypostasis, but not to the human nature.[66] Vadian's verbal legerdemain reveals his embarrassment, even though he was defending an undoubtedly orthodox position. Schwenckfeld, for his part, failed to pursue his heterodox insight to its logical heretical conclusion. He had provided himself with a solid foundation from which to build a theology emphasizing the closest of possible unions between the two natures. Paradoxically, he had also assured that the human nature would not be swallowed up by the divine. There was no need if the humanity itself was semi-divine.[67]

Schwenckfeld described Christ's life and passion as a process through which the two natures—always closely united—became even more inseparately conjoined. Whatever dissonance existed between the two was gradually erased.[68] But even during their earthly sojourn their union was, for Schwenckfeld, unutterably close. Vadian was to liken the relationship of divinity and humanity in Christ to that of the body and the soul in other human beings. Schwenckfeld accepted that comparison as only a crude approximation and a starting point. The bond between the two natures was much more intimate and thoroughgoing.[69] Both Vadian and Schwenckfeld employed time-honored terminology to describe the nature and effects of the hypostatic union. But both also redefined the terms which they borrowed. Vadian claimed to hold to *communicatio idiomatum*, whereas he actually held to the Zwinglian *commutatio idiomatum*. The two natures did not actually share properties or characteristics. Instead, under the umbrella of the hypostatic union they shared the names or words referring to those properties. It was a matter of language, what one could *say* about Christ, not what actually *was*.[70] Schwenckfeld for his part opted for a 'true' *communicatio idiomatum*.

For him, the interpenetration of the two natures was so radical that a mere sharing of characteristics, properties, or powers was insufficient. For instance, Christians worship the humanity of Christ not only because it 'borrows' the divine glory, but because it is totally bathed and suffused by divinity. This did not entail a mixture of the two natures, nor a conversion of one into the other.[71] Despite Vadian's charges to the contrary, Schwenckfeld maintained the continued existence of two essentially distinct natures. Whether that was congruent with such a deep-seated and intimate coalition was a different question.

The differences separating Vadian and Schwenckfeld became clear during the discussion of three issues: Christ's passion, his ubiquity, and his two wills. Vadian defended the orthodox position that Christ the person suffered according to his humanity. In effect, both the hypostasis and the human nature underwent the torments of the passion. The divine nature *could be said* to have suffered since it was part of the hypostatic union, but in reality it remained *per se* impassible.[72] Schwenckfeld rejected this distinction as Nestorian and forthrightly admitted that the second person of the Trinity had suffered in the passion. While accepting Theopassionism (not in itself unorthodox) he steadfastly rejected Patripassionism. Only the second person of the Trinity had been incarnated, and only the second person had suffered. But that the second person had indeed suffered was inescapable for Schwenckfeld.[73]

The status of Christ's humanity after the resurrection attracted considerable attention in the Vadian/Schwenckfeld debate, just as it had when Luther and Zwingli had battled over the eucharist. At issue for Schwenckfeld was the question of just how much the humanity in glory shared with the divinity. His answer was quite simple: just about everything. The human nature of Christ had shed all of its creaturely integuments. It was invisible, illocal, impassible, immortal, and ubiquitous. Furthermore, Christ as man was omnipotent and omniscient; he reigned over creation in God's stead. It was his spirit which effected the salvation of fallen men. All of this was summed up for Schwenckfeld by the 'the Glory of God' with which the man Christ had been endowed. And by 'the Glory of God' Schwenckfeld meant God himself, the divine essence. The humanity lived from that essence, bathed in it, but was not converted into it.[74] Vadian rejected this line of

thought out of hand. For him it was tantamount to denying
the humanity of the risen Christ. To be human was to have
a body, and a body by definition occupied space. A ubiquitous body was an oxymoron.[75] Furthermore, to ascribe all of
the divine powers and functions to Christ's human nature was
to erase the distinction between the humanity and the divinity without which to speak of two natures made no sense.[76]
It was the second person of the Trinity who reigned in heaven
and whose spirit freed man from the trammels of sin. To be
sure, the humanity in so far as it was joined to the divinity in
the hypostatic union *could be said* to share in these activities.
But in effect, its contribution had ended with the passion.[77]
These arguments only reconfirmed Schwenckfeld's suspicions
concerning the Swiss theology in general. It and Vadian failed
to realize the uniqueness of Christ. As they readily admitted,
Christ according to his humanity was no different from one of
the prophets or from Adam before the Fall.[78] This Schwenckfeld would not accept, and as a result he and his followers
would be proud to call themselves 'confessors of the Glory of
Christ.' Their opponents accused them of giving too much
honor to Christ; they responded by charging their opponents
with Judaizing.

Vadian found one more ancient heresy with which to charge
Schwenckfeld: Monothelitism. Strictly speaking this was incor-
rect. Both Vadian and Schwenckfeld held to two wills joined
together in an immutable concordance. But once again, in his
effort to get beneath the orthodox terminology Schwenckfeld
raised issues which clearly distinguished him from Vadian, in
particular with regard to the post-glorification Christ. Both
men agreed that Christ's human and divine wills were in complete agreement, but for Vadian it was a concord between two
fundamentally antagonistic entities. Only the power of the divine majesty was able to so cow the human will that despite its
essential opposition to the divine will it concurred in all that
the divinity desired.[79] Schwenckfeld, though sharing Vadian's
dualistic world view, rejected its applicablity to Christ. The
incarnation, passion, resurrection, and glorification had been
explicitly designed to overcome that dualism. Christ's new humanity, by its very nature, was conformable to the divinity in
all things in a way which far outstripped even Adam before
the Fall. Its will, its entire essence, allowed for and demanded

the closest possible union with the Godhead. In the case of Christ, this included its incorporation as the second person of the Trinity.[80]

As with the Luther/Zwingli christological debate, in the background of Schwenckfeld's disagreement with Vadian was the issue of the eucharist. In large measure Schwenckfeld's christological speculation was designed to provide the theoretical underpinnings for his teaching on the eucharist. The inner, spiritual, but real participation in the body and blood of Christ (with or without the attendant external liturgical ritual) formed the heart of the Christian experience and the salvific process for Schwenckfeld. By partaking of Christ one partook of salvation; one was reborn, remade. The ubiquity and power of the glorified body of Christ was thus essential. This presented Vadian with a very difficult problem. A Zwinglian on the eucharist by conviction, Vadian was also involved with Martin Bucer in the search for a viable concord with the Lutherans.[81] Unlike Bullinger therefore he could not deny outright a participation in Christ's flesh. Nonetheless, he rejected all of Schwenckfeld's attempts to provide an explanation of that participation.[82] Which left Vadian with much confusion, some embarrassment, and an appeal to the 'mystery' of the sacrament. In a sense he had argued his christological case too well and had had to pay the price with an unsatisfying eucharistic theology.

Both men claimed to argue from Scripture, but were forced, as were all their predecessors, to draw upon non-scriptural arguments and authorities. The Fathers, the creeds of the ancient church, and, for Vadian, the scholastics were all called upon to bolster positions and to prove orthodoxy. The difficulties arose in the first place from the nature of the issues and the limits of scriptural interpretation. Vadian explicitly rejected a literal interpretation of most of the christological proof-texts, while Schwenckfeld argued that such texts (at least in the New Testament) were the ones least in need of elaborate re-interpretation.[83] Both men accepted the standard terminology of person/hypostasis and nature, though they were not to be found in the Bible as such. Given no biblical guidance they were forced to rely on their own understanding of the terms and their significance in the context of christology. It became a battle of definitions. And therein, in Schwenckfeld's opinion, lay the cause of Vadian's Nestorian error. As Vadian himself interpreted 'definition,' it was to distinguish the thing defined from other things.[84] Applied to Christ this allowed a theologian to distinguish the two natures within the one person. But to Schwenckfeld, to imagine distinctions in Christ was to divide Christ. If one would truly understand (insofar as human beings can understand the incarnation at all), the direction of imagination must be from the two natures to the one person, that is, one must imagine the unity, not the duality. And this cannot be done by reason. Reason is limited to the division of things defined in order to grasp what lies within its reach. Only faith can reach beyond that. Only in and through faith can the unity of Christ be glimpsed. Such an understanding is a gift, not an accomplishment, and it is given to every true Christian.[85] The true understanding of Christ cannot be achieved by reason, but that does not make it anti-rational. Reason may not be able to seize it, but then it cannot disprove it either. It is consistent with reason if not discoverable by it.

With this argument Schwenckfeld had turned the tables on Vadian. Vadian had begun the battle by associating Schwenckfeld with the heresies of the ancient church. Schwenckfeld had come to the point where he implicitly accused Vadian of not having Christian faith. He had also in effect denied the competence of university trained scholars and theologians to pass judgment upon the most central doctrines of Christianity. In the end Schwenckfeld's spiritualism provided the backstop for his christology and his eucharistic theology. It was this inner consistency which lent Schwenckfeld's entire theology its strength. The various parts supported and provided a framework for each other. This inner consistency was a product of Schwenckfeld's personal experience and his own "theologizing." The historian Vadian was at a bad disadvantage trying to defend and appropriate a tradition rather than to develop his own theological rationale. While formally orthodox the various pieces did not fit together well. A biblicistic thinker, he had to deny the literal meaning of Scripture. A supporter of Bucer's semi-Lutheran eucharistic concord, he came to defend a near-Nestorian christology that undermined that concord. It is no wonder that Vadian found the entire enterprise increasingly distasteful. When the controversy ended in 1543 it was because the reservoir of good will had been exhausted and the

expanse of common ground had been so restricted that there
was little purpose in pursuing it further.

At the root of their disagreement were differing views concerning the role which Christ's humanity played in the economy
of salvation and the fate which awaits the elect in heaven. Vadian ascribed the salvific work of Christ to the divine nature
alone. The flesh, the human nature served as a passive and
passable instrument through which the divinity had worked its
will in the atonement. Its role was past. Nonetheless, Vadian
feared that by tampering with the nature of Christ's humanity
one risked the precious bridge between the mediator and fallen
mankind. Christ's humanity must be like that of fallen man,
otherwise the atonement would have no point of contact. For
Schwenckfeld the problem was different. How could a creature
save other creatures? How could a fleshly, earthly man convey
salvation to the inner man that was the Christian? If Christ
was like other men, then why was the incarnation necessary at
all? And the Kingdom of God? Was that not to be a close and
loving union of redeemed man and his loving Father, God?
For Schwenckfeld Vadian's vision of heaven was too correct,
too proper, too formal to be the goal of Christ's life and suffering. Only the most intimate reunion with God could satisfy
Schwenckfeld's longing for redemption. The saved Christian
returned as a prodigal *son*, not as a parolled convict.

At the core of Schwenckfeld's christology, as at the core of
his entire theology, was his own encounter with the person of
the Redeemer. It was as the one Christ, not as a union of two
disparate natures, that Schwenckfeld had first come to know
the Word incarnate, personally so to speak. And it was as an
adopted brother to his personal Lord, himself the natural son
of God, that Schwenckfeld felt welcomed to the company of the
elect. Compared to this, Vadian's formally correct formulation
concerning natures and hypostasis seemed a mere mental and
verbal construct, having nothing to do with the realities of sin
and individual redemption.

Notes

[1] Schwenckfeld's christology has drawn the attention of many scholars:
Ferdinand Christian Bauer, *Die Christliche Lehre von der Dreieinigkeit
und Menschenwerdung Gottes in ihrer geschichtlichen Entwicklung*
(Tübingen, 1843), 219-56; Karl Ecke, *Schwenckfeld, Luther und der*

Gedanke einer apostolischen Reformation (Berlin, 1911), 124-28, 201-03; Heinrich Wilhelm Erbkam, *Geschichte der Protestantischen Sekten im Zeitalter der Reformation* (Hamburg and Gotha, 1848), 357-475; Georg Ludwig Hahn, *Schwenckfeldii Sententia de Christi Persona et Opere Exposita. Commentatio Historico-Theologica* (Breslau, 1847); Emanuel Hirsch, 'Zum Verständnis Schwenckfelds,' *Festgabe von Fachgenossen und Freunden Karl Müller zum siebzigsten Geburtstage dargebracht* (Tübingen, 1922), 60-66; Frederick William Loetscher, *Schwenckfeld's Participation in the Eucharistic Controversy of the Sixteenth Century* (Philadelphia, 1906), 357-86, 454-500; Paul L. Maier, *Caspar Schwenckfeld on the Person and Work of Christ—A Study of Schwenckfeldian Theology at its Core* (Assen, 1959); Gottfried Maron, *Individualismus und Gemeinschaft bei Caspar Schwenckfeld, seine Theologie dargestellt mit besonderer Ausrichtung auf seinen Kirchenbegriff* (Stuttgart, 1961), 35-66; Hans J. Schoeps, *Vom Himmlischen Fleisch Christi* (Tübingen, 1951), 25-36; André Sciegienny, *Homme charnal, homme spirituel: étude sur la christologie de Caspar Schwenckfeld (1489-1561)* (Wiesbaden, 1975); Horst Weigelt, *Spiritualistische Tradition im Protestantismus—Die Geschichte des Schwenckfeldertums in Schlesien* (Berlin, 1973), 160-68. For the development of Schwenckfeld's christology see my *Caspar Schwenckfeld, Reluctant Radical*, 200-24.

2 For Schwenckfeld's early career consult my *Caspar Schwenckfeld, Reluctant Radical*, 1-119.

3 See the twelve 'Questiones' (1525), CS 3:500.26-35, 502.36-503.10. For the dating of the 'Questiones' see R. Emmet McLaughlin, 'The Genesis of Schwenckfeld's eucharistic Doctrine,' *Archiv für Reformationsgeschichte* 74 (1983), 94-121.

4 Schwenckfeld letter to Johannes Bader, (ca. 1530-1531), CS 4: 18.7-21; 'Vom Evangelio Jesu Christi,' (prior to Sept. 1531), CS 3:360.34-49.

5 'Von der Menschwerdung Christi,' CS 4:238.15-23.

6 On Schwenckfeld's battles with Frecht see Julius Endriss, *Kaspar Schwenckfelds Ulmer Kämpfe* (Ulm, 1936); for the last phase see especially 39-41.

7 For Vadian the standard work is now Werner Näf, *Vadian und seine Stadt St. Gallen* (St. Gall, 1944). But still useful is Theodor Pressel, *Joachim Vadian* (Elberfeld, 1861). An invaluable source for Vadian and for the history of the period as a whole is Emil Arbenz and Hermann Wartmann (eds.), *Vadianische Briefsammlung* (henceforth Vad. Br.), (7 vols; St. Gall, 1890-1913).

8 On the controversy itself, Näf, 452-62, and Schultz, 259-62. Neither one indulges in much theological analysis.

9 Wolfgang Rehlinger (Augsburg), Bernhard Besserer and Hans Walther Ehinger (Ulm), Hans Sachs (Esslingen). Schwenckfeld's ties to Jakob Sturm (Strassburg) are problematic.

10 Zwick to Vadian (Nov. 5, 1939). Vad. Br. 5:575 and (Nov. 21, 1539), Vad. Br. 5:578.

11 *Orthodoxa et erudita D. Ioachimi Vadiani viri clariss. Epistola, qua
    hanc explicat questionem. An corpus Christi propter coniunctionem
    cum verbo inseparabilem, alienas a corpore conditiones sibi sumat nos-
    tro saeculo perquam utilis et necessaria. Accesserunt Huic D. Vigilli
    Martyris et Episcopi Tridentini libri V. pii et elegantes, quos ille ante
    mille annos contra Eutychen et alios hereticos, parum pie de natu-
    rarum Christi propietate et persone unitate sentientes, conscripsit. Tig-
    uri Apud Christophorum Froschoverum M.D.XXXIX.* For dating the
    work, see Näf, 452-53.

12 Zwick to Vadian (Sept. 16, 1535), Vad. Br. 5:250, provided Vadian a
    brief outline of Schwenckfeld's teaching. I disagree with Näf (455) that
    Vadian had Schwenckfeld in the back of his mind when writing in 1536.
    The treatise was clearly aimed at the Lutherans whose position was to
    be debated at the Second Basel *Städtetag* for which Vadian's work was
    originally prepared, Näf, 452-53.

13 Frecht to Vadian (Jan. 28, 1539), Vad. Br. 5:530-31; Näf, 45-56. My-
    conius and Grynaeus at Basel may also have played a role in urging
    publication (CS 7:454).

14 Näf, 453.

15 In 'Verantwortung unnd Defension für Casparn Schwenckfeld' (ca. May
    154), CS 8:626-73, Schwenckfeld recounted the history of his battle with
    Vadian, but never mentioned the *Epistola*. He counted Vadian's *Antilo-
    gia* as the first in the series (CS 8:633.4-15). While Schwenckfeld took
    no notice of the work, both Calvin and Bucer took offense believing
    that it was directed against them (CS 7:455).

16 Zwick to Vadian (Oct. 8, 1539), Vad. Br. 5:573.

17 Schultz, 254-55. The two works were 'Ermanunge zum waren und selig-
    machende Erkantnus Christi,' (CS 6:501-29) and probably the 'Kurtze
    gründtliche Bewerung,' (CS 6:306-22).

18 Zwick to Vadian (Nov. 5, 1985), Vad. Br. 5:575-76.

19 Zwick to Vadian (Dec. 2, 1539), Vad. Br. 5:579. Schultz, 255, argued
    that treatise in question was the 'Summarium ettlicher Argument,' (CS
    6:531-39). The title of the *Antilogia* refers to it, see next note. This
    work had been written in reply to a letter which Zwick had written to
    von Zell (CS 7:461).

20 *D. Ioachimi Vadiani Cos. Sangallensis ad. D. Ioan. Zuiccium Con-
    stantien. Ecclesie Pastorem Epistola: in qua post explicatas in Christo
    naturas diversas, et personam ex diversis naturis unam, Iesum serva-
    torem nostrum, vel in gloria veram esse creaturam, tum oraculis scrip-
    turarum sacrosanctis, tum interpretum orthodoxorum authoritate doce-
    tur et demonstratur. Accessit huic eodem authoria Antilogia ad claris-
    simi viri Dom. Gasparis Schuenckfeldii argumenta, in Libellum qui ab
    eo Summarium inscriptus est, collecta; quibus Christum dominum in
    gloria receptum, amplius creaturam nullo modo esse, contendit. Tiguri
    apud Frosch.* For the date of publication Näf, 456. The letter to Zwick
    had originally been written June 4, 1939 (Schultz, 255).

21 Sebastian Gruebel in Schaffhausen reported receiving a copy of the book at the beginning of November, (Nov. 9. 1940). Vad Br. 5, 649. Since Schwenckfeld was able to respond as early as December 6, 1540 (in the form of a letter to von Zell, CS 7: 188-91), it would be safe to assume that Zwick sent it in November. As Schwenckfeld remarked to von Zell, he had already gotten a copy from another friend (CS 7:188.2-11). Zwick's cover letter, undated (CS 7:186).

22 For this letter see preceding note. The friendliness of Schwenckfeld's attitude to Zwick may have raised the possibility in the latter's mind that Vadian might suspect that the double-game was being played against him—Vadian—and not Schwenckfeld. In any event Zwick hastened to declare his allegiance to orthodoxy, Zwick to Vadian (December 29, 1940), Vad. Br. 5, 568. He also promised to apprise Schwenckfeld of his true opinions.

23 Schwenckfeld's letter is lost, but Vadian's reply (which was not included in Vad. Br.) is to be found in CS 7:417-18. Frecht refers to Schwenckfeld's letter(s) on July 26, 1541, Vad. Br. 6, 56.

24 'Confession unnd Erclerung vom Erkandtnus Christi und seiner Göttlichen Herrlichkeit' (CS 7:486-884)

25 Led by Bucer and Melanchthon, a group of theologians gathered at Smalcald issued a condemnation of both Schwenckfeld and Sebastian Franck, Endriss, 41-44 (CS 7:459). The text of the condemnation is in CR 3:983-86.

26 On Schwenckfeld and Kempten consult 'Schwenckfeld and the Schwenckfelders of South Germany,' above. On Abbot Wolfgang von Grünstein' (CS 7:462-63). Frecht wrote to Vadian on November 25, 1541 (Vad. Br. 6:87) and December 23, 1541 (Vad. Br. 6:92) about Schwenckfeld's work at the monastic library in Kempten. The Confession itself is dated December 1541 in the St. Gall Ms. while the prefatory letter to Melanchthon was dated January 5, 1542. Since Schwenckfeld also wrote a cover letter to Melanchthon and both letters bear the same date in later printed editions. CS believes that the January 5, 1542 was originally only that of the cover letter and that it was also applied to the prefatory letter by mistake. CS 7:465 assumes that the prefatory letter was written in early December 1541. There is mention of it in correspondence between the Schwenkfelders Alexander Held and Andreas Neff already on November 28, 1541 (CS 7:463). And as CS points out, since Adam Reissner was able to prepare at least two complete manuscript copies by New Year 1542, it would seem that the work must have been completed sometime in November.

27 On these events, CS 7:465-67.

28 On the distribution of the Confession see CS 7:467-72, and Näf, 260. Only part I of the Confession was printed in late 1542. The first complete edition was printed in 1557 (CS 7:480).

29 Pro veritate carnis triumphantis Christi, quod ea ipsa, quia facta est, et manet in gloria, creatura, hoc est nostra caro, esse non desierit, ANAKEPHALAIOSIS sive recapitulatio. Ad clarissimum virum

D.D. Ioannnem urbis Constantiensis Ecclesiasten. Authore Ioachimo Vadiano... Tiguri apud Frosch. Vadian had written it during the Summer of 1541. The prefatory letter was dated September 2, 1541. It was published by March 15. 1542, Zwick to Vadian (March 15, 1542), Vad. Br. 6:114.

30 Frecht wrote thirteen letters to Vadian in 1542, in large measure because Vadian was showing signs of fatigue and distaste for the battle, cf. Zwick to Vadian (January 17, 1542), Vad. Br. 6:96, where Zwick disclaimed responsibility for getting him into the mess. Frecht constantly reminded Vadian of other agreements that Schwenckfeld had entered into, that is, the Tübingen Concord and various agreements with Frecht, which were then broken, supposedly by Schwenckfeld, for example, Frecht to Vadian (Jan. 27, 1542), Vad. Br. 6: 99-100, and (Mar. 11, 1542), Vad. Br. 6:112. There has been some speculation why Vadian finally gave his permission to print the *Pro veritate carnis*. Näf 261 wondered if the fact that the *Confession* had been sent to others besides himself may have upset him. But as Schultz (261) points out, Vadian must surely have known that others were to get copies, especially since the prefatory letter was addressed to Melanchthon and since Held had gone on to Zurich with a letter of introduction from Vadian himself.

31 *Gründtlicher Bericht unnd Ausszug ausz Herren Doctoren Joachimen von Watt böchern/ in Lateinischer Spraach aussgangen/ anzeigend/ ob Christus der Herr auch in seiner glori nach seinem angenomnen fleisch creatur sye oder nit. creatur sein/ achtend und haltend. Durch etliche günsige der warheit brüder gestelt und zue fürderung der warheit beschriben.* The earliest reference to it was in a letter from Frecht to Vadian (Nov. 7, 1542), Vad. Br. 6, 168.

32 The diagram was on 32v. Schwenckfeld referred to the treatise's authorship in the 'Verantwortung und Defension' (CS 8:635.14-18).

33 *Von der Anbettunge Christi. Darneben auch auf das büchlin des ausszugs auss D. Joachim van Watt büchern wirt geantwurt/ wider die leere von der vermaiten creaturlichait am Herren Christo. Caspar Schwenckfeldt* (CS 8:325-99). On the dating see CS 8:319-22.

34 *Dreyzehen namhaffter irrthumb Caspar Schwenckfelds/ aussgezogen auss seinem büchern/ die er hat lassen ussgon von dem Bekenntnuss und der glori Christi: welich er zum teil nüw eyngefurt/ zum teil zue vernüweren undernommen . Diser zyt vast güt unnd nutzlich zu lösen.* On the dating see CS 8:627-28.

35 *Verantwortung unnd Defension für Casparn Schwenckfelden deren puncten und Irrthumb damit jhn Doctor Joachim von Wat/ Burgermeister zue Sanct Galle/ unrecht beschuldiget Caspar Schwenckfeld ... M.D.LXXXXI.* Reprinted CS 8:632-73. On the dating (CS 8:627-28).

36 See Vadian's letter to Ambrosius Blaurer (May 21, 1543), Vad. Br. 6, 227-28. Zwick had died in 1542, Frecht to Vadian (Dec. 2, 1542), Vad. Br. 6: 176. Though the actual controversy was at an end, Bullinger took care to have it enshrined in the Second Helvetic Confession (1562)

The Constitution of the United Presbyterian Church of the Unites States of America, Part I, Book of Confessions (New York, 1970), 5.069-5.070.

37 Letter to Wilhelm von Zell (Dec. 6, 1540), CS 7:190.1-18.

38 On the development of Schwenckfeld's christology through 1539 consult my Caspar Schwenckfeld, Reluctant Rebel, 200-24.

39 Schwenckfeld denied having changed his thinking on this issue. Instead, he claimed that he had not made clear the radicalness of his thinking out of consideration for the weakness of his audience (CS 7:864.16-865.6).

40 CS 8:378.15-20.

41 CS 7:563.10-15, margin.

42 CS 7:505.16-20.

43 The question had arisen within the ranks of the Monophysites, only to be rejected by them. It never became an issue in the wider controversy, Jaroslav Pelikan, The Emergence of the Catholic Tradition (100-600) (Chicago, 1971), 273-74.

44 Antilogia, 29v, where he draws upon Peter Lombard.

45 Antilogia, 40-40v, 53v.

46 Pro veritate carnis, 4v, 24v.

47 On Hoffman, see Klaus Deppermann. Melchior Hoffman. Soziale Unruhen und apokalyptische Visionen im Zeitalter der Reformation, (Göttingen, 1979), 189-91; Hans J. Schoeps, Vom Himmlischen Fleisch Christi (Tübingen, 1951), 37-46; William Echard Keeney, The Development of Dutch Anabaptist Thought and Practice from 1539-1564 (Nieuwkoop, 1968), 89-91, 214. On Servetus, see Jerome Friedman, Michael Servetus. A Case Study in Total Heresy (Geneva, 1978), 65-71.

48 CS 7:541.3-11.

49 On these two theories, Joseph Needham, A History of Embryology (New York, 1959), 18-74, and Keeney, 92.

50 Neither man ever made mention of a female 'seed' and tended to use terms which emphasized Mary's nutritive role. Cf. Vadian, Antilogia, 27v, and CS 7:541.3-23, 731.25-31, 732.27-30.

51 CS 7:541.3-23. Thus, God provided the Aristotelian 'act' to Mary's 'potentiality'.

52 CS 7:877.10-21.

53 On this see Auguste Gaudel, 'Chronique de théologie dogmatique: La théologie de l'Assumptus Homo. Histoire et valeur doctrinale,' Revue des sciences religieuses 17 (1937), 64-90, 214-35.

54 Vadian, Epistola, 10-10v.

55 Epistola, 12-13.

56 Antilogia, 26v.

57 Pro veritate carnis, 40.

58 In this he was in good company. Aquinas rejected the term 'Homo Assumptus' because it seemed to lead in the direction of Arianism and Nestorianism (Gaudel, 220).

59 See, for example, Pro veritate carnis, 28v-29.

60 Nestorius had argued that the eternal (the Word) could not come from the temporal (Mary), CS 8:386.34-387.7.

61 CS 7:533.22-534.8, 545.9-546.5.

62 CS 8:380.9-26.

63 *Antilogia*, 52v-53.

64 *Antilogia*, 40-40v.

65 *Antilogia*, 26v-27; *Dreyzehen namhaffter irrthumb*, fol. Aii.

66 *Pro veritate carnis*, 37-38.

67 CS 7:734.22-25.

68 CS 7:734.33-735.22.

69 *Epistola*, 19v; CS 7:626.5-13.

70 *Pro veritate carnis*, 9v-10; but compare the Zwinglian understanding of the term (15v-16).

71 CS 7:489.21-24, 714.25-26; CS 8:395.30-396.13, 630.34-671.15.

72 *Epistola*, 18-19, 21v-22.

73 CS 7:609.3-14.

74 CS 7:724.21-725.5, 734.33-735.4, 738.37-739.8.

75 *Antilogia*, 58, 59v. Schwenckfeld seems to have believed that the 'essence' of a thing, like the Platonic Ideas, need not occupy space as such.

76 *Antilogia*, 41.

77 *Pro veritate carnis*, 14-14v. *Dreyzehen namhaffter irrthumb*, error no. 9, fol. AVa. Vadian went even further, pointing out that in the ancient church only God the Father had been actually worshipped. They prayed *through* Christ, but *to* God the Father (*Antilogia*, 129).

78 *Orthodoxa... Epistola*, 25-26.

79 *Antilogia*, 18. Cf. 24v.

80 CS 7:488.17-20; CS 8:396.27-397.14, 648.4-23.

81 Näf, 422-50.

82 *Epistola*, 37-37v; *Antilogia*, 51-51v, 84v-85, 97, 99-100.

83 *Antilogia*, 60v; CS 7:642.4-643.4, 646.4-7. On Vadian's use of the scholastics, *Antilogia*, 29v, 88v-89.

84 *Antilogia*, 93.

85 CS 7:638.9-27; CS 8:526.12-15, 527.6-529.12.

Catholic Opponents of Schwenckfeld

Peter J. A. Nissen

As Max Vorburger correctly indicated during the 1982 Strasbourg conference on religious dissent in the sixteenth century, John Fabri (1478-1541), ecclesiastical adviser of Ferdinand I and later bishop of Vienna, was the only early sixteenth-century Catholic controversialist who engaged fully the theological opinions of Schwenckfeld.[1] In 1529 Fabri published his *Christenliche ablainung des erschrockenlichen yrsal, so Caspar Schwenckfelder in der Schlesy wider die warhait des hochwirdigen sacraments leibs und bluets Christi aufzerichten understanden hat* in Vienna.[2] In a letter, written to Pope Clement VII in 1533, he also mentioned a *Confutatio haeresis Manicheorum in Sacramento contra quendam Silesitam.*[3] Vorburger thinks this is the Latin translation of the *Christenliche ablainung*, published in 1537/38 in Fabri's *Opuscula.*[4] But this is unlikely. The Latin version is prior to the German and already two years before the *Christenliche ablainung* Fabri produced a composition against Schwenckfeld, entitled *Confutatio novi et antehuc inauditi erroris circa Eucharistiam sive assertio veritatis de praesentia corporis et sanguinis D. N. I. C. in sacramento altaris contra Casp. Schwenckfelder Silesitam ad Fridericum Ducem Lignicensem.* It must have been written in June-August 1527, most likely in connection with the visit Fabri paid to Breslau in Ferdinand's service in May 1527. The intention of the piece was to warn Friedrich II of Leignitz against the teachings of his adviser Schwenckfeld on the Lord's Supper.[5] The *Christenliche ablainung* is a translation and adaptation of this Latin *Confutatio.*

In any event, Fabri was, as Vorburger supposes, the main and perhaps only source of information about Schwenckfeld in the influential *Commentaria de actis et scriptis Martini Lutheri Saxonis* by John Cochlaeus, first printed in Mainz in 1549 and reprinted many times thereafter.[6] Schwenckfeld defended himself against Cochlaeus' accusations in a letter of January 12, 1552, to Balthasar von Promnitz, bishop of Breslau.[7] That Cochlaeus in his turn was the source for the scarce information on the Schwenkfeldian movement in the continuation by the Italian Oratorian Oderich Raynaldus (1595-1671) of the *Annales ecclesiastici* of Cardinal Baronius (1538-1607) is clearly indicated in the *marginalia* of this work.[8]

The *Annales ecclesiastici* by Baronius and Raynaldus are the impressive culmination of the so called 'historical school' within Roman-Catholic controversial theology, a school which, for the most part, used arguments derived from the Church Fathers and the ecclesiastical tradition.[9] Next to this school there were two others: the 'scriptural school,' less far-reaching and of less influence, willing to meet the opponents by using only arguments derived from Scripture, and the 'dogmatic school,' aiming at a synthesis of both approaches.[10]

The best known representative of this last school is certainly the *Disputationes de controversiis christianae fidei adversus huius temporis haereticos* (1586-1593) by the Jesuit Robert Bellarmine. It is striking to note that nowhere in this handbook of Catholic apologetics are Caspar Schwenckfeld or his followers mentioned by name. But Bellarmine does mention Schwenckfeld—next to a casual mention in one of his sermons[11]—in another one of his works, namely in the chronology of world history, added to his *De scriptoribus ecclesiasticis liber unus.*[12] In that piece he states that Caspar Schwenckfeld, whom he sees as a Confessionist, that is to say as a follower of the Augsburg Confession, started to distinguish himself from the other Confessionists by devising new doctrines. As such Bellarmine mentions Schwenckfeld's doctrine of the human nature of Christ turning into a divine nature after his Ascension, and the opinion that the believer has to be led by the Spirit only and that the external word and the killing, written letter have to be rejected.

Staphylus, Cassander, and Lindanus

What is interesting is the source Bellarmine uses for his information, namely a work by Friedrich Staphylus. This work leads us to another stage in Catholic polemics against Schwenkfeldianism, some thirty years later than Fabri's writing.

Staphylus, born in 1512, was a Lutheran theologian for some time, but became a Catholic again in 1552. In 1554 he became a counsellor of Ferdinand I and in 1558 of Albrecht V of Bavaria. For some time he taught in Neisse in Silesia, the cradle of early Schwenkfeldianism.[13]

In 1558 Staphylus published a work, *Theologiae Martini Lutheri trimembris epitome. De topicis praedicamentis, seu theologicis principiis, de materia praesertim controversiarum theologicarum, de successione et concordia discipulorum Lutheri in Augustana Confessione. Nuper collecta Wormatiae, durante Colloquio,* in which he denounces the mutual discord among the reformers. In only two short passages Staphylus discusses Schwenkfeldianism. Firstly, in the *catalogus sectarum inter sacramentarios* he says that Schwenckfeld denies the real presence of Christ's body in the eucharist because he believes that Christ's human nature turned into a divine one after his Ascension. Staphylus also mentions Schwenckfeld's rejection of external symbols here.[14] The second passage is to be found in the *catalogus sectarum inter confessionistas.* Here Staphylus repeats his comments on Schwenckfeld's christology and on his rejection of external religion, sacraments, and preaching. He also says that according to Schwenckfeld love, faith, and justice are particles of the divine nature, and that Judas did not really receive the eucharist at the Last Supper.[15]

Staphylus may have known some of Schwenckfeld's many booklets. At least he leaves the impression of having seen them by saying that Schwenckfeld's books circulate in great numbers among the people. 'He who wants to read them, can do it.'[16]

These short passages, clearly Bellarmine's sources, raised great excitement among Schwenckfeld's followers. One wonders about the nature of the reaction. Was Schwenckfeld perhaps gladly surprised to be attacked at last by a Catholic writer, so that he could feel that he was at last taken seriously by Catholic theologians?

Before turning to the Schwenkfeldian reaction to Staphylus' book, we first have to introduce two other Catholic opponents of Schwenckfeld: Georg Cassander and William Lindanus. Although according to Bergsma the influence of Schwenkfeldianism in the Low Countries was limited.[17] it is important to note that both Cassander and Lindanus had their beginnings in this region.

Georg Cassander (1513-1566) was born in the neighbour-hood of Bruges, and worked for the most part as an irenical theologian in Cologne.[18] We know that he seriously studied some of Schwenckfeld's writings. The University Library of Leiden has a manuscript with notes on all kinds of theologi-cal items, most of them in Cassander's handwriting.[19] Among these there are excerpts from four writings of Caspar Schwenck-feld, not in Cassander's handwriting, but with marginal notes written by him.[20]

Cassander considered Schwenckfeld's christology as his main error, and to fight it he edited the fifth-century works of Vigilius of Thapsus (still called Vigilius of Trente by Cas-sander) on christology and Trinity in 1555. In his *Commentar-ius de duabus in Christo naturis et unica hypostasis, adversus haereses huius aetatis*,[21] added to this edition, he points out that the christological errors of the first centuries of Chris-tianity have revived in the sixteenth century. Schwenckfeld's christology then, together with that of Menno Simons, is la-belled by him as Eutychianism,[22] as Protestant theologians like Vadian, Bullinger, Coccius, and Brenz did before him.[23]

Cassander was one of the sources for another Dutch polemi-cist: William Lindanus (1525-1588). After completing his stud-ies at the University of Louvain Lindanus became professor in Dillingen (1554-1557), religious commissioner in Friesland (1557-1560), dean of The Hague (1560-1561) and then bishop of Roermond (1561-1588) and of Ghent (1588).[24] In his numer-ous writings he commented on Schwenckfeld at several places. The most important of these writings known to Schwenckfeld's circle were the *Tabulae vigentium nunc atque grassantium pas-sim haereseon anascevasticae atque analyticae* of 1558. In it Lindanus speaks about Schwenckfeld in three sections.

The first one is of more or less bibliographical importance. In the second table Lindanus quotes a work by *Gaspar Zwenck-feldius* on the Augsburg Confession, in which the author re-futes the tenth article on transsubstantiation as more Papist than Protestant. This piece was not yet printed, as Lindanus states.[25] He must have meant Schwenckfeld's *Der LVIII. Send-brieff, geschrieben an etliche eifferige güthertzige Adels und an-dere Persoonen im Bapstumb, so Herren C. S. bittlich ersücht haben, sein Iudicium uber die Augspurgischen Confession und derselbigen eingeleibte Artickul mitzutheilen*, a letter which did not appear until 1570, when it was published in the *Sendbri-eff von der Bepstischen Leere und Glauben*.[26] But it is known that it circulated in manuscript before it was printed,[27] and Lindanus' statement is the first witness of this circulation.

In the third table Lindanus speaks again about Schwenck-feld. He states that his movement began in 1545 (sic!) and he briefly discusses his doctrine of the incarnation, adding that Schwenckfeld's supporters were mainly to be found in the towns of Silesia, and that they considered themselves to be en-thusiastic and divinely inspired.[28] Finally Lindanus mentions Schwenckfeld in the fourth table as a renewer of the heresy of Eutyches. Here he refers to Cassander as his source.[29]

Not only in the *Tabulae*, but also in some other writings Lindanus vents his wrath on Schwenckfeld. In the second book of his *Dubitantius de vera certaque per Christi Jesu Evangelium salutis aeternae via libri tres*, a dialogue between the doubter (*dubitantius*) and the steadfast one (*constantius*) published in 1565, Lindanus dresses up a catalogue of heretics. And of course Schwenckfeld turns up again. Lindanus attacks his doc-trine of the Lord's Supper, his rejection of the written word, and his christological teachings. The doctrine of Christ's heav-enly flesh Schwenckfeld borrowed, as Lindanus tells us, from Valentinus.[30]

Lindanus speaks again about Schwenckfeld in two later works. In *De fugiendis nostri seculi idolis*, printed at Cologne in 1580, he mentions Schwenckfeld several times, as a degener-ation of the Lutheran Reformation[31] and as a renewer of the heresies of Basilides, the Manichaeans,[32] and Eutyches.[33] In a table of eighty-five heretical sentences about the words of con-secration Schwenckfeld appears four times.[34] Finally Schwenck-feld gets a brief mention in Lindanus' letter to the citizens of Weert, printed at Louvain in 1581 as *Van d'eenicheyt des Christen gheloofs*.[35]

In his later works Lindanus quotes several sources concern-ing Schwenckfeld. Most of them are Protestant theologians, such as Flacius Illyricus, Beza, and Luther. But he also refers to Catholic writers, namely to Cassander and Staphylus, whom we have met earlier, and to Hosius, whom we will meet later. The *Tabulae* and the *Dubitantius* must have had a huge influ-ence. The first was reprinted in 1559, 1561, 1562, and 1569.[36] In 1565 it was translated into English by Lewis Evans,[37] and in 1567 into Dutch.[38] The *Dubitantius* was reprinted in 1571 and translated into French in 1566. into Dutch in 1567, and into German in 1568.[39]

A Schwenkfelder Response

All these Catholic refutations of Schwenckfeld's teachings did not remain unanswered. As early as 1558 one of Schwenckfeld's most devoted followers must have read both Staphylus' *Theologiae Martini Lutheri trimembris epitome* and Lindanus' *Tabulae.* He decided to reply to them with a booklet, published in 1558 under the pseudonym Theophilus Agricola as *Entschuldigung fur herren Caspar Schwenckfeldt, auff Friedrich Staphyli und Wilhelmi Lindani zugemessne Calumnien unnd unwarheit, mit gründlicher erklärung unnd bericht, dass sie nicht können beybringen, was sie in beschuldigen. Was auch C. S. glauben-bekandtnus und halten ist von den zweyen naturen in Christo.*[40] The writer of this booklet was aware of the fact that it was one of the first defenses of Schwenkfeldianism against Catholic polemics. He remarks,'Schwenckfeldt hat bissher nicht vil mit den Bäpstlern gestritten, weyl sie andere Deformatores haben. Es ist aber gleichwol auss irem yetzigem schreiben wider C. S. züvermercken, dass sie auch, unnd nicht allein die Lutherischen können Calumniern, und mit züchten zureden unverschampt liegen, dass schier eine parthey derselbigen scribenten ist wie die ander.'[41]

Staphylus clearly appears as the main opponent of Schwenckfeld. The center-piece of the writing is primarily directed against him: *Kurtze Entschuldigung für Herrn Caspar Schwenckfeldt, auf Staphyli beschuldigung und zugemessnen Calumnien, was in betrifft.*[42] The author tries to refute Staphylus' accusations that Schwenckfeld resumed old heresies on Christ's nature and person and on the Lord's Supper. Next to Staphylus he also addresses Lindanus and Cassander, and several Protestant opponents of Schwenckfeld, among whom were Calvin, Beza, Valerandus Pollanus, Flacius Illyricus, Peter Martyr, and Henry Panthaleon. From the three Catholic writers he must have read Staphylus' and Lindanus' works. But he does not seem to have read Cassander's commentary on Vigilius. He only quotes Cassander as Lindanus' source: that Schwenckfeld renewed Eutychianism is to be found in Lindanus 'sampt seinem lieben und falschen zeügen Cassandro.'[43]

The *Entschuldigung* is followed by a short appendix, *Was Caspar Schwenckfeldts glauben, halten und bekanntnuss ist, von den zweyen Naturen in Christo*, in which the author refutes the accusation of Manichaeism.[44] It must have been written early in 1558, because Schwenckfeld sent it together with a letter in March 1558 to his learned friend John Heid von Daun, the humanist and translator of several of his writings.[45] But it must have been written after the publication of Staphylus' and Lindanus' books, because they are both cited in the appendix.

The *Entschuldigung* was published pseudonymously under the name Theophilus Agricola. This pseudonym was used in no less than nine booklets in defense of Schwenkfeldianism, all dated between 1556 and 1558. The person behind the piece would remain mysterious if the editors of the *Corpus Schwenckfeldianorum* had not discovered a copy of the booklet on which a handwritten notice reveals the identity of the author: 'Disser Author heist Georg Mayer Jetzt Anno 72 Pfarher zu Leder oben bei Augsburck steht dem Rellinger zu. Und ist derselbige der die Institution in oder uber die Augsburgische Confession geschrieben oder gemacht hat.'[46] This Georg Mayer, who obviously was a minister at the village of Leeder near Augsburg possessed by the Augsburg family of Rehlinger, remains an otherwise unknown person.

Staphylus had another supposition about the true identity of Theophilus Agricola. He thought it to be the learned humanist John Longus or Lange. Lange, born in 1503 in Freidstadt (Silesia), received his first education in Neisse, where he was a pupil of Valentine Crautwald. He continued his studies in Cracow and Vienna, was a schoolmaster in Goldberg (1527) and Neisse (1529), city chancellor in Schweidnitz (1535), secretary to bishop Jacob von Salza (1536), and a counsellor and orator at the court of Vienna. In about 1557 he returned to Schweidnitz, where he died in 1567. He left several editions of patristic sources and published some scholarly writings.[47]

Staphylus proposes this identity in his defense of the *Trimembris epitome*, published in 1559 and reprinted several times. This defense, entitled *Defensio confutationis trimembris theologiae, quin verius Mataeologiae. Mart. Lutheri, contra Philip. Melanthonem, Suenkfeldianum Longinum, And. Musculum, Mat. Flacc. Illyricum et Iaco. Andream Shmidelinum, aedificatores Babyloniae turris*,[48] was of course not only dictated by the Schwenkfeldian *Entschuldigung*. As the title indicates Staphylus also met severe criticism from Lutheran theologians, namely Philip Melanchthon, Andreas Musculus, Matthias Flacius Illyricus, and Jacob Andreae Schmidlin.[49]

One part of the *Defensio*, the *Responsio ad tergiversationem Suenkfeldiani Longini*, is explicitly directed against the supposed author of the *Entschuldigung*, whom Staphylus calls Longinus. Christology is a major topic in this. Staphylus tries to prove his charge of Eutychianism by an exposition of the christological controversies in the early church and by comparing them to quotations from Schwenckfeld's writings. He also reproaches Schwenckfeld with the heresy of Manichaeism, because Schwenckfeld in his view teaches that faith and justice make a man essentially equal to God.[50]

Two years later Lange answered Staphylus' supposition by emphatically denying being a Schwenkfelder. He did so in an edition of poems by Gregory of Nazianzus, printed in Basel in January 1561.[51] In this collection Staphylus included some poems of his own, and among these is an *Adversus Calumniosam Friederichi Staphyli aspersionem Joannis Langi spongia.*

Lange's denial of Schwenkfeldianism was an offense to Schwenckfeld himself. He expressed his anger about it in a letter to his friend Hans Wilhelm von Laubenberg, probably written in July 1561. No one needs to be called after his name, he states, but those who confess the doctrine he teaches ought to acknowledge this. Schwenckfeld suspects that Lange denied his Schwenkfeldianism out of fear for the Emperor in whose service Lange had been.[52]

That the Emperor on the insistence of Staphylus undertook measures against Lange, is clear from a letter written by Staphylus to Cardinal Stanislaus Hosius in May 1561. Both Lindanus and Staphylus were invited to attend the third session of the Council of Trent.[53] But Staphylus refused, as did Lindanus.[54] In his friendly letter of reply to Hosius he gives as a first reason for his refusal the fact that he is a layman and that he does not want to leave his wife and children for such a long time. But' the second reason is that he wants to be present when Lange or one of his other opponents is going to move again. He then refers to Lange's treatise in defense of Schwenckfeld's doctrine, by which he must mean the

Entschuldigung. He only has one copy of it, but as soon as he receives the copy he is expecting from the court of the duke of Bavaria, he will send one to Hosius. The heart of the controversy is, as he says, the question whether Christ's human nature became divine after his Ascension: 'I deny it, he affirms it. When you receive the booklet, you will understand it more clearly.' He also states that when he visited the imperial court in Vienna a year earlier, the emperor wrote to Lange in order to forbid him to undertake anything against Staphylus in public. If he thought he was wronged by Staphylus he could fight it out before an ordinary court. But Lange, as Staphylus laments, ignored the Emperor's letter. About his *Defensio* (*libellum meum nuper editum*) Staphylus says that it proved to be fruitful; it has been printed twice and the printer just announced a third edition.[55] In fact already four printings had appeared by that time.[56]

In the meantime, Caspar Schwenckfeld several times tried to get in touch with Staphylus. He wrote to him twice in 1559. Schwenckfeld had heard that Staphylus was said to be less averse to his teaching than he was to his use of unusual words which he himself did not understand, and that he therefore invited Schwenckfeld to a friendly conference in Ingolstadt, in order to solve their misunderstandings.

In June 1559 Schwenckfeld replied to this invitation by *Der XXI. Sendbrieff, geschrieben an den wirdigen und Geleerten Herrn Fridericum Staphilum. C. S. entschuldigung, dass er kein Manicheer, noch Eutychianer, oder dergleichen sey.*[57] Schwenckfeld again refused Staphylus' accusations and asked him to read his books and give account of his errors, so that he might answer him. John Heid von Daun, who was the bearer of the letter, could give him, Schwenckfeld writes, the information and books desired, all at Schwenckfeld's cost. Schwenckfeld would have been pleased to accept Staphylus' invitation to the conference, but his age and the weakness of his body prevented him to travel, as did the fact that he was nowhere safe from the Lutherans, who were continually on the lookout for him.

Staphylus did receive this first letter, but he confided to the bearer that he hesitated to send a written reply for fear that Schwenckfeld would publish it. Heid von Daun passed this message to Schwenckfeld, who then wrote a second letter in July.[58]

He says that he never published any of the numerous letters he received, except for a letter from Melanchthon, written on February 16, 1542, which was published in 1557. Although he hopes it will be unnecessary because Staphylus might have recieved his books by now, he nevertheless briefly replies to four points of error which he was accused of by Staphylus.

But Staphylus did not answer this second letter either. He wrote to a friend of Schwenckfeld, Adam Reissner, telling him that Schwenckfeld wrote to him twice desiring a colloquy. Schwenckfeld heard about this letter, and explained to Reissner that it had not been he, but Staphylus himself who desired a conference,[59] but Staphylus never answered his letters nor replied to the books he received from him. In case Reissner would want to answer Staphylus' letter, Schwenckfeld offers to assist him by adding an appendix to his letter: *Artickel mit welchen Fridericus Staphylus C. Schwenckfelden unbillich in seinen Büchlin belegt, und beschuldiget hat.*[60]

As we have seen Staphylus published his defense of the *Trimembris epitome* in 1559, in which he repeated his accusations about Schwenkfeldian christology. It was answered only two years later by the *Zeügnis der h. Schrifft und Vätter, vom Artickel der Gottwerdunge des Menschens Jesu Christi, Das solchs die Reine Apostolische Catholische Lehre unsers Christlichen glaubens sey.*[61] According to the editors of the *Corpus* this booklet was the joint work of both Schwenckfeld and Theophilus Agricola. The style seems to be that of Theophilus—it is full of biblical, patristic, and literary quotations. And to the first defense of Schwenkfeldianism against Staphylus, the author of the *Zeügnus* refers in plural as 'unser ersten Entschuldigung.' This could indeed mean that Schwenckfeld was involved in writing the first *Entschuldigung.* In his letter to Reissner, just mentioned, he refers to 'mein und anderer verantwortung der bösen Artickel halb.'

The *Zeügnus* is accompanied with an appendix,[62] in which the author attacks another book by Staphylus that had just recently appeared: *Christlicher Gegenbericht an den Gottseligen gemeinen Layen. Vom rechten waren verstand des Göttlichen worts. Von verdolmetschung der Teütschen Bibel und von der ainigkeit der Lutherischen Predicanten*, printed in Neisse in 1560.[63] Futhermore the *Zeügnus* speaks about 'ein New Lateinische getruckte Tabula... die er mit Lindano geheckt hat.'

That this table of heretics was Staphylus' seemed obvious to
the author of *Zeügnus*: 'wiewol er seinen Namen nicht zur Tafel
gesetzt, doch verraht ihn sein genanter Gegenbericht, auch
der stilus und sprache, und die Schlesischen Calumnien des
züsatzs, die in den vorigen nit gestanden, Das er solcher Tabulae famosae auctor, und ein Calumniator ist.'[64] In all probability the author of the *Zeügnus* had the 1561 Paris edition
of Lindanus' *Tabulae* in his hands. It was printed by William
Guillard and Amalric Warancore with slight changes and the
addition of Staphylus' *Epitome* to Lindanus' work under the
title *Sectae Lutheranae trimembris epitome*.[65]

The edition of the *Zeügnus* in 1561 seems to have been the
last stage in the controversy between Caspar Schwenckfeld and
his most fervent Catholic opponent Friedrich Staphylus.[66]

Stanislaus Hosius

But there is another Catholic controversialist to be mentioned
who paid much attention to Schwenckfeld's movement, although his statements seem to have remained unnoticed by
the Schwenkfelders themselves. We already met him as one of
Lindanus' sources and as Staphylus' correspondent: the Polish
Cardinal Stanislaus Hosius.

Hosius was born in Cracow in 1504.[67] He studied in his
native city and in Bologna and Padua. He then worked for
some time in the Polish chancellery. Shortly before 1544 he
received ordination. In 1549 he became a bishop of Kulm and
in 1551 of Ermland in the eastern part of Prussia, belonging
to the Polish empire. Because of his great zeal in the Counter-
Reformation (Peter Canisius called him the best bishop of his
time) he was called to Rome in 1558 and created a Cardinal
in 1561. As a papal legate he took part in the third session
of the Council of Trent (1562-63), which he among others had
prepared from 1560 on as a nuncio in Vienna.[68] After returning
to Poland for six years (1563-1569) Hosius died as a papal
penitentiary in Rome in 1579.

Hosius strongly stressed the divine authority of the church
which is in its essence one and undivided. He assumed an irreconcilable attitude towards the reformers and fervently opposed
the endeavour of irenical theologians, such as Georg Witzel,
whom he personally excluded from the Council of Trent. Hosius' most influential writing is his *Confessio fidei catholicae*

christianae, first printed in Cracow in 1553 and reprinted or
translated some thirty times.[69]

The work that is of importance to us, however, is his treatise on the origin of heresies, which formed the first book of
the *Confutatio prolegomenon Brentii, quae primum scripsit adversus venerabilem virum Petrum a Soto, deinde vero Petrus
Paulus Vergerius apud Polonos temere defendenda suscepit.*
This work was directed against Brenz's *Prolegomena in Apologiam Confessionis*,[70] the first part of the defence of the *Confessio Wirtembergica* (1551)[71] against the criticism of the Spanish Dominican Pedro de Sodo.[72] It was first printed in Cologne
in 1558, and it went through several reprintings in Antwerp,
Cologne, Paris, and Lyon.[73] Soon the first book on the origin
of heresies was also printed separately as *De origine haeresium
nostri temporis* at Louvain in 1559.[74] It was reprinted in Paris
(1559 and 1560) and Antwerp (1565). In 1561 a French translation was published, reprinted in 1564, 1567, and 1568. And in
1565 it was translated into English as *A most excellent treatise
of the begynning of heresyes*.[75] Finally it was also included in
Hosius' *Opera Omnia*, regularly reprinted after 1562.[76] Thus, it
becomes clear that Hosius' view on the origin of heresies found
a huge dispersion within ten years all over North-Western Europe.

In the first book of the *Confutatio* Hosius gives a survey
of the rise of new heresies in the sixteenth century.[77] In his
representation the four Gospels of the Bible have been driven
out by four new gospels, namely those of the four major heresies. And these four are, according to him, those of Luther,
of Calvin, of the Anabaptists, and of Schwenckfeld.[78] None of
the other Catholic writers ever attached such an importance
to Schwenkfeldianism. To them Schwenckfeld was—the example of Bellarmine may illustrate this—nothing more than one
of the many insignificant fanatics of the Radical Reformation.
His movement only deserved attention as a historical curiosity;
from the point of view of dogmatic and apologetic theology it
was to be neglected.[79]

Hosius attached such an important place to Schwenkfeldianism perhaps because he experienced it more closely than the
other writers we have discussed. Although the bishopric of
Ermland still was some 300 kilometers from Silesia, yet this
centre of Schwenkfeldianism to Hosius' feeling must have been

situated in 'his' part of Europe. Nevertheless, Hosius did not think of Schwenkfeldianism as a local movement limited to Silesia alone. Schwenckfeld's doctrine was, as he states, spread all over Germany and even over Switzerland. Some of Schwenckfeld's followers even boasted that in several towns one could find more Schwenkfelders than Lutherans. Hosius quotes Melanchthon, who writes that Schwenckfeld (or as he calls him following Luther's example, *Stenckfeldius*) is a 'hundred-hander' (*centimanus*), having vassals everywhere who spread his booklets and who rouse to rebellion. In any event, he certainly thinks that Schwenckfeld's following is not to be neglected.[80]

We may ask whether geographical proximity is a sufficient explanation for Hosius' interest in Schwenkfeldianism. Is it possible that he had had more to do with the movement than we are able to trace now? Whether or not, some five years after the publication of the *Confutatio* the Protestant camp accused Hosius of being a Schwenkfeldian himself! Matthias Flacius Illyricus and Nicolaus Gallus made use of the accusation in a book against the Council of Trent, the *Protestatio*, published in 1563 in a German and Latin edition,[81] and Hosius himself mentions it in a letter he wrote from Trent to the Catholic theologian Julius Pflug on February 21, 1563.[82]

What value do we have to attach to this charge? Was it not more than an invention of Flacius and Gallus, possibly suggested by the attention Hosius paid to Schwenckfeld in the *Confutatio?* Or did it still contain a nucleus of truth? We simply do not know. What we do know is that Hosius received his ordination at an unusually late age; he was almost forty years old when he was ordained a priest.[83] As much as we know about the last 35 years of his life, as little do we know about the first 40 years.[84] He followed a career typical for a well-to-do humanist: *peregrinatio academica* and activity as a chancellor. And it was in the midst of well-to-do academics that Schwenckfeld found most of his adherents. Valentine Crautwald, for example, the systematician of Schwenkfeldianism, also studied in Cracow and worked during ten years at the chancellery of a bishop.[85]

In the *Confutatio* Hosius declares explicitly (but does this very explicitness not raise any suspicion?) that he has all his knowledge about Schwenckfeld at second hand, 'I do not know

the man nor have I seen his writings.'[86] His most important
source is the writings of Matthias Flacius Illyricus, one of the
major Protestant fighters against Schwenkfeldianism.[87] Besides
he refers to what Philip Melanchthon wrote about Schwenckfeld in the prologue to his commentary on the Letter to the
Romans.[88] But he does not exclusively fall back on literary
sources. He states that during a legation journey to Charles
V—and this must have been in 1549, since he then visited
Charles V in Brussels and Ghent and Philip II in Antwerp[89]—
he was able to speak to trustworthy persons who could procure
him some interesting information. They told him that the
Schwenkfelders after their joining the movement really seemed
to change, as if they were touched by the Holy Ghost, and that
they laid down the old Adam and no longer lived in the flesh
but walked by the Spirit. Anyone could see that they belonged,
as Paul says, to Christ Jesus, because they had crucified the
flesh with all its passions and desires (Gal. 5:24). But for Hosius this was only an occasion to compare the Schwenkfelders
to the Psallians, the Eutychians, the Anthropomorphites, the
Ebionites, and the Tatians, early Christian heresies which had,
nevertheless, every appearance of being pious ascetic movements. They show us how the devil can make himself out as
an angel of light.

Schwenckfeld came to his erroneous doctrines, according to
Hosius, by reading Luther.[90] He saw new heresies around him
and then got the idea of founding a sect for himself. As he
read that Luther noticed that all heretics referred to Scripture
and that the Bible therefore could be called a *liber haereticorum*,[91] Schwenckfeld drew the conclusion that Scripture can
not have any authority. It is only a creature, not more than
that. Therefore, we must not be taught by laws or by Scripture
anymore, but by God himself. We must look for the voice of
heaven. The Almighty himself will then instruct us through
dreams and visions.

Schwenckfeld was, as Hosius tells us, not the first one who
tried to talk people out of reading the Bible and who wanted
to replace the Word of God with visions. Thomas Müntzer did
this before him. But Schwenckfeld was the one who completed
these erroneous teachings. He and his followers nevertheless
referred to several passages in the Bible, and Hosius noted

some of them (Jer. 31, Mt. 23, 1 Cor. 13. Heb. 8, James 3, 2 Pet. 1 and 1 John 2).

Schwenckfeld's doctrine in Hosius' eyes is more or less the culmination of the Protestant heresy. If Luther started with abolishing the external priesthood and the sacramental sacrifice, now Schwenckfeld abolished the authority of the Bible and substituted it with dreams and visions. The false gospel, commenced by the devil in Luther, was completed in Schwenckfeld.

Hosius' position was widely spread in the third quarter of the sixteenth century, both as a part of the *Confutatio prolegomenon Brentii* and as a separate work *De origine haeresium nostri temporis*. His information was highly significant in forming the Catholic image of Caspar Schwenckfeld and his movement in those days.[92]

We have already noted that Lindanus referred to Hosius as one of his sources. In addition several later Catholic historians made use of Hosius' information. One of them was the learned French Catholic Florimond de Raemond (ca. 1540-1601), chancellor of the parliament in Bordeaux. He quoted Hosius, among others, in his often reprinted and translated *L'Histoire de la Naissance Progrez et Decadance de l'Heresie de ce siècle*, first published in 1605.[93]

Another witness is the French Jesuit, François Catrou. He made use of Hosius' information in his *Histoire des anabaptistes*, published in 1699 and meant to be the first volume of a *Histoire du fanatisme dans la religion protestante depuis son origine*. At the end of a relatively ample discussion of Schwenckfeld (whom he consistently calls 'Schuvenfeld) he quotes the passage of 'le Cardinal Hozius' about the large dispersion of Schwenkfeldianism, including the information about his legation journey to Charles V.[94]

Finally Bergsma has shown that in the seventeenth century even the Reformed theologian, Johannes Hoornbeeck (1617-1666), professor successively in Utrecht and Leiden, diligently made use of Hosius' information about Schwenckfeld in his *Summa controversiarum religionis cum infidelibus, haereticis, schismaticis* (Utrecht, 1653).[95]

That Hosius remained interested in Schwenkfeldianism even after the publication of his *Confutatio*, or at least that his correspondents expected him to be interested, is clear from the letter of Staphylus, about which we spoke earlier. It is remarkable that Staphylus only briefly mentions his Lutheran opponents but goes into details about his experiences with the supposed Schwenkfelder, Lange. He evidently expected Hosius to be especially interested in Lange's actions. In Hosius' own letters one also finds scattered information about Schwenkfeldianism.[96]

After all this it might cause some astonishment that Hosius never noted Schwenckfeld's doctrines during the Council of Trent.[97] But from the point of view of the Catholic theologians it is not altogether incomprehensible. As we said earlier, they hardly considered Schwenkfeldianism a dogmatic movement that had to be taken seriously, but only an historical curiosity, illustrating the Babylonian confusion of voices of the Reformation. And such curiosities were not considered to be relevant to the fathers gathered at Trent to formulate a new testimony of the Catholic tradition of faith. On this point of view Hosius, in spite of his great interest in Schwenkfeldianism and his possible earlier involvement in this movement, was no exception.[98]

Notes

[1] M. Vorburger, 'Die Auseinandersetzung Johann Fabris mit Caspar Schwenckfeld,' in M. Lienhard (ed.), *Les Dissidents du XVIe siècle entre l'Humanisme et le Catholicisme* (Baden-Baden, 1983), 245-49.

[2] W. Klaiber (ed.), *Katholische Kontroverstheologen und Reformer des 16. Jahrhunderts. Ein Werkverzeichnis* (Münster, 1978), 102, no. 1094. L. Helbling, *Dr. Johann Fabri. Generalvikar von Konstanz und Bischof von Wien 1478-1541. Beiträge zu seiner Lebensgeschichte* (Münster, 1941), 55-57 and 144, nos. 36 and 37. See also Chr. Radey, *Dr. Johann Fabri, Bischof von Wien (1530-1541), Wegbereiter der katholischen Reform, Rat König Ferdinands* (Wien, 1976), 18. In defense Schwenckfeld wrote *Vom waren und falschen verstandt und Glauben, sampt den ursachen dess irrthumbs und abfals im Artickel von dem H. Sacrament dess leibs und blüts Christi. Auff D. Johan Fabri calumnien, beziecht unnd unwarheyt, so er mir desshalben inn seinem aussschreiben unnd sunst zugemessen* (CS 3:615-710).

[3] W. Friedensburg, 'Beiträge zum Briefwechsel der katholischen Gelehrten Deutschlands im Reformationszeitalter,' *Zeitschrift für Kirchengeschichte*, 20 (1900), 72.

[4] Vorburger, 246.

[5] H. Weigelt, *Spiritualistische Tradition im Protestantismus. Die Geschichte des Schwenckfeldertums in Schlesien* (Berlin, 1973), 90-92. See

also K. Ecke. *Schwenckfeld. Luther und der Gedanke einer apostolischen Reformation* (Berlin. 1911). 5. In defense Schwenckfeld wrote a letter to Jacob von Salza. bishop of Breslau. in October 1527 (CS 2:637-70). Fabri is mentioned there on 644 and 658.

6   Vorburger, 245. On this work see A. Herte, *Die Lutherkommentare des Johannes Cochläus. Kritische Studie zur Geschichtschreibung im Zeitalter der Glaubensspaltung* (Münster, 1935) and A. Herte, *Das katholische Lutherbild im Bann der Lutherkommentare des Cochläus* (Münster, 1943).

7   *Beantwortung wider das falsche zeugknus Johannis Cochlei* (CS 13:3-21).

8   Vorburger, 245 and 248, notes 1 and 2.

9   H. Jedin, *Kardinal Caesar Baronius. Der Anfang der katholischen Kirchengeschichtsschreibung im 16. Jahrhundert* (Münster, 1978).

10   P. Polman, *Die polemische Methode der ersten Gegner der Reformation* (Münster, 1931). See also his masterpiece *L'Element Historique dans la Controverse religieuse du XVIe Siècle* (Gembloux, 1932).

11   In his *Conciones duodecim continentes argumenta totidem ad hominem catholicum in sua fide confirmandum et haereticum a perfidia sua convertendum*, sermon X: *de comparatione haereticorum*. See R. Bellarminus, *Opera Omnia*, ed. by J. Févre (Paris, 1873), 9:570.

12   *Chronologia brevis ab orbe condito usque ad annum Domini MDCXIII*, in the column 'Haeresiarchae'. I have used the edition Cologne, 1622, in which we find the passage on 123. See also Bellarminus, *Opera Omnia*, (Paris, 1874), 12:504.

13   J. Soffner, *Friedrich Staphylus, ein katholischer Kontroversist und Apologet aus der Mitte des 16. Jahrhunderts, gest. 1564* (Breslau, 1904).

14   I have used the edition Paris, 1561, fol. 38r. In the edition Antwerp, 1562: fol. 20r.

15   Ibid., fol. 41r. In the Antwerp edition: fol. 22r.

16   Ibid.: Libri ipsius Suencfeldii multiplices versantur in manibus hominum: legat, qui vult.

17   W. Bergsma. *Aggaeus van Albada (c. 1525-1587), schwenckfeldiaan, staatsman en strijder voor verdraagzaamheid* (Meppel. 1983) 57-73. See also his article 'Aggaeus van Albada (circa 1525-1587),' *Spiegel historiael* 20 (1985). 21-27.

18   On his 'ecumenical' theology see M. Birck, *Georg Cassander's Ideen über die Wiedervereinigung der christlichen Confessionen in Deutschland. Eine Studie* (Köln, 1876); W. Rottscheidt, 'Georg Cassander, ein rheinischer Ireniker des 16. Jahrhunderts,' *Monatshefte für Rheinische Kirchengeschichte*, 12 (1918), 105-122; P. Bröder, *Georg Cassanders Vermittlungsversuche zwischen Protestanten und Katholiken* (Marburg, 1931); M. Nolte, *Georgius Cassander en zijn oecumenisch streven* (Nijmegen, 1951); F. W. Kantzenbach, *Das Ringen um die Einheit der Kirche im Jahrhundert der Reformation. Vertreter, Quellen und Motive*

des 'ökumenischen' Gedankens von Erasmus von Rotterdam bis Georg
Callixt (Stuttgart, 1957), 203-29; A. Stegmann, 'Georges Cassander
victime des orthodoxies,' in Aspects du libertinisme au XVIe siècle.
Actes du colloque international de Sommières (Paris, 1974), 199-214.
See also my essay 'De anti-doperse geschriften van Petrus van Blom-
meveen, Cornelius Crocus, Joannes Bunderius en Georgius Cassander,'
Doopsgezinde Bijdragen, nieuwe reeks 11 (1985).

[19] Leiden, Universiteitsbibliotheek, Codices Vulcaniani 94D. See the printed catalogue Bibliotheca Universitatis Leidensis. Codices manuscripti I.
Codices Vulcaniani (Leiden, 1910), 39.

[20] On fol. 115r-116v excerpts from: (a) 'Von der hailigen Schrifft, irem
Innhalt, Ampt, rechtem Nutz, Brauch, und missbrauch etc'. (CS
12:419-541); (b) 'Confession unnd Erclerung von Erkandtnus Christo
und seiner Göttlichen Herrlicheit, das dritt theil' (CS 7:727-884);
(c) 'Ain Geschrifftliche Collation Philippi Melanthons unnd Caspar
Schwenckfelds: ob der Mensch Jesus Christus ain erschaffener Creatur oder Gottes aingeborner Son sey' (CS 7:497-509, cf. CS 15:232-
33). On fol. 122v-124r excerpts from: (d) 'Von der Anbettunge Christi.
Darneben auch auff das büchlin des auszzugs ausz D. Joachim von
Watt büchern wirt geantwurt, wider die leere von der vermainten Creaturlichait am Herren Christo' (CS 8:325-99). Marginal notes in Cassander's handwriting are to be found on fol. 115v-116v. On fol. 117r-
122r we find notes, written by Cassander, on christological errors.

[21] Klaiber, 56, no. 606. There are still many copies of this printing
(Cologne, 1555), but the text is more easily accessible in Cassander's
Opera Omnia (Paris, 1616), 576-613. A more ample discussion of this
work will be included in my forthcoming book on Catholic writings
against Anabaptism in the Low Countries.

[22] Cassander, 577.

[23] G. Maron, Individualismus und Gemeinschaft bei Caspar von Schwenckfeld. Seine Theologie dargestellt mit besonderer Ausrichtung auf
seinen Kirchenbegriff (Stuttgart, 1961) 10-16.

[24] M. Willemsen, Beredeneerd Bibliographisch Overzicht der Werken van
Wilhelmus Lindanus, eersten Bisschop van Roermond (Roermond,
1896); W. Schmetz, Wilhelm van der Lindt, erster Bischof von Roermond (Münster, 1926); P. Th. van Beuningen, Wilhelmus Lindanus als
inquisiteur en bisschop. Bijdrage tot zijn biografie (1525-1576) (Assen,
1966).

[25] I used the editions Paris, 1561 and Antwerp, 1562, fol. Blr. Lindanus
speaks about a 'scripto libello nobis.' Willemsen (12) then concludes
that Schwenckfeld had directed the writing to Lindanus himself. But by
'nobis' Lindanus must have meant 'to us, Catholics.' If Schwenckfeld's
writing about the Augsburg Confession dates from the same year as
the Confession itself, i.e., 1530, Lindanus was only five years old as he
wrote it.

[26] CS 3:862-940. In the 'Sendbrieff von der Bepstischen Leere und
Glauben,' 1570, 626-79. See also P. G. Eberlein, 'Schwenckfelds Urteil

über die Augsburger Konfession,' *Jahrbuch für Schlesische Kirche und Kirchengeschichte* 34 (1955), 60-68.

27 See the introduction in CS 3:859-62, where Theophilus Agricola's defence of Schwenckfeld (see later) is considered to be the first witness of the manuscript circulation.

28 In the edition Paris, 1561 (see note 25), fol. B7r.   ιe year 1545 is also used by Johannes Cochlaeus, *Commentaria de actis et scriptis Martini Lutheri Saxonis* (Mainz, 1549), 312, and by Raynaldus in his *Annales*. See Vorburger, 245. Cochlaeus seems to have been Lindanus' source here.

29 Ibid., fol. C3v.

30 I used the Cologne, 1571 edition. The passage on Schwenckfeld appears there on 163-64.

31 *De fugiendis nostri seculi idolis* (Cologne, 1580), 13.

32 Ibid., 41.

33 Ibid., 42.

34 Ibid., but the list has no pagination (fol. P3r-Q2r). See numbers 13, 23, 46 and 51.

35 Full title: *Van d'eenicheyt des Christen gheloofs. Dat zy ter eeuwigher salicheyt allen Christenen van noode is, ende dat geen quader peste oft grooter Zielmoorderie onder de Sonne en is te vinden, dan de Vrijheyt des geloofs, oft Vrij-Religie den gemeenen man toe te laten; soe nu ter tijt sommighe Zielmoorders onsinnelijck sijn crijsschende. Sendtbrieff Tot de borghers van Weerdt vrundtlijck gheschreven deur Wilhelmus vander Lindt, der selver plaetse Bisschop hen van Godt ghestelt.* Without paging or foliation. Cf. Willemsen, 192.

36 Willemsen, 10-14; Klaiber, 175, no. 1876.

37 *Certaine Tables sett furth by the right Reverend father in God, William Bushopp of Rurimunde, in Ghelderland, wherein is detected and made manifeste the doting dangerous doctrine, and haynous heresyes, of the rashe rablement of heretikes, translated into Englishe by Lewis Evans* (Antwerp, 1565) reprint Menston 1971 (English Recusant Literature 1558-1640, 52).

38 Willemsen, 13.

39 Willemsen, 21-31; Klaiber, 176, no. 1883 and 1886.

40 CS 16:223-66 (introduction: 219-22).

41 CS 16:263.

42 CS 16:236-60.

43 CS 16:247. Cassander is mentioned three other times (261, 263 and 264), but always in the wake of Staphylus and Lindanus.

44 CS 16:261-66.

45 CS 16:396-404, esp. 399-404. On Heid von Daun see CS 15: 258-59.

46 CS 14:957-58. See also Schultz, 345-47.

47 Schimmelpfennig, 'Lange, Johann L.,' *Allgemeine Deutsche Biographie* (Leipzig, 1883), Bd. 17, 638-39. See also CS 2: 414-16.

48 Klaiber, 271, no. 2942.

49 Melanchthon's reaction, *Responsio ad criminationes Staphyli et Avii edito a Philippo Melanthone* (Wittenberg, 1558) is not included in the *Corpus Reformatorum* but it is edited by R. Stupperich, *Melanchthons Werke in Auswahl VI: Bekentnisse und kleinere Lehrschriften* (Gütersloh, 1955), 462-81. Andreae's reaction was printed as *Ad Friderici Staphyli conflictas et calumniae plenas antilogias responsio* (Frankfurt, 1558) (copy in the University Library of the Vrije Universiteit Amsterdam).

50 We used the Paris, 1561 edition: *Defensio etc.*, fol. 26v-32v.

51 *Divi Gregorii Nazianzeni episcopi Theologi Graeca quaedam et sancta Carmina. Cum latina Johannis Langi Silesii interpretatione. Et ejusdem Joan. Langi Poemata aliquot Christiana* (Basel, 1561).

52 'Der XXIIII. Sendbrieff, geschrieben an den Edlen Vesten und Geleerten Herrn Hans. Wilhelm von Laubenberg. Auff D. Johan Langii Scriptum wider Staphilum und vom Namen Schwenckfeldisch' (CS **17**:628-32).

53 *Concilium Tridentinum VIII: Actorum pars quinta*, ed. by St. Ehses (Freiburg, 1919), 209, no. 144: letter from the legates, May 19, 1561, to Albrecht V of Bavaria. Lindanus was invited one day earlier: ibid., 206, no. 142. See also Van Beuningen, 115-17.

54 On June 28, 1561, Albrecht wrote to the legates that he would willingly delegate Staphylus to the Council as soon as it was opened, but not earlier, because Staphylus was indispensible at the University of Ingolstadt and in the struggle for the salvation of faith in Bavaria. See *Concilium Tridentinum*, etc., 230-231, no. 161. Staphylus finally did not partake directly in the Council of Trent, but he did advise the emperor Ferdinance on several subjects that were discussed during the Council, for example, communion in both kinds. In these matters he met an adversary in Hosius, who was sharply opposed to communion in both kinds.

55 *Concilium Tridentinum etc.*, 210-211, no. 145. See also H. Jedin, *Geschichte des Konzils von Trient* IV/1 (Freiburg-Basel-Wien, 1975), 71-72.

56 Klaiber, 271, no. 2942: Dillingen, 1559, Paris, 1559, Neisse, 1560, Paris, 1560. Perhaps even the Paris, 1561 edition (not mentioned by Klaiber) had appeared already.

57 CS 16:857-59.

58 'Der XXII. Sendbrieff, an den selbigen Staphilum geschrieben. Die andere entschuldigung C. S. auff Staphili beschuldigung' (CS 16: 861-64).

59 'Der XXIII. Sendbrieff, an den Eerenthafften Wolgeleerten Adam Reissner geschrieben. Die dritte entschuldigung C. S. auf Staphili zuschreiben und verleumden' (CS 17:619-21). The letter is dated July (?) 1561 by the editors of the CS.

60 CS 17:622-25.

61 CS 17:519-74.

62 CS 17:566-74.

63 Klaiber, 271. no. 2943. The editors of the CS only knew of the second edition (1561). It was also translated, and it was followed by several continuations. See Klaiber, 271, nos. 2944-2947. The book does not concern Schwenkfeldianism directly.

64 CS 17:566.

65 I studied the copy in the University Library of Amsterdam. The Antwerp 1562 edition of Lindanus' *Tabulae*, also available in the University Library of Amsterdam, is likewise accompanied by Staphylus' *Epitome*.

66 How influential Staphylus' writings proved to be is demonstrated by the fact that he is still cited in 1614 by the two parish priests of Griesingen in a short note on Schwenkfeldianism, edited by F. M. Weber in his Freiburg dissertation in Catholic theology: *Kaspar Schwenckfeld und seine Anhänger in den freybergischen Herrschaften Justingen und Oepfingen. Ein Beitrag zur Reformationsgeschichte im Alb-Donau-Raum* (Stuttgart, 1962), 126.

67 On Hosius in general, see A. Eichhorn, *Der ermländische Bischof und Cardinal Stanislaus Hosius. Vorzüglich nach seinem kirchlichen und literarischen Wirken geschildert* (Mainz, 1854-1855), 2 vols.; J. Lortz, *Kardinal Stanislaus Hosius, Beiträge zur Erkenntnis der Persönlichkeit und des Werkes. Gedenkschrift zum 350. Todestag* (Braunsberg i. O., 1931).

68 H.D. Wojtyska, *Cardinal Hosius, legate to the Council of Trent* (Rome, 1967).

69 Klaiber, 149, no. 1601.

70 Or more fully *In apologiam confessionis illustrissimi principis ac domini D. Christophori, ducis Wirtembergensis etc.*, in J. Brentius, *Opera Omnia* (Tübingen, 1590), 8:169-236.

71 Also printed in Brentius, 1-34.

72 *Assertio catholicae fidei circa articulos confessionis, nomine illustrissimi ducis Wirtenbergensis oblatae per legatus eius Concilio Tridentino*, also printed in Brentius, 35-167.

73 Klaiber, 149-150, no. 1603.

74 Klaiber, 150, no. 1605.

75 Stanislaus Hosius, *A most excellent treatise of the begynning of Heresyes in oure tyme, compyled by the Reverend Father in God Stanislaus Hosius, Byshop of Wormes in Prussia. To the moste renomed Prynce Lorde Sigismund myghtie Kyng of Poole, greate Duke of Luten and Russia, Lorde and Heyre of all Prussia, Masovia, Samogitia, etc. Translated out of Laten in to Englyshe by Richard Shacklock M. of Arte and student of the Civil lawes, and intituled by hym: The hetchet of heresies* (Antwerp, 1565), reprint Menston 1970 (English Recusant Literature, 1558-1640, 24).

76 Klaiber, 150, no. 1608.

[77] See more in general F. J. Zdrodowski, *The Concept of Heresy according to Cardinal Hosius* (Washington, 1947).

[78] I used the edition of the *Opera Omnia*, printed in 1571 by the widow and heirs of Joannes Steelsius at Antwerp. The passage about Schwenckfeld is to be found there on fol. 219v-220v. In the reprint of the English translation we find it on fol. 49r-54r.

[79] In the same way Catholic theologians looked at Henry Niclaes and his Family of Love. See A. Hamilton, *The Family of Love* (Cambridge, 1981), 4-5 and 54-55. To most Catholic writers the spiritualists were only of some importance as an illustration of the confusion to which the Reformation necessarily had to lead. The Anabaptists on the contrary had a more dogmatic interest, as my forthcoming book on this subject will show.

[80] *Opera Omnia*, fol. 220r: 'Neque vero contemnendus aliquis est Suenckfeldius hic.' And in the margin: 'Suenckfeldianorum ingens multitudo ac vis'!

[81] *Protestatio concionatorum aliquot Augustanae Confessionis, adversus conventum Tridentinum, perniciem verae Religioni et Ecclesiae molientem, et adversus eius Conventus autorem Antichristum Romanum....* (Regensburg, 1563). I studied the copy in the University Library of Utrecht. Flacius Illyricus and Gallus, the authors of the *Protestatio* that was signed by 34 Protestant preachers, blame Hosius for his treatment of the Bible: 'Facesse potius Tu mancipium Antichristi, cum tuis Stencfeldicis somniis in infernum quam ut facesset a nobis Scriptura' (p. 49 and p. 132). And at the end: 'Et denique blasphemant, per os sui legati ac praesidentis Cardinalis Hosii, Caligae aut Caligulae, hisce verbis: Sacram Scripturam esse creaturam, esse egenum elementum. Vanem esse laborem qui ei impendatur.... Sicut et singulare organon Satanae Stenckfeldius impuro ore verbum viventis Dei allatrat et lacerat.' (176). See also 99 and 129-133. They accuse Hosius of the same errors as of which he had accused Schwenckfeld in his *Confutatio*, for example, saying that Scripture is a mere creature. On 112 they also accuse the Catholic theologian Latomus of arguing against the authority of the Bible 'durch eine Schwenckfeldische behendigkeit.' The German version of the *Protestatio* is entitled: *Von dem Concilio zu Trient. Canon, Regel und Process, wie der Babst mit seinen Geistlichen in dem selben und andern seinen Concilien, Kirchen und Religionsachen pflegt zu handeln, die Kirch zu reformiren und Religionstreite zu urtheilen....* (Regensburg, 1563). Concerning both editions see W. Preger, *Matthias Flacius Illyricus und seine Zeit*, (Erlangen, 1861), vol. 2, 562-63. About the origin of the writing Preger, vol. 2, 274-77.

[82] St. Hosius, *Operum tomus secundus*, ed. by St. Rescius, (Cologne, 1584), 197-198: Epistola LI; Julius Pflug, *Correspondance*, ed. by J. V. Pollet, vol. IV, (Leiden, 1979), 508-514, esp. 513-514.

[83] Hosius writes in 1544 that he was 'paulo ante factus minister reconciliationis,' and about the 'sacerdotis officum' he speaks as 'qui reconciliationis minister est.' Hosius' first biographer Rescius draws the conclusion

that Hosius then must have received his ordination shortly before 1544 (St. Rescius, *Vita D. Stanislai Hosii Poloni S. R. E. Cardinalis majoris Poenitentiarii et Episcopi Varmiensis* (Rome, 1587), (Olivae, 1690, lib. I, c. 12, 40-41). In or about 1539 Hosius obtained a canon's prebend at Cracow (Rescius, ibid., c. 10, 35). Eichhorn, vol. 1, 45, thinks that he must have received his ordination by that time 'um dem neuen Berufe vollkomen zu genugen.' It is certainly remarkable that even Hosius' later secretary and most devoted friend Stanislaus Rescius could not say for sure when Hosius was ordained a priest.

84 To illustrate this see Eichhorn's biography of Hosius; only 60 (namely vol. I, 20-79) out of 973 (402+571) pages are devoted to the period before Hosius was ordained a bishop in 1549, so to the first 45 years of his life!

85 That there were bishops supporting Schwenkfeldianism, is demonstrated by the example of bishop Marquard von Speyer. See H.-P. Mielke, 'Schwenckfeldianer im Hofstaat Bischof Marquards von Speyer (1560-1581),' *Archiv für mittelrheinische Kirchengeschichte* 28 (1976), 77-82.

86 *Opera Omnia*, fol. 22r: 'Equidem neque novi hominem, nec eius scripta vidi.' In the reprint of the English translation: fol. 53r.

87 Preger, vol. 1, 298-353.

88 'Scribit in praefatione commentariorum, quos anno proximo superiore edidit in epistolam ad Romanos.' Hosius refers to *Epistolae Pauli scriptae ad Romanus Enarratio* (Wittenberg, 1556, 1558 and 1561), CR, 15:797-1052. The preface is dedicated to Ulrich Mordeisen: CR, 8:737-41. In column 740 we find the passage about 'Stenkfeldius'. Melanchthon describes how he is being attacked from different directions: from one side by the Anabaptists and by Schwenckfeld, and from the other side by Poole, Canisius, Ruard Tapper, Gropper, and... (H)Osius!

89 St. Rescius, *Vita D. Stanislai Hosii Poloni S. R. E. Cardinalis majoris Poenitentiarii et Episcopi Vermiensis* (Roma, 1587), (Olivae 1690), lib. I, c. 14, 49-52. See also Eichhorn, 1:89-102.

90 It would be hopeless to correct all the false representations made by Schwenckfeld's Catholic opponents. For a more shaded representation of the relationship between Luther and Schwenckfeld, see Ecke, 33-38.

91 Hosius refers to a writing about the words 'Hoc est corpus meum.' He must have meant *Dass diese wort Christi (Das ist mein leib etc.) noch fest stehen widder die Schwärmgeister*, dating from 1527, WA 23:64-283 (introduction: 38-63, comment: 284-320).

92 It would be interesting to compare this image to that in early orthodox Protestant literature, see Maron, 10-16.

93 Liber II, capitulum XVI. I have used the Latin translation: Florimundus Raemundus, *Historia de ortu, progressu et ruina haereseon huius saeculi* (Cologne, 1614), 292-95, quotation on 294, and the Dutch edition Florimond Remond, *Opgang, voortgang, en nedergang der ketteryen dezer eeuwe, uyt het Frans in't Nederduyts vertaelt door A.I. v. K.P.*

(Cologne, 1660), 144-45, quotation in right column on 144. On this work
see M. Busch, 'Florimond de Raemond et l'Anabaptisme,' in M. Lienhard *Les Dissidents*, 251-63. Busch counts 13 French, 3 Latin, and 3
German editions. The Dutch edition, printed in 1660 and reprinted at
Antwerp in 1690, remained unknown to him. There is also a German
edition from 1747, so the last edition of Raemond's work is not the 1716
printing, as Busch supposes.

94 I used a later printing Fr. Catrou, *Histoire des anabaptistes* (Paris,
1706), 246-55, quotation on 255.

95 Bergsma, 70-71. The question on 71 before note 166 Hoornbeeck evidently borrowed from Melanchthon, perhaps with Hosius as intermediary.

96 St. Hosius, *Operum tomus secundus*, ed. by St. Rescius (Cologne, 1584),
181, 183, 185, 188, 203, 251, 421 and 425. E. M. Wermter (ed.), *Kardinal Stanislaus Hosius, Bischof von Ermland, und Herzog Albrecht
von Preussen. Ihr Briefwechsel über das Konzil von Trient (1560-62)*
(Münster, 1957), 13 and 31. Julius Pflug, *Correspondance*, ed. by
J. V. Pollet (Leiden, 1979), vol. 4, 491 (no. 820).

97 As far as I could trace, Schwenckfeld was only mentioned once during
the Council of Trent, namely in an address by the Hungarian bishop
Andreas Dudith on July 16, 1562, and then only in an enumeration
of heretics: Luther, Melanchthon, Zwingli, Oecolampadius, Osiander,
Bucer and Schwenckfeld. See *Concilium Tridentinum*, 8:705-13, esp.
707, line 11. It is a piquant detail that in 1568 Dudith himself was
dismissed as a bishop because of heresy.

98 The investigations for this article were supported by the Foundation for
Historical Research, which is subsidized by the Netherlands Organization for the Advancement of Pure Research (Z. W. O.).

III

Schwenckfeld and Christian Humanism

André Séguenny

1

When the organizers of this colloquium proposed that I speak on Schwenckfeld and humanism, I accepted with enthusiasm. It was only much later, in the course of working on this paper, that the difficulties associated with the subject became clear. The primary difficulty lies in comparing these two positions, or more precisely in comparing a theological doctrine—that is, Schwenckfeld's—with such a broad cultural movement as Renaissance humanism.

The difficulty arises, too, when one looks closely at Schwenckfeld's doctrine, and the results of the research to date bear witness to the difficulties a historian encounters in defining that doctrine specifically: in it we find all the traditional dogmas in their most orthodox, literal form. The originality of Schwenckfeld's doctrine does not lie in the *rejection* either of a traditional Christianity, or of Luther's doctrine. It lies rather in the manner in which he *accepts* them both. Thus, a question of the sources of Schwenckfeld's inspiration seems to be justified: can one find them in traditional Catholic theology or rather in Luther's theology? For those who know Schwenckfeld's doctrines, the answer is unambiguous: no, neither of these two conceptions of the Christian religion taken *in itself* was the source of inspiration for Schwenckfeld. He in fact rejected them, since they only represented a part of the truth, and thus in the final analysis proclaimed a false doctrine.

2

Schwenckfeld's critique of the Roman church is severe. But it is not the critique of the church in its entirety as an institution in the fifteenth and sixteenth centuries that interests us just

now. This critique was a widely-held one. and even members
of the Catholic clergy criticized the functional degeneration of
the church. In this sense there is no way to distinguish the
spiritualist critique from the others. What is of interest is
then the question of whether the Catholic *theological* vision
and its perspective could have been the point of departure for
Schwenckfeld. In other words, the question is whether Roman
Catholicism and its teachings could have moved him to develop
the premises of his form of religion.

Our response to this question evidently depends on the definition of Catholic orthodoxy. We are not. however, in the
position to formulate such a definition. Accustomed today to
the Thomistic version of Roman theology, we must realize that
at the beginning of modern times Thomism was only one of
several intellectual options; among the others were Augustinianism, mysticism. nominalism, Scotism. The influence that
Augustinianism exerted on Schwenckfeld. at least at first. is
uncontestable. but it is necessary to know what type of Augustinianism. Was he influenced by mysticism? Mysticism. too.
represents a form of Roman religion, admittedly quite suspect
but in the final analysis never condemned by the Vatican. As
to mysticism, my response is formally negative: nothing of that
which is characteristic of mysticism was adopted by Schwenckfeld, except a certain ambience of individual religiosity. But
then again, that was postulated too by non-mystics, such as
Luther and Calvin.

If we cannot give a definition of Roman orthodoxy in the
era under consideration, we can nonetheless reconstruct on the
basis of their work the opposition's vision of the Roman Church
and of what the principle was that caused Christianity to degenerate. Thus. if we succeed in demonstrating that this principle was the basis of the Roman conception of Christian religion,
we may more easily respond to our question.

Schwenckfeld viewed this principle as the functioning of the
theory of *ex opere operato*. The theory—and here we follow
the analysis of L. Kolakowski[1]—affirms that every liturgical
act depends *not* on the moral qualities of the participants,
but rather solely on the legitimate qualification of the priest
which has been conferred upon him by the church. The moral
qualities of the participant on the receiving end. that is of the
believer, do not play in the least a decisive role. Grace is

transmitted by and through a ritual act, the validity of which
depends only upon the fulfillment of the conditions postulated
by Canon law and liturgical rules. The dispensation of grace
occurs automatically if the dispensator as well as the recipient
legally follow the rules of the institution. The institution and
nothing but the institution substitutes for and represents God
and his actions for man living in the world. Obviously, this
depiction is quite simplified, and—we should stress this—does
not correspond to the original intention of Catholic theology.
Nonetheless, the idea that the institution as founded by Christ,
administrates and dispenses the work of Christ has led fatally
to this conclusion—and it was solely the results of the principle of *ex opere operato* and not the original intentions that
have been important in the *social perception*. The automatic
distribution of grace by the church is deeply rooted in the religious mentality, and thus became the principal cause of the
degeneration of piety.

3

The degeneration of the principle of *ex opere operato* determined the position taken by Luther well before Schwenckfeld developed his. Luther rejected that principle, rejecting
at the same time the soteriology—or doctrine of salvation—
derived from it, that is, the doctrine of the possibility of being saved by external means distributed by the institution.
Nonetheless—and this is important—Luther, unlike the humanists and Schwenckfeld, placed the accent not on the fact
that the principle leads fatally to the degeneration of morals,
but rather on the fact that the principle gives the believer absolutely no assurance of being saved. It was consequently soteriological and not ethical grounds which determined Luther's
theology.

Today we know well the intentions of the Reformer which
guided him in developing his doctrine and which led to the theory of justification by faith in the the Word of God as contained
in the Holy Scripture. But we have to stress that in Luther's
conception this Word of God is transmitted and actualized
by preaching, that is, in the human speech of the of pastor.
In paradoxical fashion, Luther's opposition to the principle
of *ex opere operato* had similar results for the social perception. Schwenckfeld noted in 1530: 'Such damaging teachings

the common man soon seized upon, but through them he soon
came to doubt whether he should repent, avoid evil, do good
works.'[2]

It is true that the principle of justification by faith in the
popular perception has resulted in the conviction that it is
sufficient to be a member of the community to be saved. In fact,
the reform of Luther was dictated by the search for certitude
of God's forgiveness. Schwenckfeld, however, oriented himself
from the beginning toward the search for a morality that would
correspond to the Christian ideal. And it was this morality
alone that led him toward spiritual theology. In Luther's case,
we observe the opposite approach. It is not true that Luther
is less concerned with good works and human ethics. The
truth is far removed from that. But it is a fact that he posed
his problem exclusively at the soteriological level, considering
morals as the secondary effect which follows automatically from
the idea that man conceives of God.

Luther's theology was, nonetheless, not developed overnight: the humanists and the spiritualists considered Luther
one of their own so long as he was in the process of formulat-
ing his doctrine of man. Schwenckfeld frequently bore witness
to his debt to Luther: thus he wrote that 'teachings that are
very much true and unvarying are oft proposed and listed in his
first books'[3]; 'thus we have not done anything wrong by taking
Dr. Martin in such a work as a messenger of God who furthered
his teaching'[4]; 'I owe Luther a huge debt, because he has helped
myself and others much in recognizing truth'.[5] But homages to
Luther are, almost every time, accompanied by reservations or
direct criticisms: 'Dr. Martin has led us out of Egypt, through
the Red Sea, and into the desert. He leaves us there and wants
all the same to convince everyone that we are already in the
Promised Land'.[6] And finally we read in Schwenckfeld this as-
tonishing declaration which encapsulates in a certain fashion
his attitude toward the two expressions of Christianity that
Catholicism and Lutheranism represent: 'Personally, I want to
say frankly that I, in accordance with recognized truth, would
much rather be counted among the Papists—if in so doing my
conscience would remain free—than with the Lutherans.'[7]

4

Schwenckfeld thus rejects Catholicism, but at the same time he also rejects Lutheran theology. At the same time, he postulates the existence of a Middle Way, in his words, 'the sole correct Middle Way between Papism and Lutheranism.'[8] The quotation signifies that, despite the rejection of the practical realizations of these two doctrines, Schwenckfeld wished to retain certain of their principles.

The idea of justification, Catholic and Lutheran as well, is based on a certain vision of humanity, different in each case. The Catholic religion considers man in the image, let us say, of a pupil who is rewarded or punished by God. But this reward or punishment is distributed on the basis of man's actions and not as a function of his nature. Human nature is always the same: it is good and remains good in spite of original sin.

Luther also postulates the invariability of human nature, which in opposition to Catholicism he considered fundamentally evil as such. Even God's grace does not change that. The grace of God, his love for man, changes only the nature of the relationship between God and man. Man considers God to be a father whose forgiveness is assured; God considers man to be a child whose evil nature and evil actions are forgiven as a matter of course.

Thus, these two anthropological visions are integrated in Schwenckfeld's system: the Lutheran anthropology is the basis of the theory of the Old Man, and Schwenckfeld used Catholic anthropology for the elaboration of his theory of the New Man. Obviously the two are not used without changes and restrictions, but one may say that Schwenckfeld retains their principal intentions.

Meanwhile, comparison of Schwenckfeld's doctrine with these two theologies forces us to note that a radical change has taken place: In Schwenckfeld's religious anthropology man has become more autonomous. In Schwenckfeld's doctrine it is neither a question of saving him from hell nor of giving him a reward. What is of interest to Schwenckfeld is the possibility and actual character of moral and ontological change in man by himself, though always considered from the perspective of the absolute. In other words, his principle occupation is with the possibility of change from the Old to the New Man

and not saving him from hell or giving him a reward. We
see that traditional soteriology as a doctrine of salvation is
replaced by Schwenckfeld with the anthropology of the New
Man. Schwenkfeldian spiritualism is thus not a theology, but
rather a doctrine which brings into relief the notion of man and
not just that of God, which is the opposite of what is done in
Lutheranism and traditional Catholicism. The problem that
preoccupies Schwenckfeld is that of the action of man, and not
that of forgiveness. We encounter all of the originality of the
Silesian in his contention that man was not created in the image of God. but rather in order to *become* that image.[9] This
contention is the only one in his system—if we have read the
work of Schwenckfeld correctly—whose literal conformity to
the biblical Word may be disputed, since the other elements of
his doctrine are based literally on the Scriptures and on their
spritual interpretation.

We have tried to show what Schwenckfeld retained and what
he rejected in Catholicism and in Lutheranism. Let us reca-
pitulate the two aspects of his system. Schwenckfeld rejects
the theocentric perspectives of Catholicism and Lutheranism
in their entirety and retains certain elements of their anthro-
pologies. All the same, he does not accept their pretensions to
extend their anthropological assertions to all stages of human
existence. In other words, according to Schwenckfeld, human
nature is not always good as is asserted in Catholicism, but it
is also not always bad as is contended by Lutheranism: 'Man
is as such a being made from the earth in an earthly fashion.'
But, continues Schwenckfeld, 'he is nevertheless not so made
to remain the way he was made.'[10]

Thus, neither Catholicism nor Lutheranism may be seen as
a source of his inspiration. It is consequently unjust and historically unprovable to present Schwenkfeldianism as a radicalization of Catholicism (something which has never been said)
or Lutheranism (something which, in contrast, is often said).

5

But before taking up the problem of the source of Schwenckfeld's inspiration, we will have to take up once again our discussion of spiritualism so that certain relationships become un-
derstandable and more obvious. We have presented Schwenkfeldianism as a theory of man. We want to say, at the same

time, that Schwenkfeldianism is not a theology in the classic sense of the term, which normally defined it as the science of God.

God, of course, 'exists' in the work of Schwenckfeld. He is a transcendent God, as all orthodoxy demands, and any pantheistic interpretation should not be used if one wants to understand spiritualism. It is nonetheless true that God can become present for man through his actualization by and in the Spirit. It is equally true that Schwenckfeld was not interested in the essence of God as were the scholastics: it was rather the problem of the work of God that preoccupied him. This work of God consists precisely in the potential given to man to overcome this transcendence, that is, to be able to become one with God. At the same time, the abolition of this distance, this union with God, may not be understood in a material sense. It is a question of a spiritual act in which God is truly present for man as a father is always present for his child despite the fact that the material distance persists, and for those who take part in this spiritual union, the material distance is not noticed.

Thus, man, if he pursues his destiny to become an image of God, can enter into the schema of the Trinity, not because he becomes Christ, but rather because he becomes Christ's brother, in sum, the son of God, with this difference—Christ was not created by, but rather born of, God. The difference between Christ and man does not disappear even on the religious plane; man as man has his origins in the creature, in the Old Man. But the New Man, Schwenckfeld suggests, moves to break down of the ontological distance between created and non-created being even if this never can occur in this life. It is a process that lasts an entire lifetime. The danger of falling into the state of the Old Man is always real, and man must fight to avoid this danger. Schwenckfeld's vision of man is not a vision of facile optimism, but it is also not a fatalistic vision which makes use of the notion of predestination. The responsibilty for his future falls entirely upon man.

Christ is not interpreted by Schwenckfeld as he was by Luther, that is, as God's grace through which each individual may be saved. For Schwenckfeld, Christ and his coming are logically necessary in the divine economy. And his coming, signifying the point of departure that man may follow and imitate, may be called grace, but not in the sense of forgiveness as

in Catholicism and Lutheranism. To follow this Christ, to imitate him, signifies that man is integrated. thanks to him and
by him, into the structure of the Trinity; it means abolishing
the ontological chasm between man and God.

Next to the doctrine of Christ and of man, there is a third
doctrine we must now treat—that of the Spirit. For Schwenckfeld it is the Spirit which permits man to discover his true
being, that of a child of God. The action of the Spirit in addition shows man the possibilities of changing himself from the
Old Man to the New. This is because it shows to him and
makes comprehensible to him the divinity of the man Jesus as
well as the humanity of the God who is Christ. And let us here
forcefully stress the fact of *comprehension*. It is not. as Luther
professes, a question of presenting God's paternal love. and it
is still less a question of knowing that, except for revelation,
all that we know concerning God is negative.

Schwenckfeld insists upon the positive knowledge. sure and
self-evident. of spiritual faith. This knowledge is transmitted
by the Spirit and consists of the revelation that man has a place
in the Trinitarian economy of God, and indeed in the place side-
by-side with Christ. It is thus a question of knowledge of Christ
who can be born in us, and not solely the Christ who was sent
for us as postulated in orthodox theologies. It is the Spirit
who actualizes in us, not just the historically-unique person
who was Jesus; but this actualization concerns the *meaning* of
the life of Christ, the meaning of the flesh and of his divine
personality. It is obvious that the historical knowledge which
the Bible can give to us may play a certain initiatory role.
But this is minor and one can do without the Scriptures in
the comprehension of the Absolute. Christ, thus brought into
sharp relief by the Spirit. is the *meaning* of human existence.

The fact of conceiving our destiny as that of son of God is,
as we have said. a knowledge completely different from that
which we may have with regard to the objects of the natural
world, since the object of this knowledge is different from the
objects of natural knowledge. Schwenckfeld notes: 'To see superficially and to grasp meaning superficially is not the way
of faith. Its way is to see within, with enlightened eyes of
the heart, and to know and understand in the Spirit.'[11] The
knowledge postulated by Schwenckfeld has nothing to do with
natural knowledge because it is a *certain* knowledge, having

been confirmed by the consciousness of its self-evidence: 'Belief in Christ is no window, but rather a clear light and certain strength'[12]; it is 'a true recognition and living assurance and clarity of all that we believe.'[13]

This knowledge is the effect of the Spirit; it is through it and in it that man discovers himself in the divine perspective. Here one hesitates to speak of the *Holy* Spirit since the concept differs so greatly from that of orthodoxy. Yet Schwenckfeld says almost always: Holy. One could say with Heinhold Fast that 'it [the Holy Spirit] is simply a philosophical category of thought.'[14] but we prefer to say that it is a category of the philosophy of religion, though not a theological one. The spirit, as far as Schwenckfeld is concerned, does not enhance the image of God to man but rather makes clear the fate and the place of the human being in its absolute dimension.

6

But if Catholicism and Lutheranism are not at the root or Schwenkfeldianism. what is? Which tradition does he continue? What is his place in the history of religious ideas?

Without doubt Schwenckfeld owes much to the Fathers of the church, especially to those who desired to Christianize Platonic and Neoplatonic philosophy.

But these Fathers of the Church were read—translated, edited. commented on—by a whole generation in the fifteenth and sixteenth centuries. I am referring of course to the Christian humanists who were, like Schwenckfeld. concerned with the problems of man in all his dimensions: God as man's perspective: Christ. who shows that the absolute is the door to the realization of human potential: man's own responsibility as regards the realization of this potential: the idea of free will which again reinforces man's responsibilities: the concept of the individualization of the religious experience and the fact of a lifelong struggle; the postulate of tolerance which is linked with that of religious and cultural universality because all human history is but a witnessing of the act of God passing from creation to birth; the pedagogic postulate which consists of a liberation from all constraints: man's acceptance of his participation in the work of becoming perfect without being forced to do so by eternal punishment: and. finally. acceptance of the world of nature through its inclusion in the work of becoming perfect. that is. natural flesh may turn into celestial flesh; and this natural world is necessarily to be viewed as an environment in which man must realize his fate. If one keeps all of the above in mind, there can only be one way to proceed, and that is to turn to the Christian humanism of the Renaissance as the source of the Silesian's inspiration.

7

But what does the concept of Christian humanism mean? To be truthful, we have yet to come across a satisfactory definition in our reading. One of the greatest specialists on humanism, Prof. P. Kristeller, states that 'we must take into account the sum-total of intellectual interest that characterized the movement as a whole.... The humanists were not only moralists but also grammarians and rhetoricians, poets and writers. translators and copyists. historians and classical scholars. and many of them. perhaps the majority. were nothing but grammarians or rhetoricians.... The humanist profession as a whole was a scholarly and literary profession.... Taken as a broad group, the humanists were neither Christian nor anti-Christian....'[15]

But it seems to us that the concept of Christian humanism moves in a different direction and derives its meaning from both of the terms of which it is composed. 'Humanism' is a theory which centers its interest on man and his moral and cognitive qualities; all analyses of the natural world and of the divine transcendence have their meaning only in conjunction with man. Yet it is neither a philosophy nor an anthropology. Humanism in short is rather a general vision of man which may be expressed in many philosophical or scientific forms.

'Christianity' provides a well-defined framework for this vision of man through its conceptions of God. of the Bible. and of Christ. Since it is moreover a humanism. it is more the New Testament with its moral from the Sermon on the Mount which prevails in giving meaning to this Christianity. But not only the moral: the New Testament message is a message of religious and cultural universality which underlines the equality of man in the eyes of God. The pagan world also has a place there as a stage of development of the human species.

The Renaissance concretizes all these tendencies. They became, at this point in history. theories of man which all stress

the exceptional status of the human being to which other elements. such as religious ones, are subordinate. This can be
seen very clearly in the way God is presented. One does not
speak any longer of the problem of the essence of God as the
scholastics did, but one discovers him as God in relation to
man. There is a turn towards a negation of theology. This is
not because the cognitive powers of man are insufficient, but
rather because of a lack of interest in the discussion about
the Supreme Being taken in and of himself without regard to
the problem of man. On the other hand. other characteristic
traits of God are stressed, namely those (such as love) which
regard man. It could be said that it is in the Renaissance that
God ceases to represent a consolation for man whose being
is expressed in terms of misery and chance (as in the middle ages), and becomes instead a God who is the supreme
guarantor of the exceptional fate of man. The theory of the
double truth (nominalism) is rejected not only because it expressed doubt as to the human capability of knowing. but above
all because Renaissance man only derived *one* truth for both
worlds: that of God and that of nature. As a result, the typical theological ideas such as those of Christ, of grace, and
of the Spirit begin to lose their theocentric significance without becoming anthropocentric. Quite the contrary, we can see
that Pico della Mirandola and Marcel Ficino—to name but
two examples—categorically reject pretensions of purely natural reason in terms of its cognitive value; natural reason, if it
does not know about or refuses the prospect of the Absolute,
falls fatally into skepticism. This is what would later become
the subject of Erasmus' *Praise of Folly* and of Agrippa von
Nettesheim's work.

At the time of the Renaissance. a slow evolution in christological thought is also to be observed. Without contesting
Christ's divinity—far from it—his humanity is stressed more
strongly. Here again his divinity is used as a guarantee of human prospects. Renaissance man begins to look at Christ as
an example to be followed in order to achieve similar results.

However, in spite of a purely religious tendency. this first
generation of humanists was much more humanist than Christian.

8

But the generation which followed them—men such as Erasmus. Colet. Vives. Stapulensis—gradually changed direction in
the search for some solutions to the problem of man. For this
generation the authority of the Holy Scripture begins slowly
but surely to replace that of pagan philosophy. But man and
not God still remains the center of interest. This second generation of humanists postulated the return to original sources
as well, but for them the Bible and the Fathers of the Church
were of importance. Erasmus was to translate and to publish
them and it was also he who edited the text of the New Testament which, with its 'Annotations,' was to have a pronounced
impact on the religious landscape of the sixteenth century. But
the central preoccupation of this generation is to be seen in the
struggle between the nominalisitic theory of the double truth
and the resulting skepticism.

It would be an exaggeration to say that the sixteenth century humanists came up with a satisfactory answer to this
problem. It is only later. in the doctrine of Schwenckfeld and
of the spiritualists in general that we find a solution to it. But
in the work of Agrippa von Nettesheim and that of Erasmus,
we can already find all the elements—often of course only at
the level of suggestion—of the theory of the Spirit in the form
of a certain criterion of human knowledge and understanding.

The only way to escape from these vicious consequences
of the theory of the double truth, Agrippa says, is to find a
vantage point in the world which will not melt away and which
is not subject to the caprices of time. And it is in Christ
that man may find this immutable basis. But the problem
is still not resolved, since it is necessary to find a means to
come closer to him. To come closer means here to understand
him. One arrives at this point thanks to the internal word,
verbum internum. which enlightens the man and which gives
him the certainty and the feeling of its self-evidence. It is not
a purely intellectual knowledge, but we should stress that it is
a form of knowledge all the same. The only thing is that one
cannot understand it solely as a logical form of knowledge. It
is rather a knowledge of the heart which consists of action. It
is a knowledge by which man becomes unified with Christ and
begins to gain understanding by him and thanks to him. The

word 'Spirit' in Schwenckfeld's sense is not yet mentioned by Agrippa. but one can easily see that it requires only a small step to do it.

This spiritualizing tendency, if its principles were still not formulated, appeared more and more frequently in the writings of theologians and thinkers who immediately preceded the generation of the spiritualists. We can distinguish it in Jacques Stapulensis' method of biblical exegesis. We see the tendency as well in John Colet, who directly influenced the work of Erasmus of Rotterdam, and who in turn was a great admirer and avid reader of the Platonists of the classical Renaissance like Ficino and Pico della Mirandola. Our argument thus begins to come together, since Erasmus is the only contemporary author whom Schwenckfeld, Crautwald, and Agricola cite in support of their theses.

Here are several ideas which we encounter in Colet: In his commentary on the *Ecclesiastical Hierarchy* he writes that 'the object of our Christian religion is nothing else than our becoming like God.' 'Be ye perfect. saith our saviour. even as your Father which is in heaven is perfect.'[16] This is possible. he tells us. owing to 'the baptism with the Holy Ghost and with fire when we are born again sons of God.'[17] Thus, man— but this time. the new, spiritual man—is 'lovely and beautiful throughout... [and] consists of three natures. body, soul, and spirit: so as in its threefold constitution to resemble Christ in whom were the godhead. soul, and body.'[18]

We can see in Colet's writings the first steps toward a theory of the celestial flesh. But the theory is connected here to the necessity of justifying the Neoplatonic schema of *exitus-reditus* which of course has no place in Schwenckfeld's writings. To quote Colet once again: ... all the things belonging to man have, so far as they can, an upward aim and direction... the body towards reason. the reason towards God: the former. by obeying the soul and reason... may become in a measure rational... so long as he retains this enlightenment. man as though now fashioned in a new form more distinctly after the image of God, appears to be not so much man as of God.[19] Compare in this regard Schwenckfeld's view that man is not created in God's image, but can become so.[20]

John Colet strongly emphasizes the existence of the free will, and consequently insists that man is free to choose what

he will become. He contends further that the direction chosen
by man is pursued by the whole man, the body and the soul.
Despite the influence of Platonic philosophy, Colet, with the
majority of humanists, postulates the potential human ability
of conquering the dualism between the body and the spirit.
It is of course not necessary to mention how important this
postulate is for Schwenkfeldian spiritualism. In Colet, too, we
find the spiritual conception of the sacrament of communion,
which would become one of the principle subjects of dispute
between Schwenckfeld and the Reformers. Colet stresses the
value of the spiritual unification of man with the Christ who
has become spiritually present.

9

It is only a hypothesis that the link which unifies Renaissance
tradition with spiritualism may be found in the work of John
Colet. Nonetheless, this hypothesis seems useful. The connection between Colet, Pico della Mirandolla, and Ficino is
incontestable. On the other hand, we know well that Erasmus
owes his entire orientation to Colet. And it is precisely Erasmus, as we have noted previously, who was for Schwenckfeld, as
well as for Sebastian Franck, the sole authority among his contemporaries. It is perhaps true, of course, that Schwenckfeld
could have arrived at his conclusions without the direct influence of the humanists; in a certain intellectual atmosphere the
problems and the responses to them arise spontaneously and
independently and remain identical. But even if there were no
direct influences, our last remark would suffice to confirm the
kinship between humanist doctrines and those of Schwenckfeld.

We have access at the same time to another piece of material
evidence which is not without significance: the books in Crautwald's library, a list of which will appear very shortly in the
Bibliotheca Dissidentium. It is quite an interesting collection,
and at the same time extremely important. It goes without
saying that Crautwald is a 'pure' Schwenkfelder, and—what is
more—it is thanks to him that certain elements of the spiritualist doctrine found their distinctive form. It is impossible to
separate Schwenckfeld and Crautwald: anything we could say
about the literary predilictions of Crautwald would also apply to Schwenckfeld. We can say that Schwenckfeld's intuition

found its counterpart in Crautwald's erudition. as numerous documents published in the *Corpus Schwenckfeldianorum* confirm.

In Crautwald's library we find among other books those of Pico della Mirandola, of Battista Mantuanus, the treatises of Origen—so popular among Renaissance humanists—and above all many works by Erasmus of Rotterdam. We have mentioned all these names several times as representative for the history of Christian humanism. That which is of central interest to us just now are the works of Erasmus, given their decisive role in the formulation of the principles of Christian humanism. In the writings of Crautwald—and much later of Agricola—Erasmus is cited as an authority equal to the Fathers of the Church: and as far as Schwenckfeld himself goes, Erasmus is the sole modern author who is cited by the Silesian. Another spiritualist, Sebastian Franck. relies on Erasmus as well, as we have recently demonstrated.[21]

Thus. we find in Crautwald's library the *Moriae encomium*. one of the most renowned works of Erasmus. and considered a humanist manifesto. It is here that Erasmus mocks scholasticism, its problems, and its answers. It is here as well that he sketches out his ideal of Christian wisdom. which is composed of the abandonment of the false pretensions of the human spirit of being able to know everything on its own. and replaces it with Christian *stultitia*, a true form of wisdom. Christian foolishness is the sole approach which, in light of the fact of the Cross. can lead to true comprehension of the work of Christ. As a result. it may lead man toward the *similitudo Dei*, that is, 'toward the rebirth into the new life that signifies unification with Christ. Who is just one of us.[22] Erasmus suggests that human flesh is also included in the process of change and sublimation. It is here as well that we find the suggestion of the spiritual principle which consists of actualizing comprehension. that is, the sort of comprehension which makes present in the spirit that object which is represented by a symbol. It is a real presence. but uniquely spiritual: it is real only for those who demonstrate as well certain spiritual dispositions. This role of spiritual actualization is played by the sacrament of communion. which is in itself only a symbol and which, as Erasmus says. is always in itself useless and even harmful if not accompanied by the spiritual comprehension thanks to which

one becomes one with Christ.[23] How can we avoid the suspicion that this book, read by Crautwald, did not influence his
spiritual vision? Crautwald and Schwenckfeld highlight this
suggestion of Erasmus and push it much further in affirming
that this act of actualizing comprehension in and through the
Spirit is not uniquely intellectual, but that it brings its object
in reality, though spiritually, into existence.

We find as well in Crautwald's library Erasmus' *Paraphrasis*. This work is often cited by Schwenckfeld, Agricola, and
Crautwald himself. The *Paraphrasis* is one of Erasmus' major
works, and in it Erasmus speaks of a radical dualism that exists
at the level of natural man. This dualism is likewise something
to be combatted and vanquished at the level of the new man.
In the *Paraphrasis*, Erasmus says as well that there is no piety
other than spiritual piety, and that the ceremonies in themselves are sensual and earthbound. Erasmus speaks here as
well of the necessity of following Christ's way: it is thus the
postulate of the imitation of Christ. Erasmus notes here too
that 'the religion in Spirit taught by Christ has no need for a
Temple other than the soul.'[24] Further, he notes that 'Scriptura spiritualis est'[25] and that one may discover its meaning
in an act of spiritual comprehension without which 'knowledge
of the Scripture may be harmful.[26] He notes here as well that
the rite of Communion is neither a real sacrifice nor the bearer
of grace. It is only a commemoration which, at the same time,
like many other things, permits one to live in the same Spirit
as that of Christ.

Here we see all the themes so dear to Schwenckfeld. But, as
Jacques Chomarat says, it is obvious for anyone who has read
and reread the *Paraphrasis* that 'Erasmus desired the disap-
pearance of ceremonies, rituals, cult, liturgy, and everything
in Catholicism which has a carnal, material, earthly, Judaic
character. But he restrained himself from expressing clearly
that he wanted to do away with them completely; and the fact
is that he certainly conceived of the extinction of them as a
long, drawn-out process.'[27]

Let us now look at the *Annotations* of Erasmus, which are
quoted at length by Schwenckfeld and his associates. This is
what Schwenckfeld says on the subject of this work by Erasmus
in a letter: 'Erasmus' *Annotationes super noum Testamentum*

should be bought and read along with the Testament. This will shed great light on Christ's grace. Expertus loquor—I am speaking from my own experience. For 24 years [from 1527] it has been my primary focus of study.'[28]

It is of interest that the *Annotations* are quoted at the point where Schwenckfeld speaks of the spiritual interpretation of the sacrament of communion[29]; where he speaks of faith as a form of knowledge linked with human morality and activity; when he speaks of the process of the spiritualization of the human flesh,[30] of the ceremonies,[31] of the participation of the Spirit in the course of the reading of the Holy Writ.[32] He also says that 'Erasmus and other learned men call the scriptures "Sacras litteras." sacred letters which is the word of some-one other that God.'[33] Again. it is Erasmus who is quoted as proof that the Scripture is but a witness to the Word, a writ-ten witness but not the Word itself.[34] The humanist is quoted at the point where Schwenckfeld speaks of the divine nature. not created of Christ.[35] He takes up again the Erasmian in-terpretation of the 'logos' as a 'sermo.' and not as the Word pronounced just once. as is said in orthodoxy: '[Christ] is God's natural word... Logos... not a single word. like a word such as we humans produce... but the complete advice. will. wisdom, independence, strength, life, truth, indeed the whole speech, oratio. sermo.'[36] The postulate of the spiritual pedagogy and the School of Christ also rests on the authority of Erasmus' *Annotationes*.

Schwenckfeld uses Erasmus as a guarantee of religious free-dom,[37] and he says. concerning the birth of man from God that 'Erasmus also writes often of the seed of God.'[38] He also mentions Erasmus' name when explaining the process of the spiritualization of the flesh.[39]

It is important to point out that Erasmus' *Dialogue on the Free Will* and the *Apologia ad Jacobum Fabrum Stapulensum* are both to be found in the Crautwald library. The adoption of the Erasmian thesis concerning man's free will as well as all that he says about it is striking. Both of them consider free will a necessary condition if man is to engage himself in the path of true change.

As well. we should keep in mind Erasmus' *Enchiridion*, which speaks. as does Schwenckfeld. of a Christian struggle against the threat of a return to the state of the Old Man, and the necessity to keep up this struggle throughout one's entire lifetime.

10

In closing we touch upon a very important problem, that of the difference in the solution to the problem of man given by Schwenckfeld and the humanists. Everything we have said should not be used to demonstrate a complete identity between Erasmus and Schwenckfeld. To do so would be historically un-justified. Nevertheless, having begun researching the roots of Schwenkfeldian spiritualism, we have arrived at the contention that there is a striking resemblance between the two thinkers. However, it is a resemblance which can only be understood in the dynamism of the intentional development of their doc-trines. Erasmus—for reasons which are at the moment outside the framework of our lecture—did not wish to go as far as Schwenckfeld. The historical circumstances were also differ-ent. Schwenckfeld was acting in the atmosphere of a violent contestation against the Catholic Church. This was not the case for Erasmus who held that one could reform this religion without destroying the institution.

Nonetheless, we are convinced, thanks to the works of M. Screech, J. Chomarat. L. Kolakowski, and G. Chantraine that the spiritual intention alone can reveal to us the internal coher-ence of Erasmus' work. Schwenckfeld was the first to under-stand and to reveal this. But he did not stop at the explanation of humanist intentions alone. Prodded by the development of Lutheranism, which attacked all the achievements of human-ism, Schwenckfeld went in the direction of the radicalization of the humanist theses. It is possible, if not certain, that Erasmus would have denied his paternity with regard to spiritualism. However, his influence did not extend only to the spiritualists. Each generation of those who contested orthodox Christianity referred to him.

It can therefore be said that if classical humanism and the Christian humanism of the Renaissance demonstrated the problem, namely that of man and his dignity before God, then it was Schwenckfeld's spiritualism which proposed and formu-lated an unambiguous answer. That answer, as we know, was to give man a chance to become the son of God, and that thanks to spiritual integration into the divine reality of the Trinity. However. this thesis, presented in the sixteenth century. still did not have access to the conceptual tools which would have made it comprehensible to everyone. The spiritualists therefore formed an elite apart.

Notes

[1] L. Kolakowski, *Chrétiens sans Eglise* (Paris, 1969), 24.

[2] CS 18:307.

[3] CS 2:676 (1528).

[4] CS 3:103 (1528).

[5] CS 4:832 (1533).

[6] CS 3:105 (1528).

[7] CS 3:106 (1528).

[8] CS 9:906.26-31 (1546).

[9] CS 4:646 (1532): 'Er ist zum Bilde... nicht das Bild und gleichnis Gottes geschaffen...': see also CS 11:424 (1547).

[10] CS 11:424 (1547).

[11] CS 2:494 (1527).

[12] CS 2:449 (1527).

[13] Ibid.

[14] Heinhold Fast, *Der Linke Flüge der Reformation* (Bremen, 1962). xxiv.

[15] *Pursuit of Holiness*, ed. by Ch. Trinkhaus and H. A. Oberman (Leiden, 1974). 367-69.

[16] Colet, *Ecclesiastical Hierarchy* (London, 1869), 59.

[17] Ibid., 59-60.

[18] Ibid.. 60.

[19] Ibid., 59.

[20] *Bibliotheca dissidentium* Vol. 6 (Baden-Baden, 1985). 59-70.

[21] *Les Dissidents du seizième siècle entre l'Humanisme et le catholicisme.* (Baden-Baden, 1983). 165-74.

[22] Cf. *The Praise of Folly*, ed. L. P. Dolon (New York. 1964). 171-72.

[23] Ibid.

[24] Erasmus, *Paraphrasis*, James 1, 26.

[25] Ibid.. 250C.

[26] Ibid., 508A.

[27] Jacques Chomarat, *Grammaire et Rhetorique chez Erasme* (Paris, 1981), 663.

[28] CS 12:652.

[29] CS 3:189; 2:323; 3:645, 928; 11:1031.

[30] CS 9:685.

[31] CS 11:383.

[32] CS 12:858.

33 CS 13:748.
34 CS 14:583.
35 CS 13:262
36 CS 13:771
37 CS 16:326.
38 CS 16:791 Mg.
39 CS 18:403.

Crautwald and Luther
on the Catechism

Douglas H. Shantz

Gerald Strauss has argued recently that Martin Luther and
his followers, in an 'unprecedented venture,' sought to instil
his reform in the young and the German populace at large
through an intense program of education—mainly through the
catechism and state schools. Strauss writes, 'A conscious, systematic, and vigorous effort was made to change the human
personality through pedagogical conditioning. The chief instrument of this process was the catechism. Both Catholics
and Protestants regarded the catechism as the best medium
for propagating the right religion.'[1] Strauss speaks in terms of
an 'explosion' in the writing and publishing of catechisms in
Germany from 1529 to 1579, noting that 'something like every
third pastor drew up a substantial catechism of his own.'[2]

The present paper furthers the investigation of this catechetical phenomenon by focussing on the work of a leading Christian humanist in the Silesian territory of Liegnitz,
Valentine Crautwald. Born in 1465,[3] one year before Erasmus,
Crautwald was initially attracted to Luther's teaching in 1520.
By 1525, however, he had sided with Caspar Schwenckfeld over
against Luther in denying the real presence of the body and
blood of Christ in the Lord's Supper. In 1526 Crautwald and
Schwenckfeld broke with Luther and began to establish an
independent, 'spiritualist' Reformation in Liegnitz and other
centers in Silesia which contrasted sharply with Lutheranism
at several points. And probably by this year Crautwald had
completed his three short, undated catechetical treatises which
were designed to encourage reform in Silesia: the 'Catechesis,'
the 'Canon Generalis,' and the 'Institutiuncula de Signis.'

In examining the catechetical program of Valentine Crautwald we are dealing with a man who until recently[4] has not
received the same esteem from historians that he received

from his colleagues and many other contemporaries. There is evidence to indicate that Crautwald was in fact the careful, creative theologian of the Schwenkfeldian movement whose work behind the scenes molded some of its main contours.[5] Schwenckfeld himself constantly relied on Crautwald for advice and edited and published Crautwald's works on important theological themes.[6] Crautwald is described by his sixteenth century biographer Adam Reissner as 'Beatus theologus,' a man who 'studied the sacred writings day and night in the Hebrew, Greek and Latin language.' Through his writings, said Reissner, Crautwald 'has made known the knowledge of Christ according to the Spirit, which has become darkened ever since the time of the Apostles.'[7] Yet, because of Crautwald's reticence to publish, his works circulated mainly in manuscript form and primarily within the Schwenkfeldian circle. Reissner noted, 'He did not seek for a famous reputation and glory, but he especially fled that as much as possible.'[8] And in a revealing comment Crautwald stated, 'I would rather be blamed because I am too slow than because I rush. I will not write anything for the public before the Lord commands and promotes it.'[9] We detect here something of the scholarly perfectionism and Christian humility that motivated him.

As a result Crautwald's three catechetical treatises of the 1520s had to wait until the twentieth century to see publication.[10] The most thorough discussions of these works are those by Gerhard Eberlein in 1900, and by R. Emmet McLaughlin in 1980.'[11] Eberlein recognized Crautwald as the 'leading catechist' in the Schwenckfeld circle, and credited him with writing 'the oldest Silesian catechism.' He expressed surprise that the history of pedagogy had overlooked Crautwald entirely.[12] Careful contextual and historical exegesis of Crautwald's works has never been done.

Surprisingly, a recent study of Silesian humanism has again ignored Crautwald's work, and argued that 'the Schwenkfelders... have left only few and scattered documents. These people possessed nothing of the literary attitude of the Humanists.' The writer notes that the Lutherans in Silesia were able eventually to 'rescue' the reform movement from Schwenckfeld and his friends with their 'less literate' attempt at reform.[13]

The thesis of the present study is that the purpose and content of Crautwald's catechizing reflect his early spiritualist concern to produce the new Christian man as the basis for the new church; and Crautwald's method clearly reflects his strong humanist interest in pedagogical techniques that would maximize Christian learning in a voluntary context. In contrast to Luther, Crautwald's catechetical program had more ambitious religious goals, and more sophisticated techniques. Furthermore, we shall argue that Crautwald found inspiration for virtually every aspect of his catechetical program in Augustine's work *De Catechizandis Rudibus*. The method for the study will be contextual and comparative, using Luther's catechisms as an illuminating parallel in order to highlight the character and uniqueness of Crautwald's catechetical work.

Luther's Catechisms of 1520 and 1529

In early 1520, the year he published his three famous Reformation treatises, Martin Luther also produced another, less revolutionary work entitled 'Ein Kurze Form der zehn Gebote, des Glaubens, des Vaterunsers.' (Hereafter we shall call this the 'Short Exposition.') Described by Cohrs as 'the first evangelical catechism,'[14] parts of it appeared in altered form in Luther's 1529 *Small Catechism*. Based on sermons Luther had preached from 1516 to 1520 on the Decalogue, Apostles' Creed, and Lord's Prayer, it reflects Luther's concern with popular piety at a time when he was intensely involved in scholarly disputation.[15] The 'Short Exposition' was probably intended as an encouragement and guide for literate laymen in their private prayers. Evidently it came to have this use, for reprinted editions of it often added as a postscript these words from another treatise by Luther on prayer: 'I do not wish that all these words which I have written should be uttered in your prayers. Rather I hope I have stirred up your hearts. The heart can express these thoughts in many other words.'[16]

The prose style of the 'Short Exposition' resembles Luther's original sermons in form. It does not have the question-answer format of the *Small Catechism*. And also unlike the *Small Catechism*, the explanations were not designed for memorization.

The content of the 'Short Exposition' was structured around the Decalogue, Creed and Lord's Prayer for according to Luther 'They contain the whole substance of the

Scriptures;... they put the essentials in summary form; and also they are quickly and easily grasped.' Indeed, those 'who cannot read the Scriptures for themselves, should learn, and know by heart' these three summaries of the faith.[17] Interestingly, Luther differed from the traditional order of Creed, Lord's Prayer, and Ten Commandments. In justifying his arrangement Luther explained: 'The Decalogue teaches a man to know what is wrong with himself... to know himself to be a sinful and unrighteous man. Then the Creed shows and teaches him where to find the medicine, that is, divine grace... which will help him to know God, and also the mercy revealed and offered in Christ. And the Lord's Prayer teaches him to yearn for this grace. Then he will receive grace and... by fulfilling God's commandment, he will be saved.'[18]

Several themes received special emphasis. In Luther's exposition of the Ten Commandments the greatest sin was clearly self-love or pride. He mentioned this sin many times and in explaining both how the commandments are 'broken' and how they are 'fulfilled,' he summarized by pointing to the danger of pride: 'All such trespasses reveal nought but self-love. Well did Augustine say: 'All sin begins in self-love....' The commandments only command love and forbid self-love.... The best life is one lived quite without regard for oneself.'[19]

In discussing the Creed Luther was traditional. He affirmed that, 'belief in the Trinity is the principal article of faith, and all the other articles depend on it.' But Luther was original in sub-dividing the Creed into three articles, based on the persons of the Triune God. Luther then emphasized the way in which the Creed must be believed. One should have not only belief *about* God, but rather *in* God, in a way that 'dares to accept what is said of God, even if doing so means risking life or death.'[20] Justification by faith alone was affirmed in Luther's discussion of the article on Jesus Christ.

In his explanation of the Creed and the Lord's Prayer Luther commended the Cross of Christ as a model for Christians. By his death, Christ 'blessed all suffering and every cross, and rendered them... salutary and highly meritorious. Teach us by Thy grace rightly to understand the cross of Christ, to hold to it with all our hearts, to form our lives upon it to our salvation.'[21] And finally, we note in the 'Short Exposition' a very conservative doctrine of the church and the sacraments.

Outside of the Church there is no salvation. And it is the priest's duty, by means of the sacraments, 'to bring salvation and edification to the whole community.'[22]

Luther's *Small* and *Large Catechisms* of 1529 reflected some new concerns arising from the social and ecclesiastical crisis which threatened Germany. In the early years of the Reformation Luther had been optimistic that through the preaching of evangelical pastors and parental instruction Reformation throughout Germany would quickly be achieved.[23] However, he became disillusioned by the increasing social disturbances culminating in the Peasants' War of 1525. Also, the Saxon Church and School Visitations of 1528 further convinced him of the religious ignorance and indifference of the common people. Even the pastors, he found, 'are quite incompetent and unfitted for teaching.'[24]

It was in this context that Luther added the 'secular' concern of preserving social order to his catechetical program. Luther warned the pastors that to neglect the catechism would 'undermine and lay waste the kingdom of God and the kingdom of the world.' And so besides making Lutheran Christians, Strauss notes that for Luther the catechism had become 'a promising means for internalizing rules of moral and social conduct.'[25]

A methodological innovation by 1529 was Luther's decision to exalt the church and the state school over the home, and the professional educator over parents as the way to achieve Reformation. Catechetical instruction was to proceed in 'three simultaneous stages': pastoral instruction, school instruction, and parental instruction. In the 'Preface' to the *Small Catechism* Luther exhorted pastors to hold public catechizing and to have the young and unlearned memorize the Ten Commandments, Creed and Lord's Prayer. They were also to memorize 'brief and fixed explanations of these,' preferably Luther's *Small Catechism*. In all grades of school the schoolmasters were to 'drill boys and girls in the Shorter Catechism.'[26]

A further innovation is evident in the content of the catechisms of 1529. Their structure, like the 'Short Exposition,' was determined by the Ten Commandments, Creed, and Lord's Prayer. However, fully one half of the *Large Catechism* was taken up with the Ten Commandments. And Luther's focus was no longer primarily on individual morality and the danger of pride; instead there was a strong social thrust and extended explanation of man's duty to government and constituted authorities according to the fourth commandment. Luther wrote, 'Why, do you think, is the world now so full of unfaithfulness, shame, misery, and murder? It is because everyone wishes to be his own master, to be free from all authority, care nothing for anyone, and do whatever he pleases.'[27] Another difference from his 1520 work was that these catechisms said nothing of the Cross of Christ as a model and inspiration for Christian living. The focus of the *Large Catechism's* discussion of the Creed was on the ministry of the church more than personal piety. A definite shift had taken place from the personal to the public.

Having completed this cursory exposition of Luther's catechisms as a backdrop and point of comparison for Crautwald, we turn now to the study of Crautwald's catechetical program in the 1520s.

The Context of Crautwald's Catechizing

The immediate occasion for the Liegnitz catechetical movement was what the Schwenkfeldian reformers viewed as intolerable abuse of the sacraments among the Lutherans. This is clear from the 'Circular Letter' of April 21, 1526, probably authored by Crautwald and Schwenckfeld to defend themselves against Wittenberg's criticisms of their view of the Lord's Supper. It was distributed quite widely, responses coming in from Wittenberg, Breslau, and Prussia. In the letter they stated, 'A new indulgence of the wild nature of the flesh was introduced with the gospel under disguise, and under the appearance of the Word of God it was established and confirmed toward the damnation of many men.'[28] The Liegnitz clergy saw 'little improvement' resulting from Lutheran preaching. The reason, they felt, was due to the Lutheran failure to understand the Supper's significance and failure to restrict the sacraments to true believers and thereby establish truly reformed churches filled with truly converted Christians.

> they make no distinction with their partaking of the sacraments and they celebrate them but not at all with a proper Christian life... as if the outward thing makes someone into a Christian, and not rather a living faith

in Jesus Christ. He can... rightly proclaim the death of
the Lord who knows himself prepared to distinguish the
body of the Lord, who has examined himself carefully
beforehand and has a Christian conversion and life.[29]

Crautwald expressed the same concern over Lutheran abuse
of the sacraments in a letter to Dr. Adamus dated May 10,
1526. 'If Christ is really, substantially, and bodily in heaven,
how can he at the same time be in or under the bread?
[Luther's view] All the Fathers, Tertullian, Cyprian, Augustine, Jerome, Ambrose, Chrysostom have taught truly concerning the sacrament, but we today have neither a true observance
of the sacrament nor do we know the meaning of it.'[30]

How should Christian leaders respond to this situation in
Christendom? In the 'Circular Letter' the Liegnitz clergy
called for a cessation of all sacramental observances (*Stillstand*)
until the people were thoroughly catechized by knowledgeable
church leaders. The practice in the early church of the cate-
chumenate must be reinstituted, they felt, in order that a true
Reformation might be achieved in the church of their day.[31]
For these views the Schwenckfeld circle by 1527 were already
being branded as fanatics by other Silesian pastors. Crautwald mentioned the situation in a letter to the Bishop of Breslau: 'One who says... that catechism provides for the further-
ance of true Christian life and doctrine must be a 'Ketzer,'
'Schwärmer,' 'Rottierer.' He wants to know too much, even to
be excommunicated.'[32]

Despite this opposition Crautwald vigorously promoted the
catechetical movement for popular religious instruction in Silesia. In May 1526 Crautwald wrote two letters to Michael Wittiger, Pastor in Breslau, encouraging him to take up the task
of catechism, and confessing that

> our whole ministry of the Word is now public catechism.
> I say that this matter is timely and should be brought
> into the open and established lest the people stray and
> are seduced by the vain label of Christianity. I think
> that the glory of the gospel, which is now coming to life
> again, should be promoted by catechism.[33]

In the same year he wrote letters to Dominicus Schleupner
and Johann Hess urging them on in the same task.[34] And it
is likely that by 1526 he had begun composing the three undated catechetical works to be examined in this study.[35] The

'Catechesis' has been described as 'eine Art Katechetik,'[36] a
guide to the task of catechizing. The subtitle, 'Institutio...
compendiosa et utilis'[37] confirms that it was intended as a
ready and useful handbook that would guide pastors in their
work. Its style is that of a catechetical anthology, containing short pithy statements—mainly from the Scriptures and
Augustine—on the justification for catechism, how to conduct
the class, and what subjects to cover. The 'Canon Generalis'
has the full title, 'A General Guide Concerning those Matters
which Pertain to the Catechism of Christ.'[38] This takes the
form of a highly polished and extended meditation on the life
and teachings of Christ in the Gospels as the proper focus of instruction, with a concluding reflection on the various workings
of the persons of the Trinity in man's salvation. It also was intended as a model for Silesian pastors. The 'Institutiuncula de
Signis' discusses the signs and symbols of the faith, including
foot-washing as a third sacrament of Christ which partly renews baptism, and is a sign of mutual charity and humility.[39]
This writing resembles the 'Catechesis' in form, being comprised of numerous selections from the Scriptures as well as
from Augustine, Tertullian, Hilary, and Chrysostom. Crautwald wrote a final treatise on catechizing in German in 1534
entitled 'A Short Account of the Way to Catechize,' which we
cannot examine here. It discussed at length the 'characteristics of a good catechist,' such as diligence, godly life, use of
singing, prayer and preaching, and some sample questions to
ask of students.[40]

We now pursue a more detailed examination of themes in
Crautwald's 'Catechesis' and 'Canon Generalis,' especially pertaining to the purpose, method and content of Crautwald's
catechizing.

The Purpose, Method, and Content of Crautwald's Catechizing, Compared with Luther's

The 'Catechesis' had as its sub-title, 'Short and Useful instruction for the True Christian Man.' Crautwald's purpose in
catechizing was to establish a church comprised of 'true Christian men' as opposed to the 'nominal' Christians that then
comprised it. We note that Crautwald wanted both the catechist and the student as well to learn how to discern the genuine

Christian from the 'nominal' one: 'The one whom we instruct should be reminded that he should avoid imitation of those who are not truly Christians, but only nominally, and not be moved by the crowds of them... or refuse to follow Christ.'[41] For Crautwald true Christianity was a matter of inwardness, the heart (*animus*), rather than mere outward conformity to Christian precepts and liturgy. A true Christian man is a 'new man by spiritual rebirth,' who 'follows Christ,' 'prays continually,' 'shows kindness,' and who demonstrates 'obedience to the Word of God and devotion to the hearing of the Scriptures.'[42] It was this kind of faith which the catechist must seek to instill.

The 'Circular Letter' of 1526 explained this purpose in clear terms: 'It is pleasing to us... that we instruct men beforehand in the most challenging and important matters, such as especially the knowledge of the forgiveness of sins, *so that they may become true Christians*. We want only to establish God's honour and... a true Christian life by means of helping to establish Christian knowledge.'[43] (italics mine) Crautwald noted in the 'Catechesis' that the early church 'grew by means of catechism.' He cited the Apostle Paul in Galatians 4 as evidence that 'the "labor" of catechizing gives birth to and forms Christ [in people].'[44] Crautwald hoped by catechizing to establish people in the faith just as the Apostles did in Acts. He encouraged the clergy within the parish churches of Silesia to make their churches full of new men.

In letters to Schleupner and Wittiger in 1526 Crautwald expressed the thought that Christ might use catechizing as the means to establish a new age for the church. 'The Lord could look for a new harvest in these days. In the meantime *we must gather the church* and... educate for unity and life.' 'I also believe that *the Lord will soon gather his church*. Indeed... finally the truth will shine forth and overcome the error... and salvation will be established.'[45] (italics mine) Evidently in Crautwald's mind the 'gathering' achieved through catechizing corresponded to the Lord's gathering of his church in the last days.

Crautwald wanted the catechism to gather in young and old in every station of life: 'Somehow or other he must be instructed, be he learned, slow of mind. a fellow-citizen, an alien, a wealthy man, a pauper, a civilian, a man in office etc.

of whatever age, sex, sect etc.'[46] Further evidence of Crautwald's desire for popular instruction is provided by the open
letter he sent to Schwenckfeld in April 1526, written in German. He wrote it at Schwenckfeld's request as 'a manual of
instruction for the unlearned,' teaching the layman how to interpret biblical symbolism, especially the significance of the
Lord's Supper.[47]

How does Crautwald's purpose in catechizing compare with
Luther's? Both men sought to have the widest possible audience for catechizing—young and old in all walks of life. And
both expressed a desire to see churches full of genuine Christians, not nominal ones. However, Luther basically accepted
the parochial churches as constituted by all members of the
community, and sought primarily to educate these people in
the basics of the faith. Crautwald, however, assumed that the
mass of people were not Christians at all and so they could
not properly constitute the true church nor receive the Lord's
Supper. He therefore sought in his catechizing not only to impart knowledge but also to try and make committed Christians
out of nominal ones, and to 'gather' a church of new men that
did not yet exist. Secondly, in 1529 Luther's catechizing was
devoted to not only the well-being of the church, but also to
restoring moral conduct in society generally. This secular focus
was not present in Crautwald's catechetical concern.

We now consider Crautwald's methods in catechizing.
While Crautwald expected parents and teachers to be concerned about raising Christian children, he evidently did not
expect them to be ready to conduct catechizing to any great
extent. The 'Open Letter to Schwenckfeld' of 1526 was designed to aid lay Bible study, but provided no guidelines for
home instruction. The work of catechizing children and adults,
Crautwald felt, should be taken up by the Silesian pastors, and
so he spent much effort in telling them how to do it. In the
'Catechesis' Crautwald called for three simultaneous levels of
pastoral instruction: church classes, public meetings, and private discussions.[48]

The main focus of Crautwald's catechizing was the church
class to which people would 'come' of their own volition. Crautwald's advice in the 'Catechesis' concerning anyone who 'does
not come at all' was not to advise coercion, but merely to suggest that such a one 'neither is a Christian nor cares to become

one.' The crucial concern of these classes, for Crautwald, was to teach the 'untaught.' In the face of Catholic and Lutheran church practice, which allowed the whole parish to take the Lord's Supper, Crautwald believed only the 'mature' Christian should partake of it. All others must assume the status of the 'untaught,' and submit to instruction. Then the catechist must carefully observe, in the course of instruction, those who wanted to live as Christians and those who did not. Crautwald wrote to Schleupner in 1526 that the 'gradual gathering of the Christian church' would only occur if 'those who are redeemed by God were set apart, those remaining outside of the church excluded, and there would again be a status of catechumen and one of the mature Christian.'[49] Here we see that Crautwald divided society into three classes: unbelievers, catechumens, and mature. He and Schwenckfeld upheld the early church practice of first catechizing *all* who desired to enter the church. Crautwald's method of catechizing represented, then, a return to the approach of the early church where, in a pagan society, it was assumed that ignorance of the faith prevailed. All people needed catechizing, and those who wished to convert and join the church must first spend a period of time as 'catechumens.'

Crautwald wanted the catechism class to be as effective as possible. To this end the catechist should initially determine for each student 'from what causes he has been moved to come,' in order to determine his spiritual condition. Then, '... we can derive the subject matter and introduction of our discourse from the reply.'[50] Proper method, besides considering the *attitude* of the student, should take into account his *aptitude* as well. 'Instruction must be molded in proportion to the capacity and energies of the listener. "You should be weak to the weak, that you may win all to Christ...." The same medicine should not be administered in all circumstances.'[51] And so with small children the catechist should 'be a child for the sake of the young ones.' Likewise, 'the slow must be endured very sympathetically.' And when someone 'educated in the liberal arts' comes along, 'You will relate more quickly the things which you taught the uninstructed at more length.'[52] Rather than emphasizing intellectual content, with the educated the catechist should stress the importance of *humility* in learning, and an *obedient life* in applying what is known.

For Crautwald, method was a matter of 'prudence' and 'charity' in making the best of a particular teaching situation.

Other resources for the catechist included humour, discipline, and prayer. When the catechist caught a young student yawning on the job, the teacher should 'restore his spirits... whether by humour, by some surprise, or some punishment should be inflicted on him... that he may stay on his toes.'[53] The greatest resource was prayer; the catechist must ever be mindful of his dependence on God. When a student was particularly slow to learn, Crautwald suggested that 'many things should be said to God about him rather than to him about God.'[54] Even the most successful methods were ultimately only tools that the Holy Spirit used to change men's hearts. True catechizing only occurred, said Crautwald, when 'God speaks through us,' for 'the Spirit of God is the only teacher.'[55]

Was there any standard procedure for Crautwald amidst all of this variety? In the 'Catechesis' Crautwald spoke twice of a basic approach to instruction. 'Short maxims' of truth should be presented to the 'young or untaught' and learned from memory. These statements should be supplemented with 'brief statements from the Scriptures,' these too probably being memorized. Then the catechist's lecture should further explain the truths. Finally, 'repeated questioning' should be a part of every session to be sure the ideas had been understood. The atmosphere should be relaxed; seating was to be provided for the class, and students always free to ask questions.[56]

Besides the class, Crautwald also spoke of 'public meetings.' The format of these can be derived from the 'Liegnitz Catechism' of 1525-26. It called for services 'on a determined day in the week' devoted to considering articles of the Christian faith. The elements were as follows: a sermon clarifying an article of faith; a prayer that God 'by his Holy Spirit would be in our midst and teach us himself'; a short 'admonition' encouraging the people to act on what they have heard and amend their lives; and they should be asked individually if they have understood or not.[57] Finally, Crautwald encouraged 'private discussions concerning Christian essentials.'

Crautwald's catechetical program was surely remarkable for its energy[58] and ambitiousness. Crautwald complained to the Bishop of Breslau in 1527 that in too many parishes instruction was lifeless: 'It is enough that they perform a lecture or read a Mass although meanwhile neither in the teacher nor in the hearers is found any earnestness.'[59] We are told by Reissner, however, that in his public lectures Crautwald himself taught with unusual earnestness: 'He lifted his listeners to the heavens and often moved them to tears.'[60]

In comparing Crautwald's catechetical method with Luther's one is impressed with both how close and how far they were from each other. Both put tremendous stock in catechizing as the key to achieving reform. Both encouraged it on several levels—Luther in home, church, and school; Crautwald in church classes, public services, and private homes. Both Luther and Crautwald encouraged rote memorization of theological maxims, and a question and answer format. Both hoped that real spiritual change would result. However, it is clear that Crautwald's method made more demands on catechist and student alike. Crautwald's catechizing was entirely voluntary on the part of adults and families. No government enforcement was ever involved, and apparently catechizing in the schools was not undertaken. Also, Crautwald's method of catechizing was more obviously calculated to produce results. Crautwald the humanist spent far more effort than Luther in elaborating the actual *techniques* of skillful instruction, gearing them to individual aptitude. The loving attitude of the instructor and the role of prayer are likewise emphases not found in Luther. And finally, Crautwald's emphasis on placing before the student the need for a decision about whether he will follow Christ and join the church, is totally lacking in Luther. For Crautwald, the act of being catechized per se did not guarantee a place in the church; for Luther it did.

The content of Crautwald's catechizing focussed on Christ, faith, and the sacraments. The 'Canon Generalis,' Crautwald's exposition of the basis content of Christian instruction, is a christological treatise. Crautwald especially emphasized the role of the resurrected Christ as a spiritual physician who offers healing and wholeness to sinners, just as he performed physical healing while on earth. Crautwald argued that a fine catechism can be produced based solely on the life of Christ in the Gospels. 'Cling continually to Christ alone and to those things which he himself teaches... a versatile kind of catechism can be prepared from the individual miracles of Christ, from his teachings and precepts. These events are loaded with heavenly gifts and crammed with unspeakable mysteries.'[61] Crautwald called for an imitation of Christ's lifestyle, noting that 'extravagance of clothing and apparel. of food and buildings he utterly condemns.'[62] On four occasions Crautwald noted the importance of following Christ and making 'the way of the Cross... the course of one's Christian life.' For Christ himself 'often emphasizes the Cross so that our flesh may learn, after giving up self-confidence and its own glory which it longs for, that not until after the suffering could the glory follow, and not until after the Cross can one attain to eternal joy.'[63] And so Crautwald's christology was basically experiential and *ethical*. Christ's work was preeminently to heal men, and man's duty was to trust Christ and follow his example of humility and love. Justification by faith was taught, but true faith was not mere 'historical faith'; it involved 'experiencing Jesus Christ with your whole soul and in your deepest heart.'[64]

The sacraments also figured prominently in Crautwald's catechizing, as one would expect. The occasion for his catechetical movement had been ignorance and abuse of the sacraments. The 'Liegnitz Catechism' recommended the usual agenda for Christian instruction in its list of suggested topics. But it then devoted over half of its discussion to baptism and the Lord's Supper. It minimized the importance of external observances and symbols as avenues of grace. 'The outward baptism brings no benefit at all for the inward man.' Likewise, in the 'Institutiuncula' Crautwald wrote, 'In the sacraments... the signs are not the realities, but they point to the realities. I say the sacrament includes one thing which is subject to the eyes and senses, another which is at work in the spirits of the faithful and is received by faith.'[65] Why observe the sacraments, then? They serve as appropriate symbols and reminders for those people who already have received the grace to which they point.

Christ's healing work and exemplary life, and the true significance of the sacraments, certainly formed the main themes of Crautwald's catechizing. However, when Crautwald encouraged use of short maxims and memorization in his 'Catechesis,' he wrote: 'So that it may be done easily,... the Ten Commandments... and the Symbol in which are included Christ and his benefits, the Our Father... must be brought together.'[66] Significantly, Crautwald gives Luther's order for the three symbols, not the Catholic. Evidently he found these summaries of faith of the early church to be an invaluable guideline, to be interpreted, however, according to the themes mentioned above.

If we should ask what Crautwald considered the chief sin to be avoided. it would be pride—first in the Catechist, secondly in the educated who come to catechism. Indeed, Crautwald's emphasis on 'the Way of the Cross' essentially called for a way of life that required 'giving up self-confidence and one's own glory.'[67]

In comparing the content of Crautwald's catechizing with Luther's, one is struck by similarities to Luther's 1520 'Short Exposition.' Both Crautwald and Luther saw pride as the chief sin in man, and saw salvation as the overcoming of this sin through reliance on Christ. Both men made the cross the model for Christians, a source of inspiration in suffering and a rebuke to all self-indulgence. The great contrast comes in their opposing views on the sacraments. Crautwald utterly denied any efficacy to external observances, while Luther saw them as God's means of bringing men to faith and salvation. The closest Crautwald came to a sacrament was in his view of the institution of catechism itself, for him an effective instrument of God in gathering the church of true believers.

Crautwald's Dependence on St. Augustine's 'De Catechizandis Rudibus'

Crautwald was conscious that his catechetical program was no innovation; it merely harked back to the common practices of the early church. He wrote to the Bishop of Breslau in 1527: 'Those who have read the Fathers such as Augustine, Ambrose, Tertullian, Eusebius along with others... well know that in the early church a true catechism was pursued... so that Christians were trained and built up, and a Christian people or church was established and received everywhere the Christian doctrine and life.'[68] In 1534 Crautwald noted that 'the catechizing of Christian doctrine... is well-established' and he called as evidence 'one or two books by Augustine.'[69] And in the 'Catechesis' Crautwald cited works by Augustine, Ambrose, Gerson, Rabanus,[70] and Chrysostom as models of catechism.[71]

In all of these references Crautwald put Augustine at the head of the list. It is clear that Augustine's *De Catechizandis Rudibus* was especially influential on Crautwald's catechetical work in the 1520s. In fact, about one third of Crautwald's 'Catechesis' consists of verbatim quotations from Augustine's work! We cannot list here all of the references to Augustine. (The complete list is provided in an appendix to this paper.) However, we shall give sufficient examples to show that the purpose, method, and content of Crautwald's catechizing were profoundly influenced by Augustine.

The structure of Crautwald's 'Catechesis' closely resembles that of Augustine's work, although Augustine's is far more lengthy and detailed. Both works were written to help clerics catechize. Both works begin with general guidelines on how to catechize effectively and what questions to ask; both list the basic themes to be treated, beginning with creation and the fall and ending with the sacraments and the church. Both provide two model catechisms that pertain to sample teaching situations.

The catechism, for both Augustine and Crautwald, aimed at establishing churches of genuine Christians in contrast to the many nominal Christians who had found their way in. Crautwald's warning to catechist and catechumen to beware of the nominal Christian is taken from Augustine's words of instruction to the catechumen to 'be on his guard against imitating those who are Christians in name only.'[72] In directing and suiting catechism to various people, of every age and station in life, Crautwald again quoted Augustine's description of his all-inclusive audience including 'a highly educated man, a dull fellow, a citizen, a foreigner, a rich man, a poor man... of this or the other age or sex, from this or the other sect.'[73]

We find that Crautwald's methodological directions likewise draw on Augustine's ideas and language. He followed Augustine's suggestion that the catechist ask questions to determine the motives from which the student came. He then quoted in part Augustine's words on the difficulty of reading men's hearts: 'It is true indeed that the precise time when a man whom we perceive to be present with us already in the body comes to us in reality with his mind is a thing hidden from us. But... we ought to deal with him in such a way that this wish may be made to arise within him.'[74] Crautwald cited Augustine's comparison of the catechist to a skillful physician: 'The same medicine should not be administered in all circumstances.' To the weak, one must be weak; with children, be a child.[75] Crautwald also followed Augustine in demanding 'cheerfulness' (*hilaritas*) in the teacher, and in allowing seating for the students and plenty of questions. Crautwald's program culminated with same question which Augustine set forward in these words: 'At the conclusion of this address the person is to be asked whether he believes these things and earnestly desires to observe them.'[76]

Crautwald apparently did not follow Augustine in adding a further level of catechism as preparation for baptism for those who answered this question affirmatively. Crautwald had no need for further preparation for baptism because Crautwald was no Anabaptist![77] Much as he disapproved of infant baptism, he and Schwenckfeld were content to work within the parish churches to slowly raise the level of piety through their catechizing.[78]

Augustine's influence is further reflected in the content of Crautwald's catechizing. The 'Catechesis' follows Augustine's warnings against pride, in both teacher and student.[79] However, whereas Augustine advocated a catechetical content based on a narration of biblical history from creation to Christ, Crautwald's 'Canon' focussed much more on the life of Christ. In the 'Canon' Crautwald did quote Augustine's advice that in studying Scripture the student 'should not seek after visible miracles but learn the habit of hoping for things invisible.'[80] It is the spiritual work of Christ in the heart that should be the focus of biblical study, not externals. On the sacraments, Crautwald's 'Institutiuncula' set forth the Augustinian view,[81] with the added sacrament of footwashing.

By way of summary, we can see that Crautwald's catechetical program provides unique evidence of what would happen if a sixteenth century humanist reformer took Patristic precedents seriously. Crautwald's methodology and purpose reflect the impact of Augustinian themes on catechizing that Luther failed to take as seriously as Crautwald did.

Conclusion

If Luther's significance lay, in part, in his effort to reform church and society through a novel idea of government education, Crautwald's significance lay in his vigorous humanist attempt to revive the catechetical practice of the early church. This involved a purpose, method, and content that were distinctive from Luther's but directly imitative of Augustine's ideals as expressed in *De Catechizandis Rudibus*. It is now clear that Crautwald discovered the precedents for virtually his whole catechetical program in Augustine. Inspired by Augustine, he in turn inspired Schwenckfeld to join him in putting the program into practice.[82]

Crautwald's program is distinguished, even compared to Augustine, by its energetic efforts to produce new men through church classes, public meetings, and discussions in private homes, all on an entirely voluntary basis with no government support. His christological focus is likewise unique.

Crautwald, by his catechetical work, established himself as the co-founder and leading catechist of Silesian spiritualism. We conclude that Ferdinand Cohrs' instincts were certainly correct when he viewed Crautwald's Reformation catechizing as distinctive in his day, and granted his catechetical works of the 1520s a place among the 'monuments' of German pedagogy.

Appendix: Verbatim Citations of Augustine's *De Catechizandis Rudibus* in Crautwald's Catechesis

1. Crautwald's 'Catechesis,' ed. by Cohrs, 197, l.22 cites Augustine, *Patrologiae Latinae*, vol. 40, 322, ll.52, 53.

2. 'Catechesis,' 198, ll.1-3 cites PL 40, 328, ll.32-37.

3. 'Catechesis,' 198, ll.4, 5 cites PL 40, 322, ll.17, 18, 25, 26.

4. 'Catechesis,' 198, ll.7, 8 refers to PL 40, 323, ll.46, 47.

5. 'Catechesis,' 198, l.9 cites PL 40, 321, ll.19-21.

6. 'Catechesis,' 198, ll.10, 11 cites PL 40, 321, ll.23-25, 27, 28.

7. 'Catechesis,' 198, ll.13, 14 cites PL 40, 312, ll.54, 55.

8. 'Catechesis,' 198, ll.17, 18 cites PL 40, 318, ll.40-42.

9. 'Catechesis,' 198, l.19 cites PL 40, 324, ll.43, 44.

10. 'Catechesis,' 198, ll.20, 21 cites PL 40, 324, ll.47, 48.

11. 'Catechesis,' 198, l.22 cites PL 40, 324, l.53 to 325, l.1.

12. 'Catechesis,' 198 l.24 cites PL 40, 325, ll.54, 55.

13. 'Catechesis,' 198, l.25 cites PL 40, 323, ll.44, 45.

14. 'Catechesis,' 198, ll.28, 29 cites PL 40, 328, ll.40, 41.

15. 'Catechesis,' 198, ll.30-32 cites PL 40, 323, ll.52-54.

16. 'Catechesis.' 199, l.1 cites PL 40, 316, ll.28-30.

17. 'Catechesis.' 199, ll.3-6 refers to PL 40, 316, 11.22, 23, 25-7.

18. 'Catechesis,' 199, ll.16-19 refers to PL 40, 316, ll.34-40.

19. 'Catechesis,' 199, ll.23-25 cites PL 40, 325, ll.10-16.

20. 'Catechesis,' 199, ll.26-29 cites PL 40, 325, ll.19-25.

21. 'Catechesis,' 199, ll.30-36 refers to PL 40, 318, ll.45-319 ll.1-16.

22. 'Catechesis,' 199, ll.36, 37 refers to PL 40, 320, ll.9-10.

23. 'Catechesis,' 200, ll.1-3 refers to PL 40, 320, ll.2, 13-14.

24. 'Catechesis,' 200, ll.4, 5 cites PL 40, 344, ll.48-50. 25. 'Catechesis,' 202, ll.12, 13 cites PL 40, 318, ll.3-5.

26. 'Catechesis,' 202, ll.14-16 cites PL 40, 327, ll.9-13.

27. 'Catechesis,' 202, ll.20-22 refers to PL 40, 322, ll.50-56 and 323, ll.10-13.

Notes

1 Gerald Strauss, *Luther's House of Learning; Indoctrination of the Young in the German Reformation* (Baltimore: Johns Hopkins University Press, 1978), 175, 172.

2 Ibid., 161. At this point Strauss is relying on Ernst-Wilhelm Kohls, *Evangelische Bewegung und Kirchenordnung: Studien und Quellen zur Reformationsgeschichte der Reichsstadt Gengenbach* (Karlsruhe, 1966), 4. Between 1522 and 1529 about 30 catechisms were issued. Cf. M. Reu, *Catechetics* (Chicago, 1931), 89.

3 Daniel Sudermann, the Schwenkfelder poet, and hymnist wrote in 1603 that Crautwald 'the famous blessed theologian... died in 1545 as an 80 year old.' Cf. CS 6:193. The best biographical studies of Crautwald are by Gerhard Eberlein, 'Zur Würdigung des Valentin Krautwald,' *Correspondenzblatt des Vereins für Geschichte der Evangelischen Kirche Schlesiens* 8 (1903), 268-286; Horst Weigelt, *Spiritualistische Tradition im Protestantismus* (Berlin, 1973); Weigelt, 'Valentin Krautwald der führende Theologe des frühen Schwenckfeldertums,' *Bibliotheca Dissidentium*, No. 1, Her. Marc Lienhard (Baden-Baden: Koerner, 1983), 175-90.

4 Schwenckfeld's debt to Crautwald has recently been emphasized by Edward J. Furcha, *Schwenckfeld's Concept of the New Man* (Pennsburg, 1970), 32, 78 and Weigelt, 6, 122, 278.

5 I attempt to show this in my doctoral dissertation now being completed for the History Department at the University of Waterloo, Waterloo, Ontario.

6 For a partial listing of works by Crautwald that were edited and published by Schwenckfeld see the 1561 'Catalogus' of Schwenckfeld's writings (CS 17:698,722f).

7 Adam Reissner, 'Vita beati Valentini Crautwaldi Silesii Theologi,' CLM 718, fol. 550. (This is the Reissner manuscript of Crautwald's works preserved in Munich.)

8 Reissner, CLM 718, fol.549.

9 Crautwald, CLM 718, fol.407.

10 Gerhard Eberlein was first to edit the 'Catechesis' for publication, doing so in the year 1900: G. Eberlein, 'Der kirchliche Volksunterricht nach den Anschauungen der Schwenckfeldischen Kreise in Schlesien im ersten Drittel des 16. Jahrhunderts,' *Correspondenzblatt der Vereins für Geschichte der evangelischen Kirche Schlesiens* (1900), 1-48. And Ferdinand Cohrs published all three of Crautwald's early catechetical works in 1902 in *Die Evangelischen Katechismusversuche vor Luthers Enchiridion, Bd. IV. Undatierbare Katechismusversuche und zusammenfassende Darstellung* (Berlin, 1902), 183-225.

11 Eberlein, 'Volksunterricht'; R. Emmet McLaughlin, 'Caspar Schwenckfeld von Ossig,' (Ph. D., Yale University, 1980).

12 Eberlein, 'Der Kirchliche Volksunterricht,' 6, 21, 16.

13 Manfred Fleischer, 'The Institutionalization of Humanism in Protestant Silesia,' *Archiv für Reformationsgeschichte* (1975), 260-62.

14 As Quoted by E.-W. Kohls, *Evangelische Katechismen der Reformationszeit vor und neben Martin Luthers Kleinem Katechismus* (Gütersloh, 1971). 9. G. Seebass, 'The Importance of Luther's Writings in the Formation of Protestant Confession,' *Luther's Ecumenical Significance*, edited by P. Manns and H. Meyer (Philadelphia: Fortress, 1984), 76-80.

15 Bertram Lee Woolf, 'Introduction, A Short Exposition of the Decalogue, The Apostles Creed and the Lord's Prayer,' *Reformation Writings of Martin Luther*, trans. by B. L. Woolf (New York, 1953), 69f.

16 Ibid., 99.

17 Ibid., 71.

18 Ibid., 72.

19 Ibid., 80, 83.

20 Ibid., 83. In the *Large Catechism* Luther mentioned his originality in dividing the Creed into three articles instead of the traditional twelve. Cf. 'The Large Catechism,' *The Book of Concord*, trans. by Theodore G. Tappert (Philadelphia, 1959), 411.

21 Woolf, 86, 95.

22 Ibid., 88, 95.

23 Strauss, 4.

24 Luther, 'The Small Catechism,' *The Book of Concord*, 338.

25 Strauss, 163; Luther, 'Preface, Small Catechism,' p.340. In Luther's Preface to his *Large Catechism* he especially emphasized his religious purpose in catechizing: 'Whoever does not possess [the catechism] should not be reckoned among Christians nor admitted to a

sacrament.... All who wish to be Christians in fact as well as in name...
should be well trained in them and familiar with them.' Cf. Tappert,
362. Yet Luther did not implement structures to realize this goal as
Crautwald did. As Verduin has noted, in December 1525 Luther expressed to Schwenckfeld his desire for a church of 'true Christians.'
However, Luther was 'not prepared to sever his ties with the past, not
ready to drop the sacralist premise of a church that embraces the entire
population.' Cf. L. Verduin, 'Luther's Dilemma: Restitution or Reformation?' *Essays on Luther*, ed. by K. A. Strand (Ann Arbor, 1969),
83, 84.

[26] Luther, 'Preface, Small Catechism,' 338-41; 'Preface, German Mass,
1526,' *Liturgies of the Western Church*, edited by B. Thompson
(Philadelphia: Fortress, 1961), 126-30.

[27] Luther. 'The Large Catechism,' 381, 385f.

[28] 'Circular Letter by Crautwald, Schwenckfeld and the Liegnitz Pastors,
April 21, 1526' (CS 2:330).

[29] Ibid., 330f.

[30] Eberlein, 'Zur Würdigung,' 281.

[31] 'Circular Letter,' 331f.

[32] CS 2:661.

[33] CLM 718, fol.319, 320.

[34] Cf. Eberlein, 'Zur Würdigung.' 279f, n.6. Cohrs credits Crautwald with
inspiring Schwenckfeld and Werner to produce catechisms in the 1530s.
Cohrs, *Die Evangelischen Katechismusversuche*, p.191.

[35] See McLaughlin on the dating of Crautwald's treatises, 191. In the letter to Schleupner in 1526 Crautwald wrote, 'I consider it a worthwhile
task in future if someone note down... something concerning the catechism of Christ, that is, in what way and with what methods Christ
instructed his own disciples, the crowds, and the Pharisees...' (CLM
718, fol.289). As this is precisely what Crautwald set about doing in
the *Canon Generalis*, the latter may be dated closely to this time.

[36] Cohrs, 189.

[37] Cohrs, 196.

[38] 'Canon Generalis super his quae spectant ad Catechismum Christi'
(Cohrs, 204).

[39] Cohrs, 221.

[40] 'Kurtzen Bericht von der Weise des Catechismi der ersten Schuler im
Glauben und dem Anfang Christlicher Leere' (CS 5: 221-46).

[41] Crautwald, 'Catechesis,' 202

[42] Crautwald, 'Catechesis,' 201f.

[43] 'Circular Letter,' 331f.

[44] Crautwald, 'Catechesis,' 196f.

[45] Eberlein, 'Zur Würdigung,' 285f.

[46] Crautwald, 'Catechesis,' 198.

[47] CS 2:299.

[48] Crautwald, 'Catechesis,' 202

49 Eberlein, 'Zur Würdigung, 286.

50 Crautwald, 'Catechesis,' 199.

51 Ibid., 197-99.

52 Ibid.

53 Ibid.

54 Ibid.

55 Ibid., 198, 196.

56 Ibid., 203, 201, 198.

57 'Kadecismus Lignicensis, ca. 1525' (CS 18:8). This anonymous Silesian document, ostensibly by Crautwald and Schwenckfeld, sketches an agenda of topics for catechizing, emphasizing the sacraments.

58 Eberlein wrote that 'The special significance' of Crautwald's 'Catechesis' lay in the 'energy' with which he promoted catechism for all ages, offered guidance to teachers, and set down proper goals. Cf. Eberlein, 'Der kirchliche Volksunterricht,' 26f.

59 CS 2:661.

60 Reissner, CLM 718, fol.549.

61 Crautwald, 'Canon Generalis,' Cohrs, 210, 213.

62 Ibid., 212.

63 Ibid., 211f.

64 Ibid., 207.

65 'Kadecismus Lignicensis,' 9; Crautwald, 'Institutiuncula,' Cohrs, 219.

66 Crautwald, 'Catechesis,' 201.

67 Ibid., 198f.; 'Canon Generalis,' 212.

68 CS 2:661.

69 Crautwald, 'Ein kurtzer Bericht von der Weise des Catechismi' (CS 5:235).

70 McLaughlin has shown that 'De clericorum Institutione' which Crautwald attributed to Bede is actually the work of Rabanus, the ninth century Archbishop. Cf. McLaughlin, 188, n.245.

71 Crautwald, 'Catechesis,' 197.

72 Augustine, 'De Catechizandis Rudibus,' *Patrologiae cursus Completus, Series Latina*, Tomus 40, J.-P. Migne (Paris, 1887), 327; and for Crautwald's quotation see Cohrs, 202.

73 Augustine, PL 40, 328; and Cohrs, 198.

74 Augustine, PL 40, 316; and Cohrs, 199.

75 Augustine, PL 40, 328, 322; and Cohrs, 198.

76 Augustine, PL 40, 344; and Cohrs, 200.

77 Crautwald wrote: 'I cannot be persuaded that I should be immersed again and that I should ask for the outward ministry of baptism to be repeated. For I know that one cannot be restored... by any outward symbol or ministry' (CLM 718, fol. 408).

78 See McLaughlin, 184f, 201f.

79 Augustine, PL 40, 318, 320, 323; and Cohrs, 198f.

80 Augustine, PL 40, 317; Cohrs, 208.

81 McLaughlin, 192.

82 See n.34.

Valentine Crautwald's 'Nouus homo': Origen Lutheranized

Irena Backus

The aim of this paper is to examine the theological content, structure, and sources of Crautwald's treatise *Nouus homo* which was published in 1542 but was probably written in the 1530s. In a letter to Schwenckfeld dated January 14, 1542, Joachim Vadian compares the treatise, of which he had just received a copy, to Martin Borrhaus' propositions on *vetus homo/nouus homo* printed in the latter's commentary on *Ecclesiastes* in 1539. Vadian declares himself favourably impressed by both works: Borrhaus' propositions constitute 'ain seer fleyssig geschrieben arbait, doch gefalt mir euwers vm kürtze willen auch gantz wol.'[1] Obviously he found nothing heretical in Crautwald's treatise, and it must be said that the theme of spiritual renewal itself, although in vogue among some sixteenth century dissident theologians, was not in itself heterodox.[2] Indeed, it figured prominently not only in Luther's 1519 *Commentary on Galatians* but also in several of his sermons published in that same year. Moreover, as is suggested by *Ein tractat in dem kurtzlich durch die heyligen geschrifft anzeygt würt, wie der inwendig vnd vsswendig mensch wiedereinander und bey einander sein* (Colligiert durch ein Christlichen Burger zu Nürenberg, 1524),[3] the theme was being explored at that period in Lutheran circles. We shall here compare Crautwald's treatment of spiritual renewal with, on the one hand, Luther's treatment of the theme in his *Commentary on Galatians* and in his sermons and, on the other hand, with the anonymous author's approach to the subject in *Ein tractat*. Our object will be firstly, to see whether Crautwald has anything in common with Luther and the author of *Ein tractat* and secondly, to attempt to suggest a source for those features of Crautwald's treatise which cannot be attributed to his reading of Luther and the Lutheran theologians.

Given its sub-title, *Institutio vere Christiani hominis com-pendiosa et vtilis*, Crautwald's treatise is evidently intended to serve as a work of edification. Vast portions of the text are made up of biblical, chiefly New Testament quotations. The argument lacks a clear line and is extremely repet⊙ive. Craut-wald begins by establishing the basic distinction between the 'old' and the 'new' taking Matthew 18:3ff. as his point of de-parture. Read together with Matthew 19:14, Mark 10:15-16 and Luke 18:16-17, Jesus' words to his disciples show that all flesh is unworthy of the kingdom of heaven 'nisi conuertatur, repuerescat et rursus in Christo paruula fiat et humilis.' To enable this process of rejuvenation to take place the 'carnis vetustas' must take on 'spiritus nouitatem.' For, man incor-porates two creatures, the 'old' (carnal) descended from Adam and the 'new' (spiritual) descended from Christ. To support this claim Crautwald cites Galatians 6:15.

Having established the basic dichotomy carnal=old/ spirit-ual=new, Crautwald gives a detailed description of each of the two creatures that man embodies. The old man, being igno-rant of God, instantiates all the vices. But Crautwald speci-fies 'abluitur, sanctificatur et iustificatur, hoc est innouatur in nomine Domini Iesu et in Spiritu Dei nostri, vt deinceps seruiat iustitiae et non iniquitati ad iniquitatem. Roma. 6 [7]'(48). It is out of this old man that the new man is born, totally op-posed to the old in that he is a 'domesticus Dei,' 'plenus Deo,' 'habitaculum Dei per Spiritum.' Being born through the Spirit, the new man is of the Spirit (the old being merely *animalis*). The old man, Crautwald insists, is composed merely of the body and soul, in other words 'ex sola natura'(48). The new man is composed of body and spirit, in other words 'ex natura et gratia.'

Crautwald then makes it clear that each man is born 'vetus filius noctis et tenebrarum.' He is then reborn through the Spirit which is given by Christ. It is a purely internal process, stresses Crautwald and, to emphasize and illustrate this, he gives the example of various people being educated: 'Si rudem docueris, si ex rustico rethorem aut ciuem feceris, ex stolido prudentem... iam alius est, non foris sed intus. Iam intus doctus est peritus et rethor et pro tali etiam foris, non pro veteri deinde agnoscitur'(50). In other words the process of internal transformation, be it intellectual or spiritual, alters the whole

man, in that it causes him to act in the world in a new way:
no longer as an illiterate but as a learned man, no longer as an
incoherent speaker but as a rhetorician.

All those that are spiritually reborn through Christ, Crautwald continues, are also baptized 'lauacro generationis.' Jesus
himself is explicit about this when he instructs Nicodemus in
John 3:3 and when he asks the blind man in John 9:7 to wash
in the waters of Shilo. This baptismal water renews the 'infans
recenter Spiritu progenitus' throughout his life as its regenera-
tive force is carried on by the word. It is through hearing and
understanding the word that, after the water-baptism, the old
man begins to degenerate as his wicked desires weaken. The
new man, on the other hand, gets stronger and stronger in
the spiritual renewal, after being born as a small weak infant.
This rebirth and the subsequent process of growth, Crautwald
stipulates, is only possible because of faith in Christ and in his
sacrifice. Just as mothers take their children to the tombs of
relatives, so the newly born spiritual infant must be taken to
the cross of Christ. 'Ita hunc puerum recte ad Christum cru-
cifixum mortuumque et sepultum pro peccatoribus, primum
duxeris. Ibi enim moritur peccatum veteris Adae, concrucifig-
itur corpus peccati, mors moritur, peccatum aboletur, gratia
et remissio paratur.' In other words, the newly baptized 'spiritual infant' has to confront the full significance of Christ's
sacrifice if he is to grow into a spiritual adult. And Crautwald
emphasizes again: 'Christus sane a cruce et morte potissimum
prodest,' and his sacrifice must be preached 'toto studio et ante
omnia' so that men can learn about the nature of sin. They
will thus realize what it means to be without Christ. The rest
of the treatise is taken up with an elaborate allegory of the
birth and development of the new man.

The seed which implants the foetus of the new creature in
man is the Word of God. The mother is the grace of God
and the Spirit of Christ. The uterus is the heart in which the
new man is born, grows and lives. His bones and nerves, in
other words his strength, he obtains from the Spirit. And here
Crautwald cites Ephesians 3:16: 'Vt fortitudine corroboremini
per Spiritum suum in internum hominem.' The foetus being
thus formed is born 'Deo Patri filius et haeres per Christum.'
First he is a small boy, then an adolescent, then a grown man
in Christ. His growth and development is determined by the

growth and development of his faith. The more he grows, the greater the spiritual renewal, the more does the old man degenerate. The infant reborn 'renatus' is washed by the 'lauacrum regenerationis.' Clearly for Crautwald baptism takes place immediately after birth, that is, after spiritual rebirth. It is after its first 'washing' that the infant is fed by the 'sermo fidei et sanae doctrinae.' This food is first presented in the form of 'lac et mellis,' and then becomes more solid. A marginal note specifies that external ministry is indispensable both for the administration of baptism and for the administration of 'spiritual nourishment' or Christian teaching. The 'new creature' is not only fed but also clothed. Its clothing are the good works it performs 'dum fidem internam declarat et ornat.' He is the son of God and the brother of Christ. He is taught by God and makes spiritual progress of which his good works provide a proof. Here Crautwald stresses again that, although God teaches through the Spirit, he nonetheless uses human or 'external' ministers to administer this teaching 'qui cooperarii Dei sunt, coagriculatores et architecti.' The quality of the teaching they dispense is determined by the spiritual capacities of their pupils. The theme of the new man's development is then picked up again. He is freed from fear of death by Christ, he constantly performs good works, and he marries in Christ. He is a 'peregrinus in mundo, rex et sacerdos et miles in Christo.' In other words his life is totally given over to Christ. What happens to the old man while this process of renewal and spiritual improvement is taking place? Crautwald is quite clear that although the desires of the flesh become less strong, they never disappear in this life, and therefore the old man never dies. The new man, in spite of great efforts, can never be free from sin. A perfect spiritual renewal can occur only in after-life.

In spite of its rambling and repetitive nature, Crautwald's treatise makes several salient doctrinal points. Firstly, it emphasizes that it is only Christ that gives the Spirit and that there is nothing intrinsically spiritual about man himself. The difference between the old and the new is the presence of divine grace, which is, as it were, added on to human nature. Secondly, stress is laid on Christ and faith in him as the sole means of 'spiritualization.' The Spirit or grace which makes up the new man is the Spirit of Christ. Thirdly, the author

insists on the absolute necessity of the ministry: the Spirit is
not given independently of the preached word. Fourthly, it is
curious to note that while baptism is considered absolutely essential as initiation into the spiritual life, no mention is made of
the eucharist. Finally, we might note that for Crautwald man
does not simply become gradually spiritualized through faith:
he must show proof of his new state by performing good works.
Moreover, it is made explicit that, the 'new man' will never attain perfection in this life since the 'old man' (or flesh) cannot
totally degenerate, although he can become weaker. Undoubtedly, the most striking feature of the treatise, however, is the
detailed allegorical representation of the new man being born
and growing.

It is not difficult to see that Crautwald's doctrine of spiritual
renewal is Lutheran in essence. Luther himself in his *Commentary on Galatians* of 1519 points out at Galatians 5:17 (WA 2,
585-586) that Origen's and Jerome's division of man into flesh,
soul, and Spirit cannot be accepted. These three components
make up man but do not function independently within him.
The flesh cannot desire except by the soul, to which it is in
fact assimilated, and by the Spirit. However, one or other of
the components can be predominant. Thus, man is flesh in
so far as he obeys carnal desires. He is also Spirit 'quatenus
sapit quae Dei sunt.' He can become Spirit 'quando corpus erit
spirituale,' that is, in after life only. For in this life 'neutrum
[Spirit and flesh] extinguit alerum in hac vita et si Spiritus
inuitam carnem domet sibique subiiciat.' And in the following verse he specifies that in this life 'Nondum enim Spiritus
sumus sed Spiritu ducimur... debemus esse Spiritus, sed sumus
adhuc in ductu et, vt sic dixerim, in formatione Spiritus' (WA
2. 587). The full process of spiritualization is then summarized
at Galatians 5:21: 'vt primum de suis viribus desperantes verbum fidei audiant, audientes credant, credentes inuocent, in-
uocantes exaudiuntur, exauditi Spiritum charitatis accipiant,
accepto Spiritu, Spiritu ambulant et desyderia carnis non perfi-
ciant sed crucifigant, crucifixi cum Christo resurgant et regnum
Dei possideant' (WA 2, 591).

Thus, for Luther, as for Crautwald after him, it is wrong
to establish a distinction between inner and outer, spirit and
body. The spiritualization affects not one part of man but man
in his entirety. Moreover, both underline the importance of the

preached word in the imparting of the Spirit, both insist on a gradual process of spiritualization which cannot be completed in this life, both insist that this life is a process of being educated by the Spirit. However, in contrast to Crautwald, Luther does not insist on the process having to be outwardly visible through good works. Moreover, again quite unlike Crautwald, Luther specifies that in order for the process of spiritualization to begin, man must first despair of his own powers.

Luther makes no mention of the relationship between baptism and spiritual renewal in his *Commentary on Galatians*. He does, however, devote an entire sermon to baptism in the same year. There can be little doubt that it is Luther's views as expressed in this sermon that Crautwald adopts and adapts some years later. It is here that Luther uses the terminology of the old and the new man, the parallel between carnal and spiritual rebirth, the simile of the mother's womb. He argues 'Die bedeutung ist eyn seliglich sterbenn der sund und aufferstehung yn gnaden gottis, das der alt mensch, der yn sunden empfangen wirt und geporen, do erfeusst wirt und ein newer mensch erauss geht'(WA 2, 727). And slightly further on in citing John 3:3 as an illustration of baptism Luther explicitly links 'geyst' with 'gnade'(728). However, there is no mention of good works as a distinguishing feature of the development of the new spiritual man, and the womb simile is merely introduced without being developed.

If we examine the anonymous *Ein tractat*, a work devoted entirely to the theme of spiritual renewal, further parallels with and departures from Crautwald's doctrine can be noted. The author begins by emphasising that 'niemant kan ein kindt gottes sein, er sey dann new geboren.' This rebirth is not a matter of man's wish: it depends solely and entirely on the will of God. 'Aber Gott ist ein geist vnd nichts wirt vss gott geboren dann geist'(a1v). The rebirth therefore is necessarily spiritual. Although John 3:3 is mentioned, the exact role of baptism in the spiritual renewal is not specified. Like Crautwald, however, the author insists upon the integral connexion between the rebirth and the preached word: 'Diser geist aber vnd dise newe geberung wirt geben durchs wort Gottes durchs Euangelion als Paulus sagt, das der glaub, das ist der geist Gotts Christus selbs wesenlich wirt geben durchs wort'(a2r). Thus, the link rebirth–Spirit–faith in Christ—preached word

is common to Luther, Crautwald, and the author of *Ein tractat*. It might be noted, however, that whereas for the latter
the Spirit is Christ (*den geist das ist Christus*) for Crautwald
and for Luther the Spirit is given by Christ. since, as we saw,
both identify it explicitly with grace.

The 'christlicher Burger' then establishes the old man/new
man opposition. For him as for Crautwald, the old man is human nature unaided by grace. Without making the body–soul–
Spirit distinction the 'Citizen' makes his point quite clearly:
'Der alt mensch aber heysst vnd ist alles das das wir haben
von vatter und mutter, das ist nichts anders dann fleysch und
blut, das da begert wider Gott'(a2r). However, the new man
is not merely the old man aided by grace or Spirit which is dispensed by Christ. He is, much more explicitly than in Crautwald's treatise, identified with Christ himself. Thus, human
powers are given far less importance and any good works that
the new man performs are not his but Christ's. The author
of *Ein tractat* makes this point in no uncertain terms: 'Thue
er [der alte Mensch] und beger wie un was er vermag. er mag
nymmer meer zu der seligkeit kummen, dann nur durch den
newen menschen, durch Christum, der in vns wonet durch den
glauben vnd wir seind sein wonung, wie die Jungkfraw Maria
was die neün monat'(a2v). Therefore, it follows that 'Also lebt
vnser newer mensch Christus in vns vnd nit wir.... Dieweyl wir
nun Christen seind, allein darumb das Christus in vns wonet,
so solt man nit sprechen so einer ein gut werck thut; es hatt
der Johannes oder Wolffgang oder die Barbara gethon, wann
er hatt es nit gethon. Er ist fleysch vnd blut, darumb mag
er nichts guts thun, aber der new mensch in vns Christus hat
es gethon'(a3r). Whereas for Crautwald the new man must
perform good works to demonstrate his spiritual progress, for
the 'pious citizen,' as for Augustine, the new man is new solely
because of Christ so that any good works he performs are in
no sense his own.

Spiritual perfection in this life becomes thus even more of
an impossibility as 'Nun syhest das zwen menschen newer vnd
alter bey ein ander steen vnd doch wider einander fechten vnd
keiner den andern vsstilgt, biss das fleysch erstirbt'(a3v). Like
Luther and Crautwald, however. the author of *Ein tractat* insists that Christ can only take up residence in a man that has
faith.

There is no doubt that Crautwald's treatise shares basic features both with Luther's works and with *Ein tractat*. However, the differences are equally important. Particularly noteworthy is the emphasis on the preached word, and the impossibility of spiritual perfection in this life which is emphasized by all three. However, whereas Luther and Crautwald envisage the possibility of improvement in this life, education by the Spirit, this idea is not brought out by the author of *Ein tractat*. We might also note that while faith is a 'sine qua non' of spiritual renewal for all three theologians, Luther stresses the necessity of despair in human powers as a preliminary to the acquisition of faith while the author of *Ein tractat* leaves man out of the picture altogether: faith for him is God-given. For Crautwald, on the other hand, faith is equivalent to man's confrontation of Christ's sacrifice. All three theologians use the old man/new man figure. Luther and Crautwald, however, stress that this should not be made to correspond to the flesh–soul–Spirit distinction since spiritual renewal affects the whole person. The author of *Ein tractat* stresses the conflict, the fundamental dichotomy, between the old man (flesh) and the new man (Spirit who is Christ). Again Luther and Crautwald assign a much greater importance to baptism. The 'pious citizen' mentions John 3:3 but does not elaborate upon it in any way. Moreover, while all three theologians emphasize the Spirit, Luther and Crautwald define it as grace dispensed by Christ while for the author of *Ein tractat* the Spirit is Christ.

Luther makes no mention of the role of good works in the process of spiritual renewal. For Crautwald they are absolutely necessary as proof of increased faith. For the author of *Ein tractat* they are Christ's works and not intrinsically connected with man at all. As for the womb simile, Luther uses it to establish a parallel between physical birth and spiritual rebirth in 'Eyn Sermon von der Taufe' but does not elaborate upon it, stating merely 'Dan gleych wie eyn kind ausz mutter leyb gehaben vnd geporn wirt das durch solch fleyschlich geburt ein sundigs mensch ist vnd eyn kind des zorns. Alszo wirt auss der tauff gehaben vnd geporn der mensch geystlich vnd durch solch gepurt eyn kind der gnaden'(WA 2, 728). The author of *Ein tractat* establishes (also without any elaboration) a parallel between Christ's physical presence in Mary's womb and his spiritual presence in us. For Crautwald the elaborate allegory of birth, growth, and development of the new man constitutes the focal point in his treatise and is used to expound his doctrine of good works.

What, if any, is the source of this allegory? It might be worth noting here that, with the exception of Gregory of Nyssa, Origen is the only patristic author to figure in the catalogue of Crautwald's own library now held by the Wroclaw University Library.[4] Origen, in the famous prologue to his *Commentary on the Song of Songs* [GCS Origenes 8:64-66] establishes the basic opposition between the spiritual and the carnal. According to him Adam was composed of two men, the first 'ad imaginem et similitudinem Dei factus' (Gen. 1:26f.) and the second 'e limo terrae fictus' (Gen. 2:7). It is this dualistic conception of man, argues Origen, that was taken over by Paul when he speaks about the inner and the outer man. 'Quorum vnum, id est interiorem renouari per singulos dies memorat, alium vero, id est exteriorem in sanctis quibusque et talibus qualis erat Paulus, corrumpi perhibet et infirmari.' This for Origen shows that it is legitimate to use the same words when we are speaking about the outer, carnal man and when we are speaking about his spiritual counterpart: '... immo per eadem vocabula et exterioris hominis, membra et illius interiores partes affectusque nominantur.' Thus, he continues, words such as 'puer,' 'adulescens,' 'iuuenis,' 'pater' can be used to indicate not only the physical but also the spiritual 'age' or stage of development. Among other examples of this double usage he cites 'venter animae' in Isaiah 26:18 (*Domine, a timore tuo in ventre concepimus*).

Moreover in his tenth homily on Exodus (GCS Origenes 6:244-52) 'De muliere praegnante quae duobus viris litigantibus abortierit' Origen applies his own theory in identifying the pregnant woman (248) with the soul who has just conceived, that is, heard, the Word of God. A similar 'conception,' he adds occurs at Isaiah 26:18. However, he continues, it is not enough to merely conceive the Word of God. What is essential, is that, having been conceived, the word should be given birth to in the form of good works. Origen then elaborates the allegory adding that a soul that merely conceives the word without giving birth is weak and that is why it is called a woman at Exodus 21:22! Commenting on the following verse, he continues the allegory establishing a parallel between the 'formatus infans' and the Word of God in the soul 'quae gratiam baptismi consecuta est vel quae euidentius et clarius verbum fidei concepit.'

It would be false to claim that Crautwald adopts Origen's theology in toto. On the contrary, we saw that he denies the dualistic conception of man and, following Luther, applies the notion of spiritual renewal to the whole person. What he does take from Origen, however, is the fundamental exegetical principle whereby all physical terminology is referred to man's spiritual development. He speaks thus of birth, boyhood, and manhood of the new man and what is perhaps more significant, he adapts Origen's allegory of the 'unborn child' to his own conception of spiritual development that must be actualized through good works.

It would thus appear that Crautwald in his treatise presents his readers with the Lutheran doctrines of faith, grace, baptism, and man. Those doctrines, however, are couched within Origen's exegetical framework that postulates a perfect symmetry between the physical and the spiritual components of man. Moreover, Crautwald's doctrine of good works as elaborated in the *Nouus homo* is closer to the doctrine put forward by Origen in *In Exodum* than to any doctrine put forward by Luther or Lutheran theologians in the early part of the sixteenth century.

Notes

[1] Cf. CS 8 (1927), doc. 358, 35ff. also for details of the editions of Latin and German versions. For details of Borrhaus' treatise see my paper ' "Corpus-anima-spiritus." Spiritual renewal in the theology of Hubmaier and Borrhaus,' presented at the International Colloquium on history of sixteenth-century Anabaptism, Strassburg, July 1984.

[2] For treatments of the theme by some dissident theologians see my paper 'Corpus-anima-spiritus.' For the patristic and medieval tradition see Hugo Rahner, 'Die Gottesgeburt. Die Lehre der Kirchenvater von der Geburt Christi aus dem Herzen der Kirche und der Glaubigen' in *Symbole der Kirche. Die Ekklesiologie der Vater* (Salzburg 1964), 13-87.

[3] In 4.6 fols. a^4, b^2. Printer not named. We are referring here to the copy held by the Bodleian Library, Oxford: Tract. Luth. 37 no. 85.

[4] *Origenis in Genesim Homiliae, 16. Eiusdem in Exodum Homiliae 13 etc.... Explanatio in Epistolam Pauli ad Romanos diuo Hieronymo interprete* (Venezia, Bernardinus Benalius 1512), 2 vols.: Sign 415075, 415075+. The full catalogue of Crautwald's library compiled by Adam

Skura is due to appear in volume 6 of the *Bibliotheca dissidentium* ed. by A. Séguenny, (Baden-Baden. 1980–). On early editions of Origen's homilies on *Canticum Canticorum* see Max Schar, *Das Nachleben Origenes im Zeitalter des Humanismus*, (Basel. 1979), 112ff.

Schwenckfeld in the Netherlands: Agge van Albada (c. 1525-1587)

Wiebe Bergsma

A Dutch pamphleteer writing in 1614 draws a memorable picture of the religious pluralism prevailing in the Low Countries of his day: 'There are the Coornhertists, Arminians, Vorstians, Socinians or Polish Brethren, Papists, Mennonites, David Jorists, H. Nicolaites, and others more, whereof the country is as full as the summer is of midges.'[1] The many heterodox groups of *chrétiens sans église* noted by this seventeenth-century observor of the Dutch Republic are today classified as belonging to the 'left wing of the Reformation.'[2] Missing from the list are followers of the Silesian nobleman Caspar Schwenckfeld (1489-1561), an omission symptomatic of this spiritualist's relatively limited influence in the Netherlands.

A sixteenth century witness has it that the presence of Schwenckfeld's followers all over Europe—only the provinces of the Netherlands were free of them—was the result of the Devil's collision with a mountain as he flew through the air with a sackful of Schwenkfelders.[3] Now it is true that spiritualists such as Schwenckfeld, Franck, Niclaes, and Joris did not reveal their secrets lightly, which is why they made use of allegory, veiled language, secret organizations, and pseudonyms. And although it is also true that Schwenckfeld is routinely mentioned in Dutch sources, often in the negative context of *catalogi haereticorum* but sometimes with approval, one thing is certain: in comparison with Sebastian Franck, with whom he in fact had much in common, Schwenckfeld exercised little influence in the Low Countries. The matter is complicated by the fact that the term 'Schwenkfeldian,' like the words 'Lutheran' and 'Socinian,' was often used as a stigmatizing epithet, so that it is difficult to know if persons so labelled actually sympathized with Schwenckfeld's 'himmlische Philosophia.'

But this does not mean there were no Schwenkfelders in the country. The Dutch poet and scholar Daniel Heinsius

(1580-1655), for example, described the religious climate in
the Low Countries around 1600 in a letter to a friend,[4] pointing out that some people adhered to Castellio, Schwenckfeld,
Franck, and David Joris; others preferred Tauler and the *Theologia Deutsch*. Among these was also Agge van Albada, who
appreciated Schwenckfeld greatly. Heinsius rightly associates
the names Schwenckfeld and Albada. Thus, any consideration
of Schwenckfeld's connections with the Netherlands must begin with the Frisian jurist, politician, spiritualist, and fighter
for religious toleration, Agge van Albada (c. 1525-1587), who
in his lifetime was known as 'a chief of the Schwenkfeldians'
(*coryphaeus Schwenckfeldianorum*).

Albada's life must be viewed within the perspective of two
important developments in Western Europe—the Reformation
and the Dutch Revolt against Spain. When he was born around
1525 most of the provinces of the Netherlands belonged to
the Burgundian-Habsburg empire, and the Roman Catholic
Church still maintained her dominance. When he died in 1587
seven provinces had formed the Dutch Republic and Protestantism had gained the ascendancy.

Agge van (in Latin, Aggaeus ab) Albada was born into a
noble Frisian family. Nothing is known of his youth except
that it culminated in a *peregrinatio academica* to the French
universities at Bourges, Orleans, and Paris, where he became
an accomplished jurist and Latinist. He was so well regarded
that even at a young age he was considered a candidate for a
professorate in law. Albada preferred to return to his homeland, however, where in 1553 he was appointed to the Court
of Friesland. About this time he became alienated from the
Catholic Church, but despite his disapproval of the persecution of heretics, clerical abuse, church ceremonies, and the mass
itself—he did not believe in the *praesentia realis*—Albada refrained from committing himself to Geneva or to Wittenberg.
Owing to the persecution of the Anabaptists, Albada resigned
from the Frisian court in 1559; after a short stay in Groningen he established himself in Speyer, where he accepted the
prominent position of assessor in the 'Reichskammergericht.'

In Speyer Albada fell under under the influence of Paracelsianism and began a study of the Cabbala, astrology, and the
occult sciences. Most importantly, it was in Speyer that Albada became a follower of Schwenckfeld, thereby putting his

illustrious career at risk. An idea of just how little sympathy Schwenkfelders aroused in their contemporaries may be got by a simple consideration of the corruptions of Schwenckfeld's name one encounters in the writings of the time: Stenckfeld, Schmeissfeld, Stanckfeld, Schandfeld, Senckfeld. Secrecy offered Albada the best chance of survival, which is probably why we know so little about him and his work.

In 1570 the distinguished Dutch Calvinist Marnix of St. Aldegonde (1540-1598) wrote to Albada, warning him that nearly everyone in Europe—Philip II, Alva, and Granvelle included—were aware of Albada's Schwenkfeldian sympathies. The warning reflects Marnix's disapproval of what he called the spiritualists' 'new kind of ecstasy' (*novum genus enthousiastoon*), which he castigated in many sharp and sarcastic polemics. But Marnix's warning could scarcely have arisen out of any sympathy with Albada's Schwenkfeldian ideas, but expressed instead his respect for Albada as a person. Marnix's concern was well-founded: in 1570 the Jesuits, Alva, and Philip II made common cause against Albada so that he was declared a *persona non grata* and was forced to leave Speyer.

During the 1570s and 1580s, after his departure from Speyer, Albada would continually face the choice between a retired life in the service of Schwenckfeld or an active life of political participation in the revolt against Spain. When offered prestigious positions by various German princes and the king of Denmark, Albada would choose a quiet life devoted to the study and translation of Schwenckfeld's works. His first decision, however, taken in 1571 after a period of restless travel, was to enter the service of the Bishop of Würzburg—a staunch supporter of the Counter-Reformation! Must we regard this move as a sign of spiritualistic opportunism? Was this a case of pure hypocrisy, or did Albada live according to the adage 'intus ut libet, foris ut moris' (think what you like, but act according to custom)?[5] So it might appear, were it not for the fact that Albada had scarcely began his function as counsellor to the bishop when he refused to attend mass, provoking his employer's disapproval. The Jesuits began another campaign against him, and in 1576 he was forced to leave Würzburg.

Again Albada travelled across the German Empire and the Netherlands, finally choosing Cologne as his residence. Here, where he remained off and on until his death in 1587, Albada

would once more emerge from the shadows to play an important role in European history. The peace congress at Cologne
in 1579 would be the high point of his career.

Albada's surviving correspondence demonstrates his interest in European politics generally, and from the beginning of
the Dutch Revolt in the 1560s, his intense involvement in the
history of the Low Countries. In 1579 the Revolt had reached
a critical stage: the Unions of Utrecht and Atrecht had divided the Northern from the Southern Netherlands. One last
attempt would be made to find a *modus vivendi* for Philip II
and the rebels. At the instigation of the Emperor Rudolph
II, peace negotiations were opened at Cologne. Here Albada's
involvement in the Dutch Revolt entered its most active phase.

At the beginning of the congress Albada held the lowest
rank among those negotiating on behalf of the Dutch rebels,
but an unforseen circumstance allowed him to play a leading
role in later discussions. This occurred when a number of participants complained that they could not understand a speech
being delivered in French. Albada was brought forward because his knowledge of languages and his rhetorical skills qualified him for the function of orator and interpreter (*orateur
ende taelman*). During the Cologne peace conference Albada
made countless fervent speeches defending the Revolt against
Philip II. In these he called upon many works by known and
unknown authors to marshall political (Monarchomachic) and
theological arguments legitimizing the rebels' conduct. The
congress ended in a failure half a year after its beginning; neither Philip II nor the representatives of the rebels were willing
to make concessions. The role of the centre and mediating
groups had been played out.

To justify their conduct, the States published the proceedings of the peace congress, entrusting the editing of the memoranda, recommendations, and articles to Albada, who had defended them so well at Cologne. In January Antwerp's famous
printer Christopher Plantin (c. 1520-1589) published the *Acta
pacificationis...* in both a Latin and a Dutch version. A second
edition also appeared with many annotations, glosses, marginalia, and digressions. This official report offers us an important
source for learning about Albada's political and religious convictions. To support his own ideas, he cites scores of theologians, jurists, and political theoreticians. His two spiritual

mentors are Sebastian Castellio (1515-1563) and Schwenckfeld, whom he quotes extensively. In this way Schwenckfeld's ideas found their way into the Netherlands. Albada had high expectations for the annotated edition of the *Acta*, and when this was quickly sold out, he suspected the Spaniards of having bought all the copies to suppress his comments in the glosses. Albada's initial expectations were in fact justified, for in later years the *Acta* were often cited and read, particularly by people experiencing oppression who found comfort in the work's impassioned condemnation of religious intolerance.

After the peace congress at Cologne Albada chose not to accept any official function, preferring to spend his last years in self-imposed isolation. These were not easy years. He was plagued by kidney stones, his second marriage ended in a divorce, and he worried about the only one of his eight children to have survived an early death. Above all, he was by nature inclined to complain and his spirit seemed to be less attracted by light than shadow. His pessimism sometimes assumed the form of hypochondria. Apart from these personal circumstances was the fact that Philip II attempted to persuade the cities of Cologne and Duisburg to expel Albada from their midst because of the danger this 'heretic doctor' with his prophetic pretensions posed to the citizenry.

With his supporters, the Albadaisten, Albada devoted himself to the translation and distribution of Schwenckfeld's writings. One of Albada's best-known friends was the physician Samuel Eisenmenger (1534-1585), also known as Siderocrates, a long-time professor at Tübingen. Like Albada, Eisenmenger was interested in astrology and the Iatro-chemical theory of medicine propagated by Paracelsus (1490-1541). Each provided the manuscripts and translations of the other with commentary. Both Albada and Eisenmenger viewed Schwenckfeld and his partisan Valentine Crautwald as the two witnesses in St. John's Apocalypse, eschatological figures heralding the beginning of a new heaven and a new earth. According to Albada and Eisenmenger it was unthinkable that anyone who read Schwenckfeld's and Crautwald's books would fail to recognize these great figures as John's faithful witnesses and burning candles now shedding light on Europe and over the entire world.

It was in a certain sense the tragedy of Albada's life that while nearly all his contemporaries praised his personality and admired his knowledge. erudition, and peace-loving nature, his Schwenkfeldian sympathies were rejected all but unanimously by Catholics, Protestants of all signatures, and even by spiritualists—sometimes scornfully, sometimes in a friendly manner, but always resolutely. In this way Albada came to experience the same spiritual isolation as had characterized the life of his mentor and example, Caspar Schwenckfeld. In 1587 Albada died of pleurisy at Worms.

Albada has been characterized as a Catholic, a Calvinist, the head of the Family of Love in Cologne, and a spiritualist; he has been counted among the *mediatores*, the neutralists, and the 'tussen-beide-lopers,' but the Dutch church historian Johannes Lindeboom came closest to the mark when he described him as 'a Schwenkfeldian, the independant reformer.'[6] Albada once wrote to a friend, 'May God help me become a good translator of Schwenckfeld's writings. How happy I would be if God encouraged me in this task!'[7] Albada wanted nothing more than to serve as translator for the 'sanctissimi viri C.S. et V.C.,' the 'most holy' Caspar Schwenckfeld and Valentine Crautwald. Albada did not use initials here out of considerations of efficiency; in simply naming Schwenckfeld one burdened oneself with the odium of one of the world's worst heretics.

In the *Acta* as well as in a separately-published *Discursus*—a discussion of the political and religious situation in the Netherlands and in Europe in 1579—Albada suggests how an end to the present suffering might be achieved.[8] First, he says, we must do penance because we have despised God's light and grace and because the blood of innocent men has been spilled. We must give God's grace and light the place they deserve. From this we will learn that we should believe the simple, pure, and good teachings of Christ rather than the inventions of men. Secondly, we must serve God in the right way, not in external, human (*creatuurlijke*) affairs, but in spirit and truth. Thirdly, we should understand that to Christ alone and not to men is given the authority for the forgiveness of sins, the outpouring of the spirit, and the bestowal of grace. No matter how somber the future might appear, one comfort always remains: God's trumpets will one day sound. Albada finishes his argument with the sigh, 'May the Lord enlighten them, that they might begin to think differently, because whether they do or not, the time appears to be close at hand when it will become necessary to return to Jesus Christ, the Son of God, Lord of Lords, and King of Kings, those things I have mentioned above which have been taken away from him.' Surprisingly, this passage is an almost literal quotation from a letter which Schwenckfeld sent to a doctor in Roermond in the Southern Netherlands in 1561.

Although the *Discursus* and the *Acta* are not systematic theological treatises, they do give a summary of Albada's ideas—his spiritualism, his interest in eschatology, his christology, and his aversion to any form of religious coercion. I will now consider each of these four points.

Just as with Schwenckfeld we find in Albada's writings recurring contrasts suggestive of a form of dualism: external and internal Word, body and spirit, external and internal man, Old Testament and New Testament, Old Covenant and New Covenant, Scriptures and the Spirit, and two forms of divine revelation: through the Scriptures and directly from God. We may learn God's will from the Bible or from direct revelation— and here we recognize Albada the spiritualist: 'voluntas Dei aut revelatione aut ex scripto Dei verbo cognoscitur.'[9] God prefers to reveal himself to the simple in spirit, but these are disdained by the learned; now the adage also quoted by Schwenckfeld, 'je gelehrter, je verkehrter,' springs to mind. As a source and norm for belief, Albada considered the Bible of less importance than the spirit. He wrote to a friend: 'Nothing salutary can happen when our judgment is formed more by the words of the Scriptures than by the revelation of the Holy Ghost, when human light is held in higher esteem than the divine.'[10] Although Albada thus qualified the Bible's spiritual authority, he did not reject the Scriptures entirely; on the contrary, with the aid of Schwenckfeld's writings he wrote many commentaries on the books of the New Testament.

It should be obvious that the spiritualist Albada had little interest in the visible churches as he saw them. Like Schwenckfeld, Albada was very much disturbed by what he considered to be the laxity of many preachers, and he was disappointed by the failure of a sort of moral reformation to materialize. Completely in Schwenckfeld's spirit, Albada wished to restrict the church to conventicles without sacraments or external rituals where the 'internas loqutiones et responsiones a Deo' would take place, and the Bible would be explained. After all, sacraments and rituals were only *adiaphora* and could better be avoided: the Spirit of God is free and not bound by any external thing. Had Schwenckfeld himself not written, 'Got ist onahngebunden. Sein geist wirckt wa er wil'?[11]

Besides the qualification of the Bible's spiritual authority and a spiritualistic concept of the church, Albada shared with many sixteenth century spiritualists a great interest in all kinds of occult phenomena. The renaissance was not only the rebirth of the *bonae literae*, it was also a blossoming of the *scientiae arcanae*. Albada became engrossed in the *ars combinandi*, in the Cabbala and the occult sciences of Hermes Trismegistus.[12] In Albada's works and letters we encounter the use of allegory and references to the *Corpus Hermeticum* as well as to astrological and Paracelsian treatises; we find frequent mentions of Cabbalists such as Pico della Mirandola (1463-1494) and Johannes Reuchlin (1455-1522) and speculations concerning the tetragram JHWH. These occult interests provoked still greater reservations about Albada in the minds of some of his contemporaries.

Despite all their differences and divisions, most sixteenth century spiritualists and Anabaptists shared a strong eschatological interest and concern for the last things. Albada also dreamed of a new heaven and a new earth and longed for a kingdom where swords would be turned into ploughshares. While many spiritualists such as Joris, Niclaes, and Barrefelt (Hiel) saw themselves playing the role of messiah in the realization of these prophecies, Albada was more restrained. Though convinced of his own predictions, he did not presume to call himself a messiah. For him the eschatological figures were Schwenckfeld and Crautwald, the two witnesses from the last book of the Bible who 'have power to shut heaven, that it rain not in the days of their prophecy: and have power over waters to turn them to blood, and to smite the earth with all plagues, as often as they will' (Rev. 11:6). According to Albada, it would not be long before the new kingdom would come. As a result he withdrew 'cum libello in angello'—in this case, with Schwenckfeld's books. A certain resignation came over Albada during the last years of his life. He speculated with his followers about who would be saved in the last judgment. Albada knew it perfectly: those who possess the patience of the saints and who bear on their foreheads the sign 'tau.' References to the Hebrew letter 'tau' (see Ez. 9:4 and Rev. 7:3-4) occur more often in the words of sixteenth century spiritualists; we should not be surprised that Albada, with his interest in Paracelsianism and the *ars cabalistica*, should also mention this most secret sign.

The greater part of the *Corpus Schwenckfeldianorum* is devoted to a consideration of christology; though Albada developed few original ideas on the subject, it is clear that he followed in his mentor's footsteps by frequently pondering the theological problems posed by Christ's dual nature and the dogma of the Incarnation. Albada's interest in Schwenckfeld's doctrine of the 'coeleste corpus'—most particularly, that emphasis of Christ's divine nature which has been called the divinization of Christ's humanity—is reflected not only in his translations of Schwenckfeld's works, but also in his personal letters. Because of his adherence to Schwenckfeld's christology, Albada was forced to refuse or give up good positions. Nearly all his close acquaintances—Catholics, Protestants. Anabaptists, even Spiritualists with whom he had much in common—criticized and denigrated Albada because of his sympathy with Schwenckfeld's 'gesunde reyne lehre.' Albada made Schwenckfeld's christology so much his own that during a heated debate with the French theologian Lambertus Danaeus (c. 1530-1595), he could write in a few days forty-two closely written folios on the subject. larded with quotations from scores of church fathers. medieval theologians, and contemporary religious scholars. In this argument he often quotes 'one or another pious man,' references to the founding father.

Both Luther and Schwenckfeld endorsed the concept of freedom of conscience (*Freiheit des Gewissens* and *libertas conscientiae*), but in reality the two assumed diverging attitudes towards people who held religious beliefs different from their own. Schwenckfeld was convinced that Christians should always follow 'Christ's meekness, patience, humility, and forbearance in tolerating the adversary.'[13] Religious coercion was totally without redeeming virtue. Belief is a spiritual matter and may not be hindered by the government, fire, or sword. The wind blows where it will, the Spirit of God cannot be restrained, and persecution of belief is therefore out of the question: 'Denn wie

der wind/ bleset wo er wil/ du horest sein stimme wol/ Aber
du weist nicht von wannen er kompt/ und wahin er fehret/Also
gehets auch in geistlichen sachen zu.'[14]

Albada shared Schwenckfeld's rejection of every form of religious persecution and he worked tirelessly on behalf of those
among his fellow men who were enslaved or imprisoned on account of their beliefs. He brought all his knowledge to bear on
the task of demonstrating that heretics should not be burned.
His aversion to religious intolerance found expression in impassioned speeches delivered at the Cologne peace negotiations and published with scores of citations in the *Acta*. Just
as Schwenckfeld had done, Albada presented numerous arguments: the division of church and state and the religious pluralism this implied—that is, the idea that in a single state more
than one religion may simultaneously exist; the notion that
faith is a gift and that those who have not received this *donum
Dei* are not themselves to blame; and, most importantly, the
biblical *locus classicus* for religious tolerance, the parable of
the tares told in Matthew 13 which Bainton has termed 'the
proof text for religious liberty.'[15]

Albada's two important witnesses were Castellio and Schwenckfeld.[16] He quotes extensively in the *Acta*—anonymously,
of course —from Castellio's book *De haereticis an sint persequendi* which had appeared in 1554 under the pseudonym Mar-
tinus Bellius. Published in response to the burning at the
stake of the anti-trinitarian Servet, an execution for which
Calvin was partly responsible, the book exercised great influence throughout Western Europe. Castellio's ideological entry into the Low Countries was facilitated by Albada, who
cites with approval the various (often symbolic) names Castellio had assumed in his book: Johannes Witlingius, Augustinus
Eleutherius, Georgius Kleinbergius, and Aretius Catharus. Albada chose his citations well. For the edification of those in
power he quoted the words of Kleinbergius:

> Princes and all rulers open your eyes, open your ears,
> fear God, and consider how you will render an account to
> Him of your administration. Many have been punished
> for cruelty, none for mercy. Many will be condemned in
> the last judgment for having killed the innocent, none
> for not having killed. Incline to the side of mercy and

do not obey those who incite you to murder. They will not help you when you give an account to God. They will have enough to do to look after themselves.[17]

Albada also refers to his second important witness anonymously; Schwenckfeld is cited simply as 'a decent and pious man.' Albada saw Schwenckfeld's courage best reflected in a letter which he includes in the *Acta*: Christians should never use force or violence, they should never for religion's sake obstruct, persecute, or kill anyone who is peace-loving—not, at least, if they hope to escape judgment and punishment.[18]

Albada's contemporaries rightly regarded him as a chief of the Schwenkfeldians (*coryphaeus Schwenckfeldianorum*). Though his Schwenkfeldian sympathies were for many a stumbling block and source of irritation, Albada's political insight and diplomatic skill attracted many offers of distinguished employment in the service of Catholic bishops, German princes, and—most notably—the king of Denmark. All this makes him an interesting and intriguing figure. He did not, however, exercise much influence on his contemporaries, since few sixteenth century spiritualists held political positions of any significance. Humanistic vanity and ambition were alien to his nature, as was any longing for a place in the *respublica literaria*. He used his knowledge of Latin to translate the writings of his mentor, Schwenckfeld, rather than to serve the humanistic cult of that language. His sole desire was to live in accordance with the truth which he believed Schwenckfeld had put into words. In the midst of official proceedings, documents, protocols, and memoranda we may find Albada's personal confessions. There he lets himself go and hammers out his aversion to religious persecution, persecution which he had himself experienced. The ground of his inspiration may be discovered in the *Acta* where he writes: 'The kingdom of Christ is not of this world; it is spiritual, not material. In the same way God's word is a spirit. The gospel is the force of God. True service to God occurs in the Spirit. Because faith is a gift of God's Spirit, undeservedly bestowed, it can and may not be received or taken, protected or retained by mankind or by the material sword.'[19]

To measure a man's influence is always difficult, particularly so in the case of someone who has left behind relatively little in print. It may be said with certainty, however, that it was at least partly due to men such as Albada. the Schwenkfeldian, that the Dutch Republic came to be a place of relative tranquility for many people made homeless because of their beliefs. A Dutch historian once referred to this phenomenon by saying that while the Republic of the seventeenth century was no paradise where the wolf played with the lamb and the fox left the chickens in peace, it was indeed the most tolerant land in the *ancien régime*.[20] Contemporary documentation for this view may be found in the words of Sir William Temple,[21] the English ambassador to the Low Countries during the years 1668 to 1670, who in his *Observations upon the United Provinces of the Netherlands* writes: 'It is hardly to be imagined how all the violance and sharpness, which accompanies the differences of Religion in other Countreys, seems to be appeased or softened here, by the general freedom which all men enjoy, either by allowance or connivence; Nor how Faction and Ambition are thereby disabled to colour their Interested and Seditious Designs, with the pretences of Religion, Which has cost the Christian World so much blood for these last Hundred and fifty years.'

Notes

In order to limit the number of notes I refer the reader to my thesis *Aggaeus van Albada (c. 1525-1587), schwenckfeldiaan, staatsman en strijder voor verdraagzaamheid*, Diss. Groningen (Meppel, 1983).

[1] A. F. Mellink, 'The Radical Underground' in the Dutch Radical Reformation,' *Commissie tot de uitgave van Documenta Anabaptistica Neerlandica*, 12 and 13 (1980-1981), 53.

[2] For a discussion of terminology cf. Roland Crahay, 'Le non-conformisme religieux du XVIe siècle entre l'humanisme et les Eglises, Reflexions historiographiques.' *Bibliotheca Dissidentium, scripta et studia No. 1* (Baden-Baden, 1983), 15-35. (includes a useful bibliography). A good discussion of the literature is to be found in A. Rotondo, 'I movimenti ereticali nell'Europa del Cinquecento,' *Studi e ricerche di storia ereticale Italiana del Cinquecento* (Torino, 1974), 5-56. A neglected book is L. Kolakowski, *Chrétiens sans Eglise. La Conscience religieuse et le lien confessionel au XVIIe siècle* (Paris, 1969).

[3] G. Arnold, *Historie der Kerken en Ketteren* (Amsterdam, 1701), 2:462-63.

[4] P. Bertius (ed.), *Illustrium et Clarorum Virorum Epistolae Selectiores* (Lugduni Batavorum, 1617): 'Alij enim Castalioni, alij Swenckfeldio, alij Franco, alij Davidi Georgio haeserunt: nam et istos novi. Alij Taulerum

et Germanicam Theologiam in deliciis habuerunt. Possem infinitos numerare. quorum nominibus nunc parco. Inter eos et Albada fuit, cui placuit Swenckfeldius, quanquam, Franco quoque et postremis illis aliquid tribuere videtur. Caeterum, cum pius, sicut saepe accepi, et in primis studiosus patriae vir esset, neque opiniones suas pertinaciter defenderet aut perniciose propagaret.'

5 Nicodemising (the art of simulating) as a practical rule was defined by Carlo Ginzburg: 'Era un atteggiamento che attingeva la sua giustificazione da una religione piú pura e meno sensibile, intimamente aristocratica, in cui l'eredità esoterica dell'umanesimo neoplatonico si mescolava ad anticipazioni quasi deistiche. Il nicodemismo fu dunque una posizione religiosa precisa e consapevole, non uno stato d'animo diffuso e impalpabile, né tanto meno un miscuglio di dottrine contraddittorie.' *Il nicodemismo. Simulazione e dissimulazione religiosa nell'Europa del'500* (Torino, 1970), 16. The Jorists and the Familists, the members of the Family of Love founded by Hendrik Niclaes, advocated religious simulation. A. Hamilton, *The Family of Love* (Cambridge, 1981), 2 and W. Bergsma, 'Het Huis der Liefde,' *Doopsgezinde Bijdragen*, 8 (1982). 107-15. It is very difficult to generalize because Schwenckfeld—and Albada—attacked this religious simulation: 'Ich hab auch von dieser materia drumb dest lenger wollen schreiben/ dass ich vernommen/ wie ihren vil in denselben Landen seind/ welche die warheit des Evangelii zum theil erkant haben/ und aber darneben überredt seind/ es schade ihnen kein eusserlicher falscher Gottesdienst/haltens für recht mit den Päpstlern zu communiciren/ wollens auch vertedigen/dass ihnen alle eusserliche res externae/ oder Ceremonien frey seind/ welche von etlichen Libertini (in margin: Davidianer. Nicolaite. Die vom hauss der Liebe) genant werden. Ob ihr davon mit ihnen woltet conferirn/ wolte auch gerne wissen/ wie solch mit H. Schrifft wollen bewehren/ wir sollen je nicht Crucifugae erfunden werden/ weil das Creutz Christi der Christen edel Kleinot/ hoffarbe/ zierd und schmuck ist/ one welches wir schwärlich in himmel werden kommen/ wie vor aus Paulo/ auch auss den worten Christi selbst im Evangelio verstanden' (CS 17:600-01). Despite similarities in ideology, Albada severely criticized the members of the Family of Love, Beysura, *Albada*, 106-09.

6 J. Lindeboom, 'La place de Castellion dans l'histoire de l'esprit,' *Autour de Michel Servet et de Sebastien Castellion*, Recueil publ. sous la direction de B. Becker (Haarlem, 1953), 173.

7 E. Friedländer. *Briefe des Aggaeus de Albada an Rembertus Ackema und andere, aus den Jahren 1579-1584* (Leeuwarden, 1874), 141-42.

8 *Discursus an pax inter serenissimum regem catholicum et ordines Belgii in hoc conventu conciliabitur, an non* (Friedländer, *Briefe*, 1-10). The same ideas are expressed in the preface of the *Acten vanden Vredehandel geschiet te Colen* (Leiden, 1581). Albada paraphrases a letter of Schwenckfeld in CS 17:590ff.

9 Friedländer, *Briefe*, 117-18.

[10] *Ibid.* 57.

[11] CS 13: 421.

[12] For a treatment of Paracelsianism and the *scientiae arcanae* see the small but magnificent study: C. Webster, *From Paracelsus to Newton. Magic and the Making of Modern Science* (Cambridge, 1982).

[13] CS 5:294.

[14] CS 4:133.

[15] R. H. Bainton, 'The Parable of the Tares as the Proof Text for Religious Liberty to the End of the sixteenth Century,' *Church History*, 1 (1932), 67-89.

[16] H. R. Guggisberg, *Sebastian Castellio im Urteil seiner Nachwelt vom Späthumanismus bis zur Aufklärung* (Basel, 1956).

[17] S. Castellio, *De haerecticis an sint persequendi*, reproduction en fac-similé de l'edition de 1554 avec une introduction de S. van der Woude (Geneva, 1954), 129. See *Acten*, 104 and S. Castellio, *Concerning heretics* trans. by R. H. Bainton (New York, 1935), 219.

[18] *Acten*, 193.

[19] *Ibid.* 54.

[20] L. J. Rogier, 'De tolerantie in de Statenbond der Verenigde Nederlanden.' *Terugblik en uitzicht*, (Hilversum-Antwerp, 1964) 1:108.

[21] William Temple, *Observations upon the United Provinces of the Netherlands* (Oxford, 1972) [orig. 1673], 106. Already in 1911 Ernst Troeltsch pointed out that sixteenth century spiritualism created an atmosphere of greater religious toleration: 'Die religiöse Toleranz und Gewissensfreiheit ist überwiegend ein Werk des Spiritualismus, das Vereinskirchentum und die Verselbständigung der Taufertums und des ihm sich nahernden Calvinismus.' *Die Bedeutung des Protestantismus fur die Entstehung der modernen Welt* (Aalen, 1963), 86.

Daniel Sudermann:
Schwenkfelder Poet

Monica Pieper

Sudermann's Life

In a Schwenckfeld *Epistolar* from Daniel Sudermann's Library, an entry written in his own hand can be found which outlines his religious development in the shortest form:

> D.S. Ist geboren Anno 1550. Er ist Catholisch, aber 1558 In der Caluinischen Schul gangen. Auch zu der Lutherischen predig mit gangen. Den Teuffern auch zugehört. Ist Anno 1594 zu erkantnus der Wahrheit kommen. Und hat A[nno] 1624 dis uffgeschrieben seines alters 74, noch starck, frisch, und gesund, als lang der Herr Jesu[s] Christus will....[1]

> (D. S. was born in 1550. He was Catholic but in 1558 went to a Calvinist school and to Lutheran preaching services as well as associating with the Anabaptists. In 1594 he came to a knowledge of truth [Wahrheit] and in 1624, strong and healthy at 74 years of age he wrote this.)

The 'Wahrheit' of which Daniel Sudermann became cognizant in the forty-fourth year of his life was nothing other than the teachings of Schwenckfeld to which he remained faithful to the end of his life. The road which he had walked to this secure haven of faith was marked by aquaintance with the major confessions of his time, as can be noted from his autobiography.

Sudermann was born in February of 1550 in Lüttich, as son of the painter, graphic artist, and goldsmith Lambert Sudermann. The family formed a branch of a respected old line, living mainly in the lower Rhine region and the Netherlands. Despite apparently being baptized Catholic, Sudermann went to a Calvinist school in Aachen in 1558. Early journeys together with his father led him to Maastrich, Antwerp, Cologne,

Düsseldorf, and Frankfurt.[2] During a stay with the Duke Johann Friedrich II in Weimar, Lambert Sudermann died in 1564. Daniel, who had accompanied him, remained a guest at the court up to 1567 except for short interruptions. In 1569 he travelled to Strassburg for the first time, possibly in the entourage of Georg von Sayn-Wittgenstein who represented the Protestant party during the bishop's election of Johann von Manderscheid. In the following years Sudermann stayed in Cologne, the Netherlands, Regensburg, Düsseldorf, Rappoltsweiler, and Gemar. In 1576 he was introduced to Kaiser Rudolf in Regensburg. The travels with his father which introduced him into the circles of the German nobility, determined his prospects for the future. In the next fifteen years Sudermann was a teacher in respected families and a bailiff in German principalities. Many poems dedicated to his benefactors and pupils inform us of these relations. An extensive compilation of persons with whom Sudermann maintained such ties is given by Wackernagel in his bibliography of German hymnology.[3] The circle of his acquaintances went beyond political and confessional boundaries. Sudermann's pattern here was possibly influenced by his interest in the peaceful coexistence of all confessions.

Of great importance in this period of Sudermann's life were his visits in Jestetten and Tiengen at the Upper Rhine to the Duke of Sulz and in Wiesensteig to the Duke of Helfenstein in 1582 and 1583. He then resided near the territory of the Barons of Freyberg who had given refuge to Caspar von Schwenckfeld. Possibly, he first encountered Schwenckfeld's teachings here. The two communities, Justingen and Oepfingen, which were under the rule of the Freybergs, were a sanctuary for the Schwenckfeld religious community.[4]

Surely, his acquaintance with several Schwenkfelders of the Justingen circle, to whom he remained attached throughout his life, shaped his later convictions. To these belong the Lampertheim Pastor Hans Georg Schid who became Senior of the Justingen community in 1590, as well as Daniel Friedrich, whom the records of the Barons of Freyberg refer to as 'Schulmeister,' and whom Sudermann was determined to meet again in Strassburg.

After 1585 Sudermann lived, for the most part, in Strassburg. He received a position as tutor of young men of noble birth who were educated in the chapter house of the Protestant canons of Strassburg, the so-called 'Bruderhof.' Among his pupils were Margrave Johann Sigismund, the later Elector of Brandenburg, Johann Georg of Brandenburg, and the Barons Franz and Julius Ernst of Braunschweig.

His activities at the Bruderhof must have left Sudermann time to devote attention to his own interests, collecting and excerpting religious manuscripts and writing poetry. After 1594 Sudermann made public his Schwenkfeldian sympathies. He published Schwenckfeld's writings, the costs of which were carried by the Freyberg Barons Johann Plickard and Georg Ludwig, and he also maintained contact with the Schwenkfeldian Strassburgers among whom were the Strassburg Senator Michael Theurer and his son-in-law Michael Ellwein. Connections to Hans Georg Schid who possessed Strassburg citizenship and to Daniel Friedrich, as well as to his brother Samuel, can be ascertained. Sudermann also entertained friendly relations to the Alsatian physician, Helisäus Röslin, a resident of Hagenau. The date of Sudermann's death cannot be determined exactly, but it is probable that he died in 1631 or shortly after.

Sources of Sudermann's Work

The largest part of Sudermann's work is composed of songs and poems, believing as he did that rhyming texts had the most lasting effect upon readers or listeners:

> Geistlich spruch in Reimen ghört
> Man ehe behalt dan lange wört[5]

The number of his poetic pieces has been estimated between 2000 and 3000, but only about 435 of these were printed. If one takes a look at the extant manuscripts it is not surprising that the number of poetic works not printed cannot be ascertained precisely. In the Staatsbibliothek Preussischer Kulturbesitz in Berlin alone, where the greatest number of his manuscripts are deposited, the number of manuscript pages is over 10,000. Not all of these manuscripts are Sudermann's own work but often are transcriptions or excerpts of older Christian literature which he furnished with sententious marginalia or short rhyming comments.

My own perusal of the manuscripts led me to the conclusion that Sudermann's work is well represented by the printed material. As a result, I concentrated primarily on it and only secondarily on the manuscripts.

Apparently, Sudermann began publishing his work only late. The two earliest extant one-sheet prints stem from the years 1616 and 1617. (They are the only ones still existing in this form.) Later miscellanies like those he edited between 1620 and 1628 unite such single-sheet prints to fifty and more poems. The designing of such sheets always follows the same pattern: The upper third of the sheet is used for the title and an emblem serving to illustrate the following poetic text. The space along the margin and below the text is used to substantiate and supplement the intrinsic meaning of the poem with citations from the Bible and the Early Fathers. Sudermann had compiled five large miscellanies in this form, of which the fourth has unfortunately disappeared. All volumes bear, with small deviations in the formulation, the title: *Schöne ausserlesene Figuren und hohe Lehren von der Begnadeten Liebhabenden Seele, Nemlich der christlichen Kirchen und ihre[m] Gemahl Jesu Christo.* Sudermann's interpretation of the Song of Solomon, published in 1622, belongs to his more noted works and is titled: *Hohe geistreiche Lehren und Erklärungen: Ueber die fürnembsten Sprüche des Hohen Lieds Salmononis, von der liebhabenden Seele, das ist, der Christlichen Kirchen und ihrem Gemahl Jesu Christo.* The volume interprets chapters 1-8 of the Song of Solomon by selecting single verses from each chapter and commenting on them in poetic form. Here Sudermann pays homage to the allegoric interpretation of the Song of Solomon common since Origen and strongly enhanced in the middle ages.

A collection of rhymed quatrains appeared in two volumes in the years 1624 and 1626 designated by Sudermann as *Gleichnisse*. Their singularity lies in the fact that they are in German as well as Latin. The title is: *Centuria Similitudinum Omni Doctrinarum Genere Plenarum Sub Externarum Imaginum Aeri Incisis Umbris, Deo Devotibus mentibus, pulcherrimas res spirituales contemplandas proponentium.* The contents of the poems are always a comparison between an event out of everyday life and a Christian virtue or conduct.

The collection *Etliche hohe geistliche Gesänge* of 1626 contains forty-two songs which Sudermann partially bestowed with the melodies of well-known secular or clerical songs. Aside from the titles mentioned, a number of smaller anthologies exist of which the publishing dates are not ascertainable. Various libraries in Germany, France, and Switzerland carry them under different titles. Partially they also contain duplicates of poems. A selection of approximately 200 poems and songs by Sudermann is available in Philipp Wackernagel's *Das deutsche Kirchenlied*. The greater part of the original prints is accessible in the microfilm collection, 'German Baroque literature' edited by Harold Jantz.

A special position under Sudermann's works is given to the voluminous prose work: *Harmonia oder Concordantz* of 1613. Only the words of introduction and the epilogue were written by Sudermann, the remaining 460 pages consisting exclusively of collected extraneous material, which he extracted from Catholic, Lutheran, or Reformed authors. The excerpts are organized under dogmatic points and claim to be objectively compiled. However, they are so cleverly selected that they correspond with the religious principles of spiritualism. Sudermann wanted to prove the conformity of this teaching with the three major confessions. Thus, in the conclusion he states that the content of the three confessions treated is in accordance with that of 'N.N.' with whom none other than Caspar von Schwenckfeld is meant.

State of Sudermann Research

Only few works are devoted exclusively to Sudermann. Three types of literature deal with him. (1) There are chronologically oriented synopses which attempt a literary, theological and historical classification of the poet but are restricted to short notices. (2) More satisfying in comparison are the subject-oriented works which treat Sudermann more in depth, as a baroque poet, for example. (3) Finally, there are monographs, three of which are particularly significant. In 1857, August Friedrich Heinrich Schneider published a synopsis on the literature on Schwenkfelder lyric poets up to Daniel Sudermann. In the work he offered a description of the life of the poet reflecting his religious development and added a bibliography of Sudermann's works as well as of his library. Some of the manuscripts of the poet were apparently not known to Schneider. In 1923 in his doctoral thesis, Gottfried Herrmann

Schmidt attempted to review Sudermann's work and library closely. In addition he presented an account of the life and character of the poet and strove to cover all fields in which Sudermann was active. Despite the detailed citations, the work is somewhat obscure because Schmidt developed his own system of classification which is difficult for the reader. Finally, Hans Hornung in his doctoral thesis has dealt with Sudermann as a collector of manuscripts. The main part of his work consists of an extensive and detailed manuscript catalogue as well as an extensive biography.

Major biographical and bibliographical work has thus been accomplished. However, the works noted do not deal significantly with Sudermann's importance in the history of piety. A study of Sudermann's religious thought is still lacking.[6] What follows is based on my doctoral thesis and is offered as a contribution to this end.

Sudermann's Work

Sudermann was already known as a collector of religious literature in his own time. The stock of his library consisted largely of mystical manuscripts. But despite the time and energy he devoted to his library, all manuscripts possessed only a limited value for him. The basic precondition for properly understanding a text was for him, solely the authority of the spirit. Only the believer who was first provided by the spirit with understanding, was capable of examining books for their truth and using them to deepen his own faith.

Although a complete reconstruction of Sudermann's book and manuscript collection is not possible, a sense of his collector's activity can be gained from what remains of it. It contains two focal points: medieval German mysticism and Schwenkfeldian spiritualism. Among the manuscripts of the mystics the works of Tauler dominate; Sudermann knew most of his sermons, but often other authors are mentioned under Tauler's name. Prayers and songs which he ascribes to Tauler prove that he did not see him as an outstanding speculative mystic but as a teacher of a wider public. Meister Eckhart and Heinrich Suso are less important than Tauler for Sudermann. Occasional problems with manuscript designations make it clear that Sudermann was not concerned with these authors in themselves, but that he consulted their texts for their value as timeless and instructive messages.

With regard to spiritualism Sudermann naturally attempted to acquire Schwenckfeld's manuscripts. Frequently he transcribed them from the originals with great diligence. Beside the works of Schwenckfeld himself, he also collected manuscripts from Schwenckfeld's followers. To these belong texts of Valentine Crautwald, Adam Reissner, Bernhard Schilling, Hans Georg Schid, and Helisäus Röslin. He possessed little other Reformation literature and seems to have learned of Reformation concerns only from Schwenckfeld and his followers.

Although Sudermann openly admitted his adherence to the Schwenkfelders only in 1594, his interest in Schwenkfeldian literature commenced with his visit to the Duke Rudolf V of Helfenstein in Wiesensteig and the beginning of his relations with the von Freybergs. The first Schwenckfeld-edition of Sudermann stems for the year 1589. It is a short manuscript: *Ein christlich bedencken von dem Sprüche. Lasset die kindlein zu mir kom[m]en.* In the same year Sudermann edited Schwenckfeld's *Vom christlichen Sabbath und Underscheid des alten und newen Testaments.* According to the *Corpus Schwenckfeldianorum* the book first came into possession of Daniel Friedrich and later of Sudermann. Until then it had been printed only in extracts. Sudermann was the first to edit the complete work.[7]

In addition, an important edition originating from Sudermann is that of Schwenckfeld's interpretation of Psalm 133. First published in 1547, its first and only reprint was that of Sudermann.[8] Later, Sudermann used Schwenckfeld's interpretation in a poem which borrows almost literally from the original.[9]

In 1592 Sudermann edited Schwenckfeld's *Bekantnis und Rechenschafft von den Heuptpuncten des Christlichen Glaubens* and other pieces first published in 1547 and revised again by Schwenckfeld himself in 1561[10]. Apparently, the significance of this work lay, for Sudermann, in the fact that the central points of Schwenckfeld's theology found their expression in it and that each subject had its own chapter. Between 1594 and the turn of the century the number of Sudermann's Schwenckfeld-editions increased.

Schwenckfeld's collection of prayers *Deutsch Passional unsers Herren Jesu Christi* has a high value for Sudermann. The work was published several times before Sudermann decided to publish it. An edition from 1594 probably dates back to Sudermann, whereas an additional edition from 1601 positively goes back to him.[11] The *Deutsch Passional* is not Schwenckfeld's own creation but a translation and compilation of medieval sources which are marked by a strong mystical influence that emphasizes the transience of the flesh and the futility of the world.[12]

The Mystical and Spiritualist Features of Sudermann's Work

The classification of Sudermann's poetry evolves from its source as poem or song. In both cases he reaches back to traditional forms. The poems have features from the emblem literature or the tradition of interpretations of the Song of Solomon. Sudermann often chooses familiar melodies to which he adapts his text or he uses the form of the 'Meistersingerlied.'

Sudermann wanted to address a circle of readers belonging to the class of the 'Gemeinen Mannes' (common man). His mode of communication was suited to this group in its use of simple literary forms and the transcription of universal but abstract matters into terms that would allow laymen to grasp the 'Christliche Wahrheit' (Christian truth).

Sudermann does not present original thoughts. The basic characteristic of his work is either the consolidation of mystical or spiritualistic elements or their combination. Sudermann's own achievement is to be found in the combination of the trains of thought of both traditions and in the evaluation and accentuation by which he incorporates these elements into his poetry.

Sudermann's statements concentrate on his focal points, mysticism and spiritualism, leaving other matters unconsidered. For him dogmas are only binding as far as they are in agreement with knowledge given to mankind directly by the Holy Spirit. This means that the revelation of the Godly will must be issued to every Christian personally and cannot be effected by means of sermon or Bible. The preaching of the gospel and the reading of the Holy Scripture will confirm rather than form one's faith. Faith cannot be brought about by external mediation of the Word; it must be formed in the internal man. Sudermann's dualism, like Schwenckfeld's, separates the godly from the worldly and it also asserts the irreconcilable contrast between body and soul in every human being.

The relationship between man and Christ forms the center of Sudermann's piety. In it he reaches back to the Christ and bride mysticism of the middle ages and adopts the spiritualist christology of Schwenckfeld. He did not consider Jesus' salvific act as a unique fact manifested in faith, but saw Jesus as a goal and prototype that can be reached by man out of his own energy and in whose presence he is able to live. He described the process of this approach either with the help of Schwenckfeld's conception of the 'Wahre Erkenntnis' (true cognition) by reflecting on and becoming absorbed in the two 'Stände' (estates) of Jesus. or with the help of the mystical concept of the bridal relationship between Jesus and the soul. Both of these traditional strands are woven together, being reduced and becoming shallower at the same time.

To him, the goal of this mystical approach is not to experience the union as a trance but as an ever renewed and everlasting effort to live in closeness to God. The visions and speculation with which mysticism attempts to reach its experience are extraneous for him. He did not aim for a systematic technique which would strive toward mystical experience, but for the acquisition and spread of a new life theory which would establish pious and moral standards throughout one's whole life. He, himself, wanted to offer the methodical instructions for the realization of such piety, but above all human possibilities of communication, stood the Holy Spirit. Like Schwenckfeld, Sudermann maintains the priority of the soul over the Bible, the sermon, and the sacraments, but he did not follow Schwenckfeld's critical application of this concept in regard to church practice.

There is little deep contact with Reformed theology in Sudermann's poetry. Justification by the death and resurrection of Jesus assumes its place in the salvation events in the form of the 'Initialakt der Erlösung,'[13] but the mystical and spiritual concepts that determine the continuance of the road to salvation are more important for him.

Erich Seeberg defines the period of Sudermann's life as the 'Renaissance der Mystik' (renaissance of mysticism).[14] Freidrich-Wilhelm Wentzlaff-Eggebert sees its roots in the *Theologia Deutsch* and Tauler, characterizing them with the term 'Lebenslehre.'[15] With that the perfection of the mystical fundamentals leads to the initial steps on the road to salvation. Mysticism was revived in this form at the close of the sixteenth century in all confessions and in Sudermann it combined medieval-mystic and Schwenkfeldian piety.

Sudermann's Position in the History of Piety

The significance that this form of piety had for Protestantism can be seen in Pietism.[16] It was an important representative of Pietism who reached back to the work accomplished by Daniel Sudermann and utilized it for his own statements. In the 'Supplementa' to his *Unparteiische Kirchen- und Ketzerhistorie* Gottfried Arnold names several letters of Schwenckfeld and other documents, 'welche meist noch nie gedruckt, sondern auch von dem bekanten Daniel Sudermann fast schon vor 100 Jahren eigenhändig aus den orginalien abcopieret sind.'[17] Arnold also knew the lyric poetry of Sudermann and tried to elaborate it for his own readers.[18]

Apart from the interest that Arnold had for him, Sudermann had almost no other effect in Germany. However the Schwenckfeld communities which immigrated to North America have retained and preserved his poems.[19]

Notes

[1] Cited after Hans Hornung *Der Handschriftensammler Daniel Sudermann und die Bibliothek des Strassburger Klosters St. Nikolaus in undis*, in *Zeitschrift für die Geschichte des Oberrheins* 107 (1959), 38-97, Fig. 1: The original of this life summary is located in the Epistolar of the University Library Halle. The piece of paper in question is glued in and is also contained as a Photostat in the Wolfenbüttel Schwenckfeld Epistolar.

[2] Biographic data—if not marked otherwise—originate from the following: August Friedrich Heinrich Schneider, *Zur Literatur der schwenckfeldischen Liederdichter bis Daniel Sudermann*, in *Jahresbericht über die Königliche Realschule, Vorschule und Elisabethschule* (Berlin, 1857); Gottfried Hermann Schmidt, *Daniel Sudermann. 1550 bis frühestens 1631. Versuch einer wissenschaftlich begründeten Monographie* (Diss.

phil.; Leipzig, 1923); Hans Hornung, *Daniel Sudermann als Handschriftensammler. Ein Beitrag zur Strassburger Bibliotheksgeschichte* (Diss. phil.; Tübingen, 1956).

3   Philipp Wackernagel, *Das deutsche Kirchenlied von der ältesten Zeit bis zu anfang des XVII. Jahrhunderts* (5 Bde: Hildesheim 1964; Reprint of the Leipzig Edition 1864-1877), 1:581, 603.

4   See Julius Endriss, *Kaspar Schwenckfelds Ulmer Kämpfe* (Ulm, 1936).

5   MS. germ. fol. 403, Vol. 2, lit. 1 Staatsbibliothek Preussischer Kulturbesitz, Berlin.

6   Friedrich-Wilhelm Wentzlaff-Eggebert, *Deutsche Mystik zwischen Mittelalter und Neuzeit. Einheit und Wandlung ihrer Erscheinungsformen* (Berlin, 1969), 149.

7   CS 4:444ff.

8   CS 17:659-74.

9   Incipit of the poem:'Nun höre zu ein jeder Man' (contained in: 'Etliche hohe geistliche Gesänge').

10 CS 11:79.

11 CS 17:845 ff.

12 Paul Althaus, *Zur Charakteristik der evangelischen Gebetsliteratur im Reformationsjahrhundert* (Leipzig, 1914), 17ff.

13 Jürgen Moltmann, 'Grundzüge mystischer Theologie bei Gerhard Tersteegen,' *Evangelische Theologie* 16 (1956), 205-24.

14 Erich Seeberg, 'Zur Frage der Mystik (1921),' in his *Menschwerdung und Geschichte* (Stuttgart, 1938), 98-138 (especially 106 and 109).

15 Wentzlaff-Eggebert, 143, 167ff.

16 In the discussion concerning the roots of Pietism the term 'mystischer Spiritualismus' plays an important role in the works of Martin Schmidt ('Speners Wiedergeburtslehre,' in his *Wiedergeburt und neuer Mensch. Gesammelte Studien zur Geschichte des Pietismus* [Witten, 1969], 169-94).

17 Gottfried Arnold, *Unparteiische Kirchen- und Ketzerhistorie vom Anfang des neuen Testaments bis auf das Jahr 1688* (Hildesheim 1967; Photographic reprint of the Frankfurt/Main, 1729), 1270ff. The 'Supplementa' are found for the first time in the edition from 1703.

18 see Martin Goebel, *Die Bearbeitung des Hohen Liedes im 17. Jahrhundert* (Diss. phil.; Halle, 1914), 62.

19 Allen Anders Seipt, *Schwenckfelder Hymnology and the Sources of the First Schwenckfelder Hymn-Book Printed in America* (Philadelphia, 1909), chapters 4 to 7.

Schwenckfeld and Pietism

Horst Weigelt

The question of the influence of Schwenckfeld on Pietism has been raised repeatedly. The problem has been dealt with since 1708 when the Hungarian Samuel Zelenka[1] disputed in Wittenberg on the topic 'Schvengfeldismus in Pietismo Renatus.' Since that time a number of attempts have been made to link Schwenckfeld and the Pietists. Following Karl Ecke.[2] Selina Gerhard Schultz wrote for example: 'Schwenckfeld's influence continued to flow like an underground current through Germany. nourishing the spirituality for which the orthodox churches had little regard or understanding. Finally. after one hundred years. it broke forth anew in a sweeping. extensive movement of the seventeenth century in behalf of practical religion. by some contemptuously called Pietism.'[3] But some church historians have warned against overestimating the influence of Schwenckfeld. They would prefer having him restricted more or less to radical Pietism: Kurt Dietrich Schmidt in his *Grundriss der Kirchengeschichte* was one such writer.[4]

But these studies offer only superficial explanations of the influence of Schwenckfeld on Pietism. Reference is made to Schwenckfeld's individualism, to his insistence on experience or to his criticism of the institution of the church. Since one finds similar elements in Pietism, it is supposed that these can be traced back to Schwenckfeld. To prove this, such studies pointed out that Schwenckfeld's writings were read by Spener and Francke and especially by radical Pietists. It is. however. difficult to establish Schwenckfeld's influence on Pietism in this way. A critical edition of Pietist writings is only now in preparation and as long as such an edition is unavailable. it is only possible to investigate the influence of Schwenckfeld on individual Pietists.

On the other hand. thanks to the considerably smaller and easily surveyable source materials. it is quite possible to de-

scribe the connection or relationship between the Schwenkfelders in Silesia and the Pietists. This will be done in the
following paper. The relationship between Schwenckfeld and
Pietism will thereby appear in another light, and it should thus
be possible to explore the kind of personal contact or relationship that existed between Schwenkfelders and Pietists. From
this it might also be possible to determine which Pietistic circles were familiar with Schwenkfeldian writings. How these
writings were received by the Pietists requires an investigation
of its own.

In the first two parts of the following paper the connections between the Schwenkfelders and Spener-Francke Pietism
on the one hand and radical Pietism on the other will be considered in detail. Only a short discussion of the varied and
complex relations between Zinzendorf and the Moravians will
be given in part three, since this topic will be treated more fully
in a separate paper. The last part of this short presentation
will consider the relevance and meaning of the Schwenkfelders'
contacts with Pietism.

The Schwenkfelders and Spener-Francke Pietism

Many of the Schwenkfelders who, from the middle of the sixteenth century, settled in Silesia in the region of the Bober-
Katzbach mountains,[5] were of the opinion that Pietism was
in many ways like their own theological system, particularly
in its demands for a new birth and in its emphasis on ethical
renewal.

Their first important contact with Lutheran Pietism occurred in 1690. In this year the Schwenkfelders sent two delegates to the father of Pietism, Philipp Jakob Spener, who was
senior preacher at the court in Dresden.[6] In this position he
was the most powerful ecclesiastical authority in Protestant
Germany. One of the delegates was probably the physician
and chemist Georg Hauptmann of Lauterseiffen. These two
Schwenkfelder delegates wanted to ask Spener for a recognition of their conventicles.

What was the situation of the Schwenkfelders at that time?
They lived in open separation from the established Lutheran
church and carried on a controversy against Lutheran doctrine.
They met to pray, to sing, and to read the devotional litera-
ture of their teachers Schwenckfeld, Johann Sigismund Werner,
Michael Hiller, and Erasmus Weichenhan.

The Lutheran pastors, who had been composing anti-Schwenkfeldian writings since the middle of the sixteenth century, were afraid that this radical separatism would take root in their congregations. For this reason they did not only preach polemically against the Schwenkfelders, but incited their patrons to act against them. The result was that the conventicles of the Schwenkfelders were forbidden. It was for this reason that the Schwenkfelder delegation wanted to gain recognition of their conventicles from Spener. This seemed possible since the question of the acceptance of conventicles had been part of the Pietistic controversies in Leipzig a year before and Spener had been involved in these controversies. He was also well acquainted with Schwenckfeld's writings and had many of them in his library. The catalogue[7] of Spener's library has recently been discovered and it is now known which of Schwenckfeld's books he possessed.

In fact, Spener did not completely reject their criticism of the church, since he felt, the Lutheran pastors had brought it on themselves by their conduct. But he totally condemned their separation, as Johann Christoph Schwedler, pastor of Nieder-Wiesa, reported to August Hermann Francke on April 15, 1720.[8] Furthermore Spener expressed the hope 'that they might return from their false path and separation to our Protestant church, as a body or one by one, when more improvements have been made and more preachers begin to commit themselves more earnestly to the work of the Lord in their congregations, so that the Schwenkfelders see powerful teaching and uplifting order in the congregations.'[9] But did Spener really have this hope? Since 1695 the Schwenkfelders were also indirectly in touch with August Hermann Francke through the Silesian theological candidate Achatius Friedrich Roscius. Apparently Roscius originally wished to be a Schwenkfelder preacher.[10] But the Schwenkfelders declined: in accordance with Ezekiel 34 they believed that Christ himself must gather his scattered church, before it would be allowed to call pastors. They were also convinced that the Roman Catholic political authorities would oppose the appointment of a Schwenkfelder preacher, just as they had opposed the appointment of a Lutheran pastor in the principality of Schweidnitz-Jauer. The Schwenkfelders feared that they would only bring 'death and persecution upon themselves without the will of God.' Roscius finally found a position as a teacher in Halle in 1695.[11] From there he continued to correspond with the Schwenkfelders and conveyed kind regards from Francke.[12]

Later Johann Christoph Schwedler,[13] pastor of Nieder-Wiesa in Upper-Lusatia. undertook a similar intermediary role. He was a good friend of Francke, and he also enjoyed the confidence of the Schwenkfelders who sometimes attended his services in Nieder-Wiesa. 25 miles from Harpersdorf, the center of the Schwenkfelder communities.[14]

According to reports made by Schwenkfelder Abraham Wagner, the brilliant physician Christian Friedrich Richter, who was on the medical faculty at the University of Halle, also visited them.[15] Probably he conferred, as Andrew Berky supposed, with the 'chemist' Hauptmann and Martin John. who was a physician and botanist. on the development of *essentia dulcis*. a gold tincture held in high regard because of its healing properties.

But the Schwenkfelders themselves never had any direct contact with Francke. and they never wrote to him. Obviously the Schwenkfelders knew that the Pietism of Halle had a distinct ecclesiastical character.

The Schwenkfelders and Radical Pietism

Although the Schwenkfelders had few immediate contacts with the great exponents of Spener-Francke Pietism, they conversed with one of the most famous leaders of the radical Pietists. This was Johann Wilhelm Petersen, who visited them in 1707-1708 on his journey to Silesia and saw Georg Hauptmann in Lauterseiffen and Martin John in Laubgrund.[16] On the theological differences between them. Petersen remarked that even between him and his followers 'there are some ideas which could not stand before divine judgment. They are to be tolerated, not persecuted. On Doomsday, a different judgment will be held from what we expect.'[17]

It is interesting to see that Petersen established contacts with those Schwenkfelders who had already been in touch with mystical spiritualism. This is especially true of Georg Hauptmann and of Martin John. who had personal contacts or corresponded with numerous spiritualists. After having written to Christian Hoburg and Friedrich Breckling and others, Martin

John travelled to the western part of Germany and to Holland in the spring of 1669.[18] The journey was probably financed by money gained 'by his medical practice which had made him known in many places.'[19] First he journeyed to Bamberg where he stayed over Easter and probably visited Georg Geelmann,[20] chief[21] of the Weigelians in the southern part of Germany. Martin John had originally wished to go to Nürnberg, but went via Frankfurt and Cologne to Latum where Christian Hoburg was pastor. For a week and a half John remained in Amsterdam.[22] At this time, Amsterdam was a center of religious individualists. Here Martin John visited Johann Georg Gichtel,[23] who probably introduced him to Friedrich Breckling, Johann Amos Comenius, the Dutch chiliast Petrus Serarius, and others. He travelled home via Bremen, Hamburg, Lüneburg, Magdeburg, and Leipzig.[24] As a result of this journey a correspondence, which is, however, only partly extant, developed between Martin John and Hoburg, Breckling, Gichtel, Geelmann, as well as others in Amsterdam. He and some other Schwenkfelders were also acquainted with their publications.

It should be noted, however, that Hauptmann and especially John were to some extent outsiders among the Schwenkfelders. Of Martin John, Georg Weiss, later the first preacher among the Schwenkfelders who emigrated to Pennsylvania, wrote in 1732: 'When there was no longer any contact between Martin John and us, he longed for other friends, with whom he might have Christian and friendly communication.... Therefore, he immersed himself in correspondence with various foreign friends and acquired books of many of them, which were then being published, such as those of... Johann Wilhelm Petersen.'[25]

But there were not only personal and literary connections between some Schwenkfelders and radical Pietists. Nearly all of these radical Pietists read the writings of Schwenckfeld and were acquainted with his ideas. This is particularly true of Gottfried Arnold who was convinced that he was in theological agreement with Schwenckfeld. In his famous *Kirchen- und Ketzerhistorie* he viewed Schwenckfeld very favorably.[26] He emphasized that Schwenckfeld was chiefly concerned with the rise and development of the new man.

The Relations between Moravians and Schwenkfelders

The connection between Zinzendorf and the Schwenkfelders was historically a most significant one.[27] They met for the first time in the summer of 1723 during Zinzendorf's first journey to Silesia together with his two friends Friedrich von Wattenwyl and Pastor Melchior Schäffer.[28] Zinzendorf wanted to go to Zobten to visit a relative on his mother's side, Otto Conrad von Hohberg. Having had first-hand experience of the unfortunate situation of the Schwenkfelders, who were now persecuted by the Roman Catholic Church through a Jesuit mission, he drafted several petitions to the Imperial Court on their behalf. One month later he interceded for them when he had an audience at the Imperial Court. being held at that time at Brandeis.[29] He applied to the imperial minister Rudolph Siegmund Count von Sinzendorf and to the director of the supreme royal office of Silesia. the privy councillor Johann Anton von Schaffgotsch to obtain the right of emigration for the Schwenkfelders. but was not successful.

When in 1724 and 1725 the persecution increased daily. the Schwenkfelders asked Zinzendorf on December 19. 1725 whether he would allow them to settle in his territories.[30] The count immediately gave permission, and thus the Schwenkfelders found shelter in his territories in Berthelsdorf in Saxony.

Here they lived unmolested till 1734. But during these eight years Zinzendorf was anxious to convert them. As he wrote in a letter in August 1733 he could not imagine 'that the Silesian emigrants... are anything other than pure separatists, because they. like the Mennonites, who are generally taken to be identical with them, do not have a confession of faith of their own, and they refuse to accept any creed offered to them.'[31] In fact. the Lutheran pastors are to be blamed for the secession of the Schwenkfelders.

All attempts of Zinzendorf and the Moravians to convert the Schwenkfelders were in vain. In particular. the Silesian emigrants took offence at Zinzendorf's Christocentrism. There is no inner relationship between the doctrine of the Schwenkfelders and the Pietism of Zinzendorf. as it was sometimes supposed. And it is also wrong to suppose that Zinzendorf's concern for the persecuted Schwenkfelders was a sign of a leaning towards Schwenckfeld's teaching.

Since the Schwenkfelders had been under constant pressure to accept the Lutheran confession, they did not protest when they were advised in 1733 by Friedrich August I to leave the country.[32]

The Relevance of Schwenkfelder Contacts with Pietism

Finally we have to consider the question of the relevance of the Schwenkfelders' contact with Pietism. As I see it, their radical opposition to the church had on the one hand weakened slightly. On the other hand, their contacts with Pietism brought them in touch with another important religious movement and mitigated their former religious isolation.

Firstly, as a result of these contacts with Pietists, many Schwenkfelders began attending the services of pietistically-oriented pastors. It is important to note that they visited Johann Christoph Schwedler in Nieder-Wiesa, Daniel Schneider in Goldberg, and Johann Sturm in Adelsdorf, later in Probsthain. They allowed these pastors to perform marriages among them and to baptize their children. They accepted the established church in part.

Secondly, in their conventicles they no longer restricted their reading to the works of Schwenckfeld, Valentine Crautwald, Johann Sigismund Werner, Michael Hiller, and Erasmus Weichenhan, but included Pietistic writings, such as those of Christian Gerber. Among other such books they read Gottfried Arnold's *Unpartheiische Kirchen- und Ketzerhistorie* which, in parts two and four, contains a favorable presentation of Schwenckfeld. This is the reason why Arnold's book was found in the private libraries of Schwenkfelders.

Despite the personal and literary connections of the Schwenkfelders with the Lutheran Pietists they did not merge with them but remained distant from Lutheran Pietism. Nor did the Schwenkfelders join the radical Pietist movement. To be sure, they felt themselves connected with the radical Pietists because of their radical criticism of the church and because of their ethical rigorism. But the Schwenkfelders rejected their ideas of natural philosophy, theosophy, and millenarianism. Nevertheless, there are indications that the mystical spiritualism of the Schwenkfelders is closer to radical Pietism than to Lutheran Pietism. Conversely, the radical Pietists shared some of Schwenckfeld's central ideas, whereas the Lutheran Pietists only admired Schwenckfeld's piety and humility. Pietism is not a coherent and clearly defined movement. Future research will find it necessary to study the various connections between the different groups of Pietists and the Schwenkfelders as well as the various relations between the Pietists and Caspar Schwenckfeld.

Notes

[1] Cf. G. Maron, *Individualismus und Gemeinschaft bei Caspar von Schwenckfeld. Seine Theologie dargestellt mit besonderer Ausrichtung auf seinen Kirchenbegriff* (Stuttgart, 1961), 18-20.

[2] K. Ecke, *Schwenckfeld, Luther und der Gedanke einer apostolischen Reformation* (Berlin, 1911).

[3] Schultz, 402.

[4] See K. D. Schmidt, *Grundriss der Kirchengeschichte* (Göttingen, 1967), 428.

[5] For this and the following see H. Weigelt, *Spiritualistische Tradition im Protestantismus. Die Geschichte des Schwenckfeldertums in Schlesien* (Berlin und New York, 1973), 195-260.

[6] On this and the following see Spener to N.N., 1690, printed in Ph. J. Spener, *Theologische Bedencken und andere brieffliche Antworten*, Teil I (Halle, 1700), 314-15; Spener to N. N., July 10, 1960, printed in Ph. J. Spener, *Letzte Theologische Bedencken und andere brieffliche Antworten*, Teil III (Halle, 1711), 687-92.

[7] Cf. R. Breymeyer, 'Zum Schicksal der Bibliothek Philipp Jakob Speners,' *Pietismus und Neuzeit—Jahrbuch 1976 zur Geschichte des neueren Protestantismus* 3 (1977), 71-80.

[8] Berlin SB [Staatsbibliothek Preussischer Kulturbesitz], Francke-Nachlass, Kapsel 25.

[9] Spener to N. N., 1690 (cf. note 6), 315.

[10] On this and the following see Martin John Jr. to Achatius Friedrich Roscius, n.d., SchLP [Schwenkfelder Library, Pennsburg] VC 5-1, 782.

[11] In the list of the regular lecturers (H. Freyer, *Programmata latino-germanica cum additamento miscellaneorum vario* [Halle, 1737], 693-715) his name is not found but it is listed in the Halle University matriculation register (Fr. Zimmermann, *Matrikel der Martin-Luther-Universität* [Halle-Wittenberg 1955], 324, left column: 'Roscius, Achat. Frid. Luben. Lusat. 30. 1. 1694').

[12] Note for example Roscius to Martin John Jr., n.d. [after April 29, 1595], SchLP, VC 5-1, 803-04.

[13] On Schwedler see E. Zimmermann, *Schwenckfelder und Pietisten in Greiffenberg und Isergebirge von 1670 bis 1730* (Görlitz, 1939), passim.

14 Note for example. Schwedler to Francke, April 15. 1720. Berlin SB. Francke-Nachlass, Kapsel 25.

15 Cf. A. S. Berky. *Practitioner in Physic. A Biography of Abraham Wagner 1717-1763* (Pennsburg, 1954). 43.

16 Joh. W. Petersen, *Lebens-Beschreibung*, (2nd ed.; n.pl., 1719), 321-22.

17 Ibid.

18 On John's journey see John Jr. to Hans Brochmann. November 2, 1669, SchLP, VC 5-3, 1235-37.

19 Anonymous, 'Des zu den Quackern übergetretenen Hilarii Prachii und J. C. Matern seines Eydams Brieffe,' *Unschuldige Nachrichten von Alten und Neuen Theologischen Sachen, auf das Jahr 1706* (2nd ed.; Leipzig, 1709), 445.

20 On Geelmann see Jöcher-Adelung, *Fortsetzung und Ergänzungen zu Jöcher's Allgemeinem Gelehrten-Lexico* (Leipzig, 1787). 2: 1377; J. H. Jäck, *Pantheon der Literaten und Künstler Bambergs* (Erlangen, 1812), 302; H. Clauss. 'Weigelianer in Nürnberg,' *Beiträge zur bayerischen Kirchengeschichte* 21 (1915), 267-71.

21 Bamberg. Sterberegister der Oberpfarre Unser Lieben Frau. No. 337.

22 See John Jr. to Hans Brochmann. November 2. 1669. SchLP. VC 5-3. 1235-36.

23 Gichtel to John Jr.. September 15/25. 1669, printed in Joh. G. Gichtel. *Theosophia practica* (3rd ed.; Leiden, 1722). 1: 12-16.

24 See John Jr. to Hans Brochmann, November 2, 1669. SchLP. VC 5-3. 1236.

25 Weiss to A. W. [Abraham Wagner?]. July 9. 1732. SchLP. VA 3-12. 520-21.

26 Cf. especially G. Arnold. *Unpartheyische Kirchen- und Ketzerhistorie* (Frankfurt, 1700), 2:241ff.

27 For this and the following see my paper (The Emigration of the Schwenkfelders from Silesia to America) in the second volume of this collection.

28 See N. L. von Zinzendorf, 'Die Geschichte der verbundenen vier Brüder,' *Zeitschrift für Brüdergeschichte* 6 (1912), 99. Cf. A. G. Spangenberg. *Das Leben des Herrn Nicolaus Ludwig Grafen und Herrn von Zinzendorf und Pottendorf*, Teil II. n.d.. 262.

29 On this and the following see N. L. von Zinzendorf.' Kurze Relation von Herrnhut und Berthelsdorf seit der Abreise des Herrn Heitz.' *Zeitschrift für Brüdergeschichte* 6 (1912), 46. Cf. A. G. Spangenberg. *Zinzendorf*. Teil II. 266-67: E. Beyreuther, *Zinzendorf und die sich allhier beisammen finden* (Marburg/Lahn, 1959), 1.

30 The Schwenkfelders to Zinzendorf. December 19. 1725. printed in part in A. G. Spangenberg. *Zinzendorf*, II, 326-27. Cf. N. L. von Zinzendorf. 'Kurze Relation von Herrnhut,' 56. See also A. G. Spangenberg, *Zinzendorf*. Teil II. 324: E. Beyreuther. *Zinzendorf und die sich allhier beisammen finden*. 152.

31 Zinzendorf to N.N., n.d. [about autumn 1733], Herrnhut ABU [Archiv
   der Brüder Unität]. R 5 A 2a, 57; partially printed in English in
   E. S. Gerhard and Selina Gerhard Schultz, 'The Schwenkfelders and
   the Moravians in Saxony, 1723-34.' *Schwenckfeldiana* 1/4 (1944), 12.

32 Friedrich August II to Friedrich Caspar von Gersdorff, April 4, 1733,
   Herrnhut ABU, R 5 A 5, 18 u. Dresden LA [Landesarchiv], Cod 6854,
   fol. 82r-v; printed in N. L. von Zinzendorf, *Büdingische Sammlung*,
   vol. 3, in N. L. von Zinzendorf, *Ergänzungsbände zu den Hauptschriften*,
   hrsg. von E. Beyreuther und G. Meyer (Hildesheim, 1966), 9:12-13.

IV

Schwenckfeld, Toleration, and Liberty

Franklin H. Littell

In my book *The Origins of Sectarian Protestantism* I bracketed Caspar Schwenckfeld among the *Spiritualisten* of the Radical Reformation, along with Sebastian Frank (1499-1543) and Johannes Bünderlin (1499-1533).[1] In doing so I followed the distinctions introduced by Alfred Hegler in 1892[2] and popularized by Ernst Troeltsch in 1911. Troeltsch, in his famous work *The Social Teaching of the Christian Churches*,[3] made mention of a 'Third Type' of Christianity.

Toeltsch's 'Third Type,' a free and spiritual fellowship,[4] has scarcely been noticed—even by writers who overwork the typology for which he is best known, the 'church type' and the 'sect type.' Moreover, they have not noticed and heeded Troeltsch's own warning that the distinction between Type I and Type II was no longer useful in Europe after the nineteenth century and could not be applied to the American Free Church scene at all.

Schwenckfeld, to be sure, differed strongly from the Anabaptists in his attitude toward church discipline, the enforcement of doctrinal uniformity, and a monolithic style of life. Although he warned against putting too much trust in formal credal statements, his concern for the teaching ministry led him to prepare and widely circulate catechetical materials. Upon church discipline, however, his emphasis on the lively and unfettered conscience of the New Man in Christ led him to agree with the Anabaptists in rejecting the territorial Christendom of the Roman Catholics and the state-church Reformers, but to disagree with the Anabaptists in their stress upon the New Testament ordinances. His exchanges with Pilgram Marpeck and the elders of the South German Brethren ran over a considerable period of time and produced major writings on both sides of the dispute.

Schwenckfeld was banned by the Anabaptists for refusing to adopt and enforce believers' baptism. For them, adult baptism had become the proof that the true believer was willing to follow his Lord into martyrdom, putting himself under the Empire's death penalty for re-baptizers. For him, such enforcement involved a new captivity of conscience. The Anabaptist church discipline, later adapted by the Calvinist wing of the magisterial Reformation into a *tertior nota* of the true church,[5] smacked to him of the 'legalism' from which the Holy Spirit freed men in Christ.

In another context I have argued that Troeltsch's 'Third Type' is more applicable to American popular (or 'populist' = *völkisch*) religion than either the 'church type' or the 'sect type.'[6] Be that as it may, I have come to the conclusion that Troeltsch's 'Third Type' may be applied to Schwenckfeld only with great caution, if at all. His position seems rather to prefigure a certain kind of highly personal evangelicalism. His understanding of the Christian life owed little to the mystics' 'inner work' and 'spark of the soul' and a great deal to his optimism about the powerful working of the Holy Spirit in re-creating a New Man of the man of faith.[7]

In Marpeck's *Verantwortung*, one of the massive tracts issued by the South German Brethren against Schwenckfeld, we read the charge: 'Schwenckfeld teaches only the inward experience and the transfigured, glorified, unsuffering Christ in heaven, and not the suffering one on earth; yea, he teaches only the Word of his glory and splendor, and not of his cross and affliction as he bore it before his transfiguration and ascension and as it is still today fitting for his unglorified body to bear.'[8] But this was not strictly true: Schwenckfeld's optimism about the New Man being re-created in Christ seems very like John Wesley's optimism about the New Man being perfected in Christ. Both Schwenckfeld and Wesley met with the same kind of criticism from skeptical persons. It is worth noting that Marpeck, the leader of the South German Brethren, was—unlike most of the Anabaptist leaders—a strong Augustinian in his doctrine of sin, of the pervasiveness and stickiness of it, after, as well as before, conversion.

This introduction to a discussion of Schwenckfeld's contribution to Religious Liberty and/ or toleration is necessary, for conflicts of church and state rarely arise for the individual

mystic. It is the social nature of religion that creates bor-
der conflict. For the individual of the 'Third Type' there is
no problem, and Troeltsch comments that 'gradually, in the
modern world of educated people, the third type has come to
predominate. This means, then, that all that is left is voluntary association with like-minded people, which is equally
remote both from church and sect.'[9]

Conflict with the state authorities is unlikely for individuals
of the 'Third Type,' not considering the fact that that type
only flourishes amidst societies that are intellectually post-
Enlightenment and tolerantly indifferent to religion. But the
case is different when personhood—especially the person in relation to co-believers—is the focus of the discussion.

According to Selina Gerhard Schultz, Schwenckfeld's first
tenet was that of

> individualism.... The more I have made of myself, the
> better I can help my fellows, the more rapid will be the
> advancement of the race. This is the primary axiom
> of Schwenckfeld's system; it magnifies individualism....
> Some of the most masterly lines of German literature are
> those which Schwenckfeld wrote in defense of Christian
> liberty.... We dare to maintain that he was an apostle
> of liberty in the teeth of the established churches and
> servile universities.... Schwenckfeld advocated the right
> of religious assembly open or private, and entirely dis-
> tinct from any authorized organization. Each believer
> has the right of combining with another for religious
> meditation, exercises, conferences, prayer, and study.[10]

Precisely in this voluntary combining with others was, for
Schwenckfeld, the foundation of the renewal of Christianity to
be found. And this is the watershed: whether liberty of conscience applies only to the individual or also to the community
of faith. At this very hour it is one of the most critical—if not
the most critical—issues of all. *Item:* A public statement by
a high-level functionary in the Communist regime in Moscow,
Professor Ziffs. assured visiting American religious leaders—as
he had American publics while travelling in this country under
the auspices of the American Friends Service Committee—that
there was no persecution of Jews in the Soviet Union. He, a
Jew, had experienced none. A cynic might comment that neither a renegade Jew nor an apostate Christian had suffered

persecution. either, during the bloodiest years of the Inquisition. or the worst years of Roman Catholic and magisterial Protestant persecution in the sixteenth century. *Item:* The American Civil Liberties Union divided on support of First Amendment issues in the Wisconsin *v.* Yoder Case (1973) precisely at this point: whether religious liberty was to be defined in terms of the natural rights and limitations of the individual or conceived as a communal and historical development. *Item:* A letter recently received from a key churchman justifies limiting the constitutional freedom of belief and passing legislation to suppress 'cults' and 'sects' by stating bluntly: 'Religious freedom is the freedom of the individual and not of a movement.'[11]

At the baseline in the matter of both liberty and toleration is the question whether a society has advanced to the point where a pluralism of communities of faith is protected at law—'by constitution,' written or unwritten. In advanced societies in Christendom, such as Great Britain or the Netherlands, liberty or toleration may feel the same to minority communities. Since William the Silent in Holland and William and Mary in England, active persecution has hardly been an issue. Nevertheless, there is a fundamental difference between toleration and liberty.

Toleration derives from an action of enlightened government. A grant or patent of government, it may be withdrawn as it was once given. Generally, although the burden of persecution is lifted from minority religious groups, there is a continuance of tax support and other government assistance to preferred churches. So it has been in England since 1689 and in West Germany since 1955.

Religious Liberty, by contrast, involves a free exercise of religion—'free' in the sense of voluntary support as well as emancipation from governmental interference. Gerrit Smith, champion of the Higher Law in the fight against chattel slavery, put the case for the liberties of Americans upon its higher ground: 'To no human charter am I indebted for my rights. They pertain to my original constitution: and I read them in that Book of books, which is the great Charter of man's rights. No, the constitution of my nation and state create none of my rights. They do, at the most, but recognize what is not theirs to give.'[12] That which governments give they can take away.

That which is given of God is defiled by governments at their own peril.

Following a recent Action Conference on Religious Liberty (Nov. 1983 in Los Angeles), the following statement emerged expressing in interfaith language a conviction once held only by Radical Reformers in the sixteenth century but now widely ascribed to:

> The most dearly won of liberties is Religious Liberty. It is also a human right, and on the world map the right most rarely out of jeopardy.
>
> Religious Liberty was a fundamental human right before any government of record acknowledged its inviolability, and it is a fundamental human right whether a specific regime persecutes, tolerates, or protects.
>
> The free exercise of religion belongs to communities and individuals alike, embracing the right to practice, the right to profess, the right to propagate, and the right to convert.
>
> *Persecution* is often counter-productive and always immoral. *Toleration* may be granted by a wise government for pragmatic reasons. But *Religious Liberty* derives from a Source more ultimate than any transitory, temporal power.[13]

Where did Caspar Schwenckfeld stand in the struggle for Christian Liberty—which in his own time was a dangerous arena? Of course, in his day there were only two kinds of governments: those many that persecuted and those few, usually brief, that tolerated. His entire understanding of liberty—of the life of the new man or new woman being trained in the School of Christ,[14] being transformed by Christ through the work of the Holy Spirit—places it on a transcendent rather than pragmatic plane. Liberty was his concern, not sufferance.

In the sixteenth century Caspar Schwenckfeld knew a truth that even many late twentieth century Americans have yet to learn in spite of nearly 200 years of First Amendment rights behind them: Religious Liberty begins with the free exercise of religion, to secure which liberty there are placed constitutional barriers against governmental interference in religious affairs—either to favor or to repress it.[15]

It is an ominous fact that there are now some 6,000 cases involving the right to Religious Liberty before the courts of America, vastly more than the sum total of all Religious Liberty cases in the entire history of the republic from 1791 to 1980. Most of those cases involve principles and premises on which Schwenckfeld had already spoken a clear word more than 400 years ago. In fact Caspar Schwenckfeld wrote more letters and tracts celebrating the splendor of Christian liberty than any other leader or writer of the sixteenth century. The fact that it was not until the Virginia Burgesses acted in 1785 that any government in human history divested itself of the authority to interfere in the affairs of religious communities—more than 200 years after Schwenckfeld's testimony—and the fact that Religious Liberty has been staked out in the formal sense for less than 200 years in America, may explain to some extent the difficulties which we presently face in holding on to our rights.

In retrospect, in a season when the order and discipline of religious communities are again subject to attack—coordination or synchronization (*Gleichschaltung*) being a growing threat in America as well as a finished policy in the Third Reich and the USSR—Selina Gerhard Schultz' language in speaking of Caspar Schwenckfeld's 'individualism' may be misleading.

Since the Enlightenment and the French Revolution our ears have grown accustomed to hear the word 'individualism' used with atomistic overtones and undertones—rather than as an affirmation of voluntary association to replace the old style of religious community governmentally coerced. Dr. Schultz' last sentence, referring to the right of voluntary association, is more helpful than the opening sentence in the quotation. For with Schwenckfeld there could be no question of defining 'liberty' as an attribute of social isolates: for him, liberty is the predicate of the Christian life.[16] This liberty is never an end in itself, nor is it anti-social. Schwenckfeld was speaking of Christian liberty, not to be confused with post-Enlightenment ideas of natural freedom.

Of course in Caspar Schwenckfeld's time there was no area with Religious Liberty and precious few areas of toleration. And the rulers of those areas where toleration existed were constantly condemned by leaders of the Roman Catholic and

Protestant establishments—both bishops and princes, because they did not enforce religious conformity with sufficient force. For Schwenckfeld, by contrast, the use of violence to compel conscience is precisely the proof that the old church of Christendom is 'fallen.'[17] And the use of spiritual coercion (as he conceived it) by the Anabaptist leaders was proof that they were sliding into a like evil. He agreed with them in condemning coercion of conscience by the magistrate, but disagreed with them concerning enforcement of what they considered New Testament ordinances.

As Schwenckfeld wrote to Leo Jud, none can be made devout by coercion; Christ himself was long-suffering; the Apostle demonstrated how the faith is to be commended.[18] As Karl Ecke pointed out in his classic *Schwenckfeld, Luther und der Gedanke einer apostolischen Reformation* (1911), the Apostle Paul's method of commending the gospel by letter-writing and spiritual fellowship provided the model which Caspar Schwenckfeld emulated. The great volume of his own evangelistic and pastoral correspondence indicates how seriously he took that example. And just as Paul ministered to churches of a variety of orders and structures and doctrinal emphases, so Schwenckfeld directed his attention and his discussion not to sectarian disputes but to unity in a non-partisan (*unpartheyisch*) way.

Schwenckfeld addressed in a fraternal tone 'all those who believe in Christ among the four parties' at the same time that he rejected 'sectarian' alignment with Lutherans, Zwinglians, Papists, and Anabaptists. His perspectives were what we would today call 'ecumenical.' And like the members of the International Missionary Conference who launched the modern ecumenical movement at Edinburgh in 1910, he was moved by an understanding of apostolic Christianity that cut across ecclesiastical lines and found the sons and daughters of the Spirit in many different rooms of the Lord's house. When his irenic approach was rejected by all parties, Schwenckfeld continued his work with small fellowships, but concluded it was necessary to wait for another time for a true church in its fullness.

Just as Caspar Schwenckfeld rejected church discipline, whether dogmatic or pastoral, so he rejected for himself the role of leader of a faction or founder of a sect. He was conscious of the dangers of leading others into spiritual bondage,

aware of the temptations of the guru. On the other hand, it
would be going too far to agree with Gottfried Maron—in some
respects so perceptive—that Schwenckfeld was so individualistic as to be indifferent to others, and that the existence of a
Schwenkfelder Church that treasures his memory is an accident
of Pennsylvania 'Dutch' history.

Probably a writer lodged in the tradition of the German
magisterial Reformation like Maron simply cannot sense the
cohesiveness of a voluntary religious community. Most of our
free churches, which have prospered with voluntary membership and support and the absence of governmental interference,
also have ethnic or *völkisch* characteristics to some extent.
And many of them, like the Schwenkfelders, have a doctrine
of the Holy Spirit and his work as guide and governor which
is far fuller than that found in the churches of West European
Christendom.[19]

A high doctrine of the Holy Spirit is dangerous to all
static structures, and explosive to those that are maintained
by repressive violence. A church ruled by a professional
caste, trained with whatever theological precision, will avoid
metaphors which reinforce a general priesthood ('the priesthood of all believers'). Characteristically, the most reactionary
Popes have issued official statements identifying the church
with the Second Person of the Holy Trinity.[20] Just as characteristically Schwenckfeld, with his high level of understanding
of the ministry of every believer, developed a theology in which
the work of the Holy Spirit—a doctrine neglected for centuries
in a static Christendom—received extensive elaboration.

The Spirit of whom Schwenckfeld wrote was not, however,
the *Logos spermatikos/ synteresis/ Inwendige Wort/ Fünklein*
of the individual mystics—contrary to the popular misunderstanding of Schwenckfeld widely circulated by the beautifully
written books on mysticism by Rufus M. Jones. Rufus Jones,
whose fine books on lively Christianity found in the mystical
experience the core of high religion, introduced at the 1928
International Missionary Conference in Jerusalem the concept
which makes the conflict of 'spirituality' and 'secularism' the
major religious crisis of our age. In lesser hands, this conceptualization has led to the grave misinterpretations of the
Nazi Third Reich and its lessons and to seriously faulty esti-
mates of populist (*völkisch*) religion and secular government in

the United States. In Schwenckfeld's perception, however, the Spirit is *always* the Holy Spirit completing and channelling the work of Christ, and good government is *always* that government which does not meddle in religion.

The identification of Christ with his church presents a special problem for critics of the establishment, especially when that establishment operates on the assumption that criticism—or even suggestion of change—is 'treason' as well as 'heresy.' And this was precisely the assumption that moved the authorities in levying the death penalty against radical Christians in the sixteenth century. Practical dangers aside, however, how could a committed Christian mount heavy criticism against 'the Body of Christ'? This institution, in its Roman form, claimed to be an extension of the power and flesh of Christ, and as such endowed with divine authority and immunity.

Menno Simons, a former Roman Catholic Priest, met the problem in one way.[21] Caspar Schwenckfeld, a former follower of Luther the Reformer, met it in another. Schwenckfeld developed the teaching of the glorified, the heavenly, flesh of Christ. Christ is come to earth that through his incarnation we may be brought back to God. And—against the mystics—this is the only process by which God and man can be reconciled. In eating the spiritual food sent to us we become participants in the divine essence and become the temples of the living God. Schwenckfeld's conceptualization avoids the death of static church and dead dogma. Through Christ working in the Holy Spirit, God creates a New Man—not to be made captive in a new bondage of the mind and spirit through intellectual codes interpreted and administered by a special caste of professionals.

The 'heavenly flesh' of Christ is in no sense an other-worldly essence. Quite the contrary. He is totally present to believers. The Christian life is not a finished product, either *now* or *then*, nor can the Christian's destiny be fixed by loyalty to an institution or assent to a creed. Quite the contrary: the Christian life is a *process* in which we are created again, restored to full humanity through Christ in the Holy Spirit. Again, the similarity to John Wesley's emphasis upon the process of attaining Christian perfection is striking—a similarity which extends also to Wesley's grounds for criticism of both Roman Catholicism and the state-church Reformation.

This process, by which the Kingdom will come on earth, owes nothing to the rulers of this world except that they hold back the jungle. Thus, while Schwenckfeld's century knew only governments that persecuted and governments that might for some time tolerate, the way was opened for an understanding of *limited* government, government with only secular powers and duties. And 'secular' government, that is, government that is a human invention and limited to serving specific human needs, government that by and large restrains itself from meddling in religious affairs, is one-half of the Religious Liberty guaranteed in the First Amendment to the Federal Constitution.

Schwenckfeld affirmed this view of government repeatedly, and nowhere better than in a letter to Jakob Sturm of Strassburg, where he wrote that

> Civilian authority has no jurisdiction over the Kingdom of God; that government was divinely ordained for the sole purpose of maintaining an orderly life in human society, but has no right either to influence or to interfere with religious convictions; the individual is accountable to Jesus Christ as the head of the Kingdom of God. Christian government, a name of recent invention, is nowhere mentioned by Paul.[22]

On the other half of Religious Liberty in the First Amendment, which is a total commitment to religion voluntarily chosen, voluntarily supported, and voluntarily exercised, Schwenckfeld was just as clear. In fact, for him this principle is the primary of the two. Unlike those—whose number has greatly increased in recent years—to whom liberty is rooted and grounded in hatred of all religious practice, for Schwenckfeld the first matter is commitment to the life and process of true religion. And thereafter comes a rejection of all influences and controls and structures that improperly coerce or violate the religious sphere.

European Christendom, which even to this day tends to ascribe to government penultimate powers and sacral sanctions, and to expect of the churches certain political services and controls, has difficulty in understanding Schwenckfeld and other forerunners of Religious Liberty even today. Schwenckfeld was not without influence upon some of the leaders of his own day, even though he was a spiritual exile in his own land.[23] Today he is still in exile in his homeland, but those who carry his name have found a home long since in a land blessed by the vision of William Penn and the statesmanship which produced the First Amendment and its guarantees.

Even the most acute of the European scholars of Christian persuasion, and there are some of them left in a land mass spiritually laid waste by Nazism and Communism, typically confuse 'toleration' and 'liberty.'

On this day in America, where toleration widened during the colonial period and liberty grew more inclusive as our religious and cultural and ethic pluralism became more evident, we appropriately celebrate Schwenckfeld and the Schwenkfelder heritage of liberty. The timeliness of our celebration is also indicated by the fact that in the 1984 Presidential campaign the religious issues, and the question of the right relations of church and state, again bubbled to the surface. Obviously, some of the instructions of Caspar Schwenckfeld, the master teacher of Christian liberty of the sixteenth century, need today a wider circulation than they have yet found.

Notes

1 Franklin H. Littell, *The Origins of Sectarian Protestantism*, originally published by the American Society of Church History (1952), here cited in the revised and enlarged edition (New York, 1964), 21.

2 A. Hegler, *Geist und Schrift bei Sebastian Franck* (Freiburg, 1892).

3 E. Troeltsch, *The Social Teachings of the Christian Churches*, trans. by Olive Wyon (London, 1931).

4 Ibid., vol. 2, 729f.

5 Littell, *Origins*, 173, note 129.

6 'Community or the New Individualism,' *The Voice*, (1964), 7-20.

7 I am indebted to my student Yung-Ho Suh of Busan, Korea for new insights at this point. See his *The Spirit of Christ and Christian Living: A Study of Caspar Schwenckfeld's Christological Pneumatology* (unpub. Ph.D., Temple University, 1982).

8 Cited and critically discussed by the Mennonite scholar Robert Friedmann in *Mennonite Piety Through the Centuries* (Goshen, In., 1949), 29. The primary thrust of Friedmann's book, in which Marpeck's polemic is discussed, is to distinguish the Anabaptist-Mennonite line from later German Pietism. One has the feeling that he saw Schwenckfeld as a 'pre-Pietist' rather than as an evangelical teacher for whom Christ active through the Holy Spirit was the key to the Christian life.

9 Troeltsch, *Social Teaching*, vol. 2, 381.

10 Schultz, 370-71.

11 Letter of F-WH to FHL, dated 7/ 23/ 84.

12 Quoted in Dwight L. Dumond, *Antislavery* (Ann Arbor, Mich., 1961), 231

13 Mimeographed Conference Report in possession of writer.

14 Cf. the classic essay by Joachim Wach, 'Caspar Schwenckfeld, a Pupil and a Teacher in the School of Christ,' *Journal of Religion* 26 (1946), 1-29.

15 For documentation of the present crisis in America see Dean M. Kelly (ed.), *Government Intervention in Religious Affairs* (New York, 1982).

16 Well presented in Gottfried Maron, *Individualismus und Gemeinschaft bei Caspar Schwenckfeld* (Stuttgart, 1961), 133f.

17 On the primitivist thought of the Radical Reformation, with *restitutio Christianismi* as the constitutive element rather than *reformatio ecclesiae*, cf. Littell, *Origins*, ch. 2.

18 CS 4, Doc. 135 (1533), 752f.

19 Cf. Franklin H. Littell, 'Some Free Church Remarks on the Concept, the Body of Christ,' in Robert A. Pelton (ed.), *The Church as the Body of Christ* (Notre Dame, Ind., 1963), 127-38. For Schwenckfeld, 'the presence of Christ in the Holy Spirit is the believer's mode of experience of God.' (Suh, 162). This was as central to Schwenckfeld's theology as the experience of justification was to Luther (ibid., 178).

20 Note, for example, *Unam Sanctum* (1302) of Boniface VIII; *De ecclesia Christi* and *De fide Catholica* (1870) of Pius IX; *Mystici corporis Christi* (1943), *Mediator Dei* (1943) and *Humani Generis* (1949) of Pius XII.

21 Cf. *A Tribute to Menno Simons* (Scottdale, Pa., 1961), 53f.

22 Schultz, 311-12.

23 Among the more important figures directly indebted to him was clearly Martin Bucer. (Cf. Maron, 164-65). Another was Philip of Hesse (cf. James Leslie French [ed.], *The Correspondence of Caspar Schwenckfeld of Ossig and the Landgrave Philip of Hesse, 1535-1561* [Leipzig, 1908], 86n).

Schwenckfeld and the Anabaptists

Walter Klaassen

I have been given the task in this paper of a conjurer, a magi-
cian. I am to bring before you in words people from a century
long past. And it is expected of me as a historian that the
images I invoke, the spirits I call, will appear before you in
verisimilitude. Indeed, it is assumed that, inasmuch as I have
some reputation as an expert in seances of this kind, the people
who have these 425 years lain in unmarked graves, will in fact
appear 'as they actually were.'

We historians promote the fiction that we can do this, but
it is a fraud. We have the traces of these people, footprints of
the mind and the soul, in their writings. These reveal attitudes
and motions at particular times and their perceptions of particular events in their time, not indeed for their own sake, but
because they form part of an argument then being pursued.
The visible traces of their lives are like footprints in the sand
of the seashore. Where once there was a complete set of footprints coming onto the beach and leaving it again elsewhere,
the waves have now erased so many that one cannot be at all
certain how all the remaining prints relate to each other.

This analogy is especially important for my task here. Caspar Schwenckfeld, nobleman and scholar, and the Anabaptists,
in particular the Augsburg civil engineer and amateur theologian Pilgram Marpeck, and Schwenkfelders and Mennonites
have in the past quarrelled with each other. Small clans like
ours seem to need to be in conflict in order to maintain identity
in a cultural sea that threatens to engulf us. Thus, our description of each other has often been polemical. And that is why
the dead will hardly appear to us now 'as they actually were.'
When one considers, further, the intricate wealth that constitutes persons and their experience throughout a lifetime, we
have to admit that we have access to only a little of Schwenckfeld, the nineteen volumes of the *Corpus Schwenckfeldianorum*

notwithstanding, and even less of Marpeck. Thus willy-nilly,
our subjectivities and the scattered footprints we have of these
men may lead us astray even when we think we are most vigilant. Still the attempt must be made once more—the seance
will proceed.

I take some lines from T. S. Eliot's poem *Four Quartets*
to be a word to the wise about how we approach the notable
figures of our histories. I have kept these twenty lines from the
last part of the poem in my Radical Reformation file for a long
time. Let me recite them for you.

> Why should we celebrate
> These dead men more than the dying?
> It is not to ring the bell backward
> Nor is it an incantation
> To summon the spectre of a Rose.
> We cannot revive old factions
> We cannot restore old policies
> Or follow an antique drum.
> These men, and those who opposed them
> And those whom they opposed
> Accept the constitution of silence
> And are folded in a single party.
> Whatever we inherit from the fortunate
> We have taken from the defeated
> What they had to leave us—a symbol:
> A symbol perfected in death.
> And all shall be well and
> All manner of thing shall be well
> By the purification of the motive
> In the ground of our beseeching.[1]

Schwenckfeld and Marpeck, Schwenkfelders and Anabaptists are today folded in a single party. They appear side by
side in the pages of books on the Radical Reformation. Virtually no one knows about their little quarrel today. In terms of
today's broad outlines of religious groupings in the sixteenth
century, they are perceived as being of the same party. On the
basis of the available evidence I want to show why that is so.

But first it is important to acknowledge that Schwenckfeld and Marpeck had genuine differences. They argued and
polemicized over real issues. The fundamental difference in

their points of view was the following: Schwenckfeld, following an ancient tradition, assumed that material realities were
fundamentally different from spiritual realities, and that these
could not be communicated from God to man by any physical
means whatever. Pilgram Marpeck, following another ancient
tradition, believed that the spiritual comes by means of the material. God, he argued, adapts himself and his communication
to the fact that we live a bodily, material life. We need physical means to help us penetrate to eternal, spiritual realities.
That represents a basic philosophical difference of approach to
reality, and from this basic disagreement flowed the many arguments of detail which the two men conducted over the years.
Their differences were therefore not superficial or trivial and
we do them no justice by charging them with arguments over
trifles. Moreover, what in a radically different time may appear
to be unimportant, could have been of fundamental importance
then.

Schwenckfeld and his followers were often taken to be Anabaptists by their contemporaries. In a most obvious sense, it
was a natural mistake, for the emphasis of both Schwenkfelders
and Anabaptists on living a morally upright life and daily doing the will of God naturally suggested it. An equally obvious
fact was that both groups dissented from both Catholicism
and Protestantism, and gathered for Bible study and prayer in
small, secret conventicles. Thirdly, Luther charged Schwenckfeld and the Anabaptists with the view that the letter of Holy
Scripture must be understood according to the Spirit and not
the Spirit according the the letter (XVI, 461). Although Luther
was given to slandering his opponents, he had a sensitive nose
for the relationship of Word and Spirit, and in this case, as in
others, his judgment was quite accurate. It was also known
that, at least initially, Schwenkfelders and Anabaptists had
been friends and considered themselves to be of the same party.
Anabaptists actually banned Schwenckfeld because he did not
institute the baptism of adults. That means that they regarded
him as one of them.

Unfortunately, the early goodwill did not last. I believe that
both Marpeck and Schwenckfeld knew from the early 1530s
that they had some profound differences of perception on major elements of the Reformation debate. Marpeck had attacked

the spiritualism represented by Schwenckfeld in 1531, but without naming Schwenckfeld. Schwenckfeld, in his turn, had attempted to refute the Anabaptist view that a Christian could not participate in government, and Marpeck had responded with what can fairly be called the best presentation of Anabaptism on the question of the Christian and the use of the sword.[2]

When Marpeck appeared publicly in Augsburg in 1524, the struggle began in earnest. Since the Schwenckfeld conventicles did not practice baptism or observe the Lord's Supper, they were much less visible than the Anabaptists who did. Thus, many Anabaptists, exhausted by the unrelenting pressure of the governments, felt strongly attracted to Schwenckfeld. Marpeck worked hard to stem the flow by showing that Schwenckfeld was in error on a number of issues, especially in his interpretation of the sacraments. Schwenckfeld felt attacked at the heart since a central concern of his for two decades had been the correct interpretation of the eucharist.

Schwenckfeld had always insisted that he was no Anabaptist or sectarian, but that did not prevent him saying in 1533 that Anabaptists were better than others because they lived a truly Christian life and that he regarded them as Christians (CS 4:776, 832). He defended them against their persecutors in his writings over the years (CS 4:257-59). He could even defend Melchior Hoffman's formulation of the doctrine of the heavenly flesh of Christ (CS 4:835). But after the polemic had begun and with it the literary struggle for the loyalty of wealthy patronesses—G. H. Williams refers to this as the 'Damenkrieg'—Schwenckfeld's frustration and anger occasionally showed through in spite of his warm tolerance. In 1544 he wrote that he wanted no part of the Anabaptists (CS 8:867). He returned the hostility they harboured towards him because, as he said, he would not agree with them on their view of baptism (CS 7:89; cf. 4:834). He charged Marpeck with being an intemperate and wrathful man (CS 8:167).

Charges and countercharges appear again and again in their polemic against each other. Schwenckfeld called the Anabaptists self-called apostles, false prophets, and untaught teachers (CS 12:675), and that they built on externals and not on Christ. He complained that Marpeck constantly misrepresented him which was true. But he then did the same thing when he charged that Marpeck was interested only in the external rite of baptism and not in the inner change of heart (CS 12:673, 736, 873), and that he knew nothing about being born again (CS 11:14). He charged Marpeck with being theologically incompetent, a fact Marpeck was well aware of. Marpeck returned the injury by charging that Schwenckfeld was too haughty with his scholarship. Schwenckfeld criticized the Anabaptists for claiming that they had reinstituted the true baptism (CS 12: 775), when he in fact made the same claims for his view of the eucharist. He disputed that Anabaptists were sent by God. How could he know that he was called? And it is not hard to understand Schwenckfeld's anger that Marpeck could work openly because the Augsburg authorities needed his technical expertise whereas he, Schwenckfeld, could not. But then, he writes, 'error always has its place in the world' (CS 12:659f.).

The fact is that these two dissenters for all of their dissent were men of their time. For them as for their Catholic and Protestant contemporaries, truth was one. Therefore, if one disagreed strongly on one point, it was assumed that there must be disagreement on all other points as well. And naturally, each was convinced of having that truth. This accounts for the often laboured, repetitive hairsplitting in argument that characterized Reformation polemic in general, but especially that of dissenters. Among them there was a heightened awareness of the importance of truth because the price it demanded was so high and so final. The fact is that Schwenckfeld and Marpeck along with Luther, Zwingli, John Eck, and Servetus were one and all concerned to find and teach the truth and so to glorify God. It may be assumed with certainty that each one of them had the truth in some measure and that none of them had all of it. And that, in spite of the anger and the polemic, was what Schwenckfeld fervently believed. His only consistent company in this conviction were spiritualizers like Sebastian Franck, and the Anabaptist Hans Denck.

But I want to strike a happier note now. Despite all of the ill feeling of that time, what strikes the modern reader is the similarity betwee Schwenckfeld and Marpeck. I've read all of Marpeck and much of Schwenckfeld and would now like to present some evidence that, not only are they now 'folded in a single party,' but that even in the 1540s and 1550s this was true, although it was hidden from their eyes. And this exercise is not meant to ignore, much less negate the real differences in interpretation. This is an exercise not so much in historical research as in reminding ourselves of the experiences of our ancestors in order that we may be encouraged by their charity and avoid their errors.

Schwenckfeld and Marpeck agreed on the centrality of the Bible as the Christian's authority even though they often disagreed on interpreting the Scriptures. And they shared the same commitment to the study of the Bible for themselves and their respective groups of followers. Like virtually all anticlerical dissenters for centuries before their time, they both argued eloquently that more than scholarly equipment was needed to understand the Scriptures. That 'more' was the illumination of God's Spirit. And the Spirit dwelt only with those who had truly repented, had been born again, and walked in the law of Christ. Since it was obvious that the doctors of the church and the Reformers, all of whom were highly educated, were nevertheless lost in error, and since the Spirit came to dwell with every believer, educated or not, it followed for both Schwenckfeld and Marpeck that the simple believer could often understand the Scriptures more readily than the doctor of Scripture. When one reads Marpeck's concordance of Scripture published in 1544 and which was designed to show the differences between the Testaments, one cannot miss the close resemblance to Schwenckfeld's treatment of the same matter in a work of 1532 (CS 4:472-79).

Another important similarity was the view of both about what the church was. It was the visible gathering of Christians and further that it was the collection of congregations of believers (Schultz, 325-29). This is very concrete, and Schwenckfeld's vision of the church that transcended sectarian borders was still not the theologically abstract mystical body of Christ that was totally invisible. For both Schwenckfeld and Marpeck visibility was important. They also agreed that the church could never be defined by political borders or sovereignties.

Even on the subject on which these two polemicized constantly, the sacraments, there were agreements. Schwenckfeld, like the Anabaptists, rejected infant baptism although he did not deem the time right to make a public issue of it. For him as for Marpeck, a person had to desire fellowship with God and give personal assent to it. Both insisted on the God-given competence of lay people to take possession of the decisions regarding faith, the church, and following Christ (CS 5:385-400; 8:477).

On the Lord's Supper they were agreed in their rejection of transubstantiation and of Luther's view of impanation. The miracle of the eucharist, they believed, took place not in the bread and wine but in the hearts of believers and in the church. There was even an approximation of views on the heart of Schwenckfeld's theology, the celestial flesh of Christ. 'The flesh [of Christ] is of a creaturely nature,' Marpeck wrote in 1555, 'that is taken up into and entered into the Godhead and the Godhead is united and one essence in the flesh.'[3] It is important to remind ourselves at this point that before the end of 1538 Schwenckfeld, too, regarded Christ in his earthly existence as a creature. Thus, even here there were agreements which have been ignored.

While Schwenckfeld and Marpeck disagreed on whether a Christian could function as a magistrate, they nevertheless agreed that the government had no function in the church or in regulating matters of faith. The magistrate qua magistrate could not bring about the reform of the church. That had to come ultimately from the personal decision and personal piety of Christians. The gentle persuasion of believers through their charitable, forgiving, patient spirit and behavior was the means by which God would bring about reform. There could be no place for coercion or violence in the church in matters of faith.

Although these two gifted thinkers and leaders feuded with each other, in fact they presented a united front especially in their criticisms of the Protestants and in particular the Lutherans. They charged Luther with having begun well but then having fallen away from the truth. He had rightly depended on the Word of God at the beginning, but then switched his confidence to the worldly authorities and the secular sword. They repeatedly censured the Lutherans, whom they both referred to as 'pretending evangelicals' for their evil living, and thinking that the sacraments were a universal antidote to sin. Both criticized that appeal to faith which was accompanied by a neglect of ethics.

Both leaders and their followers experienced persecution at the hands of evangelicals and Catholics. Both were exiles from

their homes and influential positions. Both were hounded from
one place to another by the Protestant clergy for identical reasons: they represented a threat to the premises and institutions of Europe's little Christendoms and so they could not be
tolerated. The letters of encouragement Schwenckfeld and Anabaptists wrote to co-believers in prison, say the same things.[4]

In spite of their literary battle both Schwenckfeld and
Marpeck were champions of religious liberty. Schwenckfeld re-
turns to the subject again and again and reiterates that God
has his children in many places and in some we do not even
suspect. Marpeck likewise called for liberty in matters of faith.
Leopold Scharnschlager, co-worker of Marpeck, wrote a classic
appeal for toleration to the Strassburg council in 1534. And
Marpeck was also a champion of liberty within the church,
pleading especially for minimal use of the ban. There is no
doubt, however, that on this matter, Schwenckfeld gets the gold
medal in the sixteenth century. And the Sebastians, Castellio
and Franck, get the silver and the bronze. Finally on this point,
the Schwenkfelders like the Hutterites, endured the attempts
of the Jesuits to convert them back to Catholicism. In both
cases, not all were able to resist.

A final point of agreement between Schwenckfeld and
Marpeck is that both regarded the new birth as the beginning of an ontological change in the believer. They rejected
what they regarded as the pessimistic view of Luther that,
alas, one always remained a sinner, God's accepted justification notwithstanding. Rather, they believed that God's Spirit
begins the work of sanctification or glorification in the believer
which continues throughout life so that the believer begins to
be more and more Christlike, changed into the Lord's 'likeness
from one degree of glory to another' (2 Cor. 3:18).

Will anyone deny that that is a formidable range of issues
on which these two men agreed? How often, as I got involved in
their arguments, did I say to them: 'Hold on! You are talking
past each other. Don't be so concerned for your differences
that you can't see your agreements!' Although they called
each other uncomplimentary names, they were, when they were
not locked in combat, both gentle, tolerant, broadminded men;
that much at least is clearly revealed in their writings. They
were men with pastoral souls, wisely advising those who sought

their counsel. And they engaged in the major discussions of the time with a remarkable clarity of sight and lack of rancour.

I know I am presuming on your indulgence if I now also say something about Schwenkfelders and Mennonites. For as I said earlier, this is an exercise in historical reflection for our present edification. The similarities existed not only between Schwenckfeld and Marpeck; they exist also between their modern descendants. These things may be no surprise to you, but I was surprised that two tribes, or perhaps I should say tribelets, who have considered themselves to be very different one from another, should be so similar. I laughed from sheer enjoyment of the tricks time plays on us without our being aware of it.

Both Mennonites and Schwenkfelders are very history-conscious. We spend enormous amounts of energy, time, and money in publishing the materials out of which our history is constructed, the *Corpus Schwenckfeldianorum*—I love the weight and feel of those nineteen volumes!—the *Mennonite Encyclopedia*, completed in four big volumes twenty-five years ago, and now we are about to make a major addition to it. With a colleague I translated the major writings and letters of Pilgram Marpeck, and the Herald Press published the whole thing seven years ago. Mennonites have lived with the writings of Menno Simons and Dirk Philips as Schwenkfelders have with the writings of Schwenckfeld. We all love the old books with familiar family names inside, preserved in old leather and fastened with bronze clasps. We revel in the lore of ancient artifacts that have direct connections with notable people in our spiritual pedigree. We might as well call them what they are—relics. You Schwenkfelders have your Liegnitz and Harpersdorf, we have our Zurich and Witmarsum. You have your *Viehwegdenkmal*, we have our *Mennodenkmal*; in both cases a walk out of town and into a stand of trees is necessary to see it. Yours was erected in 1863; ours in 1879. Our histories are also memoralized in plaques in European cities and churches. You have one in Ossig; we have one in Rottenburg near Tübingen and one in Zurich. And we both avidly practice *Denkmalspflege*, polishing the monuments of our several histories and making considerable apologetics for our several champions of faith.

We both started out in America very simply, aware of the treasures we had to preserve and determined not to betray our ancestors with frivolous living. So our clothes and our churches were simple and austere. At first we worshipped in homes, then in plain meeting houses, and then, always in step with each other, in American gothic churches, signs that we knew that we were accepted. For a long time we eschewed musical instruments in church and nurtured *a capella* singing. Our ministers were self-taught and were chosen out of the congregation, in our case by lot, in yours bal-lot, two methods not as different from each other as we sometimes imagine. (As an aside I might mention that the word bullet also is a cognate of lot and bal-lot. There is something there to think about, but I'm not sure what.) And of course, all of us regularly went to church, since church was the social as well as the religious centre. In fact, it never occured to us that there was a difference.

O yes, and we had a very clear idea of who we were. We were simple farmer folk with simple beliefs, honest, sincere, and solid. And therefore right, more right than others, who were more 'flaky' as we say today. The Mennonites have always known that they and they alone were 'die Stillen im Lande.' Imagine therefore my surprise and indignation to discover that the Schwenkfelders made the same claim! And lest we get into a long argument about that, let us, in the spirit of these days, bilaterally conclude that Schwenkfelders and Mennonites together are the 'quiet in the land.'

We had always put a lot of stock in training and teaching children, but looking askance at higher education because our oppressors of other centuries were so often the men with university educations. Simple folk that we were, we believed literally in the adage, 'Je Gelehrter, je Verkehrter' (the more educated, the more in error). We both had our primary schools early in the 1730s where our children were taught 'das ABC' and 'biblische Geschichten.' However, both of us initially strongly resisted the introduction of Sunday School! And when the children began to talk about going to school, and, at least in the case of the Mennonites, began to enroll in Methodist and Baptist schools, we fought back and started our own schools. It was self-defence, at least in our case, and all the rationalizations about having always been interested in education were just that, rationalizations, making a virtue of necessity. And so we got the Wadsworth Institute in 1868 and you Perkiomen Seminary in 1875. And now, Mennonites at least, have their own homegrown 'scribes and pharisees' who whitewash the tombs of those who in the past took pride in their ignorance, and verbally beat up those in the present who do the same thing. And both Mennonites and Schwenkfelders claim that they have more people engaged in education, especially higher education, than any other comparable group.

Well, what else is there? Right, both groups have latterly become engaged in politics. It is true that Schwenkfelders have never been as negative on that score as Mennonites, but the fact that both have had—and in Canada still do have—involvement with political office, is a sign of their acculturation whatever other reasons may be advanced for it. I understand also that Schwenkfelders have traditionally voted Republican. That is also true of many, many Mennonites. Virtually all the elected Mennonite members in the parliament of Canada belong to the Canadian version of your Republican party. And, of course, we have both traditionally been and remain strong defenders of law and order.

But beyond all these things are also some important issues—I mean more fundamental—that our traditions have shared since the beginning and which are now cornerstones of religion on this continent. First, there is the separation of the functions of church and government, the belief that many rules that apply in government have no place in the church of Christ. Secondly, there is voluntarism, the belief that each person must choose to follow Christ and with that the view that each person with adequate intelligence is competent to make spiritual judgments. We have rightly held to this one despite all of the ambiguities which surround it. And finally, we have, since the beginning, upheld religious liberty, the view that each person should have freedom without coercion or force to worship God and do his bidding. On these we have agreed without qualification.

It is to be fervently hoped that these important truths which we hold to be self-evident and for which our ancestors did not hesitate to shed their life blood, will urge us into the lists in the long struggle for justice and truth today which desperately needs volunteers. We are very few, but we are no longer alone in these convictions. Millions within the Christian fold and beyond it now share them with us. But tyranny, technological, ideological, and political, in our own countries and elsewhere, the Antichrist, to use a term Caspar Schwenckfeld and Menno

Simons used, is always waiting for an opportunity to work its sinister will. We will honour our eponymous ancestors most if we oppose all tyrannies with conscious, intelligent, and passionate faith in God who is our Liberator. This is my wish for Schwenkfelders and Mennonites.

Notes

[1] T. S. Eliot, *Collected Poems 1909-1962* (New York, 1963), 206.

[2] CS 9:732. See W. Klaassen, 'Eine Untersuchung der Verfasserschaft und des historischen Hintergrundes der Tauferschrift "Aufdeckung der babylonischen Hurn...," ' *Evangelischer Glaube und Geschichte: Grete Mecenseffy zum 85. Geburtstag* (Wien, 1984), 113-29.

[3] *The Writings of Pilgram Marpeck*, trans. and ed. by W. Klaassen and W. Klaassen (Scottdale, Pa., 1978), 509.

[4] See for example, CS 9:435-439; *Jakob Hutter: Brotherly Faithfulness. Epistles from a Time of Persecution* (Rifton, N. Y., 1979), 49-64.

Luther and Schwenckfeld: Towards Reconciliation by Hindsight

Eric W. Gritsch

Almost 460 years ago, on December 1, 1525, Luther and Schwenckfeld met for the first time to discuss their different views of the Lord's Supper. After four days of dialogue with Luther, John Bugenhagen, and Justus Jonas, Schwenckfeld left Wittenberg, still hoping for reconciliation. Just before he left, Schwenckfeld took Luther aside, urging him to take the matter to heart; and Luther whispered in his ear, 'Wait a while. The Lord be with you.'[1]

But only a few weeks later, Luther already began warning his friends and supporters against a 'third sect' with regard to the eucharist. To Luther, Valentine Crautwald, Schwenckfeld's friend and mentor, and Schwenckfeld himself were the leaders of a sect as satanic as the sects led by Carlstadt and Zwingli.[2] On April 14, 1526, Luther wrote to both Crautwald and Schwenckfeld, telling them that the biblical and other 'proofs' of their position were not convincing; that they should renounce their obvious errors; and that he, Luther, refused to have any fellowship with them.[3] In a 1533 'table talk,' Luther contended that 'Swinefield' (*Schweinfeld*), like the pope, had taken to himself the sole power to interpret the Scriptures, thus re-crucifying Christ.[4]

That encounter with Luther may have been a contributing factor in Schwenckfeld's recommendation to his followers, the Brethren of Liegnitz in Silesia, to suspend the practice of the eucharist until institutional Christian unity could be achieved. This notion of a 'moratorium' (known as *Stillstand*) was communicated by Schwenckfeld and the other leaders to the Silesian 'Schwenkfelders' in a circular letter dated April 21, 1536, shortly after Schwenckfeld's visit to Wittenberg.[5]

Schwenckfeld was convinced that the four existing interpretations of the Lord's Supper (Roman, Carlstadtian, Zwinglian, and Lutheran) deformed the church of Christ more than they reformed it. As a consequence, the Schwenkfelders suspended the practice of celebrating the Lord's Supper from 1526 until 1877, when they reinstituted the practice in the 'new world.' They thought that in the United States there was an opportunity to form a pure church faithful to the glory of Christ.[6]

Schwenckfeld made one final attempt to win Luther's support in 1543. In a lengthy letter to Luther, he contended that Luther had not granted him the hearing he deserved before labeling him a heretic, that Luther had misunderstood the evidence, and that there was essential agreement between them, with the exception of certain interpretations of Christ's two natures.[7]

Luther was quite upset by Schwenckfeld's letter and the enclosed materials disclosing Schwenckfeld's teachings, which had been sent by messenger. Instead of a formal reply, Luther handed the messenger a hastily written note calling Schwenckfeld a 'stupid fool, who is possessed by the devil, has no understanding, and doesn't know what he is mumbling about.'[8] In 1544, in his final *Brief Confession Concerning the Holy Sacrament*, he condemned Schwenckfeld again and ranked him among the *Schwärmer* and 'slanderers of the sacrament' like Carlstadt and Zwingli.[9]

Schwenckfeld later declared that Luther and his colleagues had already despised and condemned him after the first visit to Wittenberg in 1525, but that he, Schwenckfeld, had chosen the 'middle way' between Luther and the pope, adhering to the glory of Christ.[10]

In this paper I will first sketch the differences between Luther and Schwenckfeld, as they themselves viewed them; the sketch will concentrate on the Lord's Supper and christology. Then I will attempt to show that their positions may not be as irreconcilable as they seemed to be in the sixteenth century, when viewed in the context of later sacramentological reflections. To this extent, the paper intends to contribute to the ecumenical dialogue between Lutherans and Schwenkfelders.

The Sixteenth Century Encounter

Schwenckfeld had a deep respect for Luther. During his Wittenberg visit, from December 1 to 4, 1525, he assumed that

Luther would have only 'God's honor and our salvation' in mind.[11] According to his lengthy diary entry. Luther was kind and patient, and seemed to be familiar with some of Schwenckfeld's sacramentological reflections, which he judged to be Zwinglian. He invited Schwenckfeld to look at the controversial text, 'This is my body' in both Greek and Latin.

The conversation quickly focussed on the meaning of the word 'this' (*das* in German, *quod* in Latin, *touto* in Greek). Concentrating on the Latin text, Luther maintained that the *quod* referred to the bread and wine rather than to the death of Christ, as Schwenckfeld had interpreted it. When Luther's colleague John Bugenhagen joined the discussion, Luther left the room for a while, and Schwenckfeld and Bugenhagen engaged in a lengthy debate about the meaning of the words 'This is my body.' Schwenckfeld refused to see Christ's presence in the elements of bread and wine, because the glorified, resurrected Jesus could not be equated with externals and could be present only 'spiritually,' as 'heavenly flesh,' to those who believed in him. When Bugenhagen insisted that the sacrament 'is a sign which is God's Word', Schwenckfeld replied, 'I cannot understand this unless you want to make out of the dead letter the living Word of God.... The Word is not in the sacrament.'[12]

But that is precisely what Luther and his colleagues taught: the Word of God is in the sacrament, because God so willed it. Luther himself assured Schwenckfeld that such faith in the sacrament was a matter of conscience for Lutherans. 'Verily' he said. 'in our conscience we do not believe otherwise.'[13] Schwenckfeld promised that, with the help of his friend Valentine Crautwald, he would demonstrate that the contrary was true. 'that the Word is not in the sacrament.'[14]

The position of Schwenckfeld is well summarized in a treatise published fourteen years later, entitled *A Summary of Arguments that Christ According to his Humanity Is Not a Creature, But Wholly our Lord and God* (Aug. 15, 1539).[15] This treatise was widely circulated and was also read by Luther. In fourteen propositions, Schwenckfeld attempted to show that the man Christ was not a 'creature' in the usual sense of the word. If he were a creature he could not do what the Christian tradition attributed to him: he could not be the Son of God, the head of the church, the true heavenly food in the Lord's Supper. 'The believer would be compelled to have faith in, pray to, and worship a half-Christ as God and Lord, since one may not accord a creature such divine honor.'[16]

Behind these arguments was the assumption that Jesus was truly the Son of God, the eternal, pre-existent Word, which did become human nature, but never in the same manner as any other human. God used the virgin Mary as the 'workshop, *officina*' that produced his human flesh.[17] Yet this 'flesh' was different from any human flesh: it was sinless; it was born of the heavenly Father, by way of a virgin who could not transmit Adam's sin. Thus, Schwenckfeld intended to uphold the ancient Christian dogma of Christ's two natures, born through Mary, the 'mother of God': whatever happened to one nature also happened to the other; God was born in Christ, and he died in Christ; there is a total union of person, *unio personalis*. In sum, the whole, undivided Lord Jesus Christ—human *and* divine—was involved in everything pertaining to the incarnation, whether it be humiliation and death or exaltation and resurrection. According to Schwenckfeld, the ultimate heresy, indeed the sin against the Holy Spirit, would be the notion that Christ was limited in any way by 'creatureliness,' for there can be no 'half-Christ.'[18]

This christology became the basis for Schwenckfeld's sacramentology, especially for his view of the Lord's Supper. Using the Johannine statement regarding the heavenly flesh of Christ (John 6:54, 'He who eats my flesh and drinks my blood has eternal life'), Schwenckfeld composed what he called *Arguments Against Impanation*.[19] He contended that the Lord's Supper was an external memorial, offering Christ's heavenly flesh to those who had given themselves to him in faith. Crautwald provided the formula which Schwenckfeld then used against those who, like Luther, defended the real presence of Christ in the eucharistic elements. By inverting the words 'this is my body' to 'my body is this,' Crautwald interpreted the 'this' as spiritual food for the soul, rather than relating it to the presence of Christ in the physical elements of bread and wine. Thus, Schwenckfeld could say that he never held the Zwinglian view which changed the 'this' to 'signifies (*significat*).' 'The *hoc* remains *hoc*, the *est* *est*, and the *corpus corpus*.'[20]

When a Silesian friend asked Schwenckfeld why he had written so much just to win Luther's support, Schwenckfeld replied that he had done so in order to make Christ better known, not just to please Luther. He said that Luther had helped him to come to know many points of truth and therefore deserved gratitude and an account of how he, Schwenckfeld, was arguing these points. He would neither court the pope nor Luther, 'but diligently seek to come to Christ, the Middle Way between the papacy and Lutheranism, and to confess frankly and publicly to the glory of Christ that all that is necessary to salvation must be sought and found in him alone.'[21]

Luther's treatment of Schwenckfeld was not at all as polite as Schwenckfeld's dealing with Luther. Immediately after Schwenckfeld's visit to Wittenberg in 1525, Luther wrote to friends to warn them against the sectarians in Silesia. He told them that these new sectarians disclosed the satanic symptoms of dissension on the Lord's Supper.[22] In February 1526, he returned some of the writings Schwenckfeld had sent him, commenting in a covering letter that Schwenckfeld should stop misleading the people in Silesia.[23] In other letters to Schwenckfeld and Crautwald, he told them that their interpretation of the Lord's Supper needed more scriptural proof. To Schwenckfeld he wrote:

> It is therefore my courteous request that you renounce this obvious error [of speaking of two kinds of food, 'figurative and true'] and do not join those who now lead the world so miserably astray. If this should not happen, then God's will be done. Although I am heartily sorry, yet I am not responsible for your blood, nor for the blood of all those whom you lead astray. May God convert you. Amen.[24]

Luther, of course, had already stated his basic position concerning the Lord's Supper in a rather violent attack on Carlstadt and Zwingli entitled *Against the Heavenly Prophets* published in 1525. 'God has determined to give the inward to no one except through the outward.' Luther declared. 'Observe carefully, brother, this order, for everything depends on it.'[25] Luther was committed to defending the incarnational, external order of salvation established by God in the life, death, and resurrection of Jesus. Neither Christ nor the sacraments could be 'spiritualized.' Luther went to great length to defend this point of view in 1528 against those who spiritualized the Lord's Supper, among them Schwenckfeld. If the words, 'This

is my body,' need any defense at all, beyond a literal acceptance of them, Luther contended, they must be interpreted by
means of a synecdoche, a figure of speech that ascribes two
meanings to one substance or reality. Thus, 'dove' can mean a
bird as well as 'Holy Spirit'; Christ is both 'Son of God' and
'man'; and 'cup' can refer to an instrument for drinking as well
as to 'blood of Christ.'[26] One must make proper distinctions
between 'synecdochal predications' and 'identical predications'
that do not allow two meanings for one substance or reality.[27]
Such linguistic argumentation seemed better to Luther than a
simple inversion of words, as Crautwald and Schwenckfeld had
suggested. According to Luther, they denied the ecumenical
notion, shared by Lutherans, that sacraments are 'signs and
testimonies of God's will, intended to awaken and to confirm
faith in those who use them.'[28]

The older Luther was increasingly vitriolic about Schwenckfeld. In a 1544 'table talk,' he said that Schwenckfeld invented
two Christs, 'one who hangs on the cross, and another who
ascends to his Father.' He called Schwenckfeld 'a poor wretch
who does not have talent or spirit,' and prayed that this 'ec-
static fanatic' be struck dumb so that he could no longer com-
municate. To Luther, Schwenckfeld was. at best, a Eutychian
heretic who taught that Christ has only a divine nature and
merely seems to have a human one—a heresy which had been
condemned by the Council of Chalcedon in 451 A.D.[29]

Yet Luther seems to have taken Schwenckfeld seriously as
a worthy academic opponent on at least one occasion. On
February 28, 1540, he devoted one of his famous public dispu-
tations at the University of Wittenberg to Schwenckfeld. The
topic was 'the humanity and the divinity of Christ,' and was
presented in sixty-four theses.[30] Starting with the ancient dogmatic premise that Christ is true God and true man, Luther
developed linguistic arguments to properly distinguish between
Christ's human and divine natures. According to Luther, one
should distinguish between meanings of words that have the
same spelling but different meanings (for example, the German
Hut means 'hat' as well as 'protection'). If God was incarnate
in Christ, as tradition has it, then one could say that Christ
was a 'creature,' because God's incarnation in Christ can be
expressed in various ways.

53. A grammarian can render the sentence, 'a black
person has white teeth' with 'a black person is white

in his teeth (*ist weiss an den Zähnen,*)' or 'is of white
teeth (*ist von weissen Zähnen*).' or 'is equipped with
white teeth (*ist mit weissen Zähnen versehen*).'
56. This is also true of such expressions as 'Christ, insofar as He is human,' or 'according to his humanity He is
creature.' All this means merely that He has creatureliness, or that He has taken on human nature, or simply,
'the humanity of Christ is creature....'
57. Thus, the heresy is not in the words, but in the sense
and understanding connected to them....
59. On the other hand, he who has perverted the sense,
even though he uses correct expressions and is in conversation with Scripture, should not be tolerated.
60. For Christ Himself forbade the devils to speak when
they confessed Him to be the Son of God by claiming to
be angels of light.

Unfortunately, the personal and literary encounters between Luther and Schwenckfeld did not concentrate on the
linguistic possibilities of theological discourse. Had this been
the case, some convergence might have been possible between Luther's and Schwenckfeld's christological reflections.
Schwenckfeld research seems a bit divided on the question of
whether or not Schwenckfeld was 'Lutheran' in some of his assertions. At the beginning of our century, Karl Ecke argued
that Schwenckfeld completed what Luther had begun when he
called for a church which would represent 'a practical' Christianity, thus foreshadowing the modern 'community movement (*Gemeinschaftsbewegung*).'[31] Emanuel Hirsch labeled
Schwenckfeld's christology 'a variety (*Spielart*) of Lutheran
Christology.'[32] Maier contended that 'Schwenckfeld's entire
Christology may be understood as a protest against the Nesto-
rianising tendencies of Swiss theology in favor of a near Eutychian emphasis which approximated many elements in Luther's
Christology.'[33] Gottfried Maron concluded his ecclesiological
study of Schwenckfeld with the judgment that Schwenckfeld
was committed to a 'biblicistic-gnostising mysticism' which
had nothing in common with Luther and his reformation.[34]
Heinrich Bornkamm viewed Schwenckfeld as totally opposed
to Luther whose 'biblical realism' cannot be reconciled with
Schwenckfeld's 'spiritual realism.'[35] Peter C. Erb detected a

strong influence of Eastern Greek thought in Schwenckfeld's theology, symbolized by his emphasis on the role of the glorified Christ, rather than that of Jesus' life on earth.[36]

Ecumenical Perspectives

Even a cursory reading of the encounters between Luther and Schwenckfeld warrants the observation that both could have done better than they did to understand the other's theological reflections. Luther, who left most serious ecumenical dialogues to his friend Philip Melanchthon, made little effort to find any common ground; and Schwenckfeld was seemingly too preoccupied with the systematic arrangement of his sweeping thoughts to find time to search for an ecumenical rapprochement with Luther. These factors, as well as the lack of a scholarly consensus concerning Schwenckfeld's Lutheranism, warrant raising the question regarding a possible convergence between Luther and Schwenckfeld.

Recent ecumenical dialogue has been able to achieve convergence on issues that are not totally different from those discussed between the Wittenberg priest-professor and the Silesian nobleman. In their various attempts to find agreements on classically Lutheran and Reformed interpretations of the Lord's Supper, official dialogues in the United States and in Europe have discovered significant common ground. Lutheran and Reformed theologians in the United States issued a 'Summary Statement' on christology and the Lord's Supper in 1966 (*Marburg Revisited*) which might have aroused positive feelings in both Luther and Schwenckfeld:

> We are agreed that the presence of Christ in the sacrament is *not effected by faith but acknowledged by faith*. The worthy participant is the one who receives in faith and repentance the Christ who offers Himself in the sacrament. The unworthy participant is the one who fails to acknowledge the Lordship of Christ, his presence in the sacrament, and the fellowship of the brethren in the common Lord.... The significance of the Lord's Supper is that *it brings assurance that it is the total Christ*, the divine-human person, who is present in the sacrament, but it does not explain how He is present.[37]

Luther would have appreciated the reference to the inexplicable mystery of Christ's presence; and Schwenckfeld might have empathized with the notion that a spiritually and morally worthy community acknowledges, by faith, the presence of the total Christ.

Both Luther and Schwenckfeld might also have tolerated the 'Joint Statement' of Lutheran and Reformed theologians, issued at their final meeting in the United States in 1983. This statement stressed the 'new community' Christ nurtures through the Lord's Supper; the Lord's Supper itself 'is inexhaustibly profound and awesome.'[38] Similar statements are to be found in the *Leuenberg Concord* between Lutheran and Reformed churches in Europe in 1971. There, too, the emphasis is on the gift of communion with Christ and with other Christians, rather than on finding theological explanations for Christ's presence. Luther would have agreed with the statement that 'communion with Christ cannot be separated from the act of eating and drinking'; and Schwenckfeld might have conceded that 'interest in the way in which Christ is present runs the danger to obscure the meaning of the Lord's Supper.'[39]

In recent years, there has been a strong influence of Eastern Orthodox eucharistic thought on the heirs of sixteenth century Reformation. This influence, particularly apparent in the consensus statement of the Faith and Order Commission of the World Council of Churches (Lima, 1982), is disclosed in language which echoes Schwenckfeld's concern for the visible expression of Christ's glory in the life of the faithful: the eucharist is a 'sign of the kingdom'; it depends on the work of the Holy Spirit; and 'it brings into the present age a new reality which transforms Christians into the image of Christ and therefore makes them his effective witnesses.'[40] At the same time, the Lima Document honors Lutheran concerns: the eucharist is authoritative because it is biblically instituted; Word and sacrament are intimately related; and Christ is 'really present' in the eucharist, although no attempt is made to explain how.[41]

Ecumenical hindsight does not diminish the differences between Luther and Schwenckfeld. But recent ecumenical perspectives on issues which divided them reveal the limitations imposed upon them by historical circumstances. Both were motivated by concerns and experiences in the sixteenth century context.

Luther clung to what he conceived to be the ecumenical core of Christian tradition, especially regarding worship and sacraments. He retained the basic structure of the Roman Mass, with its focus on the real presence of Christ in the eucharistic elements. At the same time, he championed the Word of God, as the gospel of God's unconditional love for sinners revealed in the life, death, and resurrection of Christ. Luther saw this Word of God revealed 'audibly' in oral communication and 'visibly' in sacraments (as Augustine defined the sacrament).[42] In his conflicts with both Rome and the *Schwärmer* (as he dubbed Schwenckfeld and others) on sacramentological issues, Luther moved from an initial appreciation of the eucharist as a 'sign of incorporation with Christ' and a 'sacrament of love'[43] towards an inflexible insistence on the bodily presence of Christ in the eucharistic elements based on a literal interpretation of the words of institution.[44]

Schwenckfeld was concerned with the moral and spiritual implications of Luther's Reformation. In full accord with the young Luther's attack on ecclesiastical abuses in the medieval church, Schwenckfeld yearned for a visible expression of the glorified Christ's power in the world through committed believers. He had experienced this power through meditation, indeed through divine visitations and private revelations, and he hoped that Luther's Reformation would create not only *Schriftsgelehrte* (those who knew Scripture and rational theological data), but also *Gottesgelehrte* (those who had been taught by the Holy Spirit to apply theological data to their personal lives). Schwenckfeld became convinced that Lutheranism, like Roman Catholicism, hindered rather than helped to improve the moral and spiritual fervor of the Christian community. To him, the sacramentological controversies were signs of a spiritual collapse which could only be prevented by a moratorium (*Stillstand*) on sacramental celebrations.

Conclusion

Could Luther and Schwenckfeld nevertheless have achieved some reconciliation? Perhaps, if they had tried to understand each other better, and if they had searched for appropriate ecumenical norms to test their theological opinions. But to become skilled in ecumenical dialogue on thorny—and often church-dividing—issues takes time and patience. Luther had not much of either; and Schwenckfeld seems to have been burdened by feelings of inferiority in the presence of Luther.

And yet they shared a christocentric vision of life: Luther from the perspective of the church militant, which shares Christ's humiliation on the cross, and Schwenckfeld from the perspective of the church triumphant, which participates in Christ's exaltation at the right hand of God the Father. At times they both used language which would not have been offensive to either of them. Luther could speak about 'the inner man' and the mystical communion of the soul with Christ, through faith.[45] He could say, 'Christ is human but not earthly (*Christus esset homo, sed non terrenus*), thus echoing Schwenckfeld's refusal to call Christ a 'creature.'[46] Schwenckfeld, on the other hand, made Christological statements that were not 'Eutychian' at all, such as, 'The human nature of Christ is the same as the divine in might, power, and honor, just as, formerly, in the personal dispensation, the divine nature was, for a time, united in the flesh to the human in shame, weakness, and dishonor.'[47]

Luther and Schwenckfeld never really gave each other a full hearing. Few theologians ever do. Both Luther and Schwenckfeld could have profited from Luther's musings on the subject of true theologians, who must follow the 'rule of David' (Ps. 119): to pray (*oratio*), to reflect and to meditate (*meditatio*), and to follow their own temptations or *Anfechtungen* (*tentatio*). Conversely, bad theologians, according to Luther, are those who think they honor God by writing fine books, preaching beautiful sermons, and using flattery. 'If you are of that stripe, dear friend, then take yourself by the ears, and if you do this in the right way you will find a beautiful pair of big, long, shaggy donkey ears.... The honor is God's alone, not the theologians.'[48]

Notes

1 CS 2: 282.5-6. English translation of the diary in Schultz, 75-96; quotation, 96.
2 Letter to Michael Stifel, December 31, 1525. WA Br. 3:653 (LW 49:141). Luther wrote similar letters also to others between December 1525 and March 1526. See Schultz, 98.
3 WA Br 4:52-53 (LW 49:149-50).

4 Table Talk, dated February 12, 1533 (No. 2971a) WA TR 3:124.25-27 (LW 54:186).

5 'Circular Letter by Crautwald, Schwenckfeld and the Liegnitz Pastors (Apr. 21, 1526), CS 2:329-33. For a summary of Schwenckfeld's reasons, quoted from his writings, see Schultz, 111-14.

6 Ibid., 111.

7 Letter of October 12, 1543. WA Br 10:420-26. See also Schultz, 286-88.

8 Table Talk dated 1544 (No. 5659), WA TR 5: 301.1-2 (LW 54:471).

9 WA 54:141.4 (LW 38:287).

10 'Defense Against Flacius' Book *Contradictiones*' (1556), CS 14:1030. 24-27. Quotation from 'Letter to Simon Ruff' (Jan. 1, 1546), CS 9:661.4-7.

11 CS 2:242.6-7.

12 CS 2:255.21-24, 28.

13 CS 2:278.25-26.

14 CS 2:278.27-29.

15 CS 6:534-39. For a detailed analysis of Schwenckfeld's christology see Paul L. Maier, *Caspar Schwenckfeld on the Person and Work of Christ. A Study in Schwenckfeldian Theology at Its Core* (Assen, The Netherlands, 1959).

16 Proposition 14 (CS 6:538. Trans. in Maier, 53).

17 'A Letter to Certain Lovers of the Glory and Truth of Christ at Augsburg' (after June 17, 1546), CS 9:800 (marginal note).

18 'Annotations on Crautwald's Letters' (ca. 1537), CS 5:743.33.

19 July(?) 1525, CS 2:132-39. See also 'Second Letter to Dr. Marx Zimmermann of Augsburg' (1556), CS 14:802.17-803.23.

20 'Second Apology' (Jan. 1 to Feb. 24, 1530), CS 3:626.23-24. Crautwald's inversion of the words 'This is my body' to 'My body is this (*daas*)' is based on the notion that such inversion is common in Hebrew. See 'Schwenckfeld's Authorized Translation of the Latin Letter Written Him by Valentine Crautwald' (Oct. 1525), CS 2:207.1-4.

21 'Letter to Simon Ruff' (Jan. 1, 1546), CS 2:661,4-7.

22 See above, n. 2.

23 The letter is not found in WA Br but in *D. Martin Luthers Briefwechsel*, ed. by E. L. Enders (Frankfurt am Main, 1884-), 5:332. It is also mentioned in Schwenckfeld's 'Second Letter to Dr. Marx Zimmermann at Augsburg' (1556), CS 14:804.16-20.

24 Letter of April 14, 1526. WA.Br 4:52.11-53.16 (LW 49:150).

25 WA 18:136.16-17, 24 (LW 40:146).

26 'Confession Concerning Christ's Supper' (1528), WA 26:472.13-31 (LW 37:330).

27 See the section on 'The Law of Identical Predication.' WA 26:437.31-445.17 (LW 37:294-303). See also the arguments against Schwenckfeld (ibid.), WA 26:433-37.29 (LW 37:288-94); WA 26:465.37-466.29 (LW 37:321-23); WA 26:490.7-18 (LW 371:352-53).

28 Art. 13 of the 'Augsburg Confession.' 1530. *Die Bekenntnisschriften der evangelisch-lutherischen Kirche* (3rd. ed. rev.; Göttingen, 1930), 68:1, *The Book of Concord*, ed. and trans. by Theodore G. Tappert (Philadelphia, 1959), 35:1.

29 Table Talk, dated 1544 (No. 5659), WA TR 5:299.4, 5-6, 14-15.

30 WA 39/2:97-100. Translations mine.

31 Karl Ecke, Schwenckfeld. *Luther und der Gedanke einer apostolischen Reformation* (Berlin, 1911), 225. This is the focus of a summary of Ecke's position by Theodor Sippel, 'Caspar Schwenckfeld,' *Christliche Welt* 25 (1911), 867. Ecke was heavily criticized by Gottfried Maron, *Individualismus und Gemeinschaft bei Caspar von Schwenckfeld. Seine Theologie dargestellt mit besonderer Ausrichtung auf seinen Kirchenbegriff* (Stuttgart, 1961), 26-27, 31-32.

32 Emanuel Hirsch, 'Zum Verständnis Schwenckfelds' in *Festgabe von Fachgenossen und Freunden Karl Müller dargebracht* (Tübingen, 1922). 165.

33 Maier, 60.

34 Maron, 60. These and other judgments are too radical in the light of Schwenckfeld's christology which is certainly closer to a Greek orthodox defense of Chalcedonian views than to a Neoplatonic gnosticism.

35 Heinrich Bornkamm, *Luther in Mid-Career, 1521-1530*, ed. by Karin Bornkamm, trans. by E. Theodore Backmann (Philadelphia, 1983), 516. It is debatable whether Crautwald's 'personal broodings became an inspiration,' as Bornkamm observed in his summary of Crautwald's letter to Schwenckfeld (ibid., 513). See above, n. 20.

36 Peter C. Erb, *Schwenckfeld in His Reformation Setting* (Valley Forge, Pa., 1978), 81.

37 Paul C. Empie and James I. McCord (eds.), *Marburg Revisited. A Reexamination of Lutheran and Reformed Traditions* (Minneapolis, 1966), 104. Emphasis added.

38 James E. Andrews and Joseph A. Burgess (eds.), *An Invitation to Action. The Lutheran-Reformed Dialogue. Series III. 1981-1983. A Study of Ministry, Sacraments, and Recognition* (Philadelphia, 1984), 15.

39 *Die Leuenberger Kondordie. Dokument der Einigung reformatorischer Kirchen in Europa.* Text in *Lutherische Monatshefte* 12 (1972) 271-74. Quotation, 273:19. Translation mine.

40 *Baptism, Eucharist and Ministry* (Faith and Order Paper No. 111; Geneva: World Council of Churches, 1982), 10:1; 13:16; 14:26.

41 *Ibid.*, 10:1; 12:12; 12:13.

42 Augustine, *Tractate 80* on John 3 cited in 'Apology of the Augsburg Confession' (1531), Art. 13, *Bekenntnisschriften* 293:5; *Book of Concord* 212:5.

43 'The Blessed Sacrament of the Holy and True Body of Christ,' (1519), WA 2:743.21; 745.25 (LW 35:51, 54).

44 See Joachim Staedtke, 'Abendmahl: Reformationszeit, Luther' in *Theologische Realenzyklopädie*, ed. by Gerhard Krause. Gerhard Müller et
al. (Berlin and New York: Walter de Gruyter, 1977-), 1:110-13.

45 'The Freedom of the Christian,' 1520. WA 7: 54.31-55.6 (LW 31:351).

46 'Sermon on the Feast of the Annunciation' (Mar. 25, 1539), WA 47:701.
11-12.

47 'A Letter to a Friend Concerning the Ascension and Session of Our
Lord' (ca. Nov. 1528), CS 3:249.2-5. Translation in Maier, 65.

48 'Preface to the Wittenberg Edition of Luther's German Writings,' 1529.
WA 50:660. 35-37; 661. 1-6 (LW 34:288).

Schwenckfeld as Classicist and Patristicist

Paul L. Maier

In its original form this paper was an after-dinner address at the close of the Colloquium on Schwenckfeld and the Schwenkfelders, and, as befits such, was written in a light, humorous, and popular vein. This, of course, provided me with a marvelous excuse not even to try to match the scholarship and eloquence of the papers presented at the Colloquium to that point, leaving me in an enviable position. I have been assured by the editor of this volume that where it now stands, at the end of the volume, the same tone might well be maintained. After several hundred pages of profundity it may be useful to approach our topic once again in a lighter and more personal vein. Kindly indulge then, the brief personal commentary originally requested by the planners of the colloquium.

I might have done a paper on *Caspar Schwenckfeld as Humorist*, and was sorely tempted to do so when I consulted the indices of the *Corpus Schwenckfeldianorum* and found the entry 'Hilarius' in each and every volume. Alas, this turned out to be Saint Hilary, the church father! But humor there is in the nearly 20,000 pages of the *Corpus*, and in the life of Schwenckfeld as well. We all know the famous episode at Schwenckfeld's hearing before the Council of Ulm in November of 1536, when Frecht quoted Melanchthon's fond wish in Latin that Schwenckfeld and his doctrines were removed to 'the Happy Isles.' Schwenckfeld translated the Latin at once, adding, with a big smile, 'Gentlemen, they wish that I were in Calcutta.'[1] This, of course, was no Indian mission effort they desired in behalf of Schwenkfeldianism: Calcutta was the 'Siberia' of that day.

There were other humorous moments in Schwenckfeld's life. Anyone who could devise for himself such a pseudonym as J. Dinopedius von Greissenecker is not without wit! Or have

friends such as Bernhard Unsinn of Augsburg, and enemies like
the almost-bacterial Friedrich Staphylus of Konisberg! We do
not, however, look for cascades of rollicking wit in Schwenckfeld, as, for example, in Luther's *Tischreden*, simply because
the life of a persecuted exile, fleeing from place to place—
sometimes in fear for his very life—is not the sort of fun-
and-games atmosphere in which humor flourishes. Nor did
Schwenckfeld have wife and children to wring humor from himself for very survival, or a flock of disciple-students jotting down
his every witticism at table.

A Personal Pilgrimage

While pursuing studies in church history at Harvard University under Professor George H. Williams, whose words opened
this colloquium. I discussed with him several possible areas
for my doctoral research. Like so many Lutheran students,
I wanted to do something on—who else?—Martin Luther.
Dr. Williams, however, pointed to the vast amount of research
already expended on Luther's life and theology, and the com-
paratively slight amount devoted to the Radical Reformation,
particularly in the case of such an arresting figure as Caspar Schwenckfeld, whose works were now ever-so-conveniently
available in the *Corpus Schwenckfeldianorum*.

Raised in a somewhat chauvinistically Lutheran tradition, I,
of course, knew all the anti-Schwenckfeld jokes: Luther's familiar misspellings of his name—always good for a cheap laugh—
or the item in the *Table Talk* recorded by Jerome Besold in
1544. about Schwenckfeld's visit to Wittenberg. To quote
Luther: 'When he [Schwenckfeld] came from Silesia he tried
to persuade Dr. Pomeranus and me that his view of the sacrament was right. Since he couldn't hear well, he asked us to pray
for him. Yes, I wanted to pray that he become dumb as well.'
Even Katy, Luther's wife, interrupted him at that point to object, 'Ah, dear Sir, that's much too coarse.'[2] Unfortunately,
Luther could get much coarser than that!

But Schwenckfeld never was coarse, as I soon learned in
taking up the *Corpus Schwenckfeldianorum*, at first somewhat skeptically. Continuing my studies at the Universities
of Heidelberg and Basel, I soon fairly *wallowed* in the luxuri-
ous convenience of this research: rather than having to spend

months, if not years, tracking down the primary documents for my doctoral dissertation, all this enormous work had already been done for me, thanks to Chester David Hartranft, Elmer E. S. Johnson, Andrew S. Berky, and especially Selina Gerhard Schultz, Wayne C. Meschter and their associates. The joy of reading Schwenckfeld himself, rather than the screeds of his detractors, was something of a revelation, for here was a gentleman in an age where there were few, an almost Christ-like figure above and beyond the often murky level of Reformation Era controversy and the *rabies theologorum*. So I easily became a convert, perhaps not directly to Schwenkfeldianism per se, but to a new appreciation of one of the very noble figures and great personalities of the sixteenth century.

On this occasion of the centennial of the publication of the *Corpus Schwenckfeldianorum*, let me stop for a moment and commend enthusiastically the editors, associate editors, scholars, and sacrificial contributors to this mighty project. The obstacles were daunting, but they had the courage to continue, and were not afraid to adjust and change over the seventy-seven years of publication. For example, had the *exhaustive* approach of Hartranft in Volume I continued, the *Corpus* would have numbered about 400 volumes and been completed by, say, 2500 A.D.—and been read by almost no one! Wars intervened, manuscripts had to be hidden from bombs, destroyed volumes reprinted, but they brought it off. Schwenckfeld would be proud of them, but so too, I think, would Luther and the other reformers—now possessed of higher, heavenly wisdom—since the *Corpus Schwenckfeldianorum* brings the Reformation Era to life as few similar works.

This also demonstrates the power of dedication rather than the power of numbers. For so tiny a church—by the usual statistics—the *Corpus* project must have seemed impossible. But the statistical probabilites of landing one Schwenkfelder, not to say two, on an American President's cabinet would have been deemed impossible too. (Had proportional religious representation been the rule, President Reagan's cabinet would have to have included, say, 10,000 Roman Catholics!) Schwenckfeld's free-church approach and interior theology was not conducive to church-building, but if it had been, and if all his followers had the spirit of the Pennsylvania Schwenkfelders, they would probably be the largest Protestant faith in Christendom today!

The *Corpus* enabled me to complete my doctorate at Basel in record time, and the title of my published dissertation, *Caspar Schwenckfeld on the Person and Work of Christ*,[3] also stands prominently printed on my diploma. Then, in 1961. when, with beautiful symmetry, the *Corpus Schwenckfeldianorum* was finally completed on the quadricentennial of Schwenckfeld's death, I was also invited to deliver an address on Schwenckfeld before a joint session of the American Historical Association, the American Society of Church History, and the American Society for Reformation Research at their annual convention in Washington, D.C., which was subsequently published in the *Archiv für Reformationsgeschichte*.[4]

To deliver 'A Quadricentennial Evaluation' of the life and thought of someone as productive as Schwenckfeld in the time alloted seemed an unlikely task. All the great Reformation era scholars were there, ranging from Roland H. Bainton to George H. Williams. But throughout the address, I watched the reaction of the one person who mattered most to me, and when Selina Gerhard Schultz told me afterward that I had succeeded even to her satisfaction, I was in my own version of the Happy Isles!

The two things which struck me most in reading Schwenckfeld were: (1) his comprehensive, even exhaustive use of Scripture, as witness the scores of columns of biblical texts at the back of each volume in the *Corpus Schwenckfeldianorum*—there was no stronger biblicist in the Reformation Era; and (2) his wide use of the Greek and Latin church fathers. In documenting his writings and his theology with such authorities, he was heartily responding to the cry, '*ad fontes!*' In a sense, I've followed him: for a Reformation historian to edge back into the ancient world is not unusual, and much of my subsequent professional life has been a happy slip in that direction, thanks, in part, to Schwenckfeld and his classical-patristic consciousness. Perhaps, then, it is appropriate that I try to gauge on this occasion how Schwenckfeld handled the Greek and Latin sources—secular and religious—which so influenced his own theology.

Schwenckfeld as Classicist

Precursor to the Reformation and its contemporary secular counterpart. of course, was the Renaissance, defined, in those days, as 'Humanism'—not to be confused with the misuse of that term now being exploited by the new Religious Right. As both sides in the Roman Catholic/Protestant dispute scrambled to capture the past for their side, via tradition, the church fathers, and Scripture, a great impetus was given to humanistic studies of—not so much Latin, which every scholar knew—but also Greek and Hebrew. Schwenckfeld eventually immersed himself in all three languages, and had absolute facility in Latin, as the many documents in the *Corpus Schwenckfeldianorum* testify, where he easily lapses from German into Latin and back again in the text or marginal notes. To be sure, others in his era and following, Crautwald or Agricola, for example, were more classically inclined than he—as he was the first to acknowledge; but he had no trouble whatever in editing their works for the common cause.

Although details of Schwenckfeld's earliest studies are sketchy, his education itself was not, as is clear from *Corpus Schwenckfeldianorum* references to Cicero, Horace, Livy, Lucretius, Ovid, Plautus, Quintillian, Seneca, Terence, and Virgil among the Romans, and such Greeks as Homer, Socrates, Plato, Aristotle, and Epicurus. Later on, he familiarized himself with the church fathers, the medieval scholastics, Renaissance humanists, contemporary reformers, and others. His wide reading equipped him as well as any university degree.

Furthermore, his close association with Valentine Crautwald meant that a truly first-class humanist was near, much as Melanchthon served this role for Luther. Many of the detailed, even oblique, classical references in the *Corpus Schwenckfeldianorum* are from the pen of Crautwald, a highly gifted scholar, whose knowledge of Greek would be particularly serviceable in the Silesian interpretation of the Words of Institution in the Lord's Supper.

But Schwenckfeld was no mean humanist himself. In one of the first documents in the *CS*, a letter he wrote to Johann Hess in 1522, he comments, 'What you have written to Luther and what he may have replied, you keep silent about, because I am a pitcher full of cracks and I let the water out on all sides,' managing not only good, self-deprecating humor but a quotation from Terence as well.[5]

Later, the mature Schwenckfeld had nearly the same view of the 'pagan' or 'heathen' classical authors as did Luther: disdain wherever they were exploited by the adversary for sophistic, casuistic, or mere dialectic ends, since they were on a lower, non-biblical, pre-Christian level, but praise and citation where they provided the *bon mot* for a given situation. Thus, we find Schwenckfeld repeatedly objecting that the universities taught little of Christ or Paul, but much of Aristotle. Like other reformers, he also had little use for Aristotle-inspired scholastic distinctions in the sacrament between *substans* and *accidens*,[6] arguing that the Holy Spirit did not require dialectic.[7] Classical authors, in fact, demonstrated that the ruin of human nature in the Fall was greater than human reason could appreciate, otherwise 'such intelligent and wise pagans as Seneca, Plato, Socrates, and the like would also have understood the Adamic evil.'[8]

The classics, for all their charm, were still on a niveau below the Bible. In a letter to Andreas von Baden, an Anabaptist, in 1542, Schwenckfeld complains that people read the Bible without imploring help from the Holy Spirit, handling it like a regular piece of literature: 'Today the Bible is treated much as Livy or Cicero, in that one presumes to understand it and teach it to others merely through the exercise of human effort....'[9]

So much for his negative view of the classics, born primarily of what he deemed his opponents' misuse of the Greco-Roman authors. But Schwenckfeld, too, can involve them in the theological enterprise, and cite them in a positive context. While Crautwald assembled a whole constellation of classical authors to support his *touto* in the Lord's Supper controversy ('My body is *this...*'), Schwenckfeld could reject Virgil's pantheism— '*Jovis omnia plena*'[10]—but happily enlist Seneca's help in opposing Luther's doctrine of the ubiquity of Christ in the eucharistic controversy: 'Es haben sich zwar die Heiden auff das Vbique / das Gott allenthalb ist / weder unsere jetzige Theologi verstanden / dauon auch Seneca sagt: *Nusquam est, qui vbique est*' ['What is everywhere is nowhere!'][11]

He had high regard for Aristotle's *Ethics*, and, in fact, used the Greek philosopher to quash the old and trite argument that if the Holy Spirit were not guiding the established church and sacrament, then the Devil must be. 'Aristotle and the other pagans have written extremely well about moral virtues,' wrote Schwenckfeld, 'as one can see in the *Ethics*. That he did not have the Holy Spirit, however, is obvious, and yet who would then immediately assert that all of this stems from the Devil?'[12]

Perhaps the most poignant classical reference in the entire *Corpus Schwenckfeldianorum* comes when Schwenckfeld writes Hans Wilhelm von Laubenberg in October, 1545, just after news reached him of Valentine Crautwald's death that September. After providing the religious reaction—God had delivered the departed from the tribulations of this life—Schwenckfeld goes on to a strong classical reference concerning friendship: 'Ich möcht vol von ihm schreiben / was Cicero in seinem buch...*de coniunctione & amicitia*... hat geschrieben / wiewol diese unser Christliche Freundtschafft viel höher... gewest ist....'[13] Crautwald, the quintessential classicist, would have treasured that comment!

Schwenckfeld as Patristicist

As is obvious in any volume of the *CS*, Schwenckfeld was far more a biblicist and patristicist than a classicist. The total number of classical references in his writings is sparse when compared with the myriad citations from the Old and New Testaments and the church fathers.

A preliminary count of the patristic references in the indices of the *Corpus Schwenckfeldianorum* yields the following ranking for the sixteen most cited authorities: Augustine (1,034); Ambrose (572); Cyril of Alexandria (390); Jerome (348); Hilary (307); Tertullian (244); Chrysostom (161); Athanasius (147); Irenaeus (132); Gregory Nazianzus (132); Cyprian (124); Origen (96); Epiphanius (73); Cassianus (59); Eusebius (42); Basil the Great (33). These references are not evenly distributed throughout the *CS*. The index of Church Fathers, for example, expands dramatically with Volume II—the years 1524-27—since the debate on the Lord's Supper had commenced, and Schwenckfeld was finding support for his views in Tertullian, Cyprian, Jerome, and Hilary. He was delighted to find Ambrose and Chrysostom relating John 6 to the Words of Institution as well. But it is with Volume VII that the patristic index suddenly explodes, and understandably so, since the years 1540-41 mark the publication of his *Great Confession*, which is rich in patristic documentation. Cyril and Irenaeus become more important to Schwenckfeld here, although he does not discover Epiphanius until the next volume, years 1542-44.

What shall we make of the list above? To compare the theologies of these church fathers with Schwenckfeld's own system is extremely illuminating and suggestive. The primacy of St. Augustine, of course, is both dramatic and obvious. The North African church father seems to have been patron saint of all the reformers, since a basic Augustinianism, emphasizing the grace of God over human works, lay at the very heart of the Reformation. But Schwenckfeld would find in Augustine also some support for his dualistic theology—the inner and outer man, Word, sacrament, hearing, and the like. Not surprisingly, his earliest patristic reference is to Augustine's comment to Cassulanus, 'He who conceals the truth of God sins no less than he who speaks falsely.'[14] His hermeneutical principles—that Scripture is to be interpreted by Scripture—were admittedly Augustinian.[15]

St. Ambrose of Milan, another of the great doctors of the Western church who aided in the conversion of Augustine, ranks a strong second in the list of Schwenckfeld's patristic sources. Exuberantly anti-Arian in his theology and thus Christ-exalting, Ambrose and Schwenckfeld would have found each other congenial. More importantly, Ambrose helped introduce the thought of the Eastern Greek fathers into the Latin church of the West, a point to which we shall return.

St. Cyril of Alexandria holds a powerful third place in Schwenckfeld's writings, and even the briefest overview of his theology tells us why: Cyril stressed the intimate union of the divine and human natures in Christ, the oneness of the incarnation. He vigorously opposed the Antiochene school which separated the natures and stressed the humanity of Jesus. Nestorius of Constantinople was Cyril's *bete noire*—and Schwenckfeld's too! Had Schwenckfeld been born instead in the fifth century during the christological controversies raging between Alexandria and Antioch, his address would unquestionably have been Alexandria.

One of the four great doctors of the Latin church, St. Jerome is also one of the big four in Schwenckfeld's patristic arsenal. In life style, the two had much in common: celibacy, ascetic inclinations, and immersion in Scripture. In using his hermeneutics, Schwenckfeld was more influenced by Jerome the exegete than Jerome the theologian, although this father also helped funnel Eastern Greek thought into Western Latinity.

St. Hilary of Poiters was styled the 'Athanasius of the West' for his anti-Arian crusades. While exiled in the east, Hilary learned the Greek mind, and his works on the Trinity emphasize the deity, the consubstantial deity, of Jesus. As a 'Confessor of the Glory of Christ' in his own day, Hilary later returned to Gaul, where he *also* served as a channel for Greek thought to the West. The pattern continues.

Tertullian, as patristic source, seems somewhat puzzling, since a number of his accents seem quite different from those of Schwenckfeld. But the latter used his ethical strictures to strong advantage in his complaints about the morals of the Reformation Era. Too, he learned some of Irenaeus through Tertullian, and some of Tertullian through Cyprian.

St. John Chrysostom, one of the four great doctors of the East, and his enormous surviving literature would be difficult for any theologian to overlook, and nearly all the reformers quote him as second most cited source, after Augustine. Schwenckfeld admired his Scriptural commentaries; pithy, incisive sermons; and strong moral applications.

Athanasius of Alexandria, hero of anti-Arianism and credal orthodoxy, predictably influenced Schwenckfeld's christology via *De Incarnatione* and other works, which stress the restoration of the divine image in man. Union with the Word confers a special illumination of the mind, Athanasius taught, which, in mastering the lower impulses, can begin to approximate Christ, who is both cause and exemplar of our redemption and the near-mystical re-establishment of the divine image. The parallel Schwenkfeldian accents here are startling and clear.

Irenaues, early bishop of Lyons and predecessor to many of the above, was one of the earliest exponents of Eastern theology in the West. His concept of salvation bears formidable resemblance to that of Schwenckfeld. To this church father, salvation is the restoration to mankind of divinity in view of the union of the human and divine natures in Christ, which, in the believer, must result in ethical change as well. This almost sounds as if Irenaeus were a main contributor to the *Corpus Schwenckfeldianorum!*

Space prevents any further canvas of the church fathers, but the nine above are by far the most influential in Schwenckfeld's life and theology. In summary, let me state again what I asserted about patristic influences on Schwenckfeld in the

'Quadricentennial Evaluation' at the American Historical Association convention:

> Probably the heaviest influence on Schwenckfeld was the real, physical redemption of Greek-Anatolian theology, and in the sense that he preached this Eastern soteriology in the West, we could perhaps designate Schwenckfeld as the 'Irenaeus of the Reformation,' and there are other striking parallels—though also differences—between the reformer and the church father.[16]

It must be remembered, of course, that mere patristic citation does not necessarily imply indebtedness. Some of the reformers, as well as their Roman Catholic opponents, often conceived of theological opinions—with or without the use of Scripture—and then ran to the church fathers to see which ones agreed with them! Ideas ran both ways.

Schwenckfeld, however, began with Scripture, wrestled with Scripture, relied on classicism for the linguistic tools necessary for its interpretation, arrived at some preliminary opinions, and then tested these against the writings of the church fathers, where, unquestionably, he was also influenced by what to him would be their fresh insights. Beyond all debate, he found the nine fathers cited above to be the most congenial and useful for his theology of the Middle Way. Schwenckfeld, thus, had to make his own pilgrimage back to the early church, and so must his interpreters today, if they would understand him correctly.

Notes

[1] CS 5:543.

[2] LW (Table Talk), 469-70.

[3] Paul L. Maier, *Caspar Schwenckfeld on the Person and Work of Christ.* (Assen, The Netherlands, 1959).

[4] Paul L. Maier, 'Caspar Schwenckfeld—a Quadricentennial Evaluation,' *Archiv für Reformationsgeschichte*, 54 (1963), 89-97.

[5] Terence, *Eunuchus*, i, 21, cited in CS 1:38.

[6] CS 11:307, 318, 1052, 1055.

[7] CS 17:357-8, where Schwenckfeld adds: 'die Dialectica von den heiden Aristotele / Platone und andern Philosophis nicht umb Christi noch umbs Christlichen glaubens willen ist erfunden und beschriben / Wie solche natürliche kunst auch inn götliche heimlicheit nicht vermag zureichen.'

[8] CS 3:886.

9 CS 8:94; cf. 14:567.
10 CS 17:306 *et passim*; Virgil, *Eclogues* iii. 60.
11 CS 17:318.
12 CS 5:135.
13 CS 9:496.
14 CS 1:36.
15 CS 1:266.
16 Maier, 95.

Directory
of Authors

George H. Williams is Hollis Professor of Divinity Emeritus, Harvard University

Walter Klaassen is Professor of History at Conrad Grebel College, University of Waterloo, Waterloo, Ont., Canada.

Werner Packull is Associate Professor of History at Conrad Grebel College, University of Waterloo, Waterloo, Ont., Canada.

Gottfried Seebass is Professor of History at the University of Heidelberg, West Germany.

Fred Grater is a Catalogue Librarian at Pitts Theological Seminary, Emory University, Atlanta, Ga.

Daniel Liechty is a lecturer at the American International School, Vienna, Austria.*

R. Emmet McLaughlin is Associate Professor of Religious Studies at Villanova Univeristy, Villanova, Pa. At the time of the Colloquium he was Assistant Professor of History and Religious Studies at Yale University.

Klaus Deppermann is Professor of Early Modern History at the University of Freiburg, West Gemany.

Peter Nissen is a research fellow at the Katholieke Theologische Hogeschool, Amsterdam, The Netherlands.*

André Séguenny is a research fellow at the Centre National de Recherche Scientifique, Strasbourg, France.

Douglas Shantz is Assistant Professor of Church History and Theology at Northwest Baptist Theological College, Vancouver, B.C., Canada.

Irena Backus is a maître d'enseignement et de recherche at the University of Geneva, Switzerland.*

Wiebe Bergsma is at the Frisian Academy, Leeuwarden, The Netherlands.

Monica Pieper is an instructor in religious education and German literature at the Integrierte Gesamthochschule Ernst Bloch, Ludwigshafen, West Germany.

Horst Weigelt is Professor at the Institute for Protestant Theology at the University of Bamberg, West Germany.

Franklin H. Littell is Professor of Religion at Temple University, Philadelphia, Pa.

Eric Gritsch is Professor of Church History and Director of the Institute for Luther Studies at the Lutheran Theological Seminary, Gettysburg, Pa.

Paul L. Maier is Professor of Ancient History at Western Michigan University, Kalamazoo, Mich.

Peter C. Erb is Associate Director of Schwenkfelder Library and Professor of Religion and Culture at Wilfrid Laurier University, Waterloo, Ontario, Canada.

*Paper prepared for Colloquium but author unable to attend.